SELF-TAUGHT

SELF-

The John Hope Franklin

Series in African American

History and Culture

Waldo E. Martin Jr. and

Patricia Sullivan, editors

Heather Andrea Williams

TAUGHT

African American Education in
Slavery and Freedom

The University of North Carolina Press

Chapel Hill and London

Designed by Jacquline Johnson
Set in Bembo
by Keystone Typesetting, Inc.

The paper in this book meets the guidelines for permanence and
durability of the Committee on Production Guidelines for Book
Longevity of the Council on Library Resources.

Parts of this book have been reprinted with permission in revised form
from the following works: *Southern Manhood: Perspectives on Masculinity
in the Old South*, edited by Craig Thompson Friend and Lorri Glover,
196–219 (Athens: University of Georgia Press, 2004); and " 'Clothing
Themselves in Intelligence': The Freedpeople, Schooling, and
Northern Teachers, 1861–1871," *Journal of African American
History* 87 (Fall 2002): 372–90.

Library of Congress Cataloging-in-Publication Data
Williams, Heather Andrea.
Self-taught : African American education in slavery and freedom /
Heather Andrea Williams.
p. cm. — (The John Hope Franklin series in African American history
and culture)
Includes bibliographical references and index.
ISBN 0-8078-2920-X (alk. paper)
1. African Americans—Education—Southern States—History.
2. Slaves—Education—Southern States—History. 3. Freedmen—
Education—Southern States—History. 4. Self-culture—Southern
States—History. 5. Literacy—Southern States—History.
6. Education—Social aspects—Southern States—History. 7. Slavery—
Southern States—History. 8. Southern States—Race relations. I. Title.
II. Series.
LC2802.S9W55   2004
370'.89'96073075—dc22   2004022755

09 08 07 06 05   5 4 3 2 1
THIS BOOK WAS DIGITALLY PRINTED.

For Clay
and in memory of my mother,
Linda M. Williams

CONTENTS

ILLUSTRATIONS

ACKNOWLEDGMENTS

This book grew out of a dissertation, and Glenda Gilmore was the ideal dissertation director. She was thoroughly supportive, getting excited with me when I made new discoveries, pushing me to explore further. She helped me to grow as a historian and writer and continues to be an enthusiastic and insightful reader of my work. I am grateful to her beyond words. The late John Blassingame ignited my love of the discipline of history in his courses on slavery and the Civil War, and I continue to consult his copious writing on African American history. I am thankful, too, to Matthew Jacobson and David Brion Davis, who taught and inspired me from the very beginning of this project. Knowing that Matt is eager to teach my book has made me work even harder at it.

Several other historians have been important to my growth over the years. I would like to thank John Demos, whose class on narrative history made a difference, and Jennifer Baszile, whose comments have helped me to better clarify and articulate my own thinking.

While writing the last chapter of my dissertation, I began to realize that the University of North Carolina Press had published some of the most important books on African American education in the twentieth century. My first meeting with Kate Torrey confirmed my interest in working with the Press: Kate understood the importance of this history and appreciated the way that I told the story. Chuck Grench has made the process of publishing this book a pleasant experience from the start. He very patiently answered my many questions and gave me encouraging feedback. Working with Chuck has been all the more satisfying because of our mutual love of quilts. Bethany Johnson is a brilliant copyeditor. She has what is to me an astounding ability to pay attention to the most minute details while remaining completely engaged with the narrative. I am immensely grateful to the outside readers for the Press, James Anderson and Ira Berlin. Their comments and suggestions were invaluable to me as I revised the manuscript.

I received a great deal of support both during graduate school and after to make this work possible. Most recently, a Woodrow Wilson Postdoctoral Fellowship in the Kahn Liberal Arts Institute at Smith College gave me the time to revise the manuscript. I would like to thank especially Marjorie Senechal, René Heavlow, and Cyndee Button of the Kahn Institute; Ann Ferguson and Kevin Quashie of the Afro-American Studies Department; and

Mendenhall Fellow Crystal Lewis-Colman. I also learned a great deal from the students in my courses on race, slavery, and emancipation. Most of all, I thank my colleague and neighbor Tracy Vaughn for her friendship during my time in Northampton.

I would like to thank the Yale University Graduate School for accepting and offering financial assistance to someone who had already had one career. It meant a great deal to me. I am extremely grateful to the Ford Foundation for the Predoctoral and Dissertation Fellowships that enabled me to research and write almost without interruption. Receiving the Spencer Dissertation Fellowship was a great honor that came with the added benefit of introducing me to scholars working on a wide range of educational issues. I also received a number of research fellowships. I would first and particularly like to thank the Institute for the Advanced Study of Religion at Yale for the summer research fellowship that enabled me to travel to archives in New Orleans, Louisiana, and Richmond, Indiana. I am thankful also to the Oberlin College Archives for the Frederick Artz Research Grant, to Yale University for the John F. Enders Research Fellowship, and to the North Caroliniana Society for the Archie K. Davis Fellowship that enabled me to use the resources at the University of North Carolina at Chapel Hill.

Numerous archivists and librarians have been extremely helpful to me. First, I would like to thank Brenda Square at the Amistad Research Center in New Orleans. Her excitement about my project gave me extra energy for the weeks spent in the archives. Reginald Washington and Michael Musick at the National Archives Research Administration patiently helped me to navigate through Military Service Records and Regimental Books. Ronald Baumann, the Oberlin College archivist, was also very kind and helpful, as were Leigh Troutman at the Kentucky Department for Libraries and Archives and Teresa Roane at the Valentine Richmond History Center. I am thankful to archivists and librarians at the Quaker Collection at Earlham College in Indiana, the Schomburg Center for Research in Black Culture in New York City; the Massachusetts Historical Society in Boston; the Connecticut Historical Society in Hartford; the New Orleans Public Library; the Memphis/Shelby County Public Library; the Tulane University Library; the Filson Society in Louisville, Kentucky; the State Historical Society of Missouri in Columbia, Missouri; the Hampton University Archives in Hampton, Virginia; the Beinecke Rare Books and Manuscripts Library and the Yale University Manuscripts and Archives in New Haven, Connecticut. I would also like to thank Ira Berlin and Leslie Rowland for making the materials of the Freedmen and Southern Society Project at the University of Maryland available to me. I would like to thank Nancy Godleski, Librarian for History and American Studies at Sterling Memorial Library at Yale, for all her support. Finally, I am grateful to the staff of the Cross Campus Library at Yale for always making me feel at home.

I was the beneficiary of a tremendous system of support among my colleagues in the Yale Graduate School. Members of our quilting group who have become intellectual partners and family include Qiana Whitted, Françoise Hamlin, Leigh Raiford, Lisa McGill, Brian Herrera, Catherine Whalen, Kimberly Brown, and Danielle Elliott. My dissertation group, Qiana, Françoise, Leigh, Eric Grant, and Cheryl Finley, read my work and offered much appreciated support. Lisa McGill left footsteps for me to follow all along the way. Sonya Winton was a good study partner who paced me during the last months of writing. Qiana Whitted and I became compatriots at the very beginning of the graduate school experience; her friendship continues to mean the world to me. Thanks to Victorine Shepard, Registrar of the American Studies Department, for her strength and warmth and integrity.

Before Yale there was Saint Ann's School in Brooklyn. I would like to thank Stanley Bosworth for thirty years of faith. I thank the late Jacquelyn Lee for exposing me to African American literature, history, and performance. I thank Linda Kauffman for her love and for planting the seeds that first made me think about attending graduate school. And I thank my students at Saint Ann's for sending me to Yale.

Before Saint Ann's there was my family. My brother, Donny, is no longer here, but he is with me often. My sisters Patricia and Sonia have always believed in me. I thank them. My brother-in-law Errol feeds me. I thank him. I thank my father, Andrew Williams, for first teaching me to play with words and to question what I thought I knew. I thank my stepmother, Daphne Williams, and my nephew Derrick Huggins for being my vacation partners and for being so proud of me. I thank my nephews and nieces, Donavon Williams, Sheena Williams, Christopher Nembhard, and Nicole Nembhard, for their unlimited supply of love. Christopher's calls to check up on me have always come at a good time. I thank William Bell, who encouraged me even when it was not in his own best interest.

Most of all, I thank Clay Williams, my nephew, whose pure love, wisdom, and pride in me keep me going. I dedicate this book to Clay, and to the memory of my beautiful mother, Linda M. Williams. Her students knew her simply as "Teacher."

SELF-TAUGHT

INTRODUCTION

This study emerged from one central historical question: What did ordinary African Americans in the South do to provide education for themselves during slavery and when slavery ended? To get at the answers, I have cut across traditional constructs of periodization and have therefore been able to see African Americans in slavery, in the Civil War, and in the first decade of freedom. Reading in this way made it possible to discern a continuity of people and ideas; and I was able to observe the visions of enslaved people emerge into plans and actions once they escaped slavery. Looking at African Americans' creative and surreptitious efforts to become literate while enslaved provided a rich context for their eagerness to attend schools in the aftermath of the Civil War. Literate men who escaped slavery to enlist in the Union army, for example, became teachers in regiments of black men, and once the war ended, these same men taught in local communities. They also advocated for political and economic equality, underscoring with each letter or petition precisely why literacy was such an urgent priority to an oppressed group living within a literate society.

I relied on a vast number of sources to tell this history of freedpeople's role in educating themselves. I returned, in the first place, to the same missionary archives that other historians have used, and I learned to read between the lines, to pull out people who are mentioned only in passing. I learned to overlook white missionaries' paternalism at times and to expose and challenge it at other times. But relying on sources produced by white people to tell a story about black people can be frustrating. One day after spending many hours in Union records and American Missionary Association (AMA) manuscripts, my craving for black sources was palpable. I walked around the library muttering, "Where are the black people? I have to find the black people." That day I found Elijah Marrs in a bibliography of black autobiography, and he became an important guide who took me from the time he learned to read while enslaved in Kentucky, to his decision to lead other black men into the army, to his teaching in his regiment, his agitation for African American political rights, and finally to teaching black children into the twentieth century. Other guides appeared for short portions of the journey: among others, John Sweney, Mattie Jackson, London Ferebee, Margaret Adams, and E. D. Tilghman. I encountered them in military records, slave narratives, autobiographies, black college archives, the records of the Freedmen's Bureau, and in the collections that historians have painstakingly compiled over the years.

Sometimes I can tell only part of a story because the freedpeople in a particular episode drop out of the sources, but even these small bits become significant when placed with other small pieces to create a larger picture. Although many sources, including the missionary manuscripts, do not foreground them, African Americans are present in the interstices, in the negative spaces that comprise such a substantial part of the picture. African Americans move out of the background first when you look for them, and second when you read several sources together. Because I insist on acknowledging their presence, African Americans are much more present in this narrative of freedpeople's education.

I tell the story in nine chapters. Chapter 1 explores what literacy meant to enslaved people and recounts the methods they used to acquire literacy even when state legislation and local practice forbade it. Chapter 2 follows enslaved people out of slavery into contraband camps and freedpeople's villages, where some immediately began teaching and implored white missionaries to provide trained teachers. Chapter 3 also follows African Americans out of slavery, but this time into the Union army. There, literate men taught and donated money, time, and labor to build schools for communities of freedpeople, even as they engaged in combat, built fortifications, and reflected on the roles they would play as free men in a world being transformed by war. Chapter 4 looks at early political organizing by freedpeople and identifies self-help and self-determination as important values. The chapter also traces African Americans' efforts to establish education as a civil right, which they called on state governments to enforce. Chapter 5 examines freedpeople's implementation of schooling in local communities. It recounts as well some of the conflicts that arose between African Americans and white northerners over who would be in control of schools for black people. Chapter 6 enters classrooms with African American teachers from southern and northern states and discusses their need for supplies, adequate school buildings, and sometimes even more education themselves. African American teachers in Georgia in 1866 form the core of this chapter. Chapter 7 examines the content and availability of textbooks for freedpeople's schools and analyzes texts that Confederate states created to convey a proslavery ideology to southern white children. Chapter 8 turns to African American children and adults as students. It examines their motivations for attending school, their adjustments to the schoolroom, and their expectations of teachers. Further, the chapter examines how teachers perceived students, how they assessed their intellect and potential. Finally, chapter 9 traces African American influence on white people's interest in education in the South and argues that freedpeople's schools motivated poor whites to attend school and convinced elite whites to call for the establishment of schools for poor whites. The schools became reality while African Americans and other Republicans held power in state legislatures.

The history of education among former slaves was by no means an untold story when I came to it. Several historians have written about the missionary teachers who went to southern states to teach former slaves. Historian Henry Lee Swint of Vanderbilt University was perhaps the first to devote a monograph to the northern teacher in the South. Writing in 1941 within a tradition that celebrated the white antebellum South and was contemptuous of African Americans, Swint mostly concerned himself with explaining and justifying white southern hostility toward black education. White southerners did not so much oppose the education of former slaves, he argued, as they resented the intrusion of white northern schoolteachers who carried abolitionist beliefs and a complete disregard for southern strictures into southern communities. Black people appear in Swint's narrative almost incidentally. To his way of thinking, they exhibited little if any agency.[1]

Robert C. Morris, whose work on textbooks for freedpeople is invaluable, also focused more on missionary teachers and organizations than on freedpeople in his monograph, *Reading, 'Riting, and Reconstruction*. In Morris's view, "Black education was a cooperative venture involving the Freedmen's Bureau, benevolent societies, and a corps of teachers that by July 1870 numbered 3,500." Although Morris discussed black teachers in one chapter, it seems that by not explicitly including freedpeople as participants in the "cooperative venture," he continued to treat them as subjects who were acted upon, rather than as actors themselves.[2]

More than other historians, Jacqueline Jones, in *Soldiers of Light and Love: Northern Teachers and Georgia Blacks, 1865–1873*, portrayed African Americans as active participants in the movement for education. She documented, for example, conflicts that arose in Savannah, Georgia, between AMA missionaries and blacks over who would control the administration of schools that blacks had established. Still, the work is principally concerned with the missionary teachers, their motivations for going south to teach, their approaches to teaching, and their reception by black and white southerners. Jones's interest was in telling the story of the predominantly white northern women who courageously ventured into the South after the war.[3]

Admittedly focused on "white northern objectives and actions," historian Ronald E. Butchart, in crafting a convincing argument that land ownership was essential to African Americans in the aftermath of the Civil War, contended that missionary associations' decision to provide education instead was a costly mistake. "The Afro-Americans were on the threshold of freedom," Butchart argued. "They needed land, protection, and a stake in society. They

needed and demanded meaningful power. They were given instead a school."
Butchart placed the impetus for the educational movement squarely in the
hands of northern benevolent organizations such as the American Missionary
Association and blamed them for, in effect, imposing education on African
Americans.[4]

Butchart, Morris, and Jones helped me to understand the inner workings
of the missionary organizations that sponsored teachers and that so greatly
influenced the institutionalization of schools for African Americans in the
South. Their work provided me with insight into the teachers' motivations
for going south as well as an appreciation of the teachers' reception and
service once there. I turned to these books many times as I researched and
wrote. Still, their emphasis on northern white actors might be seen as helping
to reproduce beliefs that African Americans' role in the educational mission
was largely one of dependence. In particular, Butchart's argument that the
decision by northern whites to provide education was not in the best interest
of freedpeople did not ring true to me. I wanted to poke at that assertion, to
test it to see if Butchart was correct. What I have found is something quite
different. In community after community, state after state, I found freedpeople placing education on a short list of priorities that included land ownership, fair contracts, suffrage, and equal treatment in legal proceedings. And, I
found them building schools, teaching, paying tuition, and working to garner
additional resources.

I received encouragement to center African Americans in the telling of the
history of emancipation-era education from the work of W. E. B. Du Bois
and historians James D. Anderson and Herbert Gutman, each of whom credited African Americans with launching the educational movement in the
South that led to the establishment of public school systems to accommodate
white children as well as black. More broadly, Leon F. Litwack's depictions of
newly free people in *Been in the Storm So Long* held me enthralled. His detailed
history allowed the former slaves to speak, and as I listened, I felt as if I were
there with them, and I wanted to stay. Litwack introduced me to the period
of emancipation, and he showed me a way of telling history.[5] As I went into
the archives myself I was even more spellbound. During the period of emancipation, bureaucrats, journalists, individuals, and organizations generated a
host of sources that include information about African Americans. Reading
those documents it sometimes seemed as if African Americans had been
speaking while enslaved, but we could only hear a few of them. The new
sources produced after the war enrich our understanding of the lived experiences of enslaved people as well as of freedpeople.

I have found issues of power to be ubiquitous in freedpeople's efforts to
obtain schooling. Writing about our contemporary moment, Michael W.

Apple and Linda K. Christian-Smith have observed, "Education and power are terms of an indissoluble couplet. It is at times of social upheaval that this relationship between education and power becomes most visible."[6] This coupling was no less salient in the South in the 1860s. Varying and persistent conflicts arose between and among southern blacks, northern blacks, northern whites, and southern whites as each constituency realized that an educated black population could bring about a seismic change in the American South. Sometimes struggles over power were articulated economically or politically; sometimes they were acted out in brutal attacks against freedpeople and white teachers. Indeed, I include accounts of southern white violence in several chapters because I want to establish the centrality of violence as a foil to freedpeople's educational efforts. My analysis of the issues of power that were implicated in this educational movement is grounded in the work of James C. Scott, who contends that oppressed, relatively powerless people, unable to openly express their true thoughts, develop public transcripts steeped in deference and loyalty. At the same time, out of their submerged anger and resentment, the powerless produce "hidden transcripts" of subversion that represent a critique of power. The hidden transcript enables the powerless to achieve some degree of autonomy and dignity and, combined with the public transcript, deflects suspicion that the powerless may pose a threat to the status quo. Once again, by looking at African Americans across a wide timeline, I am able to identify shifting transcripts from slavery into freedom.[7]

By concentrating my attention on African Americans, I was able to see important elements that have been overlooked. It became overwhelmingly clear, for example, that freedpeople, not northern whites, initiated the educational movement in the South while the Civil War was being fought. This made sense to me in light of what I had already uncovered about some enslaved people's determination to become literate and the drastic and creative measures they took to learn to read and write. It made perfect sense that someone who had climbed into a hole in the woods to attend school would, in freedom, sacrifice time and money to build a schoolhouse. It rang true that people who waited up until ten o'clock at night to sneak off to classes on the plantation would want to establish schools in the open as soon as they possibly could.

I began to see, too, that in many places schools that history has labeled American Missionary Association schools, for example, could just as easily have been called freedpeople's schools. Certainly missionary employees taught in the schools, but time after time, the sources revealed that in fact former slaves conceived of the school, donated their churches to house it or built new cabins from scratch, provided fuel, and paid tuition. Sometimes a freedperson even taught the school until a better trained northerner arrived.

In the end, through all the struggle to establish schools, through all the wrangling with northern white missionaries over control of schools, and for all the violence and hostility from some southern white people, the freedpeople's educational movement transformed public education in the American South, to the great benefit of both black and white people. The sources argue for a shift in perception that enables us to see the vision and persistent work of African Americans to become an educated people.

CHAPTER 1 ▪ ▪ ▪ ▪ ▪ ▪ ▪ ▪ ▪ ▪ ▪ ▪ ▪

In Secret Places

Acquiring Literacy in
Slave Communities

No child, white people never teach
colored people nothing, but to be good
to dey Master and Mistress. What
learning dey would get in dem days,
dey been get it at night. Taught
demselves.
　　Louisa Gause, South Carolina

I have seen the Negroes up in the
country going away under large oaks,
and in secret places, sitting in the
woods with spelling books.
　　Charity Bowery, North Carolina

Despite laws and custom in slave states prohibiting enslaved people from learning to read and write, a small percentage managed, through ingenuity and will, to acquire a degree of literacy in the antebellum period.[1] Access to the written word, whether scriptural or political, revealed a world beyond bondage in which African Americans could imagine themselves free to think and behave as they chose. Literacy provided the means to write a pass to freedom, to learn of abolitionist activities, or to read the Bible. Because it most often happened in secret, the very act of learning to read and write subverted the master-slave relationship and created a private life for those who were owned by others. Once literate, many used this hard-won skill to disturb the power relations between master and slave, as they fused their desire for literacy with their desire for freedom.

Placing antiliteracy laws in dialogue with the words of enslaved people enables an examination of the tensions that slave literacy provoked between owned and owner. Masters made every attempt to control their captives' thoughts and imaginations, indeed their hearts and minds. Maintaining a system of bondage in the Age of Enlightenment depended upon the master's being able to speak for the slave, to deny his or her humanity, and to draw a line between slave consciousness and human will. The presence of literate slaves threatened to give lie to the entire system. Reading indicated to the world that this so-called property had a mind, and writing foretold the ability to construct an alternative narrative about bondage itself. Literacy among slaves would expose slavery, and masters knew it.

Understanding how enslaved people learned not only illuminates the importance of literacy as an instrument of resistance and liberation, but also brings into view the clandestine tactics and strategies that enslaved people employed to gain some control over their own lives. While it is common to view Frederick Douglass's antebellum struggle for literacy as exceptional, slave narratives, interviews with former slaves, and other documents offer a view of more widespread communities of learners who also forged the crucial link between literacy and freedom.

The story of Mattie Jackson illustrates the radical potential that enslaved African Americans perceived in literacy. Although Jackson came of age as the institution of slavery faced its final challenge, her personal efforts to free herself are suggestive of other people's experiences in slavery. Once free, Jackson told her story to a more literate black woman who wrote it down. This narrative helps us to understand the key role that literacy—and gender— could play in the crusade for freedom.

As a child in Missouri, Mattie Jackson experienced the family disruptions that so often characterized the experiences of enslaved people. When she was three years old, her father was sold, but he escaped before he could be transferred to his new owner. Months passed before the family received word that he had reached freedom. Two years later, Jackson's mother, Ellen Turner, attempted to escape to Chicago, where her husband now preached. With two children accompanying her, however, Turner was quickly captured and returned to her owner, who promptly sold her and the children. It was not unusual that the man would successfully escape while the woman remained behind, as responsibility for childbearing and child-rearing circumscribed slave women's movement. Work assignments also restricted women's mobility. Men were more likely to be hired out or sent on errands into town, thus acquiring greater knowledge of how to move about without detection as well as greater opportunity to meet people who might shield them from discovery. Turner's attempt to leave, then, spoke of her determination to be free even in the face of the discouraging odds against success.[2]

Four years after her initial escape attempt, Turner remarried, and this second husband too escaped, once again to avoid being sold. Now left with four children, Turner went about her job as cook in the household, attending to her domestic duties, even at the expense of caring for her fatally ill son. Her owners, Mr. and Mrs. Lewis, might well have thought that all was in good order with this family of slaves. Turner, it appeared, had been tamed. With the loss of two husbands and a child, she seemed to have given up any hope of ever being free.[3]

In truth, Turner had not surrendered and had in fact managed to pass on some of her resolve to her daughter, Mattie. The coming of the Civil War stirred their hopes to the surface. With Union troops stationed nearby, tension grew in the household. The Lewises' agitation at news of Union victories emboldened Mattie Jackson and her mother in their challenges to being owned. Gathering information through eavesdropping became an important weapon in their private war with their owners. According to Jackson, when husband and wife talked about the war, Mrs. Lewis "cast her eye around to us for fear we might hear her. Her suspicion was correct; there was not a word that passed that escaped our listening ear."[4]

To learn most of their news, the Jackson women had to listen hard and remember well, tasks that slaves had perfected across the South. Such eavesdropping constituted a vital and accessible component of the intelligence network within slave communities. As important as literacy was to the slaves who employed it in service of their own freedom or for the benefit of others, enslaved African Americans also had other ways of knowing. They relied heavily on oral and aural systems of information. Those with access to white people's conversations listened closely when masters gathered and developed acute skills of perception and memory. As Henry Bibb noted, "slaves were not allowed books, pen, ink, nor paper, to improve their minds. But it seems to me now, that I was particularly observing and apt to retain what came under my observation." Specifically, Bibb recalled, "all that I heard about liberty and freedom to slaves, I never forgot. Among other good trades I learned the art of running away to perfection."[5]

As an enslaved boy in Winchester, Virginia, John Quincy Adams similarly honed his eavesdropping skills. When he learned there was no one to teach him to read and write because whites did not want blacks to become literate, the prohibition only stoked his curiosity. Whenever he heard a white person reading aloud, he lingered to listen, replying "nothing" when asked what he wanted. Then, at the first opportunity, he repeated to his parents everything he had heard. They, in turn, encouraged him to "try to hear all you can, but don't let them know it." By listening in this manner, Adams was able to inform his parents of an impending election that the owners wanted kept from their slaves. His information-gathering skills likely helped the family to escape to Pennsylvania during the Civil War. Other slaves worked as scouts for the one literate person among them. A woman in Beaufort, South Carolina, recalled that her mistress and master spelled out any information they did not want her to understand. As she was unable to read, she memorized the letters and repeated them as soon as she could to her literate uncle. He then decoded her memories into words or scraps of words.[6]

Long after he had transformed himself from enslaved child to prominent African American leader, Booker T. Washington reflected on the eavesdropping that had fed the "grape-vine telegraph" among slaves, which had kept them so well informed of the "questions that were agitating the country" leading up to the war. Enslaved people, he recalled, had developed reliable means for acquiring and dispersing information. For example, the man sent to pick up mail at the post office tarried long enough to overhear white men discussing the letters and newspapers they had just received. On the three-mile walk back to the plantation, the mail carrier relayed the news he had gathered. In this way, slaves often heard of important occurrences before the white people at the big house did.[7]

In addition to this traditional and widely available tactic of eavesdropping, Mattie Jackson and her mother had a device that John Quincy Adams would have coveted: they could "read enough to make out the news in the papers." According to Jackson, "The Union soldiers took much delight in tossing a paper over the fence to us. It aggravated my mistress very much." Although the soldiers likely considered the newspapers to be propaganda directed at white residents, Jackson and her mother appropriated them for their own purposes, sitting up late at night to "read and keep posted about the war." They then strategically deployed the information against their owners. During Mrs. Lewis's visits to oversee her slaves in the kitchen, the women taunted her with their knowledge of Union activity. In one kitchen skirmish the infuriated owner declared, "I think it has come to a pretty pass, that old Lincoln, with his long legs, an old rail splitter, wishes to put the Niggers on an equality with the whites." She went on to vow "that her children should never be on an equal footing with a Nigger, she had rather see them dead."[8]

Slave owners grew keenly aware that all around them African Americans were increasingly taking advantage of the Civil War to mount challenges to the institution of slavery. Perhaps spurred on by his wife's diminishing sense of authority over their human property, Mr. Lewis searched Turner's room and, upon finding a newspaper picture of Abraham Lincoln pasted on the wall, angrily demanded an explanation. When Turner, refusing to suppress her own feelings, replied that she had hung the picture because she liked it, a livid Lewis knocked her to the ground and "sent her to the trader's yard for a month as punishment."[9] It must have occurred to Lewis then that Ellen Turner had not been tamed at all; she had merely changed her tactics of resistance. Instead of running away, she now used the newspaper and, by implication, her literacy as a mechanism for destabilizing the master-slave relationship. For her part, Turner fully knew that both she and her room were Lewis's property and that he could enter the space at will. By cutting Lincoln's image from a newspaper and hanging it on a wall in Lewis's house, Turner reinforced for herself the possibility of imminent freedom. At the same time, she issued a challenge to her owner's power by asserting that she and other slaves had allies in high places. In displaying the image of a potential liberator over her bed, she declared that slavery would not last forever and that she fully supported its demise.

In the domestic battle between owners and slaves, literacy persisted as a symbol of resistance. Despite Turner's severe punishment for brandishing Abraham Lincoln's likeness, order in the household continued its decline. While Mrs. Lewis mourned over a Union victory, the enslaved women rejoiced. "The days of sadness for mistress were days of joy for us," Jackson recounted. "We shouted and laughed to the top of our voices. My mistress was more enraged than ever—nothing pleased her." One night, Mrs. Lewis flew into an unprovoked rage. She announced that Jackson would be punished, selected a switch, and placed it in the corner of a room to await her husband's return. Countering Mrs. Lewis's assertion of power, Jackson proclaimed both her recalcitrance and her literacy by bending the switch into the shape of an "M," the first letter of her name. With this symbolic challenge to her master and mistress, Jackson and another enslaved girl walked away from the house.

Jackson's display of literacy, paired with her departure, telegraphed to her owners the clear message that she refused to acquiesce in her enslavement. She sent them word that despite their prohibitions she had learned to write and was intent on marshaling every means at her disposal to undermine their authority. By asserting that Mr. and Mrs. Lewis could not stop her from learning to write, could not whip her, and could not prevent her from running away, Mattie Jackson utilized at once all the oppositional strategies that her mother had used over a lifetime.

The two girls made their way to the arsenal to find the Union troops, who they believed were a new form of protection. But they could gain neither admission to the arsenal nor the protection they sought. Even so, the girls had made a point. Upon returning to the Lewis household, "not a word was spoken respecting [their] sudden departure."[10]

Silence, however, did not signal peace. Slavery was a negotiated relationship maintained by the power of owners' violence.[11] Sometimes, though, enslaved people overwhelmed shocked owners with displays of their own force. Within weeks the stalemate in the Lewis home erupted into a violent confrontation. Once again the incident began with Mrs. Lewis's complaints. Mr. Lewis intervened, asking Jackson if she had done her work. Jackson said she had, in essence contradicting her mistress, who "flew into a rage and told him I was saucy, and to strike me, and he immediately gave me a severe blow with a stick of wood, which inflicted a deep wound upon my head." When Jackson disobeyed Mr. Lewis's order to change her bloody clothing, he "pulled me into another room and threw me on the floor, placed his knee on my stomach, slapped me on the face and beat me with his fist, and would have punished me more had not my mother interfered." In Jackson's estimation, her mother's refusal to leave the room angered Lewis, but it also intimidated him as he assessed his chances of winning a fight against these two women.

Unlike slave women narrators such as Harriet Jacobs, who felt constrained to present themselves to white northern readers as demure and genteel, Jackson spoke unabashedly of her physical confrontation with her master. "I struggled mightily, and stood him a good test for a while, but he was fast conquering me when my mother came. He was aware my mother could usually defend herself against one man, and both of us would overpower him, so after giving his wife strict orders to take me up stairs and keep me there, he took his carriage and drove away."[12] With his departure Lewis conceded that even the man of the house could no longer control his slaves, which encouraged Jackson to place even more pressure on the weakening slave power. Still wearing her bloody clothing as evidence of her mistreatment, Jackson once again set out for the arsenal to seek protection from the Union army. This time, she was able to convince an officer to hear her complaint and give her shelter.[13]

Mattie Jackson's search for freedom and protection openly asserted her opposition to her owners' control and violence. Her actions were tantamount to a declaration of domestic civil war.[14] By calling on authorities who might exercise some power over her owners, she publicly declared her intention to be free. Certainly Jackson's will to make this declaration gained momentum from the Civil War, yet early in the war, particularly in border states such as Missouri, Union officers refused to interfere in the established relationships of the South. When Jackson turned to Union officers to help execute her private war, they failed to provide long-term protection. Thus, three weeks later when Mr. Lewis appeared to claim his property, the Union troops handed her over. Before long, Lewis sold Jackson, her mother, and her siblings to different owners. Jackson's actions had only served to further infuriate her owners, who retaliated by simultaneously liquidating their investment and disrupting this enslaved family once more.[15]

Like Mattie Jackson and her mother, Ellen Turner, other enslaved people folded literacy into the store of strategies that they called upon both to challenge slavery and make slavery bearable. Becoming literate itself required them to employ creative tactics. Jackson does not reveal how her mother learned to read, but presumably mother taught daughter at night in their room in the Lewis home. Accounts of such efforts make it evident that even in slavery, with its violence, insults, and punishing labor, many African Americans yearned to become literate, to have access to the news and ideas that otherwise would have been beyond their reach. For similar reasons, southern white elites continued their efforts to place literacy itself beyond the reach of African Americans.

Indeed, literacy constituted one of the terrains on which slaves and slave owners waged a perpetual struggle for control.[16] Cognizant of the revolutionary potential of black literacy, white elites enacted laws in slave states to proscribe teaching enslaved and sometimes free blacks to read or write. The timing of these antiliteracy laws often exposed the close association in white minds between black literacy and black resistance. Whether the threat to slavery came in the form of a slave rebellion or talk of abolition, southern lawmakers linked black literacy to the institution's demise and invested powers of surveillance and punishment in a host of officials, including justices of the peace, constables, sheriffs, marshals, police officers, and sergeants. Although antiliteracy statutes are often associated with Nat Turner's rebellion in 1831, they in fact had their beginnings a century earlier. In 1739, in an effort to escape to Florida, South Carolina slaves killed more than twenty whites in what became known as the Stono Rebellion. One year later, suspecting that slaves had communicated their insurrectionary plans in writing, the colonial legislature of South Carolina inscribed its fear into a statute that outlawed teaching any slave to write or employing any slave to write. The legislature reasoned that this prohibition was necessary because permitting slaves to engage in writing "may be attended with great inconveniences."[17]

Black people in South Carolina, however, devised methods to circumvent the law, and in 1800 the legislature explicitly acknowledged that earlier laws had been insufficient to keep blacks in "due subordination." Teaching had moved farther underground. The legislature hoped to root it out by enacting a statute that declared any assembly of "slaves, free negroes, mulattoes and mestizoes," among themselves or with whites, for the purpose of "mental instruction," an unlawful meeting. The new law broadened both the scope of prohibited activity and the categories of individuals covered. Rather than solely criminalizing the teaching of writing, the 1800 statute outlawed "mental instruction," which could include reading, writing, memorization, arithmetic, and much more. Furthermore, while the 1740 statute had only prohibited teaching slaves, the 1800 law prohibited teaching slaves *and* free blacks. Finally, the 1800 law aimed specifically to prevent African Americans from gathering in secret places to learn "either before the rising of the sun, or after the going down of same." The legislature had undoubtedly become aware of clandestine schools meeting before dawn and late into the night. By way of enforcement, lawmakers required magistrates to enter into such "confined places," to "break down doors," and to disperse such unlawful assemblages. The law subjected each person of color in the group to corporal punishment not to exceed twenty lashes.[18]

In 1829 David Walker's *Appeal to the Coloured Citizens of the World*, with its militant attack on slavery and its call for armed resistance, stirred fears in southern whites that the essay would inspire slaves to rebel. Rebellion, of course, was exactly what Walker hoped to provoke. Born to an enslaved father and a free mother, he had left his home in Wilmington, North Carolina, eventually settling in Boston, where, although free, African Americans led severely circumscribed economic and political lives. In the *Appeal*, Walker declared white Americans the natural enemies of African Americans, and he both predicted and urged warfare that would bring about the destruction of slavery. Moreover, Walker linked literacy to slavery's demise. Powerful whites went to great lengths to deprive blacks of education because, he argued, "for coloured people to acquire learning in this country, makes tyrants quake and tremble on their sandy foundation," knowing that "their infernal deeds of cruelty will be made known to the world." Walker hoped "all coloured men, women and children, of every nation, language and tongue under heaven, [would] try to procure a copy of this Appeal and read it, or get some one to read it to them." Published in September, the pamphlet quickly made its way south.[19]

On December 11, 1829, the Savannah, Georgia, police department seized sixty copies of the *Appeal*. Walker would no doubt have proposed severe punishment for the black Baptist minister who handed the *Appeal* over to officials after receiving copies from a ship's steward.[20] The Georgia legislature wasted little time in responding. Ten days following the seizure, the legislature passed a law to quarantine any ship that carried a free black person or a slave into Georgia ports. In addition to outlawing teaching any "slave, negro or free person of colour" to read, the statute provided punishment for blacks or any person bringing into the state and circulating "any printed or written pamphlet, paper or circular, for the purposes of exciting to insurrection, conspiracy or resistance among the slaves, negroes, or free persons of color" of the state.[21] Although a black minister may have betrayed his brethren, white legislators clearly feared that other African Americans would not be so afraid or so loyal.

Louisiana lawmakers were also afraid. In 1830 that state's legislature criminalized teaching slaves to read or write. Sections of the statute resonated with the panic that Walker and other abolitionists had inspired. The law punished with death, or imprisonment at hard labor for life, "whosoever shall write, print, publish or distribute any thing having a tendency to produce discontent among the free coloured population of the state, or insubordination among the slaves therein." Further, the statute specifically targeted anyone who "shall knowingly be instrumental in bringing into this state, any paper, pamphlet or book" that tended to excite insubordination or to cause discontent among African Americans, free or enslaved.[22]

As the northern abolition movement, prodded by African American abolitionists, shifted from a position of gradualism to immediatism, slave states ratcheted up their efforts to sustain a way of life that depended on slavery.[23] In 1830, a critical turning point for the abolition movement, North Carolina enacted a statute that articulated the perceived kinship between slave literacy and slave control. "Whereas the teaching of slaves to read and write, has a tendency to excite dissatisfaction in their minds, and to produce insurrection and rebellion, to the manifest injury of the citizens of the State," the law read, "any free person, who shall hereafter teach, or attempt to teach, any slave within this State to read or write, the use of figures excepted, or shall give or sell to such slave or slaves any books or pamphlets, shall be liable to indictment in any court of record in this State." The law further specifically forbade any slave to teach another slave to read or write. Significantly, North Carolina's antiliteracy stance constituted part of a larger scheme of surveillance and control over African Americans, enslaved and free. In the same legislative session, lawmakers promulgated limiting conditions for the manumission of slaves by owners, targeted runaways and those who harbored them, imposed restrictions on free black peddlers, and sought to exclude northern-produced literature that might "excite insurrection, conspiracy or resistance in the slaves or free negroes."[24] As was often the case, the North Carolina statute punished blacks more harshly than whites. White men and women could be imprisoned or fined between $100 and $200. Free people of color faced fines, imprisonment, or the public humiliation of whipping. Slaves convicted under the statute could be punished with "thirty-nine lashes on [the] bare back."[25]

Notably, North Carolina's antiliteracy law permitted teaching slaves arithmetic, likely because mathematical skill was necessary for trades such as carpentry and would therefore inure to the benefit of slave owners. Writing was strictly forbidden, however, even when a slave might use the skill to benefit his owner. Similarly, an 1833 Georgia statute made it unlawful for any person to "permit a slave, negro or person of colour to transact business for him in writing." Legislators assessed the costs and benefits of having literate slaves in their midst. They concluded that the risk was too high that slaves would use writing skills to subvert owners' power.[26]

A few months after North Carolina did, Virginia moved against African American literacy. In the spring of 1831, Virginia rendered unlawful "all meetings of free negroes or mulattoes, at any school-house, church, meeting-house or other place for teaching them reading or writing, either in the day or night, under whatsoever pretext." The statute also specifically outlawed the compensation of any white person for teaching slaves to read or write.[27] Three months after the August 1831 insurrection in which Nat Turner, a literate slave, and several other slaves killed fifty-five whites in Virginia, Alabama enacted a legislative package intended to severely curtail African American activity.[28] In addition to forbidding any person to teach any free person of color or any slave to spell, read, or write, it forbade slaves to associate with free blacks without permission of their owners, made it unlawful for five or more male slaves to assemble outside of their plantation, and made it unlawful for any person of color to "preach to, exhort, or harangue any slave or slaves, or free persons of color, unless in the presence of five respectable slaveholders." The statute also attempted to legislate paternalism by imposing a duty on all slaveholders to "feed and clothe their slaves with a sufficiency of food and clothing for their comfort." Legislators hoped that satisfying physical needs would stave off insurrectionary fervor.[29]

In 1836 the Alabama legislature voiced its fear that prohibitive laws notwithstanding, some African American slaves were literate and had access to antislavery literature. In a memorial addressed to the legislatures of all other states, Alabama lawmakers condemned the "dark, deep, and malignant designs of the Abolitionists," who were "sending into our country their agents and incendiary pamphlets and publications, lighting up fires of discord in the bosoms of our slave population." The legislators charged that abolitionists "have presses in the various parts of the Union, from which they issue millions of essays, pamphlets and pictures and scatter them amongst our slave population, calculated to urge them to deluge our country in blood." "This cannot be tolerated," Alabama's leaders concluded.[30] As David Walker had urged, some slaves were getting their hands on antislavery writings.

It is clear, too, that enslaved and free black people operated schools, particularly in urban areas.[31] An 1834 South Carolina statute suggests that the state's two earlier attempts to prevent slaves from becoming literate had not succeeded. This third attempt at control punished anyone who taught or assisted any slave in learning to read or write. In a revealing move, the statute added a new level of detail that presumably targeted contemporary practices; it punished by fine, imprisonment, or corporal punishment "any free person of color or a slave [who] shall keep any school or other place of instruction, for teaching any slave or free person of color to read or write." This statute aimed at African Americans who did not rely on sporadic teaching, but who instead established schools to make education more formal and methodical.[32]

White Americans' opposition to black education was not limited to the southern states. At the same time that Virginia and Alabama enacted legislation to prohibit African American education in the 1830s, the northern free state of Connecticut used both legal and extralegal means to curtail education options for black people. When the Convention of Colored Men of the United States met in 1831, delegates proposed establishing a college on the manual labor system in New Haven. Following up on a proposal by the convention's education committee, Arthur Tappan, who along with fellow white abolitionists William Lloyd Garrison and Simeon Jocelyn attended the convention, went so far as to purchase several acres of land to house the school. However, the white people of New Haven vehemently opposed any plan to provide higher education for African Americans. Supporters of the school suggested that opponents particularly objected to the impertinent idea of building a *college* for African Americans. The city's political leaders declared that a college to educate the black population would be "incompatible with the prosperity, if not the existence" of Yale College and the city's other educational institutions. The mayor and city council resolved to "resist the establishment of the proposed college in this place by every lawful means."[33]

Convention delegates abandoned the idea of building a black college in New Haven, but the struggle to provide education for African Americans in Connecticut did not end there. In 1832 Prudence Crandall, a white Quaker schoolteacher, along with black abolitionists James Forten, Reverend Theodore Wright, and Reverend Peter Williams, founded a boarding school for African American girls in Canterbury, Connecticut. In response, in May 1833 the state legislature outlawed the establishment of schools that provided instruction to "colored persons who are not inhabitants of this state." Crandall was prosecuted and convicted for violating the statute, but an appellate court reversed the conviction. Not long after, angry white residents set the occupied school on fire, then vandalized the building with clubs and iron bars, forcing Crandall to close the school.[34]

Back on southern plantations, purveyors of advice warned white masters, or more probably white mistresses, against giving in to any impulse to teach enslaved people to read the Bible to save their own souls. Prizewinning essayist Nathan Bass argued in 1851 that although a literate slave, if provided with appropriate reading material, might learn to "respect and venerate the authority of his owner," the risk was too great. Bass blamed "the spirit of bigotry and fanaticism which are abroad in the country, seeking to disseminate a spirit of insubordination in the bosom of the slave, by the circulation of incendiary publications, inducing him to throw off the authority of those to whom his services are due." Bass thought it wiser for owners to take responsibility for inculcating their own precepts of morality and religion into their slaves. A Mississippi planter also writing on slave management agreed with Bass. "I would gladly learn every negro on the place to read the Bible," he proclaimed, "but for a fanaticism which, while it professes friendship to the negro, is keeping a cloud over his mental vision, and almost crushing out his hopes of salvation."[35] Bass and the Mississippi planter would have considered naive the opinion of a Georgia planter who encouraged teaching slaves to spell and read; he found these skills convenient for slaves engaged in weighing cotton and erecting buildings. "Hurricane," as the planter called himself, saw no danger in the practice because he considered African Americans too stupid to become literate enough to undermine white authority.[36]

Enslaved people realized that those who owned them brought their awesome and arbitrary power to bear against any effort slaves made to learn to read and write. Interviewed years after slavery had ended, many recalled the barriers that whites had placed between literacy and themselves. Some slaves experienced the threats or punishment directly. Gordon Buford remembered that he and fellow slaves never learned to read and write because their master threatened to "skin them alive" if they tried. Charlie Grant's mistress beat him with a plaited cowhide when she caught him with a book. And Belle Caruthers's master struck her with his muddy boots when he caught her studying a Webster's blue-back speller.[37] Others experienced secondhand the violence that could be visited upon a slave who was caught reading or writing. James Lucas reported that his owner "hung the best slave he had for trying to teach the others how to spell." Literacy could also disrupt a sale. When Lucas's master realized that some of the people he had purchased at auction in Baltimore could read, he sent them back. Similarly, when Tom Hawkins's owner discovered that his carriage driver had learned to read and write while taking the owner's children to and from school, he cut off the driver's thumb and assigned another enslaved man to drive the carriage.[38] Still other former slaves had a broad and daunting sense of the punishment that might be meted out. Charlie Davis believed that he would get one hundred lashes if he so much as picked up a book, and George Washington Albright thought a Mississippi statute provided that if any slave learned to read or write, "he was to be punished with 500 lashes on the naked back, and to have the thumb cut off above the second joint."[39] The Mississippi statute actually prescribed punishment of thirty-nine lashes, but the expectation of even more violent punishment would surely have been enough to terrorize all but the most courageous and persistent.[40]

As slave owners and legislators suspected, African Americans, free and slave, designed all manner of strategies to elude the laws against learning. At about the same time that Virginia first put into writing its prohibition of teaching blacks to read and write, Mary and Thomas Peake, free people in Norfolk, Virginia, sent their six-year-old daughter Mary to live with an aunt in the District of Columbia so that she could attend school. She remained there until, according to Peake, the District of Columbia, too, prohibited teaching blacks. In 1847 she moved to Hampton, Virginia, where she taught black children and adults until the Civil War.[41] In Georgia, Susie King Taylor participated in an intricate web of secrecy to become educated. Born enslaved in Georgia in 1848, Taylor's owner permitted her to live with her free grandmother in Savannah. The port city of Savannah afforded a fair amount of mobility to hired slaves and had a large free black population.[42] Taylor's nominally free status released her from labor and from oversight by an owner, enabling her to pursue an education. Even so, she was constrained to learn in secret and with a patchwork of teachers because both the state of Georgia and the city of Savannah made it illegal to teach slaves or free people of color to read or write.[43] Carrying schoolbooks camouflaged with paper, Taylor and her younger siblings stole, one at a time, into the home of a free black woman each morning, careful not to be spotted by the police or any white person. Twenty-five children studied their lessons in Susan Woodhouse's kitchen each day and slipped out, one at a time, each afternoon. After two years with Mrs. Woodhouse, Taylor went to Mary Beasley, another black woman, who, after teaching everything she knew to Taylor, recommended that Taylor's grandmother find a more advanced teacher. That next teacher was a white playmate, who gave Taylor lessons for four months before joining a convent. Finally, the son of her white landlord gave Taylor lessons for several months until he was conscripted into the Confederate army.[44] Roughly pieced together as it was, Susie King Taylor's education would have appeared veritably formal to many other enslaved people who managed to become literate.

Sometimes masters' wives, inspired by evangelical Christianity, took it upon themselves to teach slaves to read. While some owners turned a blind eye to their wives' efforts, others badgered them into understanding the dangers inherent in teaching slaves. A few owners, however, not only tolerated but even encouraged their slaves' interest in education, particularly when it could benefit the owners. In one unusual instance, Lucy Skipwith in Hopewell, Alabama, kept up a correspondence during the 1850s and 1860s with her absentee owner, John Cocke, in Fluvanna County, Virginia. In her letters she informed Cocke of activities on the plantation, including the progress of her plantation school for other slaves.[45] In Virginia the state legislature passed a special law in 1842 granting permission for an enslaved man, Randolph, to learn to read and write. Randolph's owner, Henry Juett Gray, was blind and wanted to become a teacher of the blind. According to the special act, Gray needed the services of a "servant capable of reading and writing, which object cannot be permanently secured otherwise than by the education of a young slave named Randolph." Despite his usefulness to the young white man, the state considered a literate Randolph a potential danger and required that Henry Gray's father, Robert Gray, "indemnify the public against any possible injury which might be apprehended from the misconduct of said slave."[46]

Most enslaved people were not so fortunate; theirs was a covert mission to become literate. They truly had to "steal" an education. Some slaves hid spelling books under their hats to be ready whenever they could entreat or bribe a literate person to teach them. Some turned to white children, too young to understand that they violated the slave code, or to poor white men who did not care. Former slaves recounted stories of trading food and money for letters and words. In exchange for writing lessons, G. W. Offley fed a white boy whose father had gambled away the family's money. Offley later traded boxing and wrestling lessons with white men for writing instruction. James Fisher gave an old man money to buy whiskey in exchange for his writing lessons. As a young enslaved boy, Richard Parker picked up old nails and traded them for marbles that he then used to pay white boys for reading lessons. He carried a primer under his hat to be ready for class at any time. In addition, he received instruction from his owner's daughter until they were caught. "Uncle" Charles, a former slave in North Carolina, recounted that he also carried a primer under his hat and challenged white boys to tell him what a letter was, until he managed to learn the alphabet. He once traded a knife for a reading lesson from a white boy.[47] These particular means of acquiring literacy had important gender implications, as once again enslaved males tended to have greater mobility than enslaved females. Boys and men were more likely to accompany white children off the property to school and often had wider access to public spaces in which they could convince white males to teach them.

At the same time, women who worked inside the owner's household could entice their young white charges to pass on what they learned in school. Alice Green recalled that her mother had learned to read by keeping a schoolbook in her bosom all the time and asking the white children to tell her everything they had learned in school each day. In this way, she learned enough to teach school once slavery ended. Likewise, Allen Allensworth's mother encouraged him to "play school" with his young master who attended school every day.[48]

Enslaved people put the resources they could garner to maximum use. Mandy Jones knew of a young man who learned to read and write in a cave. She also recalled that there were "pit schools" near her Mississippi plantation. Slaves would dig a pit in the ground way out in the woods, covering the spot with bushes and vines. Runaways sometimes inhabited the pits, but they also housed schools. According to Jones, "slaves would slip out of the Quarters at night, and go to dese pits, an some niggah dat had some learning would have a school."[49] In South Carolina Edmund Carlisle cut blocks from pine bark and smoothed them into slates. He dropped oak into water to make ink, and he used a stick as his pen.[50] Some slaves copied letters and words whose meanings they could not yet decipher onto fences and in the dirt.[51] And, more than one hundred years later, when slave cabins were excavated, archaeologists were surprised to find, along with the predictable shards of colonoware pottery, food bones, and oyster shells, the remains of graphite pencils and writing slates, some with words and numbers still written on them.[52]

Sundays proved to be an important day for enslaved people to learn to read and write. Some slaves took advantage of the opportunity that a few missionaries offered to learn to read. Others relied on their own resources. Since the colonial period, slave management on the Sabbath had presented a vexing challenge to slave owners. Whites struggled to maintain control over black movement on the day when slaves were not required to work, the day when whites attended church and socialized away from their homes. In South Carolina, for example, legislation passed in 1712 aimed to limit the movement of blacks who congregated in Charlestown on Sundays in such great numbers as to "give them opportunity of executing any wicked designs." Twelve years later the colony's assembly directed white men to ride armed on Sundays in order to defend against slaves who congregated in large numbers. Evidently the legislation did not effectively curtail black behavior because over the next thirty years grand juries made several attempts to mandate stricter enforcement. Their concerns were not unfounded; in September 1739 slaves staged the Stono uprising while whites attended "divine service."[53]

In similarly radical fashion, African Americans took advantage of their leisure time and whites' absence on Sundays to become literate. They lurked in their designated places until masters left for Sunday outings, and then they pulled out books and pencils. Former slave Charity Bowery recalled that on Sundays on her Edenton, North Carolina, plantation, she saw "negroes up in the country going away under large oak trees and in secret places, sitting in the woods with spelling books." In Maryland G. W. Offley, who later paid white men and boys for writing lessons, received his first reading lessons at age nineteen from an old black man, who taught him at night and on Sunday mornings. Here were the clandestine schools that legislatures sought to eliminate, schools that convened after dark and on the Sabbath, when masters were likely to be more concerned about their own souls and their own pleasure than about the activities of the people who worked for them on the other six days of the week.[54] In Person County, North Carolina, James Curry began his illegal lessons with his master's son. Curry's mother bought him a spelling book, and the lessons continued until his owner found out and forbade further teaching. According to Curry, though, "when my master's family were all gone away on the Sabbath, I used to go into the house and get down the great Bible, and lie down in the piazza, and read, taking care, however, to put it back before they returned." Just as the slaves who congregated in

Charlestown, South Carolina, had used Sundays to resist their owners' control over their bodies, slaves like James Curry took advantage of Sundays to undermine owners' attempts to control their intellect.[55]

But why was literacy so sought after and so forbidden? The motivations on each side were very much the same. Whites feared that literacy would render slaves unmanageable. Blacks wanted access to reading and writing as a way to attain the very information and power that whites strove to withhold from them. Literacy had practical implications for enslaved people. When James Fisher's owner sold him away from his mother in Nashville, Tennessee, Fisher quickly decided that he must learn to write in case he ever had the opportunity to forge a pass and escape. "I copied every scrap of writing I could find, and thus learned to write a tolerable hand before I knew what the words were that I was copying," Fisher recalled. After a while he met the old man who taught him to write in exchange for money to buy whiskey. When his mistress entered his room and discovered his writing materials, she reported him to her father, Captain Davis, who immediately made the same connection between liberty and literacy that Fisher had made. Davis began by threatening Fisher, saying that if Fisher belonged to him he would cut off his right hand. Since he did not have authority to carry out such a threat, Davis attempted instead to convince Fisher to forsake ideas of freedom, arguing that he was better off enslaved than free. Both Davis and Fisher clearly equated wanting to learn to write with wanting to be free. Davis's arguments notwithstanding, Fisher eventually escaped to Canada.[56]

As both James Fisher and Captain Davis understood, African American literacy portended a profound threat to slavery by providing slaves with an advantage for greater movement within a system that relied on individual owners' providing passes for their slaves, rather than on some method of universal registration. Susie King Taylor's clandestine educational efforts in Savannah, for example, provided an immediate reward when she was able to write passes for her grandmother, who, although free, was required to produce a pass from her white guardian in order to move about at night.[57] In Kentucky field hand A. T. Jones cobbled together enough education to write himself a pass to freedom. When Jones learned that his master had sold him instead of allowing him to buy himself as they had previously agreed, he decided to make his way to Canada. "I could hardly put two syllables together grammatically," Jones later confessed, "but in fact, one half the white men there were not much better. I wrote my pass—'Please let the bearer pass and repass, on good behavior, to Cincinnati and return.'" His ability to write, along with the marginal literacy of potential captors, helped Jones to execute the escape.[58]

Owners' fears of slave literacy materialized in the loss of their property. In

$50 REWARD.

RUNAWAY FROM THE SUBSCRIBER, on the 25th day of November last, my boy WILLIS, aged about thirty years. WILLIS is about 5 feet 10 inches high, of dark complexion, has a down cast look, a little stooping, and limps slightly in his walk, caused by a severe burn on (I think) his left thigh and leg : When last heard from said boy, he was in the neighborhood of Laurinburg, N. C., and I have no doubt is trying to make his way to the free States, either by way of Wilmington, N. C., to the Yankee fleet, or through the country in some other direction. I have good reason to believe that he has been passing on a permit written by himself, fictitiously signed, and may attempt to pass himself as a free negro. I will pay the above reward for his apprehension and delivery to me, or one half the amount for his lodgment in any Jail within the limits of the Southern Confederacy, so that I can get him.

W. R. MEDLIN,
Clio, Mar'boro' District, S. C.

January 29-18-6t

Newspaper advertisement placed by a South Carolina slave owner offering a reward for the capture of a slave who may have written a pass to enable his escape. From Wilmington Journal, *February 12, 1863.*

February 1863 a South Carolina slave owner placed a newspaper advertisement in search of an escaped slave. He suspected that Willis, a thirty-year-old man with a "down cast look" and a limp, was making his way north through North Carolina and possibly attempting to enlist with the Union army. He also suspected that Willis was using his literacy to effect his escape. "I have good reason to believe," the advertisement read, "that he has been passing on a permit written by himself, fictitiously signed, and may attempt to pass himself as a free Negro." The erstwhile owner offered a $50 reward for Willis's return.[59]

In addition to providing concrete information about the physical location of freedom and the means to get there, literacy had the potential to help enslaved people articulate intellectual objections to the very existence of the institution of slavery. Reading catapulted some slaves beyond the limited sphere to which owners hoped to keep them restricted and enabled them to engage vicariously in dialogues that raised moral challenges to the enslavement of human beings. When James Curry sneaked into his owner's library on Sunday mornings and carefully took down the family Bible, he somehow made his way to a passage that reinforced the condemnation his slave community had long made of slavery. He "learned that it was contrary to the revealed will of God, that one man should hold another as a slave." Curry recalled that he had always heard it said among the slaves that their ancestors had been stolen from Africa and should never have been enslaved. By reading the Bible, he discerned that "God hath made of one blood all nations of men to dwell on all the face of the earth." Curry interpreted the Apostle Paul's message to mean that since God had made all people, no one group was justified in enslaving another. While his owners attended "divine worship," Curry used the words in their own revered Bible to fashion his own condemnation of their unjust practice.[60]

Another literate slave, C. H. Hall, invoked Patrick Henry, hero of the American Revolution, to support his claim to freedom. Hall's mistress internalized her Baptist teachings of each believer's individual relationship to God and thought it her duty to teach her slaves to read the Bible. Her husband urged her to stop, but she had refused, and thus Hall learned to spell and to read fairly well. As he grew, his master became even more threatened by his literacy and accused Hall of becoming just like his brother, a literate preacher who "was raising the devil on the place." His master's watchful criticism forced Hall to stop reading, but only for a while. When after several years he began reading again, his owner's fears were realized, for according to Hall, "the more I read, the more I fought against slavery. Finally I thought I would make an attempt to get free, and have liberty or death." Hall's invocation of this language suggests that he used the lessons he learned from his mistress to venture beyond the Bible into the writings of American revolutionaries and adapted their language of liberation to his own circumstances. He escaped from his Maryland owners and made his way to Canada in the 1830s.[61]

On the Shelbyville, Kentucky, farm where he was enslaved, Elijah Marrs early in life became interested in learning to read and write. "I was convinced," he later wrote, "that there would be something for me to do in the future that I could not accomplish by remaining in ignorance. I had heard so much about freedom, and of the colored people running off and going to Canada, that my mind was busy with this subject even in my young days."[62] It is perplexing to consider what might cause an enslaved child to think that he would have important things to do, and what propelled him to make the link between education and effectiveness. Nevertheless, as many other slaves did, Marrs "sought the aid of the white boys" to teach him. He then practiced his lessons by reading the newspapers and the addresses on letters that the "white people" sent him to pick up at the post office. After a while, Marrs attended a late-night school that Ham Graves, an old black man, secretly taught. It was Graves who taught Marrs to write, and Marrs, too young to realize that he was leaving evidence of his illicit behavior, practiced his new skill all over the farm: "on every gate-post around the stables, as on the plow-handle, you could see where I had been trying to write."[63]

In the Bible, books, and newspapers, literate slaves found a language of liberation that augmented what they learned in slave quarters.[64] Reading gave a larger voice and conceptualization to ideas they had heard expressed by other slaves. Frederick Douglass, the most famous slave to become literate, demonstrated this progression. In a letter to his former master, Douglass wrote that at the age of six he decided to be free some day. Like James Curry, his first understanding of why he was enslaved came from hearing older black people say that their parents had been stolen from Africa by white men and sold into slavery. These narrations enunciated the community's foundational belief that its enslavement was illegitimate, a belief that was reinforced when Douglass's aunt and uncle escaped to freedom.[65] His desire for freedom grew when his master made a link between literacy and freedom, and the possibility of freedom became real for him when he read a dialogue between a slave and a master. Finally, the idea that all blacks might some day be free took root when he first read a definition of the word "abolition." Reading, then, did not introduce Douglass to the concept of freedom; rather it buttressed and augmented a developing consciousness.

While a boy in Baltimore, Douglass's mistress began teaching him to read, but he had not yet made much progress when Hugh Auld, Douglass's master, forbade his wife to continue. Auld also made the mistake of proclaiming his rationale to Douglass. "If you give a nigger an inch, he will take an ell. A nigger should know nothing but to obey his master—to do as he is told to do," Auld contended. Then he declared that teaching a black person to read would render him forever unfit to be a slave. As Captain Davis had, Auld saw literacy and liberty as indivisible concepts, and he thus considered a literate slave to be an inherent threat. Auld's outburst inspired the young Douglass to make the same transformative link. Taking Auld at his word, Douglass came to see literacy as power and illiteracy as mental darkness. However, convinced by her husband that a literate slave was a dangerous one, Mrs. Auld took up a new mission to keep Douglass from learning. "Nothing seemed to make her more angry than to see me with a newspaper," Douglass recalled. "She seemed to think that here lay the danger." As some other enslaved men and boys did, Douglass adopted a plan in which he befriended every white boy whom he met on the streets and "converted" as many as he could into teachers. He took a book and bread with him on errands, traded the bread for lessons, and so learned to read.[66]

In childhood Douglass may have believed that the mere ability to read would be a magical elixir that would lead to freedom, but in actuality it was the content of the reading material that transformed his life. Caleb Bingham's *The Columbian Orator*, for example, profoundly influenced Douglass. Originally published in 1810, this palm-sized volume contained speeches and essays intended to "improve the youth and others in the ornamental and useful art of eloquence." Bingham's instructions regarding pronunciation, cadence, pitch, and gesture had been read by thousands of American schoolboys before they found their way into the hands of a slave boy in Maryland.[67]

Douglass recalled the particular impact of two items in the book. First, he read a speech delivered in the Irish House of Commons in 1795 in favor of the bill to emancipate the Roman Catholics. The speaker asserted that England could not turn back the tide of the world's movement toward freedom and suggested that England's recent loss in America "should serve as a lasting example to nations, against employing force to subdue the spirit of a people, determined to be free."[68]

Second, in the "Dialogue Between a Master and a Slave," an African American slave who had twice run away challenged his master's right to keep him enslaved. The master, hurt by the slave's desire to be free, questioned whether he had not treated him well, to which the slave responded that no manner of good treatment could ever compensate him for being deprived of his liberty. The slave further contended that as he had been kidnapped and sold into slavery, there could be no moral justification for his enslavement. Finally, he assured his master that as long as he had legs, he would continue trying to escape because "it is impossible to make one, who has felt the value of freedom, acquiesce in being a slave." In the end, the slave's moral argument and his threat of continued resistance, prevailed over the owner's defense of slavery and the owner freed him.[69] Before reading this dialogue, Douglass may never have imagined that a slave and master could speak to each other "man to man," or that their conversation could come to such a positive end. However, Douglass could certainly identify with the slave who had been kidnapped, as his own oral tradition placed him in a genealogy of ancestors who had been kidnapped into slavery. Douglass lived in a world in which members of his slave community, at least among themselves, challenged the legitimacy of their enslavement, and at the same time, his owner expected him to accept enslavement without question. Exposure to the dialogue and speech delivered Douglass intellectually from this restricted, incongruous space to a place where slavery was not only openly challenged but defeated.

Douglass read the speech and the dialogue over and over, finding that they "gave tongue to interesting thoughts of my own soul, which had frequently flashed through my mind and died away for want of utterance." The thoughts, then, were not all new, but seeing them in print provided Douglass with a vocabulary for expressing them, as well as an added confidence derived from the new knowledge that his own thoughts had life and meaning outside of himself and his small community. As he meditated on the readings, he came to "abhor and detest" his enslavers and to experience the torment of hatred. "As I writhed under it," Douglass wrote, "I would at times feel that learning to read had been a curse rather than a blessing. In moments of agony, I envied my fellow-slaves for their stupidity. I have often wished myself a beast. It was the everlasting thinking of my condition that tormented me."[70]

Thus, Douglass suggested that had he not learned to read, he would not have become dissatisfied with slavery. This, of course, contradicted his assertion elsewhere that his initial desire for freedom came at age six when his aunt and uncle escaped. Rather than introducing the idea of freedom, reading, it seems, reinforced an existing desire and expanded his conception of the possible. The possible became even more enticing when Douglass learned the meaning of the word "abolition." He had heard the word and knew that it was significant and somehow opposed to slavery. When he got hold of a newspaper and read about petitions being filed in Washington, D.C., calling for the abolition of slavery, the increased possibility of freedom fired his existing desire to be free. Before he ever mounted a stage to deliver an antislavery speech, Douglass had inserted his consciousness into the national dialogue about the future of slavery.[71]

If legislative proscriptions in tandem with limited resources and the wrath of owners effectively kept most enslaved people from becoming literate, they never fully succeeded in arresting black literacy, as Frederick Douglass, Ellen Turner, and Mattie Jackson could have attested. Indeed, the battle between those who would impede black learning and those who would facilitate it continued right up to the Civil War. In 1853 Margaret Douglass, a southern white woman, was sentenced to one month in jail for teaching free black children in Norfolk, Virginia. Douglass, a seamstress, fell into the role of teacher when a free black barber asked if she would teach his children. She was visiting his shop one day and noticed his two sons reading a spelling book. The boys attended a local Sunday school where they received reading lessons, but they could not advance quickly because Norfolk had no schools for black children. Douglass decided that she and her daughter, Rosa, would teach the barber's children. As it happened, he could not spare the boys from their work, so he sent his three daughters instead, and what began as a private tutorial soon developed into a school with twenty students when other families got wind of the lessons. Douglass excluded enslaved children, but she claimed not to know that the law also prohibited her from teaching free black children. The school continued for several months without disturbance, and the state might have continued to turn a blind eye, as it did regarding the Sunday school, had Douglass not made a public declaration of her association with African Americans.[72]

When one of her students died, the white teacher joined in the funeral procession. Shortly thereafter, constables entered her home and ordered Douglass, her daughter, and the students to report to the mayor's office.[73] Margaret and Rosa Douglass were subsequently indicted by a grand jury on charges that they did "unlawfully assemble with divers negroes, for the purpose of instructing them to read and write, and did instruct them to read and to write, contrary to the Act of the General Assembly." Representing herself before the court, Douglass argued that as a former slaveholder herself, she was no abolitionist or fanatic and was strongly opposed to northern interference with southern institutions. However, she asserted, "I deem it the duty of every Southerner, morally and religiously, to instruct his slaves, that they may know their duties to their masters, and to their common God." She would no longer violate the law, Douglass told the jury, but she would continue her good work by "endeavoring to teach the colored race humility and a prayerful spirit, how to bear their sufferings as our Saviour bore his for all of us. I will teach them their duty to their superiors, how to live, and how to die."[74]

Perhaps swayed by Douglass's expression of loyalty to southern values and her sanction of African Americans' subservience to whites, the jury found her guilty but imposed a fine of only $1 instead of the maximum $100. In the two-tiered sentencing structure, however, the judge also had a say, and he imposed an additional sentence of one month in prison. In imposing the sentence, the judge informed Douglass that he had not been convinced by her argument that literacy was vital for religious training. Intellectual and religious instruction often go hand in hand, he wrote, but the fact that in many parts of Virginia, and other parts of the country, more than a quarter of whites were illiterate and still abided by moral laws proved that literacy was not a prerequisite for understanding moral law.[75] The judge further asserted that the law prohibiting teaching African Americans was a matter of self-preservation and protection, having its foundations in Nat Turner's memorable insurrection. He blamed the need for such a law on "Northern incendiaries" who clogged the mails with "abolition pamphlets and inflammatory documents, to be distributed among our Southern negroes to induce them to cut our throats."[76]

As late as 1861, the city of Savannah, Georgia, publicly whipped Reverend James Simms, a black man, for teaching slaves. A carpenter by trade, Simms purchased his freedom with money he earned by hiring himself out. Even after being whipped, he persisted in teaching slaves, and the city fined him $100. Refusing to pay, Simms left Savannah for Boston, where he remained until after the war.[77]

But what of Mattie Jackson with whom we began? After several escape attempts, Jackson finally made it to freedom in Indiana through the help of some "colored people" who "assisted slaves to escape by the Underground Railroad." In 1866, at the age of twenty, she dictated her narrative, hopeful that its sale would fund her education so that she, in turn, could teach other former slaves. Where slaves' narratives had previously been sold to raise funds to get rid of slavery, this narrative, produced in a new time, was sold to educate those who had outlasted the institution. In a plea to potential readers, Jackson confided, "I feel it a duty to improve the mind, and have ever had a thirst for education to fill that vacuum for which the soul has ever yearned since my earliest remembrance." Jackson believed that she and her race had been oppressed through no fault of their own, but now that the "links have been broken and the shackles fallen from them" through the efforts of the "beloved martyr President Lincoln," they needed education to become full participants in society. "Thus," Jackson implored potential purchasers, "I ask you to buy my little book to aid me in obtaining an education, that I may be enabled to do some good in behalf of the elevation of my emancipated brothers and sisters." Jackson had survived slavery and appealed to "the friends of humanity" to assist her in rendering her freedom meaningful.[78]

As a free woman, Jackson made a declaration that was arguably as significant as her earlier determination to end her physical enslavement. She asserted that she would become educated and began the process of making this new goal a reality. In Indianapolis Jackson boarded with people who became interested in "teaching and encouraging me in my literary advancement and all other important improvements, which precisely met the natural desires for which my soul had ever yearned since my earliest recollection. I could read a little but was not allowed to learn in slavery. I was obliged to pay twenty-five cents for every letter written for me. I now began to feel that as I was free I could learn to write, as well as others."[79]

In publishing her plan for education, Jackson made three claims on behalf of African Americans. First, she challenged notions of black intellectual inferiority by asserting that she was educable and could learn to write as well as anyone else. Second, she rejected notions of black degradation and made the radical claim that the soul of an enslaved black child had always yearned for enlightenment. Finally, Jackson sought to eliminate any assumption of exceptionalism by including other former slaves in her claims of intellectual curiosity and capacity. Implicit in her desire to educate other blacks was the confidence that they also wanted to learn, and she encouraged them to do so. "Manage your own secrets, and divulge them by the silent language of your own pen," she counseled. She hinted, too, that once educated, she would write a second book, with her own pen, recounting her experiences in slavery.[80] In Mattie Jackson's view, freedom, combined with education, would empower her to finally take control of her own life, keeping her secrets and speaking her mind.

CHAPTER 2 ■ ■ ■ ■ ■ ■ ■ ■ ■ ■ ■ ■ ■ ■

A Coveted Possession

Literacy in the First Days of Freedom

> Probably with the children that are coming up no white men will not be needed. They are learning to read and write—some are learning lawyer, some are learning doctor, and some learn minister; and reading books and newspapers they can understand the law.
>
> Harry McMillan, Beaufort, South Carolina

> Of course, in our struggles, many of us felt sorely the need of an education in the midst of the new surroundings. Many of the old ones passed away from earth without realizing this coveted possession.
>
> Peter Randolph, Virginia

As Mattie Jackson did, thousands of enslaved people seized on the turmoil of the Civil War to make a final move for freedom. In sites of Union occupation, so many African Americans fled slavery that they began to influence Union policy, ultimately transforming the military's treatment of slaves seeking refuge. From an initial policy of noninterference with slave property, the Union came to understand two things. First, it was powerless to stop the flow of enslaved people into Union camps. Second, it could not successfully conduct the war without African American assistance.[1] These realizations, however, came only gradually.

The social and political power with which former slaves invested literacy initiated an educational revolution in the American South as African Americans' persistent demand for teachers and schools ignited and fueled a movement of northern teachers into southern black communities. Even as they risked everything to reach freedom, African Americans' once secret acquisition of literacy emerged as both public demand and support for education. Their determination to acquire literacy and numeracy generated the energy to build schoolhouses even while they tackled the physical challenges of hunger, disease, and homelessness. Indeed, during the transition from slavery to freedom, many African Americans simultaneously attempted to satisfy material needs along with intellectual longings. Tracing the movement of former slaves throughout war-torn southern states is critical to grasping the context within which they attempted to begin new lives. As African Americans carved out provisional spaces of freedom during the chaos of war, literacy ranked high among their priorities.

Ellen Turner would surely have been crestfallen had she known that early in the war her revered president disavowed any intention of ending slavery. In the inaugural address he delivered in 1861, Abraham Lincoln sought to assure slaveholders of the security of their property rights in African Americans. "Apprehension seems to exist among the people of the Southern States," the new president observed, "that by accession of a Republican Administration their property and personal security are to be endangered." But, he consoled southern interests; "I declare that—I have no purpose, directly or indirectly, to interfere with the institution of slavery in the states where it exists. I believe I have no lawful right to do so, and I have no inclination to do so."[2] Although Lincoln's proclaimed intention to leave slavery intact would not be a static one, well into the war he and other representatives of the Union refused to embrace emancipation as a goal.

Southern African Americans, however, intended to use this occasion of unrest and division among white Americans to liberate themselves from bondage, just as some of their ancestors had used the War for Independence and the War of 1812 as escape valves from enslavement. Their strategy capitalized on the networks of communication they had developed over generations, including what even Abraham Lincoln knew of as "the telegraph grapevine."[3] African Americans listened for the gunshots that signaled the presence of Union troops nearby. Then, not fully trusting northern soldiers, who were after all white, they sent two or three ahead to voice their petition for protection. Others followed when they learned of a positive reception.[4]

This movement of African Americans into freedom began as a persistent trickle of slaves leaving masters to seek asylum with the Union and grew into a groundswell. On May 6, 1861, just one month into the war, several African American men in King George County, Virginia, provided an early, silent signal of black intentions. Slave owner John T. Washington and six other white men began their patrol of neighborhood estates at about ten o'clock that night. When Washington returned home the following morning he "discovered that five of his negro men had packed up their clothing and absconded." Tracks suggested that the men had moved north toward Fredericksburg. When Washington inquired of his neighbors, he learned that "their negro men" had also disappeared. Recalling the previous night's patrol, Washington realized that he had seen only three black men on the seven estates under his surveillance. Confederate officials responded to Washington's alarm by "dispatching mounted men to intercept the slaves supposed to have escaped," but with no immediate results.[5]

African American men had begun to absent themselves from their place as slaves. Later in May 1861, three such men presented themselves to Major General Benjamin F. Butler at Fortress Monroe, Virginia, initiating an episode that became a critical turning point in Union policy toward African American slaves. The men, field hands belonging to a Confederate colonel, convinced Butler that without his intervention they would shortly be sent away from their families to Carolina to aid Confederate forces. Butler, who only one month earlier had assured the governor of the loyal, slave state of Maryland that he had no intention of interfering with property rights in slaves, made a bold move. Reasoning that Virginia, having seceded, was now an enemy foreign country, Butler concluded that it was within his province to seize property belonging to the enemy. "Shall they be allowed the use of this property against the United States, and we not be allowed its use in the aid of the United States?" Butler asked rhetorically. In response, he declared the men contrabands of war and set them to work constructing a new bake house for the fort.[6] Congress and the secretary of war endorsed Butler's decision.[7] The grapevine went to work, and within three months nine hundred former slaves lived at Fortress Monroe under Union protection.[8] One woman traveled two hundred miles, disguised in men's clothing, to claim freedom at the "Freedom Fort."[9] Their very presence at the fort, however, raised ideological and pragmatic questions that haunted the federal government throughout much of the war.

Despite Butler's 1861 maneuver, freedom did not always await African Americans who reached Union lines. More than one commander wrote superiors from the field to express his disgust at being dragged into association with slaves and slavery. As these officers saw it, the war was about securing the Union, and they had no intention of staining their hands with the nasty southern business of slavery. They wanted "nothing to do with the slaves at all" and considered them the property of their owners—"no better than horses in that respect," as one commander remarked.[10] For these northern white men, determining whether runaway slaves should be given refuge or returned to their owners constituted a "delicate" and "embarrassing" matter, thus their approach fluctuated according to command.[11] Many officers echoed the sentiments of J. H. Lane, commander of the Kansas Brigade: "My brigade is not here for the purpose of interfering in anywise with the institution of slavery. They shall not become negro thieves, nor shall they be prostituted into negro catchers. The institution of slavery must take care of itself."[12]

Even with the risks associated with escape and the uncertainty of their fate, enslaved people continued to make their way to Union lines because for them

freedom was both a place and a concept. In contrast to American revolutionaries of the eighteenth century who imagined themselves enslaved by Brit-
ain's tyranny, African American slaves daily experienced slavery's toll both
physically and psychologically. Claiming emancipation, then, necessitated re-
moving themselves from the homes they had known; often it meant ventur-
ing into the line of fire between North and South. On the Union-occupied
Sea Islands, Edward L. Pierce recorded the arrival of a community of slaves.
"Forty-eight escaped from a single plantation near Grahamville, on the main
land, held by the rebels, led by the driver, and after four days of trial and peril,
hidden by day and threading the waters with their boats by night, evading the
enemy's pickets, joyfully entered our camps at Hilton Head."[13] As Pierce's
observation suggests, it was hazardous for enslaved people to abandon owners
in hope of freedom. To leave the plantation was to enter into a war in which
their color immediately identified them as property to be seized and returned
if not killed. The risk of being captured by Confederate soldiers, hit in
crossfire, starving, freezing, or being imprisoned was all too real.[14] Yet they
made the choice for freedom. In North Carolina, during the battle of New
Bern in early 1862, "rebel masters shot at a group of fifteen men, women, and
children as they made their way up the river in a dingy to the Union headquarters." By 1865 more than ten thousand contrabands lived in and around
New Bern, having "stolen in singly, or in squads from time to time."[15]

African Americans' movement out of slavery into contraband or freed status
mirrored the movement of the Union army. As Union troops began to occupy
Confederate territory—first the Virginia Tidewater in May 1861, then the
South Carolina Sea Islands in November and December 1861, New Bern,
North Carolina, in March 1862, New Orleans in April 1862, and Vicksburg,
Mississippi, in July 1863—they encountered thousands of black people intent
on gaining freedom.[16] In the Union-occupied part of Tidewater, Virginia, the
number of blacks within Union lines grew from 17,500 to 26,000 between
1861 and 1863. In North Carolina in 1864 there were 17,419 blacks within
Union lines.[17] In some states, like Alabama, the Union army never penetrated
far beyond the northernmost regions, but when the army prevailed in the
Tennessee Valley region of the state in April 1862, slaves fled plantations and
became contrabands building fortifications. Farther south and west, freedom
came late to most blacks, who remained enslaved until the end of the war.[18]

In these far-flung and growing communities, African Americans did not
constitute a monolithic mass.[19] Not all African Americans in the South were
newly freedpeople—some had been free before the war. Not all freedpeople
became contrabands seeking refuge from the Union army. And not all contrabands relied on charity for subsistence. In New Bern, North Carolina, African Americans who were free before the war and newly freed people took on

numerous skilled jobs around the city, including work as carpenters, painters, blacksmiths, butchers, oyster men, engineers, cooks, and masons.[20] Throughout Union territory, many newly freed people worked for the government for low, unreliable pay.[21] Men served as teamsters, blacksmiths, and wheelwrights. They built fortifications and bridges, dug ditches, chopped wood, picked cotton that the federal government sold, and performed many of the labor-intensive tasks of the war that white soldiers complained about doing.[22] Women labored in camps as cooks or laundresses and alongside the men in fields that fell under Union control. Both men and women worked as spies. Not surprisingly, many newly freed people lived under deplorable conditions; some freedpeople in Hampton, Virginia, for example, lived in an old tobacco barn with chalk lines drawn on a dirt floor to demarcate each family's living space. And in Columbus, Kentucky, five hundred contrabands lived in the stalls of stables.[23]

Within contraband camps and in freedmen villages, amid the poverty, newly freed people and those who had been free before the war debated political strategies for the future of the race, a future clouded with ambiguity.[24] Reverend Lewis C. Lockwood, the first representative of the American Missionary Association at Fortress Monroe, had an opportunity to listen in on some of those discussions and debates, as freedpeople in Fortress Monroe and Hampton, Virginia, assessed their new status and their treatment by the United States government and pondered the possibilities for creating the kind of freedom they had long envisioned. Living among the freedpeople, visiting their churches, and attending their meetings, Lockwood learned of their values and their fears. While some procured lumber and began building cabins, others lost faith that freedom would be long-lived. With the army severely restricting civilian movement, some freedpeople felt betrayed by the very Union commanders they had looked to as liberators. This was not the freedom they had contemplated. Phillip Kirby complained that although he worked for the government for seven months, he had only received one item of clothing and one dollar in payment. In response, Thomas Walker urged patience. He too worked for the government for several months and had only received two dollars and a few articles of clothing. "But, if I had received nothing," he vowed, "I should feel like continuing on, like Job waiting till a change come." "And what if we suffer hardships, so we gain freedom in the end?" he continued. "Will that not make rewards for all?"[25]

In the chaos and uncertainty, many former slaves publicly sought to prepare themselves for the future by becoming literate. Their conception of education would take on greater complexity when they later studied mathematics and Greek, but in this early period the widespread desire to learn to read and write was foremost. Even as ironclad war ships pulled into nearby harbors, throughout the South former slaves seized opportunities to become literate. In the very early months of the war when African Americans first thronged to Fortress Monroe in 1861, Edward L. Pierce noticed a "very general desire among the contrabands to know how to read."[26] When he transferred to the Sea Islands of South Carolina in February 1862 to work as a U.S. Treasury agent, he detected similar interests among the freedpeople: "all of proper ages," he noted, "when inquired, expressed a desire to have their children taught to read and write and to learn themselves." On this point, he said, "they show more earnestness than any other."[27]

It was this earnestness that prompted Pierce to urge northern religious societies to send the first cadre of teachers to the Sea Islands in 1861.[28] He was inspired by a visit to a school for freedpeople taught by three black teachers and headed by white Massachusetts clergyman, Solomon Peck. During a visit to the school, Pierce observed that the sixty or so pupils, aged six to fifteen, were "rapidly learning their letters and simple reading." Pierce taught several of the children the alphabet for a few hours, then, "during the recess heard the three teachers, at their own request, recite their spelling-lessons of words of one syllable, and read two chapters of Matthew." "It seemed to be a morning well spent," Pierce mused. He also commented on a "great apparent eagerness to learn among the adults" on the Sea Islands. "They will cover their books with care," he wrote, "each one being anxious to be thus provided, carry them to the fields, studying them at intervals of rest, and asking explanations of the superintendents who happen to come along." Pierce noted, however, that after a while some of the adults lost interest, finding it too difficult to learn. According to Pierce, parents continued to appreciate "the privilege for their children," but often gave up on acquiring the skills themselves.[29] Some adults, who as slaves had harbored a desire to read and write, apparently found it too challenging to master memorization and the other skills literacy required, yet they remained intent on providing the opportunity for their children.

Large numbers of newly freed people manifested this intense interest in becoming literate. In 1862, upon visiting a Quaker-run school in Cairo, Illinois, where adults and children studied together, an army chaplain remarked on the "avidity" with which many of the freedpeople who sought refuge in this border city tried to learn to read. The chaplain remarked that the students could be seen "all about after school hours, with books in hand, learning their lessons."[30] Another chaplain, this one in Corinth, Mississippi, also wrote of the long hours that students invested in becoming literate. He wrote, "You will find them every hour of daylight at their books. We cannot enter a cabin or tent, but that we see from one to three with books. I visited a cabin one night about half past nine o'clock and found a boy studying with pine chips for a light, and thus he had been for over an hour." The chaplain remarked that he and the missionary teachers were greatly encouraged by the eagerness of the students and by their rapid advancement.[31]

From Vicksburg, Mississippi, Chaplain G. L. Rankin requested spelling books to pass on to the freedpeople.[32] Vincent Coyler, Superintendent of the Poor in North Carolina, also commented on this keen desire for learning. "The colored refugees," he wrote, "evinced the utmost eagerness to learn to read. I had taken with me some spelling books and primers, and these were seized with great avidity." Coyler, too, badgered the AMA to send more books.[33] The Superintendent of Colored Schools in Memphis reported to John Eaton that when the city fell under the control of Union forces in June 1862, "the colored people began soon to manifest a strong desire to learn to read. Those known to be friendly were therefore persistently importuned to open colored schools."[34] In New Bern in the winter of 1862–63, Captain Whipple, a disabled officer in the Twenty-third Regiment of the Massachusetts Volunteers, "strove to satisfy the intense eagerness of some twenty or thirty blacks, of all ages from ten to fifty years, to learn to read." Using a dark-painted window as a makeshift blackboard, Whipple taught students who arrived one and two hours before the scheduled time for classes. Men of the regiment recalled seeing black men whose job it was to take logs from the river to the saw mill pull out spelling books during their short breaks to study their lessons.[35] Finally, from Columbus, Kentucky, AMA missionary S. G. Wright reported that when he visited among the freedpeople and the "born free," he discovered that they were collecting funds for building a "rough house" to serve as a school.[36]

These were by no means isolated observations. Following visits to Washington, D.C., Eastern Virginia, and North Carolina in June 1863, the American Freedmen's Inquiry Commission concluded that "sufficient evidence is before the Commission that colored refugees in general place a high value both on education for their children and religious instruction for themselves." The commission learned that in various places "one of the first acts of the negroes when they found themselves free was to establish schools at their own expense." Further, the commission found the freedpeople in each area it visited "eager to obtain for themselves, but especially for their children, those privileges of education which have been jealously withheld from them." Based on these findings, the commission concluded that the freedpeople could be depended upon to support, in part, both teachers and ministers sent by missionary societies. This assessment would subsequently be reflected in Freedmen's Bureau policy toward black education; the bureau often based its support of schools on the freedpeople's own involvement.[37]

In 1863 James E. Yeatman, a representative of the St. Louis–based Western

Sanitary Commission, toured contraband camps from Cairo, Illinois, to Natchez, Mississippi, to observe the conditions of the freedpeople and gauge which of them were likely to become dependent on the government or charity. Commencing his tour in the camps of Illinois, and traveling through Tennessee, Arkansas, Louisiana, and Mississippi, Yeatman estimated that approximately 25,000 freedpeople lived in camps and towns along the Mississippi River. He reported on the conditions of the camps, complaints by freedpeople regarding unfair wages, and the recent arrival of a few missionary teachers from the North. He also noted that African Americans were already at work teaching freedpeople. The black teachers were not sufficient to meet the need either in skills or numbers, but their presence and the presence of students anxious to learn communicated volumes about how much the freedpeople valued education, and how determined many were to become literate.[38]

It is challenging to develop a cohesive narrative about these early black teachers. Yeatman, for example, recorded brief sightings of indigenous black teachers in Arkansas, near Goodrich's Landing, where recently arrived white Presbyterian teachers were readying a school. "[T]here is at Groshon's plantation," he wrote, "a school taught by Rose Anna, a colored girl." Rose Anna had between forty and fifty students. "Uncle Jack," Yeatman continued, "a colored man, at the Goodrich place, is teaching a school of eighty-nine scholars." And, he recorded, "Uncle Tom, a colored man, at the Savage plantation, has a school of thirty scholars. He is infirm, and teaches them remaining himself in bed." Nearby, "Wm. McCutchen, a colored man, has commenced a school on the Currie place." McCutchen had sixty students who badly needed books. "They are using books of every kind and description, scarcely any two of them alike," Yeatman commiserated. "One had a volume of Tennyson's poems, out of which he was learning his letters." Noting that McCutchen "had but one arm, having lost the other by a cotton gin," Yeatman promised to send books and slates.[39]

Reading Yeatman's brief descriptions of these teachers and students is like awakening from a dream and struggling in the dark to catch hold of the elusive strands of memory. The few lingering threads provoke a host of questions. How had Rose Anna, Uncle Jack, Uncle Tom, and William McCutchen learned to read and write? How proficient were they? Had they taught others during slavery? If so, had their students met in groups then, or would congregating over books have unleashed the wrath of owners Groshon, Goodrich, Savage, and Currie? Once emancipated, had the adults on these estates demanded that plantation owners permit them and their children to attend school as a condition of remaining on the land? How long had that one student held on to the book of Tennyson's poems—had he possibly purloined it from his owner's collection, hoping some day to crack the code that would reveal to him what lay within the book's covers? What did he hope he would find there, once he learned to read? Was Uncle Tom preparing someone else to take over when his infirmities would no longer permit him to teach? On these questions, the historical record is silent. The last names of Rose Anna, Uncle Tom, and Uncle Jack were not recorded. Yeatman's mention of William McCutchen, a former slave living on a plantation, may be the only surviving record of his existence.

In contrast to Yeatman's relatively quick trip through southern states, the AMA's Lewis Lockwood stayed a while at Fortress Monroe in Hampton, Virginia. Lockwood pioneered a religious and educational mission that would eventually involve hundreds of ministers and teachers representing several freedmen's aid and religious organizations from the northern and western states. In Hampton, Lockwood became a strident advocate for the fair treatment of former slaves by the federal government. It was there that he encountered Mary S. Peake, whose parents had skirted Virginia's law against teaching blacks by sending her to school in Washington, D.C. As she grew to womanhood, Peake in turn had violated the state laws by holding school for black children in Hampton. After initial wartime disruptions, she began teaching newly freed children. The front room of her house served as a classroom, where she taught fifty-three students during the day and twenty students at night.[40]

The relationship between Mary Peake and Lewis Lockwood offers some insight into how northern white missionary men understood their role among the freedpeople. Men like Lockwood brought a complex range of values and behaviors to their work with the freedpeople. They could be concerned, committed antislavery men and, at the same time, self-promoting competitors for black people's souls and the applause for working among them. They could be simultaneously selfless in their dedication and obsessed with their own heroic allure. Lockwood was in Virginia to wrench proslavery white ministers from black pulpits, preferably replacing them with AMA Congregational ministers, and he was there to establish schools for the freedpeople. Formerly enslaved African Americans already had ministers, however. They were more interested in enlisting his assistance to establish schools.

Lockwood admired and respected Peake, regarding her as a martyr of sorts, "a blessed saint." He included frequent updates on her failing health in his letters to AMA staff in New York. He observed Peake at her work and researched her history, even writing a book that has helped to preserve the historical memory of this "colored teacher at Fortress Monroe." Lockwood seemed entranced by Mary Peake, when he wrote "in her presence I was a learner, and, under the inspiration of her words and example, obtained new strength for fresh endeavors in the cause of God and humanity." Accompanying his admiration though, was a hint of possessiveness that foreshadowed conflicts that would arise in some interactions between AMA ministers and local black people as they struggled over control of freedpeople's education.[41]

In Lockwood's adoration, one senses that he was bent on possessing Peake's image, on claiming her legacy for the AMA. When former slave children preempted him by asking Peake to teach them, Lockwood went so far as to suggest that the children had somehow read his mind. He said that he had intended to start a Sabbath and weekday school, but in the meantime, "some of the children of the vicinity, getting perhaps some hint of my intention, or prompted by an impulse from on high, called on Mrs. Peake, and requested her to teach them, as she had taught the children in Hampton."[42] Here Lockwood sought to claim responsibility for planting a seed among black children to seek an education. Perhaps realizing that it was a stretch to impute mind-reading ability to the students, he then sought to attribute their initiative to "an impulse from on high." Lockwood, of course, was well aware that Mary Peake had taught blacks long before he ever arrived in Virginia. He also knew that she was so committed to teaching freedpeople that even when too ill to sit up, she lay in her bed, surrounded by students, teaching them to read.[43] As with Uncle Tom, whom James Yeatman had met on the Savage plantation in Arkansas, any space that the teacher occupied was transformed into a classroom. Circumstances were changing dramatically as the Civil War unraveled slavery and black people peeled away its prohibitions. Formerly enslaved children and their parents now had direct access to Mary Peake and her education. She in turn could openly teach them in front of white men. Yet Lockwood found it difficult to admit that he and the AMA were not responsible for sowing the seeds of their desire.

Although not acknowledged by Lockwood and most of his northern contemporaries, a synergistic relationship developed between the freedpeople and missionary ministers and teachers.[44] Between 1862, when the first missionaries landed in the Sea Islands to teach and work among the freedpeople, and the early 1870s, when most white northern teachers had left the South, several hundred teachers, mostly white and mostly female, went south to teach. In 1866, for example, approximately 1,400 teachers worked in the South for northern organizations. Some were local teachers, but most were sent by religious and secular organizations with a mission to assist the freedpeople.[45] These teachers made great sacrifices to teach in sometimes unhealthy and often hostile territory, and much of the historical literature about black education during this period has focused on such northern white women, or "Yankee schoolmarms," as they were called. It is certainly true that without northern teachers many freedpeople would not have received any education at all.

However, the history of freedpeople's education is also the story of former slaves' determination to become educated and their efforts to help themselves and to reach out to others who could help them. Even when northern whites served as the teachers, freedpeople built schools, paid teachers, and made other contributions to the educational effort. The mutuality of this relationship became evident as soon as the northern ministers began their service. When Lewis Lockwood spoke to black audiences in Hampton, for example, he stressed the importance of starting schools. But it was equally true that many in these audiences already agreed with his message and had long yearned to attend school. Lockwood and other missionaries encouraged blacks to seek education. At the same time, blacks' intense desire to learn fueled the passions of northern whites to make education available. Lockwood needed only reflect on the evidence around him to understand that African Americans' interest in becoming literate predated his arrival and existed far beyond his sphere of influence.[46]

From the towns and cities surrounding Fortress Monroe, freedpeople sent messages conveying their interest in having schools and teachers. Lockwood and the New York AMA leaders received such messages from Newport News, Harpers Ferry, Norfolk, Williamsburg, Yorktown, Downey Farm, and Camp Hamilton. The freedpeople of Norfolk, Lockwood reported, "signify a desire for a school teacher." He thought it likely that they would build a log house for a teacher, but because there were only about one hundred freedpeople, he recommended to the AMA that if funds were limited, "it would be best to let this field wait—content with the efforts of soldiers and the more intelligent among themselves."[47] From Harpers Ferry, a chaplain informed the AMA that "the colored people are anxious for a school." He proposed opening a school as soon as they could procure books.[48] In a request for books from Yorktown, the AMA received word of a "large number of contrabands anxious to learn to read."[49] Later that year, when Lockwood visited Yorktown, he found "a colored man named Peter Cook, of moderate abilities in reading," teaching about a dozen students with books sent by the AMA.[50] Likewise, an African American man and woman held school for 140 students in nearby Suffolk.[51] And when an AMA official visited Newtown, the freedpeople showed him a schoolhouse they had built and begged him to send them a teacher.[52]

The utopian missionary views of white northerners answered, rather than generated, the call for education. In July 1862 freedpeople in Norfolk sent a message to the Superintendent of Contrabands at Fortress Monroe. The messenger "expressed a desire for school privileges for the colored people there." He also stated that the people were restless under their slaveholding and proslavery pastors. The superintendent advised the freedpeople of Norfolk to petition military authorities for permission to start a school, and he told them to get rid of their ministers as soon as they could.[53] Lockwood further reported that, in that same month, the AMA was "also urgently solicited by the colored people in Williamsburg to establish a school there." "I think we should listen to the call," Lockwood urged.[54] When the AMA responded to the call from Norfolk, teachers were overwhelmed by "a multitudinous host seeking instruction." On the first day of classes held at the Bute Street Baptist Church, 350 students attended the day session and 300 came to the night session. Soon the numbers had more than doubled, causing the organization to staff an additional school at the Methodist church.[55]

As in slavery, African Americans' motivations for acquiring literacy were often pragmatic. An eighty-five-year-old woman wanted to read the Bible for herself and teach the young. She felt that she must do it then or not at all.[56] Some people regretted their lack of education because it hampered meaningful practices such as recording the birth of a child.[57] Others saw education as a privilege—a "coveted possession"—to which they had been denied access.[58] The American Freedmen's Inquiry Commission began to get at this last motivation when it noted that the freedpeople were "eager to obtain for themselves, but especially for their children, those privileges of education which had hitherto been jealously withheld from them."[59] Similarly, Booker T. Washington elucidated the feelings of other freedpeople when he recalled the sense he had as a child that getting an education was a prize of inestimable value. "I had no schooling whatever while I was a slave, though I remember on several occasions I went as far as the schoolhouse door with one of my young mistresses to carry her books. The picture of several dozen boys and girls in a schoolroom engaged in study made a deep impression upon me, and I had the feeling that to get into a schoolhouse and study in this way would be about the same as getting into paradise."[60] In January 1862 William Davis, a contraband at Fortress Monroe, put it a little differently when he accompanied Lewis Lockwood to New York to seek support for the freedpeople and to pressure the government into treating them more decently. Davis "spoke of the advantages of education to the slave, and the eagerness with which the contraband children learned. They thought it was so much like the way the master's children used to be treated, that they believed they were getting white."[61]

In other words, in the aftermath of slavery black people like Booker T. Washington and Mary Peake's students in Hampton, whom Davis described, finally saw an opportunity to accrue some of the privileges of whiteness that had been denied them. As slaves they had seen the impact of education firsthand. They had carried young masters' and mistresses' books and lunch to school, then seen some of them off to college. Upon their return, educated masters and mistresses moved into positions within the white gentry, oor whites and blacks, with little or no education, remained poor and ess. At emancipation, many freedpeople were anxious for education y because of its direct relationship to power within the society.

very linkage of education and power created tensions, however, be- ome freedpeople and those northern whites who sought to use the provision as well as the substance of education to enlarge their own power and control. The mere willingness to provide education, some whites believed, could be an inducement of great value. Writing from Port Royal, Edward Pierce articulated his sense that the offer of education was a way to gain the freedpeople's trust. He believed that northern educational efforts had produced an unexpected subsidiary effect. "At a time when the people were chafing the most under deprivations, and the assurances made on behalf of the Government were most distrusted," he wrote, "it was fortunate that we could point to the teaching of their children as a proof of our own interest in their welfare, and of the new and better life we were opening for them."[62] The New England Freedmen's Aid Society, established in February 1862 in response to Edward Pierce's appeal for teachers, articulated in its first annual report a similar understanding of the mission among the freedpeople. Commenting upon the earnest desire by the freedpeople to learn to read, the society concluded that "they prize every opportunity for instruction, and the confidence inspired by the establishment of schools is one of the chief means of influence and control over them." The society conjectured that its provision of teachers signaled to freedpeople that they could trust northern whites unlike southern whites.[63]

Some white northerners, then, believed that black people wanted education so badly that its provision could become a mechanism for controlling their behavior. Promise the freedpeople literacy for themselves and their children, and they would quietly accept whatever new places white northerners carved out for them in a South reconstructed in the northern image. As it happened, both white and black southerners had other notions of who should be in control and whether education would be a palliative for blacks or a threat to white supremacy. Black education would become a site of contention as each party wrestled for control over its delivery. For their part, white northerners were often shocked to find that former slaves were not passive, degraded human beings who simply sat awaiting enlightenment. White southerners, who had long contended with black resistance despite the myths they created to convince themselves of black acquiescence, were not so much surprised as infuriated when African Americans stepped forward to openly express claims for power.

African Americans had their own visions of freedom. They had had generations to contemplate a world in which they could claim the benefits of their own labor and make choices for themselves and their children. These critical choices often included becoming literate. Mattie Jackson, for example, believed that freedom, combined with education, would empower her to finally take control of her own life. As such, an inherent tension existed between her perception that education would allow her to make her own choices and thus assert more control over her life, and some white northerners' belief that providing education would enable them to direct the lives of freedpeople. Jackson had fought for control over her labor when a slave; now she claimed control over her mind. Although she dictated her first book, Jackson declared that once her education was completed she would "endeavor to publish further details of our history in another volume from my own pen." The pen, she thought, would endow her with unique power: only she could make the decision to sell her story, and only she would decide how to spend the proceeds. With education, she could decide which of her secrets to write down and which to keep hidden. Jackson envisioned a life independent of white southern or northern domination.

Much as it did for Mattie Jackson, education signified empowerment and self-determination to former slave Harry McMillan. McMillan, who had worked on a Beaufort, South Carolina, plantation for nearly forty years, became one of the black people whose testimony the American Freedmen's Inquiry Commission heard.[64] In June 1863 the commission asked him if he thought "the colored people would like better to have this land divided among themselves and live here alone, or must they have white people to govern them?" McMillan began his response by saying that the freedpeople needed whites to administer the law. "The black people," he said, "have a good deal of sense but they do not know the law." He believed that they would need white people, not to be masters, but to interpret the law. He likely thought immediately of the law because that was the tool that might protect black people and would create rights for them. Then he projected into the future. "Probably with the children that are coming up no white men will not be needed," he testified: "They are learning to read and write—some are learning lawyer, some are learning doctor, and some learn minister; and reading books and newspapers they can understand the law; but the old generation cannot understand it. It makes no difference how sensible they are, they are blind and it wants white men for the present to direct them. After five years they will take care of themselves, this generation cannot do it." In McMillan's view, within as short a period as five years, black youth would have attained enough education to direct their own affairs and those of the older generation within the laws of the United States. At that point, blacks would be able to manage without white interference or assistance.

Parents' hope for literacy, nurtured during slavery, might not be fulfilled, but their children raised in freedom would learn to read and write.[65] For Harry McMillan, Mattie Jackson, and the thousands of other former slaves who attended school, taught school, or sent their children to school in the early years of emancipation, the freedom they had long hoped and fought for would become even more substantive with education.

The Civil War opened several new paths to freedom. For some, freedom came when they escaped and became contrabands of war, for some it came with the Emancipation Proclamation, and for thousands of black men, particularly in the loyal border states, freedom came when they ran away and enlisted in the Union army.

CHAPTER 3 ▪ ▪ ▪ ▪ ▪ ▪ ▪ ▪ ▪ ▪ ▪ ▪ ▪ ▪ ▪

The Men Are Actually Clamoring for Books

African American Soldiers and the Educational Mission

We wish to have some benefit of education To make of ourselves capable of business in the future.

Sergeant John Sweney, Kentucky

The progress which the soldiers are making in trying to acquire an education, surpasses the most sanguine expectation. The soldiers themselves pay all the expenses incurred by the employment of teachers.

Reverend Henry McNeal Turner, South Carolina

By the fall of 1864 the Union had dramatically changed its war strategy. The president's Emancipation Proclamation in January 1863 freed the slaves in territory under Confederate control and announced the Union's intention to enlist black soldiers. Five months later, the War Department created a Bureau of Colored Troops, and finally the Union officially accepted African American men as soldiers. Thus it was that in September 1864, when Elijah Marrs walked away from the Shelby County, Kentucky, farm where he worked alongside thirty other enslaved people, instead of seeking protection as a contraband of war, he marched toward enlistment as a soldier in the Union army. At twenty-three years of age, Marrs set out to claim his freedom by taking up arms against slavery. As a small boy he had learned to read and write because he thought he would have something important to do in the future. Now the literacy that had distinguished him as a leader within his community of slaves would also influence the role that he carved out for himself within the military structure.

When Marrs decided to enlist in the Union army, he did not go alone. He spent the daylight hours rounding up a network of "old comrades" to join him on the march to Louisville, twenty miles east of Shelbyville. As night fell, twenty-seven men met Marrs at a local black church. There, they elected him their captain.[1] Choosing Marrs was a logical move. His physical stature alone marked him as a leader. At five feet, ten inches, Marrs was nearly a head taller than most of the men around him.[2] More important, as a literate man, others in the slave community in Shelbyville had long recognized him as a leader. Indeed, the farm on which he lived was considered a secret "general headquarters for the negroes," where Marrs read newspapers to the gathered slaves, an act that provoked angry local whites to brand him the "Shelby County negro clerk." As black men, like his older brother Henry, began enlisting in the army, Marrs ignored his owner's cautions and persisted in reading letters that these men sent home to illiterate family members. "The colored soldiers had confidence in me," Marrs recalled, "and knew that their letters would be faithfully delivered."[3] Finally, the men chose Marrs as their captain because it was he who conceived of and activated their collective movement toward freedom.

Even as they met to map out the route to Louisville, however, Marrs's capacity for leadership met its first test when a rumor spread "that the rebels were preparing to make a raid upon the church." Shouting at the backs of men who fled, over the screams of women in the church, and above his own terror at the prospect of a rebel raid, Marrs encouraged the men to remain, exhorting them "that if we staid [sic] at home we would be murdered; that if we joined the army and were slain in battle, we would at least die in fighting for principle and freedom."[4] Marrs's words to his men convinced them to maintain their resolve to enlist in the army, and they marched through the night, armed with "war clubs and one old rusty pistol." As the sun rose on Marrs's band, they reached the recruiting office in Louisville. They had arrived just in time. By noon, their owners had reached Louisville in pursuit of their former slaves—slaves no longer, but soldiers in the Union army. The former slave owners returned home empty-handed.[5]

Marrs and the more than two dozen black men from Shelby County joined a growing force that escaped slavery by enlisting in the military. Black enlistment varied by state and by African Americans' legal status. Northern states, whose small black populations were already free, offered up fewer recruits than border states such as Kentucky and Missouri, where the Emancipation Proclamation had left slavery intact. Enlistment in the military became the escape hatch from slavery for thousands of black men in these loyal states. For example, Kentucky, which had 5 percent of the black men in the country, was home to 13 percent of the black men who enlisted nationwide. More than half of that state's enslaved men between the ages of eighteen and forty-five joined the army.[6]

Although they engaged in combat and performed some of the most difficult work associated with the war, many African American soldiers also took time to become literate. Black men who had learned to read and write in slavery taught others. Chaplains, officers and their wives, and missionary teachers joined them in creating a fragile structure of schools within black regiments. Because these schools were so sporadic and unreliable, as only one component of an incipient educational movement among freedpeople, black soldiers and chaplains appealed to the government to provide schooling for the thousands of soldiers eager to become literate. And the soldiers did not restrict their concern about education to their own needs. Several regiments gave their money and labor to build schools that would educate larger African American communities.

If the war provided pathways into freedom, enlistment in the military enabled black men to expand educational opportunities that they hoped in turn would improve their ability to intervene in civic governance. Military service combined with education would, they believed, enable them to claim and exercise the rights of citizenship. Far from simply soaking up whatever lessons northern whites offered in classrooms, African American soldiers actively participated in working out what they could gain from military service as they prepared for engagement in civil society once the war ended. Elijah Marrs and other southern black men who enlisted to gain freedom both transformed the Union army and were profoundly changed by their service. Their location in a chain of command that led to the president of the United States opened up a new forum for men who had until recently been checked by the power of an owner. The ability to read and write, they knew, could provide them with access to centers of power and could enable them to both shape and gain access to rights for the freedpeople.[7]

Elijah Marrs's secretly acquired literacy had afforded him an elevated status within the community of slaves in Shelbyville, Kentucky. Now, as he constructed his identity as a free man within the confines of military service, literacy again proved critical. Shortly after enlisting, Marrs developed "a reputation as a writer," and many fellow soldiers came to him to write letters home to their families. What Marrs had been obliged to do in secret while a slave, he was now able to do openly as a soldier. When the regiment's officers discovered that Marrs was "skilled in the use of the pen," they sought him out and found him "surrounded by a number of the men, each waiting his turn to have a letter written home." Satisfied that they had found someone who was a "penman," the officers promoted Marrs to duty sergeant.[8] He accepted the position with the understanding that he would receive "personal instruction in army tactics" to enable him to fulfill his new role. However, a painful incident threatened the stature that literacy seemed able to bestow in freedom. The new sergeant was sorely disappointed when the commanding officer ordered him to take a squad of men to clear ground for the erection of barracks. Although literate, and despite his promotion, Marrs, like most black soldiers, was relegated to the most grueling, distasteful tasks of war, drawing fatigue duty, as white soldiers grew tired of war.[9]

Insulted by the order, Marrs reflected on the disparity between his actual situation and the notions of freedom that he had cultivated over many years of enslavement. "While I felt myself a free man and a U.S. soldier," he complained, "still must I move at the command of a white man, and I said to myself is my condition any better now than before I entered the army? But the idea would come to me that I was a soldier fighting for my freedom, and this thought filled my heart with joy. I thought, too, that the time will come when no man can say to me come and go, and I be forced to obey."[10]

Marrs was not alone in the hopeful equation of soldiering and manhood. Following the Emancipation Proclamation, Frederick Douglass and other black abolitionists had issued an urgent manifesto to black men in which they made the same link. "Men of Color To Arms! To Arms," their recruitment broadside called, imploring black men to fight for the Union to gain their freedom and prove their manhood. "Our enemies have made the country believe that we are craven cowards, without souls, without manhood, without the spirit of soldiers. Shall we die with this stigma resting upon our graves?" it asked. "Shall we leave this inheritance of Shame to our children? No! A thousand times NO! Let us rather die freemen than live to be slaves." In exchange for a display of manly courage, the abolitionists promised free and enslaved black men a new social order. "A new era is open to us," they pledged: "For generations we have suffered under the horrors of slavery, outrage and wrong; our manhood has been denied, our citizenship blotted out, our souls seared and burned, our spirits cowed and crushed, and the hopes of the future of our race involved in doubt and darkness. But now our relations to the white race are changed. Now therefore is our most precious moment. Let us rush to arms."[11]

Douglass expounded on the sentiments expressed in the recruitment broadside in an article published in his newspaper, *Douglass' Monthly*. In his enumeration of nine reasons in response to the question "Why Should a Colored Man Enlist?" Douglass argued that enlistment would benefit the esteem of each black soldier. "Decried and derided as you have been and still are, you need an act of this kind by which to recover your own self-respect," he told his audience. They had to some degree rated their own value according to the estimate of their enemies, he argued, and therefore had underestimated their self-worth. "You owe it to yourself and your race to rise from your social debasement, and take your place among the soldiers of your country, a man among men."[12]

But the abolitionists' promises were not fulfilled. Elijah Marrs's freedom was tenuous and evolving. He had picked up arms, but his commanding officer now ordered him to pick up a shovel. Enlistment in the army, instead of allowing him to fully exercise his freedom, imposed new constraints that insulted his stature in the black community and prevented him from using his own judgment or achieving his own desires. Although he believed that his ability to read and write had elevated him above taking orders from white men, he found himself still subject to their commands. Furthermore, their commands relegated him to menial labor, a stinging reminder of slavery. He now imagined a new meaning for freedom: equality with white men. It was no longer sufficient not to be owned by white men; Marrs wanted to escape their domination entirely. He longed to be "a man among men." While Marrs awaited equality and achievement of his vision of manhood, he returned to the methods that had previously given him some sense of leadership as a slave. He continued to write letters for fellow soldiers, and, now stationed at Camp Nelson, Kentucky, he began to teach as well. He and a sergeant major taught vocal music and the rudiments of English grammar while in camp.[13] By teaching, Marrs hoped to pass on his skills and to salvage his self-respect.

Elijah Marrs and other literate former slaves constituted part of a loosely defined teaching corps for African American soldiers, who, much as their civilian counterparts in contraband camps and freedmen's villages, believed that learning to read and write was essential to performing new roles as free people. Other teachers included chaplains, officers' wives, missionary teachers, and even a contraband woman, Susie King Taylor. With scant resources, they taught men anxious to throw off the limitations of slavery.

Early in the war, when Union forces captured the Sea Islands in April 1862, fourteen-year-old Susie King Taylor, the Savannah girl who had learned to read and write through an intricate web of secrecy and perseverance, escaped to freedom with her uncle and his family. They took refuge on St. Simon's Island, from which white slave owners had fled. At the same time, Major General David Hunter was forming an unauthorized regiment of black soldiers. Taylor's uncle, several of her cousins, and her future husband Edward King joined the regiment. The War Department later recognized the regiment, the First South Carolina Volunteers, Thirty-third Regiment, and placed it under the leadership of Colonel Thomas Wentworth Higginson. Taylor became an adjunct to the regiment. She served as a laundress for the men and nursed them after battle.[14]

Taylor also taught. Working with the first officially recognized African American regiment, she was one of the earliest teachers of black soldiers. Forty children attended her day school, and a number of adults took lessons from her at night. She found "all of them so eager to learn to read, to read above anything else." In addition to the civilian students, she taught many of the men of the regiment. "I taught a great many of the comrades in Company E to read and write, when they were off duty," Taylor wrote. "Nearly all were anxious to learn." According to Taylor, "I was very happy to know my efforts were successful in camp, and also felt grateful for the appreciation of my services."[15]

African American soldiers were indeed anxious to become literate, as they stood to become leaders in their communities after the war. As Susie King Taylor did, northern white teachers also commented on the men's dedication to acquiring literacy. A teacher in Pine Bluff, Arkansas, reported seeing many of his soldier-students "stand guard with book in hand," so determined were they not to waste any time. When Indiana native Lizzie Edwards visited the school that a fellow Quaker missionary taught in Arkansas, she was particularly impressed by a class of soldiers. She thought the soldiers "the most interesting of any class to teach. They seem to feel the importance of learning and study very hard, helping themselves along very much."[16]

In the summer of 1863, Frances Beecher, wife of James Beecher, colonel of the First North Carolina Colored Volunteers, helped teach a school for black soldiers in Jacksonville, Florida. The regiment had been raised in New Bern, where the African American women, assisted by the colonel's sister, Harriet Beecher Stowe, sent their men off with a handmade battle flag. This regiment, like many other African American ones, spent much of its time digging trenches and doing the other laborious work of the war, but it also fought in battles, including one alongside the Massachusetts Fifty-fourth.[17] Setting up a school tent wherever the regiment made camp, Frances Beecher, along with the chaplain and a few officers, spent her mornings teaching the men of the regiment to read and write. She was impressed by the soldiers' intense desire to become literate: "Whenever they had a spare moment, out would come a spelling-book or a primer or Testament, and you would often see a group of heads around one book." According to Beecher, by the time the men mustered out, each one could legibly sign his name to the payroll, where only two or three could do so upon enlistment.[18] This was a fairly common occurrence: men enlisted illiterate and mustered out able to read and write.[19]

Freedom, military service, and literacy brought about noticeable transformations in these former slaves. The men stood guard with pride, spelling books in hand, and they displayed a sort of assertiveness that would have been unavailable to most of them while enslaved. Reverend Joseph Warren, Superintendent of Colored Schools for the Department of Tennessee, observed "one of the most gratifying facts developed by the recent change in their condition is, that they very generally desire instruction, and many seize every opportunity in intervals of labor to obtain it." He reported that he "saw a small detachment of infantry soldiers, who had previously been unable to secure any attention from a teacher, placed within reach of a mission family. The soldiers had not been there an hour when those not on sentry duty had, of their own motion, procured spelling-books, and begged one of the ladies to aid them occasionally. Soon, he said, they were "busily at work on the alphabet." Black men, emboldened by their uniforms, not only felt free to approach white "ladies" in the street, but felt secure in publicly professing and displaying their imminent literacy.

Alongside this new assertiveness, soldiers carried with them methods that had served enslaved communities well: self-help. When they learned to read and write, the men passed on their knowledge to others. As Superintendent Warren reported, "I find that in the colored regiments the men often find assistance from their comrades. A chaplain of one of these regiments, who has done very much for his charge, tells me that they have done more for one another."[20] Following a visit to Virginia, Reverend Charles Lowe noted that he "found everywhere manifested an earnest desire to learn. In hospitals I found them teaching each other to read. Nowhere among our soldiers were papers and books more acceptable than in these colored hospitals; and, though usually only one or two men in a ward could read, they would all gather about one of these, who would read aloud; and the ability to read and write appeared to be an almost universal desire."[21]

Soldiers, then, taught as they learned, sometimes substituting for absent missionary teachers or assisting them in classrooms.[22] Jason Spratley, who had managed to learn the fundamentals of reading and writing as a slave, recalled attending school in the army while his regiment was stationed in Portsmouth, Virginia. "That was the first time I ever was allowed to enter a school room," he wrote. Teachers from a missionary organization staffed the regimental school; however, when the regiment moved out of Portsmouth, the men had learned enough so that "we could help ourselves some."[23]

A nighttime study session of black soldiers profoundly affected the life of a young runaway slave. John McCline was only about eleven years old when he escaped from the Clover Bottoms Plantation near Nashville, Tennessee. The white regiment he fell in with assigned him to care for the quartermaster's mules. One night while stationed in Chattanooga, McCline wandered off from his regiment and stumbled upon a camp of black troops, the first he had ever seen. Entranced by the sight, he investigated further: "Going up a light rise where stood several large square tents," he later recalled, "I stopped, and was cordially invited to enter. There were four or five in the great tent, and to my great surprise, some were reading, and others writing. All were neatly dressed and looked so nice in their uniforms." During the day the chaplain taught the men; at night they studied together. The sight of black men reading so impressed McCline that he soon got hold of a Webster's blue-back speller and began taking lessons from a member of his regiment.[24]

Schooling within black regiments was sporadic and dependent on volunteers; as a result, some African American soldiers, from their unprecedented position within the military hierarchy, sought to institute a more reliable system by mounting campaigns to obtain the resources they needed from the government. When First Sergeant John Sweney penned a letter asking the government to establish a school for his regiment, he articulated other soldiers' desire for education, predicted that many of them would become community leaders once literate, and declared a wider African American intention to be self-supporting. Although he was born free, Sweney had only acquired rudimentary literacy skills, but, like Elijah Marrs, he was likely promoted to first sergeant because even this limited literacy enabled him to perform clerical duties. The extant morning reports for Company F of the Thirteenth Regiment document Sweney's daily count of officers, enlisted men, and serviceable weapons, endorsed by his carefully etched signature.[25] Sweney wrote to the government out of a sense of duty to the other men of his regiment, as well as to the larger black population of his home state of Kentucky. The punctuation and spelling that betrayed the flaws of the self-taught by no means impaired his reasoning.

"Sir," Sweney wrote to Brigadier General Clinton B. Fisk in October 1865, "I have the honor to call your attention To the necessity of having a school for The Benefit of our regiment We have never had an institiong of that sort and we Stand deeply inneed of instruction the majority of us having been slaves We wish to have some benefit of education To make of ourselves capable of business in the future." Sweney anticipated a future in which he and other African American men now serving in the military would use their education in order to carry out the business of their communities. He was determined to help build self-supporting African American institutions. "We have establesed a literary Association which flourished previous to our march to Nashville," he continued. "We wish to become a People capable of self suport as we are Capable of being soldiers." Then, in his role of advocate for the soldiers of his regiment and the communities from which they came, Sweney wrote, "my home is in Kentucky where Prejudice regns like the mountain Oak. I had a leave of absence a few weeks a go on a furlough and it made my heart ache to see my race of people there neglected And ill treated on the account of the lack of Education being incapable of putting Their complaints or applications in writing For the want of education totally ignorant of the Great Good Workings of the Governement in their behalf."[26]

John Sweney, who might have hidden his literacy before the war, now publicly asserted that education would empower African Americans to claim their rights. By noting what he considered the ignorance and neglect of fellow blacks in Kentucky, Sweney made an explicit link between education and empowerment. Once taught to read, the black people of Kentucky would have knowledge of the workings of the government and would be able to petition for their rights as white men had long done, and as the literate

Sweney was now able to do as well. Further, Sweney intimated that the black soldiers' education could not be contained. Literacy would spread to blacks in Kentucky and the other states from which the soldiers hailed. Sweney ended his letter with a nod to the beneficence of his regiment's white officers and proposed a coherent, regiment-wide system of education. "We as soldeirs," he wrote, "Have our officers who are our protection To teach how us to act and to do But Sir what we want is a general system of education In our regiment for our moral and literary elevation."[27] Sweney's connection between military service, education, and civil rights was precisely what many white northern men had feared when they sought to keep black men out of the military forces of the Union. The new social order that Frederick Douglass and other abolitionists promised in their recruitment broadside was being established in small increments even during the war as black men such as Sweney coupled their fight for freedom with a struggle over access to literacy and empowerment.

Several black chaplains joined in this struggle by appealing to the government to help black men to become literate. Henry McNeal Turner, one of fourteen African American chaplains during the Civil War and a future bishop of the African Methodist Episcopal (AME) Church, beseeched his superior officers for teachers and books to meet the need. Bold and contentious, Turner's demands turned sarcastic at times. Frustrated by the army's recalcitrance, he even attempted to bargain for education in exchange for promotions. Unlike John Sweney, Turner felt no need to avow the goodness of white officers. Sweney had lived his entire life in the South and was well versed in public transcripts that demanded deference and loyalty when addressing powerful white people.[28] Turner, in contrast, was now a well-educated northerner. He faced the white military hierarchy just as resolutely as he had faced the AME Church when he petitioned to become a minister.[29] And, whereas Elijah Marrs questioned when he would feel like a free man, Turner reveled in his freeness, regarding it as the core of his being. In his interactions with blacks or whites, Turner drew upon the confidence this status provided him.

In June 1865, after his regiment, the First United States Colored Troops, had settled in Roanoke Island, North Carolina, in quarters that afforded them "favorable conveniences," Turner took up the question of education for black soldiers with his superior officer. He said that he had "constantly kept the subject of education before our soldiers" and that they had advanced well even under the conditions of war. However, all progress was at a virtual standstill because he was unable to supply the men's heavy demand for books. Turner's tone turned angry and scornful when he insisted that had his repeated requests for a leave of absence been granted, he would have purchased books for the men, even at his own expense. Instead, they had nothing. Hundreds of books he had previously provided the soldiers were destroyed in their knapsacks when their boat sank in the Cape Fear River. Turner mockingly hoped that it would not be "an outrage upon the right of petition" to request the government's help in procuring additional resources.[30]

Turner asked for five hundred advanced spelling books because many of the troops "who can read and write some, need to be much better drilled in spelling." In the negotiations, he challenged the military powers to reward the men of his regiment for their "bravery, courage and invincibleness" in the face of the enemy. "I claim this favor for my regiment," he declared, "upon the ground that she is the mother of colored Troops, and that in nine battles, regardless of skirmishes, she has never faltered, given way, or retreated unless ordered by the General Commanding. I challenge mortal man to stain her career with one blot of cowardice." Turner then made the same linkages that Sweney had, asserting that the spelling books were necessary "as a means to make brave soldiers, good and intelligent citizens." Like Sweney, Turner viewed literacy as joined to good citizenship, and he contended that the army owed it to these troops to prepare them for meaningful participation in the new America that would emerge after the war.[31]

When by August 1865 Turner's regiment still had not received the books, he again solicited the adjutant general. Hoping to shame the army, he wrote, "The progress which the soldiers are making in trying to acquire an education, surpasses the most sanguine expectation. It is indispensable however that I renew my application, asking that you have my Regiment furnished with five hundred advanced spelling books. The soldiers themselves pay all the expenses incurred by the employment of teachers." In Turner's estimation, the men had done all they could do for themselves. Now, they had no alternative but to rely on the government to send them the spelling books they needed in order to make further progress. The final twist came when Turner attempted to hold the army accountable for discriminating against black soldiers. He proposed to trade medals for spelling books, arguing, "as there are no promotions made in colored Regiments for gallantry or merit, it would be but a very small manifestation of regard to supply those at least who are trying to improve their minds with the necessary books for the purpose."[32]

Turner did not try to veil his cynicism. As pastor of Israel AME Church in Washington, he had recruited African American soldiers for the Union army, but now he was frustrated in his efforts to provide the men of his regiment with something that they both needed and wanted. On their behalf he proposed this sneering trade of medals earned for books deserved. Turner's correspondence does not indicate whether the regiment ever received the advanced spelling books, but by the end of August he reported that there were several company schools in operation, "employing the leisure hours of all the soldiers who are off duty." According to Turner, "the men learn with flattering success. I have never seen the fruits of my labor so visibly as I do now since I have held my position."[33]

Several other black chaplains embraced education as part of their mission. Some months after announcing plans to start a regimental school, William Waring, chaplain of the 102nd United States Colored Troops, noticed increasing interest in literacy among the soldiers. Writing from Beaufort, South Carolina, in November 1864, he noted that "there is a growing desire for something to read—when some months ago I began furnishing reading matter I could scarcely get rid of what I would get, but now I am frequently called upon when I have not got it and men find themselves enjoying an hour over a tract or newspaper that would perhaps, otherwise, be worse than uselessly spent." Presumably, a regimental school had been established, and as the men became more competent readers, the demand for reading material increased.[34]

Not only did recently freed men need training in rudimentary literacy; some northern black troops did as well. According to Benjamin Randolph, the chaplain of the Twenty-sixth U.S. Colored Troops, organized at Rikers Island, New York, many of the men from rural areas of New York State had "quit the plow and the field, and fled to their country's rescue."[35] Several hundred men in the regiment could not read or write. However, as Randolph, an Oberlin College graduate, reported, the men showed a great deal of interest in learning, and they were already putting more than two hundred primers and other books to good use. "In passing the company streets now," Randolph wrote, "we find men with books in hand and not so many cards as formerly. And our Colonel who manifests much interest in such things has promised to have a school house built, and then we expect to keep up an interesting and profitable school." Randolph provided what he considered important statistics regarding the moral and educational standing of the regiment, including: "Whole number of church members—64; Whole number of soldiers learning to read—200; Whole number of soldiers learning to write—70; Whole number of soldiers detected gambling—4; Whole number of soldiers detected playing cards upon Sabbath—4." Like Chaplain Waring, Randolph believed that once the soldiers learned to read they would be less likely to engage in "useless" or immoral activities like playing cards. He predicted that many of the men would return to their homes "better scholars and better morally."[36]

The young black chaplain of the 109th United States Colored Troops also made education a priority during his brief and tumultuous term. Twenty-one-year-old Francis A. Boyd, a former house servant and ordained minister, enlisted as a private in Lexington, Kentucky, in June 1864. Within a few weeks he was promoted to color sergeant. In November Major General Benjamin Butler appointed him chaplain of the regiment. However, by January 1865 Boyd's position was threatened. He complained to Butler that he had been "coolly and contemptuously treated" by the officers of the regiment. "Prejudices are dark, and bitter," he confided, "and I feel that my life is in peril." The former surgeon of the regiment vouched for Boyd, asserting that he had friends within the regiment who considered him "capable of doing more good in that Regt. than many white Chaplains could do." The defense failed, however, and in February Boyd's chaplaincy was revoked, allegedly because he had been appointed by the general, rather than elected by the white commissioned officers of the regiment as mandated by Congress.[37]

Inspired by the soldiers' eagerness to become literate, Boyd advocated for books, a school, and a teacher during his brief tenure as chaplain. "The men are actually clamoring for books and readers," Boyd related in one of his written reports. "As regards the matter of education, although the Men, so far as teachers are concerned, have had a meagre chance, nevertheless, enter their quarters at what time you may, and you will find them engaged in trying to decipher lessons in their spellers." He illustrated their potential with his own experience teaching one soldier to read and write: "What they would do if blessed with opportunity, and teachers, you may imagine from the instance of our color corporal, Preston Paterson, who was entirely ignorant in books, on the first of last August. In that month I commenced teaching him, and learned him to write his name, in two days. He is now able to write his Company Sick List, read his bible, and Cury's Practice." Boyd conjectured that all the men would perform as well as Paterson if given the chance. Boyd was ambitious in his plans for education within the regiment and reported that he had made arrangements with the Christian Commission "to secure eight-hundred Websters elementary and a tent 30 by 20 feet long, and a teacher, which I expect soon, and as soon as they arrive every exertion shall be used to push forward the educational interests of the Regiment."[38]

Boyd quickly grew impatient waiting for the Christian Commission to deliver the tent and asked the colonel of the regiment to assign men to build a schoolhouse. Boyd's concise letter stated simply, "In view of the pressing Demand for moral improvement, and Education Exhibited in the condition of our Regiment, I would respectfully request a Detail of Men or volunteers, with axes, to fell timber, and build a schoolhouse, to be used also for Chapel purposes."[39] Within a month, however, Boyd's chaplaincy was over, and his campaign to bring large-scale education to the regiment abruptly ended.

While Francis Boyd failed to build a schoolhouse, some African American soldiers did manage to leave physical monuments to their commitment to black education. Black soldiers contributed to newly established schools for freedpeople and, in some instances, founded schools with their donations. Soldiers of the Eighth United States Colored Infantry stationed in Petersburg, Virginia, for example, donated $241 to the endowment of Wilberforce University in Ohio. Black soldiers at Benton Barracks in Missouri donated $50 to a school for freedpeople in Brooklyn, Illinois.[40] Likewise, black soldiers from the 107th Colored Regiment in Georgia donated funds to support an orphanage and school in Atlanta; and in 1866, members of the Thirteenth Colored Regiment donated a melodeon, an early American organ, to the fledgling Fisk Colored School in Tennessee.[41] Similarly, in Greensboro, Georgia, officers and enlisted men of the 175th Battalion of New York Volunteers, working with African American residents, raised approximately $65 toward purchase of land for a school building. John J. Jackson, a black member of the regiment, served as the first teacher.[42]

On a larger scale, officers and soldiers of the Sixty-second and Sixty-fifth United States Colored Infantry in Missouri contributed more than six thousand dollars to launch Lincoln Institute (today's Lincoln University) in Jefferson City, Missouri. Most of the men had pulled heavy fatigue duty, digging trenches in Baton Rouge, Louisiana, where more than four hundred of them died as they carried out their duties. Still, many learned to read and write. As the surviving soldiers prepared to muster out of service, two of their officers remarked on how unfortunate it would be that so many men who had learned to read while in the army would have no school to attend when they returned home to Missouri. The idea of creating a school caught on, and white officers as well as black soldiers contributed funds. Officers of the Sixty-second Regiment contributed $1023.60, soldiers gave $3,966.50, and soldiers from the Sixty-fifth Regiment added $1,379.50. Samuel Sexton, a soldier in the Sixty-fifth Regiment, made a particularly notable contribution to the nascent school. From a weekly salary of $13, he donated $100.[43]

Born in St. Charles, Missouri, Sexton gave his occupation as "farmer" when he enlisted in March 1864 at age thirty. He was promoted to corporal but was reduced to private after one year. He worked as a nurse in the regimental hospital during much of his service.[44] In the estimation of Richard Baxter Foster, a white officer in the Sixty-second Regiment and the first president of Lincoln Institute, Sexton's contribution, coming as it did from such limited income, was "an example of liberality that may well challenge comparison with the acts of those rich men who, from their surplus, give thousands to found colleges."[45] Foster credited the black men of the two regiments with having established the school, noting that Lincoln was not established on the contributions of philanthropic whites.[46]

The Lincoln Institute Board of Trustees began its work with the approximately six thousand dollars that the two regiments raised. It chose Jefferson City, the capital of Missouri, as the site for the school, but it had trouble finding a schoolhouse. In Jefferson City, as in many towns in southern states at the end of the war, there were two black churches, one Baptist, the other Methodist. According to Foster, the black Baptist church already housed a school. The black Methodist church rebuffed Foster because he was white and would be the teacher. The white Methodist church in town refused to house the school because the students would be black. In the end, Lincoln Institute was founded in a "shell, a wreck, a ruin of a house" with two small rooms. The school began in September 1866 with two students, Henry Brown and Cornelius Chappell, and quickly grew beyond the capacity of one teacher.[47] Students received lessons in orthography, reading, phonetics, mental arithmetic, written arithmetic, geography, map drawing, penmanship, vocal culture, elocution, composition, vocal music, synthetic drawing, and calisthenics.[48]

In 1866 African American soldiers of the Arkansas-based Fifty-sixth United States Colored Infantry purchased thirty acres of land and built a school, first called the Helena Orphan Asylum, then Southland College, and finally Southland Institute.[49] The regiment deeded the real estate and buildings to the Indiana Yearly Meeting of Friends, a Quaker organization whose members had been working with black orphans in Helena for two years. The story of Southland provides an illustration of collaboration among black soldiers, local freedpeople, and northern missionaries, a collaboration that has rarely been examined.

Contemporary Quakers gladly recognized and even lauded the work of the black soldiers. In their newspaper, the *Freedmen's Record*, and in accounting statements and minutes of meetings, the Indiana Yearly Meeting of Friends consistently acknowledged that the soldiers' financial and physical contributions to Southland were critical to its existence. They expressed gratitude that the soldiers had stepped in when the institution was threatened and, by purchasing land, made it possible for the school to continue to operate. However, when Eli Jay, himself a Quaker, wrote the first history of Southland College in 1904, he risked eliding the full significance of the role of the men of the Fifty-sixth. In his handwritten history, Jay first wrote:

In 1866 the 56th regiment of colored soldiers, Colonel Charles Bentzoni commanding, purchased 30 acres of land lying about 9 miles north west of Helena, erected suitable but cheap buildings for the accommodation of the Asylum and deeded it to Indiana Yearly meeting. Each officer and private contributed a percent of his wages to cover the cost; and men were detailed each week to work on the building till completed. The land and buildings were valued at $4000.

This account credited black soldiers' agency and involvement. However, whether for editorial or substantive reasons, Jay crossed out the original version and shifted to a passive voice. The new text read instead:

> Accordingly, 30 acres of land lying about 9 miles north west of Helena was purchased on which were erected suitable but cheap buildings for the accommodation of the Asylum and deeded to Indiana Yearly Meeting. Each officer and private contributed a percent of his wages to cover the cost; and men were detailed each week to work on the building till completed. The land and buildings were valued at $4000.[50]

Jay's second version of the history nearly erased the role of the black soldiers. In the new rendering, there was little sense that the men wanted to build the school, or that it could not have been done without them. In fact, it almost intimated that they were ordered to build the school. It is not sufficient to say that schools were built, blacks were educated. In Helena, Arkansas, black soldiers and Quaker missionaries from Indiana worked together to create an institution that would care for the physical as well as the educational needs of local black children. The account of the creation of the school begins with the Quakers' presence in Arkansas during the Civil War.

Years after large numbers of Quakers abandoned the South for the Midwest, due in large part to their opposition to slavery, a few returned as missionaries working among newly freed blacks.[51] In October 1863 the Indiana Yearly Meeting established a "Committee on the Concerns of the People of Color" to see to the "relief of the physical necessities of those who have recently been released from slavery, and to their advancement in knowledge and religion."[52] One year later, the members met to consider how they could best use their resources to attend to the needs of the freedpeople. The group appointed Elkanah Beard to go south with three mandates: to inspect the condition of contraband camps, hospitals, and black settlements; to set up a network for distributing clothing; and to "establish schools at such points as may be deemed advisable."[53] Shortly thereafter the Indiana Yearly Meeting received an urgent request from the Union commander at Helena, Arkansas, for help with black orphans who were "suffering greatly from neglect and exposure."[54] The meeting sent four missionaries, among them Calvin and Alida Clark, who would serve in Helena for more than a quarter century.

From the beginning of the interaction between freedpeople in the South and the Quakers, education emerged as a priority for both. From Tennessee, for example, the Indiana Yearly Meeting received word that large numbers of freedpeople had arrived within Union lines "in a very destitute condition." When the Quakers sent clothing and an agent, the agent reported that "there were large numbers of freedmen at Pulaski and other points, who were anxious to have schools established among them." In their destitute condition, freedpeople in Tennessee, much as freedpeople in Norfolk and Hampton, Virginia, and on the Sea Islands, made it clear that they wanted not just clothing; they wanted schools as well. In this instance the Quakers declined to send teachers to Tennessee due to the "indifference, and in many instances, the hostility evinced toward the cause of education among them by their employers and the white citizens in general."[55]

Wherever Quaker missionaries went, however, they observed freedpeople's commitment to education. In Pine Bluff, Arkansas, for example, they learned that the black people were very willing to board and pay a teacher.[56] In another instance, the *Freedmen's Record* noted, "one of our teachers writes that soon after their arrival they found the colored people had heard of their coming, organized a board to forward their work, and raised a considerable sum of money to help towards meeting expenses. We are informed that some of the Freedmen partially pay for their tuition, and generally show a disposition to try to help themselves." The Quaker newspaper editorialized, "We wish to say for the encouragement of those who contribute to this benevolent cause, that, we believe, experiment has fully demonstrated that the quickest and shortest way to relieve ourselves of the burden of contributing to the relief of this class; and *only* way to elevate them above the depressing effects of the deep-rooted prejudices with which they are surrounded, and enable them to enjoy the full blessings of freedom is, after relieving their pressing physical wants, to *educate!*"[57]

Quakers already had a long history of prioritizing education for their own children as well as those of oppressed people whom they considered "under their care." In the antebellum period, once blacks made it to freedom, Quakers offered support to black schools. In most instances black teachers taught the children, and white Quakers advised and assisted financially.[58] Quakers also established boarding schools for Shawnee children in Kansas, although as of 1861 the Shawnee schools were not successful as parents did not want their children separated from them.[59] Whether working among Indians or African Americans, the Quakers saw their mission as first to relieve physical suffering, then to "supply, according to our ability, the demands of their higher nature, by sending Christian laborers to instruct their minds, and to aid in leading them to Christ."[60]

Among former slaves, Quakers took a twofold approach to education, teaching with an eye toward appealing to a "higher nature" as well as equipping them with practical, usable skills. Encouragement of self-reliance underlay their missionary impulse. For example, although they first supplied do-nated clothing to the former slaves, they soon determined that this method was ineffective because the freedpeople did not learn to help themselves; and moreover, the clothes did not fit. As a result, they instead decided to establish industrial schools. Thus, in Helena, one missionary teacher established an industrial school to teach sewing to poor women, many of whom were solely responsible for the support of their families. The women crafted surplus military overcoats into capes, coats, and skirts.[61] But the Quakers' focus in Helena was on caring for and educating orphaned, destitute, or abandoned African American children.

In the antebellum South, being an orphan only made a black child more vulnerable to sale and sexual abuse.[62] Predictably, the number of orphaned children multiplied during the Civil War, and African American children were particularly susceptible because as slaves they often lived separately from one or both parents. During the war, with slave owners sending highly valued enslaved people into hiding from Union soldiers, with black men running away to enlist in the army, and with women and children thrown out of their homes by embittered owners, the probability increased that a child would be left without support. The war and extreme poverty that often accompanied the nominal freedom of contraband status also stretched fictive and extended kinship ties that had previously protected children without parents.

Children entered asylums like the one in Helena in one of several ways. In one instance, a white man brought in two orphan boys who had belonged to his father. He did not wish to keep them any longer and left them at the asylum. In another case, an African American widow brought her three children seeking a place for all four of them to live. The mother said she thought she could manage with one child, but no one wanted to hire a woman with so many children. The Quakers accepted two of the children. At the asylum, which was in actuality an orphanage and a school, the children received food, clothing, and education.[63]

For two years the Quakers operated the school and orphanage at Helena on property abandoned by local whites who had fled the area during the war. However, in the autumn of 1865, after the fall of the Confederacy and with the North intent on reconciliation, southern landowners began to return to claim their land, and the Union government acquiesced in returning seized property. In November 1865, when John Henry Douglas visited Helena on behalf of the Indiana Yearly Meeting, he found Calvin and Alida Clark healthy but worried about the future of the asylum. They were caring for twenty children and "feeling very much discouraged," Douglas wrote back to Indiana. "Everything is uncertain; they are liable to have to give up their work at the house they now occupy any day, and the officers informed us that there was no other place that they could give them, as Government is turning over everything to the owners as fast as they can, and as to what the white people will do in the place when left to themselves, we cannot tell; that remains to be tested." Douglas concluded that the Quakers' continued success in Helena would depend on getting a "permanent foot hold either by leasing or by purchasing some real estate, or by the Freedmen's doing so."[64] One month later, in December 1865, Calvin and Alida Clark confirmed Douglas's fears and seemed resigned to eviction. Matters became even more hopeless when the government stopped the food rations that the children and teachers relied on for sustenance. According to the Clarks, "The various officers of the army, and the colored people generally, are expressing the greatest regret at the prospect of giving up the Asylum here."[65]

Regret evolved into action. The *Freedmen's Record* reported in March 1866 that the government still planned to return the property to its owners, but the Quakers were "encouraged by the spirit which the officers in charge have shown, as well as the colored people. They are trying to buy a lot and erect suitable buildings on it for a permanent Asylum near by and seem likely to succeed in their undertaking."[66]

Local black people played a role in supporting the school. In April 1866, for example, when the Helena school and orphanage celebrated its second anniversary, "the colored grocers in the city presented six cans of oysters, four of sardines, three large cocoanuts [*sic*], one each of peaches, grapes, black-berries and pineapples, three gallons cream nuts and filberts, four pounds crackers, two pounds sugar cakes, fancy candies, etc, which, added to the rations drawn for the children, made them an extra nice dinner, which was spread in the schoolroom"[67] Further, several local black people worked with the Quaker missionaries at the asylum. Stephen Patton, usually referred to in the missionaries' letters as "Uncle Stephen," was a "colored minister, who has felt it to be his duty to devote himself to the temporal and spiritual interests of the children."[68] In addition to Patton, Mildred Williams cooked for staff and children, Betsy Dawson was the washerwoman for the asylum, and Henrietta Kitteral filled in when needed.[69]

The regiment's commander was also critical. The enlisted men certainly could not have participated in the enterprise without the approval and even leadership of their colonel, Charles Bentzoni. Born in Prussia, Bentzoni arrived in the United States in 1857. He took command of the Fifty-sixth Regiment in 1864.[70] Bentzoni appears to have had some abolitionist tendencies. When he ordered musical instruments and sheet music for the regiment, along with the patriotic "Star Spangled Banner" and the playful "simple quick steps and waltzes," he also ordered the abolitionist favorite, "John Brown."[71] Bentzoni further demonstrated his interest in the well-being of the former slaves who served as soldiers in his regiment by encouraging them to open savings accounts, so that they would not be "compelled to work for small wages, and lead a life of trial and deprivation with no recognition as worthy and substantial members of society."[72] With these values, it is not surprising that both the Quakers and historians credited Bentzoni with leading the men of the Fifty-sixth Regiment in raising funds for the asylum.

The soldiers, however, were central in creating this educational institution in Helena. While Colonel Bentzoni certainly encouraged and enabled the soldiers to assist the asylum, it is equally clear that the soldiers did not act merely on orders from their colonel. They voluntarily raised funds, cleared the land, and built the school. Though it was certainly possible for Colonel Bentzoni to order them to work on the land, he could not order the men to give money from their salaries to make the initial purchase. Yet, each company donated funds, totaling $2,093, to the school project.[73] In addition, they held two concerts to raise funds.[74]

Some of the soldiers developed ongoing relationships with the teachers and children at the school. One evening in late February 1866, three young soldiers, Thomas Watson, Samuel Cole, and Josiah Hale, gave the children a special treat. According to the *Freedmen's Record*, the men had benefited "from the various instruction, religious, moral and literary, emanating from the Asylum, and wishing to manifest their gratitude for it and their respect for their teachers, superintendents, etc, as well as to gratify the orphan children, they asked and obtained leave to have a candy pulling at their expense." The soldiers, children, and a few other young people piled their plates with candy and began "pulling, eating and playing until the drum tapped and away the soldier boys had to run to roll call." These men acted out of a sense of personal commitment when they gave their funds and labor to create a permanent home and school for the children.[75]

The men of the Fifty-sixth Regiment used the money they raised to purchase thirty acres of land at a cost of $900, plus lumber, cement, lime, and other building supplies, cisterns, three cows, and a calf. Then the regiment began the work of transforming the property into a residential school.[76] Located nine miles northwest of Helena, the property was heavily timbered woodland with oak, sweet gum, poplar, and ash. One oak measured twenty feet in circumference and stretched forty-five feet high. The soldiers cut down trees, built fences, and dug ditches for drainage. They built the schoolhouse, residential buildings for the teachers, and outbuildings. The effort did not always go smoothly, however. In July 1866 Calvin Clark wrote to inform Indiana Friends that they were completely out of funds, and he promised to lend the money needed to purchase lumber. When the lumber arrived the regiment would resume building. With only one house for the children completed, the school was overcrowded, and healthy children were forced to sleep in the same rooms with the sick. "There is no backing out now, Friends," Calvin Clark urged. "We must go on till houses and cisterns are made to enable us to live."[77]

Despite the shortages, the Quakers and soldiers were eager to celebrate their joint venture. In July 1866, with the project still underway, the officers and soldiers of the Fifty-sixth Regiment dedicated the new school at Helena. They "came out in military style, marched nine miles to our front yard, and hoisted the flag on the staff previously planted precisely in the center of the walk," Alida Clark reported. Soldiers, staff, children, and local white visitors then paraded to the grove where the quartermaster had spread a table. There, the colonel announced the amount of money that each company had raised. On behalf of the Fifty-sixth Regiment, he ceremoniously handed the deed to the property to Clark who received it on behalf of Indiana Yearly Meeting. Following speeches and refreshments, the colonel called on the children to sing. The girls, wearing new calico dresses and neatly trimmed "Shaker bonnets," and the boys, in new linen pants and shirts with new straw hats, "acquitted themselves honorably," according to Alida Clark.[78]

The project was still not complete when two representatives of Indiana Yearly Meeting visited the school in September 1866. But the soldiers had made considerable progress. They had built two cisterns, dug a well, and laid out a road within the compound. The men had plowed the farm, and it was in good condition with acres of corn, cotton, and vegetable and pasture lots. It was stocked with a horse, two mules, four cows, and three calves. The school compound was designed to form a hollow square with two buildings, each ten feet long with a veranda on one side, forming two sides of the square. The soldiers had not yet built the two other buildings that would complete the square. The visitors noted that the lumber was ready, but "the colored regiment was ordered away a few days before we arrived probably to be mustered out of the service. They had hoped to have remained long enough to have put up this building."[79]

The soldiers probably never returned to complete the buildings. The war was over, and regiments were being discharged. In September 1866 sad news reached the Quakers. The *Freedmen's Record* reported: "LATE NEWS from St. Louis state[s] that nearly two hundred soldiers of the colored regiment who built the Asylum at Helena, have died of Cholera, which is said to have been caused by eating raw sugar whilst coming up the river."[80]

Still, the men of the Fifty-sixth Regiment made an invaluable contribution to the children of Helena. Calvin and Alida Clark's missionary work among the freedpeople might have been thwarted or, at the least, diminished had not the regiment provided a permanent home for the school and orphanage. The

Clarks' fears of being evicted had not been hyperbolic. Other Quaker-run asylums closed or endured substantial reduction when the government returned land to former owners. In August 1866 the asylum at Lauderdale, Mississippi, could not afford to purchase the 40-acre property it occupied and was forced to move the buildings to an adjacent 1½ acres.[81] This was a great loss as the institution relied on farming for financial as well as instructional value.[82] In September 1866 the Quakers shut down the asylum at Little Rock for similar reasons and made plans to move those children to Helena. The officers and black soldiers of the Fifty-sixth Regiment thus left a monument of black education. Working with the Quakers, they built a lasting institution in which black children could live and learn. At a time when the Helena Asylum was threatened, the regiment gave it a sense of permanence that could only have come through owning the property on which it stood.[83]

The soldiers of the Fifty-sixth Regiment, like so many other black men who fought in the Civil War, participated in a growing movement to educate formerly enslaved people. Whether building schools, advocating for education, learning to read and write, or teaching others, a common theme resounded among the soldiers: they had to construct new lives for themselves and their communities, and education was central to that charge. As a child, Elijah Marrs had "stolen" an education because he felt that he would have something important to do. John Sweney urged the government to provide an educational institution within his regiment so that the men could prepare to carry out the important roles of citizenship. And Lizzie Edwards thought the soldiers at a school she visited studied harder than other students because they "feel the importance of learning." Black soldiers were men in a world ruled by other men, and they sought to prepare themselves to take on leadership roles in their own communities. Once mustered out, some of these student-soldiers would attain political office. For example, three black sergeants from Colonel Thomas Wentworth Higginson's regiment served as delegates to the South Carolina Constitutional Convention of 1868.[84] Other men taught in schools back home or petitioned the government on behalf of freedpeople. As John Sweney had predicted, their education could not be contained.

African American soldiers, perhaps even more than black civilians, burned with a special fervor to learn to read and write. By joining the military they had not only freed themselves, but had also emancipated their wives, children, and mothers.[85] Perhaps they studied extra hard because they believed that education would help them to throw off the smear of inferiority that whites had inscribed upon them during slavery. These black men's very presence in the uniform of the United States military proved that the old system of slavery was dying and that when they emerged from war, the whole world would have changed.

But the change came slowly, and black men knew it. As Elijah Marrs wrestled with continuing to obey the commands of white men, he knew that it would take more than freedom to make them consider him their equal. Henry McNeal Turner understood that the Union failed to recognize black men's valor precisely because they were black. Even as black men gained their freedom and fought for others to be free, white men challenged their right to be considered "men among men." Northern white commanding officers such as Thomas Wentworth Higginson inspected and examined, scrutinized and measured, poked and prodded black men's bodies as if to assess whether they could indeed take a place alongside white men in the great chain of being; and southern white men continued to make claims of ownership over black men's bodies even after the war ended.[86]

On December 10, 1866, more than two years after Elijah Marrs enlisted, and nearly eight months after he mustered out of the service, his former owner filed a claim with the War Department "For Compensation For Slave Named Elijah Marrs." In bargains struck by President Lincoln, Radical Republicans in Congress, and the governor of Kentucky, the government agreed to compensate slave owners for each slave who had enlisted in the Union army. In an affidavit witnessed by two residents of Shelby County, slave owner Jesse Robinson swore an oath of loyalty, attesting that he had not participated in the rebellion and had never borne arms against the United States of America. He further swore that as he owned Elijah Marrs's mother when Elijah was born, Elijah had belonged to him since birth. Robinson averred that at the time of enlistment, Marrs was worth $800, but he entered a claim for $300, the maximum amount allowed by the government. Robinson also filed a claim for Henry Marrs, who, like his brother Elijah, was literate and achieved the rank of sergeant in the army. Neither brother was a party to these transactions. It was a matter between the former slaveholder and a government that recognized a claim of property in a veteran of the Civil War.[87] Freedom had taken generations to come and then only through struggle. But as Jesse Robinson's claim so clearly illustrated, the struggle for true freedom and equality continued.

CHAPTER 4 ▪ ▪ ▪ ▪ ▪ ▪ ▪ ▪ ▪ ▪ ▪ ▪ ▪ ▪

We Must Get Education for Ourselves and Our Children

Advocacy for Education

Whereas, Knowledge is power, and an educated and intelligent people can neither be held in, nor reduced to slavery . . . we will insist upon the establishment of good schools for the thorough education of our children.

Proceedings of the Colored People's Convention of the State of South Carolina, 1865

We are the substrata, the foundation on which the future power and wealth of the State of Arkansas must be built, and as the future prosperity of the State cannot afford to rest upon ignorant labor, therefore, we respectfully ask the legislature to provide for the education of our children.

"Proceedings of the Convention of Colored Citizens of Arkansas, 1865"

Sergeants Elijah and Henry Marrs mustered out of the army into a world transformed by war and freedom. They and other black men had enlisted on the run from slavery; now astonished former owners looked on as black soldiers returned home in Union uniforms, armed with pistol and pen and paper, issuing public appeals for African American civil rights.[1] When freedpeople gathered in local communities to enunciate their shared goals and to design strategies for fighting the discrimination that stood in the way of their progress, they selected men who could put their concerns into writing. Often, these men had been soldiers, part of the liberating force. Henry Marrs served as spokesperson for such a group of freedpeople in his hometown of Shelbyville, Kentucky.[2] He wrote to the secretary of war in May 1866 on their behalf to give voice to their concern that even though free, they remained shut out from public accommodations unless an authorized white person granted permission. To make matters worse, blacks could not instead associate with one another in their own establishments because local whites also barred them from operating businesses. They needed grocery stores, coffeehouses, and rooming houses for black travelers. Marrs inquired whether all black people, even the soldiers who had served their country, must now return to former masters and work for twelve or thirteen dollars a month. "If you call this Freedom, what do you call slavery?" Marrs wanted to know. He implored Secretary of War Edwin M. Stanton to "send some word to our relief" and assured him that there were no idle blacks in Shelbyville. All of them, he said, were engaged at something.[3]

Two years later and a few miles away, Elijah Marrs emerged as the representative voice of the freedpeople of La Grange, Kentucky. He, too, wrote to Secretary Stanton, "after seeing the Great Sufferings of my nation of people in the State of Kentucky." The black people in La Grange, he told Stanton, stole away at midnight to a mass meeting at which they "passed a resolution that I shold Rite to you on this Subject and let the congressman know our distress in Kentucky." According to Marrs, so imbalanced was the power between blacks and whites, that African Americans dared not even look a white man in the eye. Where the people of Shelbyville were most concerned with gaining access to public accommodations and establishing businesses, the people in La Grange focused on the right to testify in court. Elijah Marrs complained that the law deeming black men and women incompetent to testify against whites allowed white people to abuse them with impunity. African Americans, he said, had been murdered at night by whites who dared witnesses to report their offenses. He offered to investigate the murders if the Freedmen's Bureau would empower him to do so. If something is not done, Marrs told Stanton, "we will hafter leave this country." As Henry had, Elijah also questioned the substance of this freedom that seemed to grant few rights to former slaves.[4]

As sergeants in the army, the Marrs brothers belonged to a clerical bureaucracy whose authority they now hoped to draw upon by writing to the secretary of war. Before the war their literacy made possible communication among separated slaves and informed black communities of local and national news. With the experience gained from soldiering, they now enlarged their roles to include advocating on behalf of the freedpeople of Shelbyville and La Grange. Both men intended that their literacy should carry the freedpeople's thoughts and desires beyond the black community to officials in the president's cabinet, whom they believed had the power to mitigate their repression. On behalf of fellow freedpeople, they rejected the new system of domination that southern whites were putting in place, and they articulated a demand for agency and self-determination. If southern whites would not allow them into white coffeehouses, they wanted the right to operate their own. If whites would not allow black travelers to lodge in white-owned inns and hotels, black communities and individuals wanted the right to provide their own accommodations. Further, they rejected the idea of returning to work for white people—former masters—for a pittance, when they were industrious enough to establish their own businesses. Henry, Elijah, and the freedpeople of Shelbyville and La Grange realized that petitions to the very local whites that sought to exclude them would be meaningless and would be sure to trigger reprisals. In this moment, with some northern whites still considered allies, they could write down their aspirations and send them north, hoping that powerful northerners would intervene and help them to realize their claims for fair treatment and self-determination.

In the postemancipation South, with freedpeople's stubborn hope and optimism butting up against a resolute determination to maintain white dominance, Henry and Elijah Marrs blended their energies with a large force of African Americans who set about fashioning political, economic, religious, and educational institutions within black communities. In newspaper editorials, letters to public officials, speeches at conventions, and statements to white citizens, black individuals and organizations demanded land, enfranchisement for black men, the right to testify in courts, fair compensation for their labor, and the right to compete economically. They also asserted a right to education.

Acquiring literacy in conjunction with freedom had the potential to open access to democratic political activity, and that in turn held a promise of enabling African Americans to participate in shaping the civil society in which they had hitherto been considered chattel—insurgent chattel, but chattel just the same. Former slaves, who had always had a public presence, sought upon emancipation to enter the public sphere as individuals distinct from owners. They stood on the verge of being counted for the first time not as part of an owner's inventory for tax assessment nor as a percentage of a man for political apportionment. Freedpeople wanted to ensure that they counted as voters and as legislators who could govern their own futures. Illiteracy, they knew, would impede their ambition for full participation in this public, political sphere.[5] Therefore, alongside traditionally defined civil rights of suffrage and jury service, freedpeople propounded a new right: the right to attend school. Across the South, African Americans employed the literacy they possessed to argue for a meaningful freedom, and, realizing the limits of their self-taught literacy, they urged the federal government to acknowledge and protect their right to education. Simultaneously, they appealed to state governments to provide public schooling.

The idea of a right to education was a radical one indeed. Most slave states had not only criminalized teaching blacks, they had also failed to confer on whites anything resembling a right to an education. Schooling in the antebellum South constituted a privilege that wealth purchased. Less wealthy whites attended school sporadically, if at all, with little or no assistance from states. Following the war, many freedpeople realized that their illiteracy would play into the hands of white southerners who argued that blacks were incompetent to participate in civic activities. The freedpeople therefore resolved that they and their children would have access to schools. They shaped their desire for education into a right that they believed warranted governmental protection.

Parents made public claims for the right to educate their children. In February 1864 the Superintendent of Negro Labor in New Orleans testified before the Freedmen's Inquiry Commission that "a negro soldier *demanded* his children at my hands; I endeavored to test his affection for them, when he said: 'Lieut., I want to send them to school.'" When the superintendent replied that the children had a good home with their former owner, the African American soldier insisted, "'I am in your service; I wear military clothes; I have been in three battles; I was in the assault at Port Hudson; I *want those children*; they are my flesh and blood.'" The superintendent relented and ordered the children's former owner to bring them to his office. Over her objections, the superintendent handed the children over to their father.[6]

In March 1865 the African American men of Roanoke Island, North Carolina, wrote directly to the president of the United States. "We Colored men of this island held a meeting to consult over the affairs of our present conditions and our rights, and we find that our arms are so short that we cant doe any thing with in our Selves so we Concluded that the best thing we could do was to apply to you or some of your cabinets." The men had been told that they were free, but they wanted to know if they had any rights, or were they to be "stamped down and trodden under foot" by the very superintendent to whom they looked for assistance. Among their complaints against the superintendent, whom the federal government paid to oversee plantations on the island, was the fact that he had interfered with the education of their sons. "We want to know from the Secretary of War, has the Rev. Chaplain James which is our Superintendent of negros affairs has any wright to take our boy Children from us and from the School and Send them to New Bern to work to pay for they ration without they parent Consent. If he has we thinks it very hard indeed." The men alleged that the superintendent tricked some parents into sending their sons to collect rations. Many parents, suspicious of "Cesesh plots," suspected that the superintendent was playing games and kept their boys at home. Guards forced the other boys onto a boat and took them to New Bern, where they put them to work. The superintendent, the men claimed in their letter, ignored parents' pleas to return their children. The men of Roanoke Island wanted to know if the president had issued any rations for schoolboys. In other words, wasn't it possible for their sons to attend school and collect rations as well?[7]

Both parents and children, moreover, negotiated labor contracts that included a right to education. In April 1867 Carter Holmes, a twelve-year-old black apprentice in Maryland, wrote a letter to the Freedmen's Bureau in Washington, D.C. Three years earlier, he said, he had been bound out by government officials to a Mr. Suit who promised to clothe, feed, and educate him as compensation for his labor. Holmes complained that while Suit had been generally kind to him, he had neither clothed him decently nor sent him to school. Holmes was so tired of being cheated out of his labor, receiving "no clothing, no chance for school—nothing but *whippings*," that he ran away to Washington. He begged the Freedmen's Bureau not to let Suit take him back; "I have a mother and a father who would care for me if they knew where I was." He believed they were somewhere in Washington. The Freedmen's Bureau superintendent sent Holmes to the District of Columbia Orphan Asylum.[8] Even in the former Confederacy, the mother of a seven-year-old boy in Muscogee County, Georgia, made sure to include education in her son's apprenticeship contract. In exchange for the child's labor, the employer agreed to "provide for all his temporal wants and learn him to read and write if he will take it."[9]

These four episodes depict freedpeople attempting to insert a right to education into their newly gained freedom. For the parents, freedom meant nothing if it did not mean taking control of their children's lives and deciding what was best for their well-being. The soldier in New Orleans wanted his children to live with him and their mother. He believed that as parents, they had the right to care for their own children, and for them, this included sending the children to school. The men of Roanoke Island admitted that it was a sacrifice for families to send their sons to school rather than put them to work, but it was a sacrifice they were willing to make. They believed it was their right to make that choice and so resented the superintendent's interference with their decision to place education above immediate income that they took their complaint to the highest office in the land. For the young apprentice in Maryland, freedom meant wearing decent clothing and attending school. Significantly, freedom also meant being cared for by his own parents, not by a mistress or master, and he probably presumed that his own parents would understand the importance of sending him to school. The mother in Georgia similarly asserted her right as a parent to ensure that her son received an education. For each of these freedpeople, and countless others, a meaningful freedom included access to schooling.

Like Harry McMillan, the freedman in Beaufort who predicted that in less than one generation African Americans would acquire enough education to govern their own communities, these freedpeople foresaw an immediate future in which neither white southern mistresses and masters nor white northern superintendents would hold sway over their lives. They looked forward to the day when they would have the tools they needed to live without interference from whites. They were certain that education would provide those tools. Now out of slavery, they openly expressed dissatisfaction with the very limited freedom that seemed acceptable to the federal government, and they moved to transform long-coveted access to education into a right whose enforcement they insisted upon. The soldier *demanded* his children; the men of Roanoke Island challenged the authority of the superintendent; the young boy in Maryland unilaterally revoked his apprenticeship contract; and the mother in Georgia negotiated a contract that provided schooling for her son. Education was now not only something jealously yearned for, nor was it something to be secretly "stolen." Many African Americans in the South construed it as a right that they were prepared to fight for and protect, and one that they believed the government should force recalcitrant whites to honor.

As individual freedpeople formulated the right to education, they publicly articulated arguments in favor of public education for former slaves through embryonic African American political institutions that they launched. Freedpeople began this work of organizing in nighttime meetings where they devised strategies for activating their freedom in places like Hampton, Virginia, La Grange, Kentucky, and New Bern, North Carolina. Intent on developing a political life as soon as the war ended, freedpeople also began meeting in more public forums in statewide conventions modeled after the antebellum ones that African Americans had held in northern states since 1817. At the antebellum conventions, delegates organized against colonization and proclaimed their opposition to the institution of slavery. They also developed plans for educating free African Americans.[10] Later, when African Americans in the free border state of Kansas held a convention in 1863, and when freedpeople in former slave states including Louisiana, Virginia, Tennessee, Missouri, Arkansas, South Carolina, and North Carolina held conventions in 1865, they called for civil rights including jury service and suffrage, and they pressed states and the freedpeople themselves to make education available to former slaves.

The North Carolina convention provides texture and context for understanding the circumstances under which these post–Civil War conventions took place. In August 1865, at the urging of a group of freedpeople who met in New Bern, Abraham H. Galloway, John Randolph Jr., and George W. Price issued the convention call: "Rally, old men, we want the counsel of your years and experience; rally, young men, we want your loyal presence, and need the ardor of youth to stimulate the timid."[11] At the end of September, 117 black men representing half of the counties in the state arrived in the capital of Raleigh. Some of the men wore Union uniforms, others ministerial robes, and some wore still the cheap, course, homespun clothing that slave owners had once doled out.[12] Some delegates arrived without proper credentials, having left their homes hastily and in secret to avoid retribution from local whites. They had stolen away in the night to shape their freedom as they might have done to escape slavery just a short while earlier. All the delegates were men.[13] Most were freedmen, not men who had been free before the war. Roughly half were literate, a much higher percentage than the literate among the larger African American population. Most were skilled laborers—barbers, blacksmiths, carpenters. Some were ministers and some teachers. Freedpeople in towns around the state chose their most educated, articulate, spokesmen to represent them.[14]

Delegates began their deliberations on September 29, 1865, in the Loyal African Methodist Episcopal Church in Raleigh. The church, also known as Lincoln Church, was a plain, wooden, white structure located on a back street of the city. Inside, the floors were carpeted, the seats cushioned. Devoid of ornament, the sanctuary offered nothing to detract the eye from its focal point. At the front of the church, above the pulpit, in the space where one might expect to see a cross or a representation of Jesus, hung a "large and elegant and life-like" plaster bust of Abraham Lincoln. Above the assassinated president's head African Americans had inscribed the last lines of his second inaugural speech: "With malice toward none, with charity for all, with firmness in the right, as God gives us to see the right, let us strive on to finish the work we are in, to bind up the nation's wounds, to care for him who has borne the battle, and for his widow and orphan; to do all which may achieve and cherish a just and everlasting peace among ourselves and with all nations."[15]

So much had changed. In the early years of the war in Missouri, Ellen Turner's owner beat her for daring to hang a picture of Abraham Lincoln on her bedroom wall. In 1865 a black congregation publicly honored the memory of the man whom they considered a liberator. But so much had stayed the same. The delegates who delivered speeches from the pulpit longed to cloak themselves in the protections of the American nation, but they also knew that merely seeking those protections pitted them against those who already enjoyed the privileges of citizenship. The delegates understood, moreover, that their mere presence, and certainly their assertion of political rights for African Americans, would disturb any peace that might have been established between them and the white nation.

Under the scrutiny of the more than four hundred spectators who filled the church's main floor and balcony, delegates spent the better part of an afternoon debating a resolution that urged the employment of black teachers in black schools and black preachers in black churches. Proponents argued that having black teachers would stimulate interest in education among young black men and women. Abraham Galloway and other opponents of the resolution argued, however, that expressing such a preference would only erect one more wall between blacks and whites. In the end, many delegates who supported the premise of the resolution voted against it not because of the potential effect on race relations, but because they believed some black parents would take the ideal too far and refuse to send their children to schools with white teachers. Believing that freedpeople had to make the best use of the resources available to them, the majority voted down the resolution, opting instead to express their gratitude to northern aid societies and the Freedmen's Bureau for work on behalf of freedpeople's education.[16]

In an address drafted to send to the whites-only state convention that would soon meet a few blocks away to ratify a new Reconstruction state constitution, the delegates refrained from making demands. Careful not to antagonize white politicians, they even went so far as to thank "those among former slave masters who have promptly conceded our freedom, and have manifested a just and humane disposition towards their former slaves." African Americans, they said, were primarily concerned with gaining fair treatment and compensation. With regard to education, the delegates simply stated: "We desire education for our children, that they may be made useful in all the relations of life."[17]

But even these muted expressions by the black convention met with resistance. On October 2, 1865, the state constitutional convention received the so-called Freedmen's Address. For the most part, the convention deflected freedpeople's concerns about labor and education to the state legislature. Two or three delegates argued for freedpeople's education, but instead of supporting the rights that freedpeople sought, the convention made the vague suggestion that it was in the interest of the white race who now had to live with free blacks to elevate them by enacting laws that would encourage them to work the land and take responsibility for their own welfare. Further, the white delegates made it clear that they did not support legislation aimed at ending prejudice, as such laws would tend only to "influence and strengthen" prejudice, and thus disrupt the delicate relations that existed between blacks and whites who had formed bonds of affinity in slavery. The convention discouraged any "premature introduction of any schemes that may disturb the operations of these kindly feelings, or inflame the inherent social prejudice that exists against the colored race."[18]

The black convention was temperate in its requests. The white convention, while outlawing future enslavement of African Americans as required for readmission to the Union, upheld black people's second-class status. It would take Congressional Reconstruction to bring about any dramatic shifts in state policy and law.

Taken collectively, other African American conventions in South Carolina, Georgia, Missouri, Arkansas and even the free state of Kansas enunciated a three-pronged education agenda. First, they encouraged African Americans to pursue education for themselves and their children. Second, they urged southern whites not to use illiteracy as an excuse to exclude African Americans from civil government. To support this request, they pointed out that whites were responsible for former slaves' educational deficits, and they noted that illiteracy did not exclude white men from voting. Third, playing to white people's self-interest, the conventions attempted to persuade white southerners that black education was not only inevitable, but would ultimately inure to the benefit of whites.

Self-help often appeared at the forefront when convention delegates spoke of education. Fully cognizant of the history of white suppression of black education and aware of continuing white hostility, delegates urged black people to establish their own schools and to take full advantage of educational opportunities provided by other blacks or by northern associations. South Carolina delegates meeting in Zion Church in Charleston in November 1865 acknowledged that the "measures which have been adopted for the development of white men's children have been denied to us and ours." Still, they embraced the truth of the maxim "God helps those who help themselves" and entreated African American parents and guardians to recall the *"forced ignorance and degradation"* of the past and to see to it that schools were immediately established in every neighborhood. The delegates pledged to "contribute freely and liberally" of their means and promised to "earnestly and persistently urge forward every measure calculated to elevate us to the rank of a wise, enlightened and Christian people." They urged parents to ensure that their children attended regularly once schools were in operation.[19]

Similarly, when Kansas delegates met in an AME church in Leavenworth in October 1863, convention president Reverend John Turner emphasized morality, self-help, and education as essential to black people's progress in the United States. He admonished fellow delegates that while they should be thankful to God for the good that He was doing for them through the works of men, they could not rely on others but had to do for themselves as well. "If we would be great, we must be good," he told his audience; and to be considered good, black people would have to be even more "industrious, sober and truthful" than others. "Knowledge is power," Turner reminded his audience, "therefore we must get education for ourselves and our children.

Each of us ought to consider the character and elevation of the colored people of Kansas as in his own keeping and labor with that view." The convention endorsed the president's emphasis on education by resolving that "Whereas, 'knowledge is power,' we recommend our people to seek education for themselves and children, and that they insist upon their educational rights everywhere in Kansas."[20]

Delegates aimed the second prong of the educational agenda directly at whites in positions of political power. Arguing that former slaves should not be denied access to the vote and to jury service on the basis of illiteracy, they also made it clear that to do so would be unjust and hypocritical as white people were responsible for blacks' illiteracy. Furthermore, convention attendees alleged, since illiteracy did not preclude whites from voting, it should not exclude blacks either. Delegates to the South Carolina Colored People's Convention employed the language of America's defining documents to lay African Americans' illiteracy at the feet of whites. In a "Declaration of Rights and Wrongs," the convention argued that black people had been denied their inalienable rights in violation of the principles on which the country was founded. Specifically, they contended, "We have been deprived of the free exercise of political rights, of natural, civil, and political liberty. The avenues of wealth and education have been closed to us. The strong wall of prejudice, on the part of the dominant race, has obstructed our pursuit of happiness." The declaration concluded by charging that black people had "bled and sweat for the elevation of those who have degraded us, and still continue to oppress us."[21]

In a document directed to the Congress of the United States, South Carolina convention delegates asked to be included on juries, to have the right to bear arms, to be free of discriminatory "black laws," and to receive the free land that the government had promised them. They also wanted "the three great agents of civilized society—the school, the pulpit, the press—be as secure in South Carolina as they were in New England."[22]

The State Convention of the Colored People of Georgia sounded a similar chord in its address to the Georgia legislature in January 1866. "Suffering from the consequent degradation of two hundred and forty-six years' enslavement," the delegates reasoned, "it is not to be expected that we are thoroughly qualified to take our position beside those who for ages have been rocked in the cradle of education." The Georgia delegates attempted to negotiate. African Americans, they claimed, were willing to bury the past and forget the ills of slavery. In exchange, they expected white people in Georgia to create equitable laws. They hoped Georgia lawmakers would take past oppression into consideration when it decided who would be admitted into the body politic. In other words, the illiteracy of many former slaves should not exclude them from political participation.[23]

Delegates to the Missouri convention took up the second part of the argument. Illiteracy, they asserted, should not exclude African Americans from civic activity if it did not also exclude whites. They called for an "impartial discrimination which shall affect white as well as black," and they argued that "the entire ignorance and stupidity of the people should not by any presumption be wholly charged to the account of ourselves." That is, if literacy were to be a prerequisite for voting or jury service, some whites should be excluded and some blacks should be included.[24] The Missouri delegates went even further. "Our asserted ignorance is not a condition from choice or disposition, as is now everywhere made evident in the zealous efforts of our people to educate themselves and their children," they said, "but arises from the black code legislation of our illiterate franchised masters." In one move they asserted that whites had kept blacks from becoming literate, acknowledged the efforts of vast numbers of newly freed African Americans to become educated, and condemned their former masters, who whether or not educated, still exercised the franchise.[25]

Finally, the third prong of the educational agenda declared black educational progress inevitable as well as indispensable to the progress of the entire region. "A few years will materially change our status," the State Convention of the Colored People of Georgia insisted. "Education and wealth, which are bound to be distributed in our ranks, will tell in power upon the resources of the state." To bring about the changes in African American education with its resulting benefits to all the people of Georgia, the delegates asked the legislature to establish schools and colleges for African American children and promised, or perhaps threatened, that "our young men will be aspiring to the positions of doctors, lawyers, ministers, army officers, and every capacity in which they can represent the interest of their people." Georgia's newly elected white legislators under Presidential Reconstruction must have cringed when they read these former slaves' bold claims of equality and declarations of intent to attain the very highest in social and political status.[26]

Black people emerged from slavery ambitious and determined to direct their own path. Former slaves, convention delegates contended, had created the economic base of southern states, and as free people, they would continue to be fundamental to white American success. However, they intended now to move out of fields and other places of forced servitude and into professions including law and medicine. Education would be essential to their ability to concretize their still ephemeral freedom, and black convention delegates wanted powerful whites to know that African Americans refused to revert to positions of subservience. William Grey, a minister who was at one time owned by the governor of Virginia, issued a statement on behalf of the Arkansas convention entitled, "The Present Condition and Future Prospects of the Colored People of the South." He recalled with his African American audience a time when a black man dared not put on even the cast-off uniform of a white soldier. Since that time, he said, African American men had not only put on uniforms but had fought for their rights as citizens. "God in his providence," Grey pronounced, "has permitted the seeming ignorant stolidity of the negro to be more than a match for the learning of the Saxon. After an acquaintance of two hundred years, he woke up in '62, and found the negro not half as big a fool as he thought he was." He continued, "True, [whites] had always been accustomed to hear their advice received respect-fully, in short monosyllables—yes, sir, massa; or no, sir, massa. They never once dreamed that under this seeming respect there was a human soul, with a will and a purpose of its own." Grey challenged the white people of Arkansas and beyond: "We have now thrown off the mask, hereafter to do our own talking, and to use all legitimate means to get and to enjoy our political privileges." The convention backed him up with a resolution that stated, "we are the substrata, the foundation on which the future power and wealth of the State of Arkansas must be built, and as the future prosperity of the State cannot afford to rest upon ignorant labor, therefore, we respectfully ask the legislature to provide for the education of our children."[27]

Bolstered by the liberating power of the Emancipation Proclamation, the performance of African American men in the Union army, the protection provided by the Freedmen's Bureau and federal troops, and the political support of Radical Republicans in Congress, delegates to the black conven-tions stood in pulpits in southern states and demanded education. With trenchant rhetoric, these men who had recently been enslaved or nominally free, attempted to transform education for African Americans into a right, just as the black soldier in New Orleans, the young apprentice in Washington, D.C., the men of Roanoke Island, and the mother in Georgia did. Further-more, believing that southern whites would be more motivated by self-interest than generosity, they sought to attach black children's education to the future well-being of the South.

Despite the fact that education was not an enumerated right, African Americans continued to publicly claim it. As the delegates to the South Carolina convention put it, "whereas, Knowledge is power, and an educated and intelligent people can neither be held in, nor reduced to slavery, we will insist upon the establishment of good schools for the thorough education of our children."[28] Yet with no constitutional amendment to guarantee educa-tion, convention delegates and, more generally, African Americans, faced a dilemma. They had to attempt to convince the very same people they blamed for having deprived them of education—the people from whom they declared their independence—that it was in their best interest to support education for African Americans. Thus, African Americans stood in a difficult spot: as they declared that they were free, equal, and ready to undermine the racist assumptions that undergirded southern white belief systems, they also needed white southerners to agree to black legal equality. Through the Reconstruction Act and the civil rights constitutional amendments, Congress could codify blacks' new status, but southern white recalcitrance and outright hostility could stymie congressional intent. Funding for education was principally a state prerogative. This is precisely why suffrage was at the top of freedpeople's list of priorities, and why they could not postpone universal manhood suffrage until they had achieved higher levels of literacy. In fact, literacy devolved from suffrage: if black men could vote on budgetary priorities, or if political parties were forced to compete for their votes, blacks would then have a chance to implement public educational systems throughout the South that included them. It would take time to realize African American entreaties for state-supported schools for their children.

But there were inherent tensions between their bold assertions and their lowly economic and political status. The young apprentice in Maryland, the delegates at African American political conventions in southern states, and the black parents in Louisiana and Georgia confronted those tensions directly. In each case, African Americans formulated educational agendas, and in each case they had to submit those agendas to whites in whose hands power still rested. Whether these whites were northerners or southerners was of little consequence as blacks had to tailor their requests to please them. The young apprentice turned to Freedmen's Bureau employees to mediate between him and the man who denied him education. Black delegates at the North Carolina convention who wanted to encourage blacks to have black teachers had to sublimate their principles for fear of alienating whites. Until they gained political power during Congressional Reconstruction, the self-help prong of the educational agenda held the greatest promise. African Americans had to rely on their own resources to ensure access to education for themselves and for their children.

CHAPTER 5 ▪▪▪▪▪▪▪▪▪▪▪▪▪▪

We Are Striving to Dwo Buisness on Our Own Hook

Organizing Schools on the Ground

I find the col'd people with six little schools averaging say 30 each taught and paid for *by themselves*. No white man to help.

John Alvord, Tallahassee, Florida

This is the first application that had been made to any source for help since we have been free. But have been doing the best we could.

Emanuel Smith, Apalachicola, Florida

As African Americans struggled to bring schools into being, they experienced the complex, textured relationships that evolved as the constellation of participants—northern whites, southern whites, southern blacks, and sometimes northern blacks—interacted with one another to teach freedpeople. Relations with white northern missionaries sometimes proved challenging, for southern blacks and northern whites could be partners in the educational mission, or they could be combatants for dominance over the educational agenda. African Americans were now free, but free in a land where power and resources yet rested in white hands. The very decision to communicate with the white men who headed the Union army, the Freedmen's Bureau, and missionary associations signaled freedpeople's determination to enter onto new terrain, to push beyond the boundaries that sought to define and delimit their existence. Their resolve did not dissipate once the teachers and missionaries arrived in the South with their own ideas and agendas.

As articulated in the rhetoric of the black conventions, two closely enmeshed values—self-help and self-determination—figured prominently in African Americans' strategies for becoming literate. Freedpeople most often had no choice but to rely on one another: southern whites rarely helped and northern whites were scarce. Moreover, self-help could enact self-determination. The ability to interpret laws for themselves, or to apportion funds for schools, or to teach their own children would give them control over their lives and their communities.

John W. Alvord remarked on this tendency toward self-reliance when he made his first trip through the South as General Superintendent of Schools for the Freedmen's Bureau. In 1865 this Congregational minister and former agent of the American Anti-Slavery Society toured eight southern states to assess freedpeople's educational condition. He noted in his report to General O. O. Howard, head of the Freedmen's Bureau, "Throughout the entire South an effort is being made by the colored people to educate themselves. In absence of other teaching they are determined to be self-taught; and everywhere some elementary textbook, or the fragment of one may be seen in the hands of negroes." The freedpeople, Alvord observed, "quickly communicate to each other what they already know, so that with very little learning many take to teaching." They also showed "a willingness, even an ambition to bear expenses." He concluded, "They often say we want to show how much we can do ourselves, if you will only give us a chance."[1]

Still, African Americans often had to concede the limits of their own training and resources. At those times they struggled with the tensions that surfaced with their new status. African Americans wanted to be independent yet were challenged by hostile whites who erected barriers at every turn; they wanted to be self-sufficient yet were forced to ask for assistance. When freedpeople appealed to missionary associations or the Freedmen's Bureau to send help, they frequently couched their requests in a language of shame tempered by two factors: first, a reminder of why African Americans lacked material resources, and second, a demonstration of their determination to quickly overcome past deprivations. When Simon Ryall, a "crippled" teacher from Thomasville, Georgia, reached out to the Freedmen's Bureau in 1866, he combined a request for financial assistance with an assurance of self-help. At a cost of $100, local freedpeople had built a school capable of holding a hundred students. However, they were too poor to continue paying the balance due on the building. Ryall appealed to the Freedmen's Bureau: "we would Be Glad of sum assistance we are striving to Dwo Buisness on our own hook but are Destitute of means."[2]

This effort to act on their own behalf was repeated over and over. In Tallahassee, Florida, when former slave and Methodist minister James Smith wrote to the AMA in October 1865, instead of money he requested a teacher. Relying on his self-taught spelling and punctuation, he informed the AMA that "the peopall hear is joust out of the house of Bondage and have not had a chance to make eney thing but a common Support for themselves and famileys the government hav not done eney thing hear for them. We hav 5 Small Schools but no one can teach them the English language properly." He added that while local black teachers could teach the rudiments of spelling, they needed the AMA to send someone who could teach reading and writing. In the same breath that he asked for help, Reverend Smith hastened to assure the AMA that the freedpeople were making efforts to be self-sufficient: "the colard people is trying to dow what They can for them Selves."[3]

Later that month Smith pressed his petition when John Alvord visited Tallahassee. Alvord confirmed Smith's claim of self-help. "In this place," Alvord informed the AMA's George Whipple, "I find the col'd people with six little schools averaging say 30 each taught and paid for *by themselves.* No white man to help." Although Alvord reported that there was relatively little anti-black violence in Florida, he added that only a strong military force held hostile whites at bay. The freedpeople "bear it with fortitude and are determined to do what they can to support and educate themselves." "Do what you can for them," he urged Whipple, "It *is a strong case.*"[4]

South of Tallahassee, on the coast of the panhandle, Emanuel Smith, another black minister, had more organizational support than did James Smith because the freedpeople of Apalachicola had formed a school board to oversee school development. Still, Emanuel Smith and the trustees found it necessary to ask outsiders for help, requesting the AMA to send a female teacher to take charge of Apalachicola's black school. Smith specifically asked for a woman, he said, because he believed that women could be hired on "cheaper terms" than men. He explained that although there had been schools for black people in Apalachicola, they had been of poor quality and had operated for only short periods. Further, most freedpeople could not afford to pay the tuition of $1.50 per month. Good local teachers—meaning white southerners—would not teach black people.[5]

Emanuel Smith assured the AMA that the freedpeople were trying to provide for themselves and did not wish to be dependent on others. "We have Plodded along this far. The Best we could. Som children has learnt some. But [they are] far Behind all other Parts we hear of." To further demonstrate their attempt at self-reliance, Smith told the AMA, "This is the first application that had been made to any source for help since we have been free. But have been doing the best we could." He promised that although his community was poor, "we expect, and are willing to pay some."[6] When the AMA finally offered to send a teacher, Smith replied that he would inform the "Committee of Colored men who are managing the school which we are carying on." He also thanked the organization for its offer to send books and spellers, which he intended to sell at cost to counteract the high price of books in Apalachicola.[7]

As the AMA prepared to send a teacher to Apalachicola, however, Smith abruptly withdrew his request. He and the members of the board of trustees had "engaged a young man (colored) who has been a U.S. Soldier." Smith considered him fully competent to teach for the present. Although he wondered if the former soldier would continue teaching for long, Smith thought it best to give him a chance. Several factors may have influenced the board's decision to hire this young black man. The former soldier was willing to work "pretty cheap"—a convincing characteristic, given their limited funds. The board may also have preferred to rely on their own resources rather than seeking outside help. In this way, trustees could continue to exert control over how the school operated. It may well be, too, that as some of North Carolina's convention delegates had, the Apalachicola board of trustees preferred to hire a black teacher, believing that his presence would motivate other young black people. Without listing the reasons for declining the offer, Smith expressed the black community's gratitude for the AMA's generosity, but said the freed-people "were glad not to ask so much." He added, "We are under renewed oblagations to you and your association for favors rendered, and hope that you will still do what you can to aid us in this dark, and much forgotten part of our country."[8]

The AMA continued to send books. Smith paid the freight charges himself and sold the books at small sums to those who could pay, giving them away to those who could not. After several months, he was forced to ask the AMA to stop sending even books because the parents were too poor, and many had taken their children out of school.[9] Despite the pervasive poverty, some interest nevertheless remained. In November 1868, one year after canceling his book orders, Smith sent the AMA a list of books that he now wanted to purchase. "Our people are very poor out here," he wrote, "but have to try to get good books at any cost, and every school teacher wants different books." Not only were the freedpeople still interested in obtaining books, clearly there were now several schoolteachers in Apalachicola. The board of trustees had managed to establish schools on its own terms.[10]

By choosing to hire local teachers, the freedpeople of Apalachicola averted the conflicts that sometimes arose between freed communities striving for self-assertion and self-determination, and those representatives of northern benevolent associations who arrived in the South certain that their education, experience, northern-ness, and whiteness ordained them to control freed-people's educational experiences. Northern white missionaries and local African American community leaders and parents sometimes had conflicting answers to the critical questions of who would direct hiring and who would make pedagogical decisions in freedpeople's schools.

In New Orleans, where freedpeople were anxious to have some say in their children's education, Margaret Adams interjected herself and African American parents into a feud between two AMA employees. She argued for the retention of C. L. Tambling, a white teacher who had gained the devotion and love of black parents, she asserted, because of the "kindness and delight he takes in instructing our race." In rare public documents produced by a southern African American woman regarding freedpeople's education, Adams argued for parental influence over who would teach. She and other parents had found themselves on the sidelines while the AMA representatives engaged in

Letter from Margaret Adams to the American Missionary Association, May 9, 1864. Courtesy American Missionary Association Archives, Amistad Research Center, Tulane University.

both external and internal contests over control of freedpeople's schools.[11] The parents had lost all faith in Tambling's adversary, Dr. Isaac Hubbs, who they believed was not sufficiently concerned with the welfare of their children. In contrast, Adams expressed confidence that if Tambling were permitted to remain for another six months, some of the wealthiest black people in the city would send their children to the school, thus increasing the attendance from six hundred to eight or nine hundred. Feeling like powerless observers of multiple layers of antagonism, Adams and the black parents wanted to ensure that the teacher they thought most committed to their interests would remain in the school. They chose sides.[12]

Margaret Adams was decidedly frustrated with the limited degree of control that she and other parents could exercise with regard to their children's education. She had referred many students to the school and had listened with pleasure as their parents expressed satisfaction with Tambling's instruction. Now the students stood to lose him because the AMA, not the parents, had authority over school administration. The parents organized and tried a number of strategies to assert their preference. First, they considered with-drawing their children from the school. Some followed through, but Tambling advised them to send the children back. Then, they petitioned the city school board, but the board said it could do nothing. Finally, Adams appealed to the AMA, simultaneously vouching that African Americans would not long have to make such requests for intervention. Like Reverend James Smith in Tallahassee, Adams assured the AMA that the freedpeople intended to become self-sufficient. "We hope it will not be long before we are enabled to take care of our selves without being a heavy burden to the Government so much for Assistance," she wrote. She foresaw a time when her community would stand able to support its own education. She also made sure to expose the source of freedpeople's dependence on outside assistance. Every bit as politicized as black convention delegates, Adams let the AMA know that she understood the historical role whites had played in oppressing blacks, denying them both wealth and education. As she put it: "we are really ashamed but we cannot do any better at present for we have been kept down so much by our enemies notwithstanding we love our rebel friends and do not wish to harm them but we want to see them love God and become good Christians as we have raised their children cultivated their ground, and enriched them and all we ask of them now is to give us our rights."[13] Like the men of Roanoke Island, the young apprentice in Maryland, the mother in Georgia, and the former soldier in her own city of New Orleans, Adams included education among freed-people's new rights. Further, she joined convention delegates in asserting that although whites had held African Americans back, with fair and equal treatment freedpeople would transcend both their poverty and limited education.

It is interesting to consider what made Margaret Adams step into the public sphere with such a political agenda at a time when men dominated African American public discourse. We do not have much information about her. Missing from the New Orleans census, city directories, marriage records, and newspaper obituaries, she is also absent from historical studies of black New Orleans.[14] The two letters that she wrote to the AMA must be relied upon to begin to speak about her life. Her high degree of literacy was surely an important factor that qualified her as a spokesperson. Her handwriting, spelling, and grammar suggest that she was not solely self-taught; she had had some teaching. The absence of punctuation in her letters, however, suggests that her education had not been so formal as attending seminary or college. She was the type of African American whom northern whites identified as "intelligent" when they interacted with freedpeople in the South, meaning that she was relatively well educated, articulate, and able to engage easily in conversations with whites. A resourceful woman, who was clearly able to navigate distinct social worlds with facility, she was equally at ease with whites as with other blacks. She had recruited many of the black parents, and on the day following an offensive speech by Hubbs, many of them sought out her opinion of it. She in turn visited Tambling at his residence for the "purpose of reviving the drooping spirits of our young brother." She evidently looked upon the "young brother" as a friend and an equal, at least before God.

In the end, the black parents won a Pyrrhic victory. Hubbs left the school under suspicion resulting from charges of corruption and immoral behavior. But before departing, he fired the favored Tambling. In her second letter to the AMA, Adams reiterated the imbalance in power between parents and the benevolent organization: "Mr. Tambling has been cast from the board of education and if it is possible we would like to get him back, we have not the power ourselves, but the association has and it is our earnest request that you will do all you can do for us, in obtaining him again." She signed "In behalf of the Colored people attending school."[15] In this instance, freedpeople's reliance on outside help subjected them to the AMA's judgment of who would teach them and their children.

The imbalance in power and resources between formerly enslaved people and northern whites could challenge even freedpeople with far more sophisticated organizational structures than the parents in New Orleans. The African American–run Savannah Educational Association, which sponsored eight schools with 425 students, became a source of contention between the AMA's S. W. Magill and local black leaders. Within a month of Union soldiers' arrival in Savannah, freedpeople began the work of organizing schools. On January 2, 1865, African Americans held a mass meeting in the First African Baptist Church in Savannah. During the meeting, a group of black ministers met with John Alvord, then employed by the American Tract Society, and Reverend James Lynch, an AME minister from Baltimore who helped them in establishing the Savannah Educational Association. Realizing that they might need additional resources, the association invited "the patronage and assistance of the American Missionary Association in the great work, now devolving upon us." The founders returned to the mass meeting, where they appealed to the people to donate funds to establish schools. Men and women made their way to the table at the front of the church with a "great rush" and "fast as their names could be written by a swift penman, the greenbacks were laid upon the table in terms from one to ten dollars, until the pile, footed up the round sum of *seven hundred* and *thirty dollars*."[16] The next day, John Alvord and Reverend Mansfield French, former missionary in the Sea Islands, examined candidates for teaching positions in the Savannah schools. Judging several individuals competent to teach, they hired fifteen black teachers.[17]

With teachers selected and school buildings secured, the Savannah Educational Association was ready for business. Organizers met five hundred freed children at the church. In a dramatic gesture, the children marched through the streets of the city to the buildings assigned as schools. One observer wrote, "Such a gathering of freedmen's sons and daughters, that proud city had never seen before! Many of the people rushed to the doors and windows of their houses, wondering what these things could mean!" AMA representatives expressed surprise at the African Americans' initiative and at the fact that not only were a "goodly number" of the children already able to read and spell, some also had experience with arithmetic, geography, and writing. These AMA employees, new to the city, would not have known that some of these students may very well have attended the illegal, antebellum schools that African Americans such as Susan Woodhouse taught in Savannah.[18] One agent commented, "We are all surprised to find so much intelligence and money ability among the freedmen of Savannah. They have already contributed some *eight hundred dollars* for the support of schools among themselves." By quickly organizing schools and readying their children to attend, freedpeople in Savannah meant to claim the privileges of education for their children. In so doing, they asserted their intention to control their educational and civic affairs.[19]

Rather than recognizing or encouraging the effort that Savannah blacks expended in creating an educational institution, S. W. Magill, a white native of Georgia and an AMA employee, complained that black people expected him to work *with* them rather than hand over authority to him.[20] When Magill arrived in Savannah in February, he immediately contemplated white control of the schools that the black people had begun. On February 3, 1865, before he even observed black teachers in their classrooms, Magill wrote to the AMA regarding the Savannah Educational Association: "They know nothing of managing, and how much of teaching I am yet to ascertain—I fear they will be jealous and sullen if I attempt to place the management in the hands of our white teachers."[21] Without even evaluating the local black teachers, Magill assured himself of white teachers' superiority.

But the black leaders of the Savannah Educational Association thought differently. With the help of three educated northern men, they had already hired teachers whom they considered competent. They wanted Magill and the AMA to help them, but they did not intend to hand over control; they were bent on self-help and self-determination. In several letters to the secretary of the AMA, Magill lamented African American resistance to his benevolence. "My object was a definite one," he wrote, "the intellectual and moral improvement of the colored people—and I applied myself immediately to the study of the field of beneficent effort on their behalf." He soon discovered, however, that Savannah's blacks had not been waiting for his generosity. Instead, they had established the association to "demonstrate what the colored man could do if left to himself." Magill bemoaned an indiscriminate "spirit of exclusiveness" that he found prevailing in the minds of some members of the association. This spirit was all the more offensive to Magill because it was directed not "at their old white neighbors simply, which would have been quite justifiable considering the past, but including all white people." He thought it would be unfortunate if those members of the association who supported black control prevailed because he was certain that the black people, inexperienced as they were, would fail. Magill considered it "preposterous" that the Savannah Educational Association intended to "work the ship exclusively by their own wit and will." He was particularly annoyed that the association intended to maintain black principals and teachers in charge of schools and to place northern white teachers as their assistants. The association, it seemed, planned to rely on northerners primarily for much needed financial help.[22]

Once again, however, freedpeople's authority proved tenuous. Although the Savannah Educational Association wanted to maintain control over who would lead in the classroom, it also needed funding that could only come in sufficient quantity from outside the freed community. Given Magill's objection to black supervision of schools, financial assistance from the AMA was not forthcoming. Magill considered it a "great point gained" when the association relented and asked him to manage its schools. He thought it a victory that the black people finally realized "their inability to work [the schools] on the plan proposed, excluding white control." Although he had been impatient for the opportunity to run the schools, Magill nevertheless expressed some reluctance to intervene. "I anticipate trouble," he wrote. "Leading men among negroes, especially their preachers are jealous of their honor and influence and as they have started on the principle of managing things themselves it may be very difficult if not impracticable to bring them back to a different course."[23] As soon as he did take control of the schools, Magill put white northern teachers in charge and demoted the black teachers, whom John Alvord and Mansfield French had considered qualified to teach, to assistants.[24]

To justify the demotion of black teachers, Magill pointed not only to deficiencies in their ability to teach academic subjects, but to moral and social ones as well. His plan to bring about the "intellectual and moral improvement of the colored people" was deeply embedded in a philosophy of northern white supremacy and, as such, fit well with the AMA's goal in entering the educational field. The association wanted to take the freedpeople "by the hand, to guide, counsel and instruct them in their new life, protect them from the abuses of the wicked, and direct their energies so as to make them useful to themselves, their families and their country."[25] Implicit in this paternalistic goal, of course, was the assumption of white northern superiority and black southern inferiority, assumptions that left scant room for freedpeople's own initiative and plans.

To be sure, whites representing missionary associations had far greater educational training and experience than most local black teachers and administrators in the South. Many black teachers and community leaders recognized this fact and asked for help. Nonetheless, particularly in urban centers like Savannah, where black people had surreptitiously taught for decades, some blacks were indeed qualified to teach. Of course academic qualification was not the main concern for Magill and others who considered black independence a threat. A more progressive man such as John Alvord could applaud and encourage blacks' determination to do for themselves; those who were far more concerned with amassing personal power and exporting so-called northern values to the South could see black self-determination only as an impediment to their own course.

In Georgia, as in other parts of the country, conversations about freedpeople's education were very much part of a discourse about race, racial equality, and the abilities of African Americans both as teachers and students. Philanthropists in the North generally thought like Magill. According to the missionary associations, assessing teaching ability required a dual measurement: first, did the teacher have the substantive knowledge and training required; and second, did the teacher bring appropriate character, values, and civilization or culture to the job? The New York National Freedman's Relief Association articulated this philosophy quite definitively in response to criticism of its educational committee regarding the hiring of black teachers. The association said that it had not refused to hire black teachers. It had in fact supplied some when demanded in Maryland and had been forced to hire a few in other places where no white teachers were available. However, the association made clear that its goal was to hire the best teachers available and for them that meant white. "That good white teachers, on the whole, are the best will hardly be disputed," the organization wrote in its annual report. "It must be remembered, too, that the men and women who go down from our Normal and High Schools carry more than their education," it continued. "They carry their race, their moral training, their faculty, their character, the influences of civilization, the ideas, sentiments, principles, that characterize Northern society, and which we hope will one day characterize southern. We want to introduce persons as well as pedagogues, and persons will be worth all they cost."[26]

The National Freedman's Relief Association saw its role as inducing the entire South to embrace Yankee values. In the organization's view, this practice of primarily hiring white northern teachers would meet no opposition since no one else was either willing to or capable of establishing a system of education. Southern whites and blacks did not trust each other, and blacks did not trust themselves; therefore, white Yankees would be most popular. "We want, not schools merely," the organization asserted, "but Northern schools, Northern men and women, down south, teaching, mingling with the people, and instituting the North there among the old populations. In this way we civilize all at once, by communicating simultaneously all the chief intellectual elements of civilization." Northern white teachers were not only better suited to teach black southern people—they had a thing or two to teach white southerners as well.[27]

Yet, on the heels of this affirmation of white northern supremacy, the National Freedman's Relief Association demurred that it would by all means encourage "the blacks" to establish and take control of their own schools. "The quicker they do this the better," the association claimed. But these schools could not be the only ones since they would not inculcate northern white values. For this missionary association, as for Magill, the prospect of black-controlled schools was, if not preposterous, certainly not to be the primary way to educate blacks.[28]

Magill and the AMA may have won the battle by taking control of black schools and discouraging other northern associations from entering the educational field in Savannah, but their actions stirred resentment among the city's African Americans. James Lynch accused the AMA of discriminating against blacks when hiring teachers. And some freedpeople exhibited a preference for black teachers even when they were not as qualified as northern whites. Further, some African Americans established private schools for children who could afford it, leaving the poorest children dependent upon the AMA schools.[29]

A similar conflict in St. Louis ended differently when the white AMA missionary packed up and left in the face of resistance from freedpeople. AMA missionary George Candee, a man dedicated to establishing integrated public schools, encountered resistance from the local black school board that was determined to have a black-run system of schools. In June 1864 white administrator A. K. Spence traveled to St. Louis at Candee's invitation to consider taking over the role of superintendent of freedpeople's schools. Spence concluded that this was not the job for him. He quickly realized that the African American board was not interested in hiring a white man to run its schools. He informed the AMA that "there seems to be a growing prejudice on the part of the Board against your society; or perhaps I should rather say a desire to act entirely independent of any outside control, a desire to hire and direct their teachers and that these should be *colored* including the superintendent, and plant their own schools." "In short," he concluded, "the reins have been put into their hands and they are inclined to drive." Spence thought this experiment in self-reliance should be given a chance.[30]

Despite antislavery credentials and a commitment to freedpeople's education, Candee, for his part, also found himself rebuffed by a large percentage of the African American school board. He concluded that "as this disturbing element wishes to operate independently of the AMA and through colored agencies altogether, that the Association better give up this city to their exclusive controll [sic]." Although disappointed, he conceded that the board could adequately run the schools "on an exclusively colored basis."[31] He recommended that the AMA concentrate on other areas of the state. As Candee left St. Louis to do just that, the board members wrote to the AMA to ask if the organization could "procure a well educated colored man to serve our Board in the capacity of Superintendent." They would provide housing if the AMA would pay his salary.[32] The board wanted to make all hiring decisions, yet it was compelled to turn to northern whites to solicit assistance.[33]

Despite numerous instances of tension and competition between northern missionaries and southern blacks, it was neither inevitable nor universal that northern whites would perceive African Americans' efforts at self-help and self-determination as a threat to white supremacy. Another possibility existed. Quaker interactions with freedpeople in Helena, Arkansas, and Columbus, Mississippi, for example, demonstrate working relationships that more closely resembled partnerships. The Quakers' institutional ego appeared to be less obtrusive than the AMA's and other missionary organizations. Quakers freely and publicly thanked freedpeople for their support and acknowledged them as critical participants in the educational mission. When reporting to their northern sponsors, Alida and Calvin Clark consistently credited the black community of Helena as well as the black men of the Fifty-sixth Regiment for their roles in building the school and orphanage in Helena. Likewise, white Quakers in Columbus worked hand in hand with African Americans and frequently acknowledged the mutuality of their interactions.

Late in 1865, Indiana Quaker missionaries in search of a safe place to work with freedpeople in Mississippi settled on the city of Columbus in Lowndes County, after encountering stiff white opposition to black education in several other parts of the state.[34] They considered Columbus "one of the most liberal places we have found."[35] At the first organizational meeting, freedpeople filled their largest church, and hundreds stood outside in the rain. Whites of the "first class" who attended the afternoon meeting also expressed approval of the establishment of schools for African Americans. Following the meeting, freedpeople asked to meet with Quaker J. H. Douglass and Freedmen's Bureau official R. S. Donaldson to "talk over educational matters, and to learn what they could do towards supporting schools." Douglass reported that he had never seen "greater anxiety manifested to have a school." The people were in fact so anxious to begin that they raised $658 on the spot. A few days later they added $250 to the fund. In addition, they agreed to pay tuition of $1 per month. Douglass was confident that the freedpeople would financially sustain schools in the city. He only needed to find teachers.[36] Four white Quaker teachers soon arrived, and they taught school along with "a colored man of this place and one of the officer's wives to assist."[37]

Classes began in February 1866. The Quakers remarked on the students' interest in learning and thanked the freedpeople of the town for accommodating them. In March they wrote, "We are so fortunate to have some quite independent colored friends who own as fine horses and carriages as are to be found here, and we are often favored with rides through the country."[38] But by April things were heating up in Columbus as federal troops left the city. On April 19, Quaker Jonathan Wilson received a letter that read: "DR WILSON:—We, the undersigned, have determined that you shall not stay in this country, and teach a negro school; and if you do not leave, we will hang you and your whole crowd. Do as you please—leave or not—there is one thing we are determined on, that you shall not stay if we can procure rope that will hold you. Leave immediately. 'Your many Enemies.' "[39]

The Columbus city council passed several resolutions to the effect that so long as the Quakers minded their own business and obeyed the law, city officials would protect them. A newcomer, Jonathan Wilson was ready to put his faith in the "good white citizens who appear[ed] ashamed" of the white antagonists. However, the freedpeople of Columbus did not put much stock in such promises or resolutions. Two days after the many enemies of black education penned their threats, former slave John Edwards, a self-employed shoemaker and secretary of the Freedmen's Aid Society, wrote his own letter to the Quakers. "We don't think a *citizen's* guard *reliable* protection for you and the teachers, and therefore we, of the Freedmen's Aid Society, pledge our *lives* to you, if it comes to the issue, for it is our indispensable duty, and it is our *right* as Freedmen, and hope you will *leave* us the pleasure of guarding you."[40] The Freedmen's Aid Society confessed its distrust of even seemingly supportive southern whites, thinking it unwise to rely on local white citizens to protect those who would teach black people. Protecting the teachers, in this instance, amounted to protecting the future prospects of the freed community, and freedpeople stood ready, they said, to give their lives to secure both. Ten armed African American men guarded the pacifist Quakers' residence, inside and out. Other black men stood guard at the schoolhouse.[41]

With the threat to hang the teachers still pending, the freed community started planning a celebration to mark the anniversary of their freedom. They intended to stage a large parade through town to the fairgrounds where they would give speeches. The specter of hundreds of black people marching through town sent shudders through white civic leaders who feared that while the better set of whites would be tolerant, "some drunken wretch might fire a pistol as they passed along the street, and perhaps make a Memphis riot out of it." The mayor requested that the Quakers intervene and prevail upon the freedpeople to have a less public demonstration. The black community acquiesced and held their celebration in a schoolroom instead.[42]

Columbus officials were justified in their fears. Freedom threatened white southerners in so many ways. The prospect of former slaves attending schools induced rage enough in some to threaten to hang teachers. And the sight of African American women, children, and men marching through the streets memorializing the end of slavery could be so galling as to trigger a riot. The combination of black education and black people's presence in the public sphere could indeed be lethal. In Memphis, where white rioters and white police killed forty-six black men and women in May 1866, a government committee concluded that "the most intense and unjustifiable prejudice on the part of the people of Memphis seems to have been arrayed against teachers of colored schools and against preachers to colored people."[43] But the riots began in the streets, triggered by the presence of a group of three or four black men. The Freedmen's Aid Society in Columbus successfully guarded the Quaker home and school for a time, but in January 1867 the schoolhouse burned. The Freedmen's Bureau official in charge reported that an investigation by a committee of citizens left little doubt that the fire was "the work of some evil disposed person, and not the effect of accident." Freedpeople and the Quakers continued the school in the teachers' homes but half of the students could not be accommodated.[44]

The Columbus, Mississippi, story points to the complexity of the relations that freedpeople negotiated in their interactions with whites after emancipation. Within Columbus, not all southern whites opposed black education; some expressed a willingness to protect the teachers of freedpeople. However, the freedpeople of the city could not bring themselves to trust even these whites. Further, the Quakers demonstrated that not all northern whites coveted control over freedpeople's affairs. It appears that the freedpeople trusted the Quakers to teach them and their children. The freedpeople participated and exerted their will in other ways, by giving money to start the school, by paying tuition, by providing transportation to the teachers, and by defending with their bodies both the school and the teachers. In turn, Quakers shared credit with African Americans for building institutions, and in contrast to some other benevolent groups, they worked with an eye toward bolstering the freedpeople's goal of relying on their own resources. Whereas many AMA ministers predicated their commitment to abolition on a perception of African Americans as lowly beings whom the ministers would raise up, Quaker missionaries were more likely to see that African Americans were capable of functioning on their own.[45] In their interactions with both the AMA and the Quakers, African Americans understood literacy to be closely associated with freedom, and they conceived of freedom as meaning self-determination, not subordination to paternalism.[46]

CHAPTER 6 ■ ■ ■ ■ ■ ■ ■ ■ ■ ■ ■ ■ ■ ■ ■ ■

We Are Laboring under Many Difficulties

African American Teachers in Freedpeople's Schools

I was a perfect curiosity to the white people of Simpsonville, simply because I was the first colored school-teacher they had ever seen.

Elijah Marrs, Kentucky

We do not make a living at the present time, but hoping to do something for our emancipated race, we are willing to labor and to wate.

Bartley Townsley, Griffin, Georgia

Amid the contention over white missionaries' efforts to control freedpeople's education, amid struggles over free or public schools, and amid attempts by some white southerners to impede black education, African Americans entered classrooms as teachers. Rather than simply waiting for help to come, they used what learning they had to begin to teach. John Alvord narrated this phenomenon in one of his reports. "Not only are individuals seen at study, and under the most untoward circumstances," he observed, "but in very many places I have found what I will call 'native schools,' often rude and very imperfect, but *there they are*, a group, perhaps, of all ages, *trying to learn*. Some young man, some woman, or old preacher, in cellar, or shed, or corner of a Negro meeting-house, with the alphabet in hand, or a torn spelling-book, is their teacher." Alvord encountered such a school in Goldsboro, North Carolina, where two black men who had only recently begun learning to read, taught 150 students, whom they charged a small tuition. The men told Alvord that before him, no white man had ever come near their school.[1]

Like the two young men in Goldsboro, many teachers had only rudimentary literacy skills. Others, like Elijah Marrs, though self-taught, had had more practice. Still others, such as Mary Peake in Virginia or Susie King Taylor in South Carolina, managed to acquire more sophisticated skills during slavery. Through these teachers, we are able to enter freedpeople's classrooms and discover what learning and teaching meant in the early days of southern black education.

Teaching amounted to a political act for African Americans in the emancipation period. And it was an act of courage. Entering the classroom to teach other black people was an open challenge to slavery's insistence on illiteracy, as well as to southern whites who sought to maintain antebellum power relations, even in the face of military defeat. With this act, African American teachers asserted at once that black people were educable, and they demonstrated that some possessed the knowledge required to instruct others. Many African American teachers, whether from the North or South, entered freedpeople's classrooms out of a sense of racial commitment that sometimes reached beyond lines of class and color. By teaching, they meant to put freedpeople into a position to at least claim the social, political, and economic benefits that derived from education.

Elijah Marrs, self-taught slave, sergeant in the Union army, and advocate for freedpeople in Kentucky, easily fit into John Alvord's classification of "native" teachers. When Elijah and Henry Marrs mustered out of the army in the spring of 1866, they returned to Shelby County, Kentucky, where they applied their literacy to civic advocacy as well as to teaching. Entrepreneurs, the brothers first pooled their savings to purchase horses and a harness; Henry became a teamster, while Elijah farmed a rented twenty-five-acre plot. Before long, however, members of the black community in Simpsonville, Kentucky, importuned Elijah to teach their children. Although he protested that he was not qualified to teach, he relented and decided to leave "the corn-field and enter the school-room to labor for the development of [his] race." Three black trustees hired Marrs at a salary of twenty-five dollars per month, paying him from the one-dollar monthly tuition from each student. With 150 students, the school was fully self-sustaining, receiving no assistance from the Freedmen's Bureau or any missionary association.[2]

White people in Simpsonville regarded with wonderment a black man teaching black students. Marrs recalled, "I was a perfect curiosity to the white people of Simpsonville, simply because I was the first colored school-teacher they had ever seen, and yet I was no stranger to them, for just three years from the time I left Simpsonville, a slave, to join the United States Army, I returned a free man and a school teacher." But this manifestation of Elijah Marrs did indeed render him a stranger to local whites. The Civil War had radically and fundamentally transformed his life and his relationship to the white people of Simpsonville. Among other things, he no longer had to attempt to keep his literacy secret, and he could even publicly pass on his knowledge to any African American who paid the dollar to attend his school. Whites in Simpsonville were simply stunned. "They would come to visit me and stare, and wonder at the change," Marrs recalled. His former owners were particularly fascinated. They sent him arithmetic problems to solve. What was $146 + 12 - 19 + 200$, they wanted to know? When Marrs solved the problems, one remarked, "That Elijah is a smart nigger!"[3]

After one year in Simpsonville, Marrs took over his brother's school in La

Grange, Kentucky, near the Indiana border. There, too, whites marveled at the phenomenon of a black teacher. Marrs described a visit to the home of some of his students. Their white neighbors had heard that Marrs was coming and poured out of the house to take in the sight of a black teacher. As he walked past them, they tussled with each other to get a good look at this oddity and followed him as he made his way. Finally, one member of the crowd asked, "Teacher, can you read?" When Marrs responded affirmatively, they requested that he read something for them. According to Marrs, as he read a passage from a book, the crowd was "wonderfully astonished that a colored school teacher could read."[4] Marrs's experience in Kentucky speaks to the dramatic nature of the change brought by emancipation. This transformation from slave to teacher, free to demonstrate his literacy, was just one more unsettling phenomenon that threw southern whites off balance. Yet, as odd as Elijah Marrs appeared to the white people in Simpsonville and La Grange, he was by no means unique. Marrs and his brother Henry belonged to a vast body of African Americans who taught freedpeople.

From Delaware to Florida, Freedmen's Bureau officials counted blacks as teachers, owners of schoolhouses, and financial supporters of schools, reinforcing the tendency toward self-education that Alvord had observed in his 1866 report. In the loose partnership that sometimes developed, missionary associations paid northern teachers' salaries and sometimes provided books. The Freedmen's Bureau paid for transportation for northern teachers and sometimes paid for the rental, repair, and construction of school buildings, often deeding them to missionary associations, especially to the American Missionary Association. Local black residents purchased land, constructed school buildings, provided churches for use as schools, paid tuition when they could afford to, and frequently operated completely self-sustaining schools.[5]

Information about African American teachers is often obscured and frequently anecdotal. Beginning in 1867, the Freedmen's Bureau reported the number of white and black teachers in each state, but the figures were limited to the schools that state superintendents knew of, usually through their own travels. Superintendents, therefore, likely did not count the most informal schools, and they would not have been able to penetrate all areas of the states. Still, despite the influx of northern, predominantly white teachers and despite the fact that institutionally sponsored white teachers had a higher chance of being counted, at midyear in 1868 the total number of African American teachers exceeded the total number of white teachers in the fifteen states from which the Freedmen's Bureau collected data.[6]

Although the figures in these reports for black teachers included black, northern missionary teachers, the majority by far were local people, often self-educated during slavery or immediately afterward. Of the 303 teachers

Teachers by Race, July 1868

State	White Teachers	Black Teachers	Total
Maryland/Delaware	260	414	674
Virginia	818	837	1,655
North Carolina	582	863	1,445
South Carolina	178	205	383
Georgia	378	298	676
Florida	112	110	222
Mississippi	124	69	193
Louisiana	252	291	543
Texas	65	48	113
Arkansas	80	68	148
Tennessee	403	345	748
Kentucky	385	503	888
Missouri/Kansas	154	162	316
Total	3,791	4,213	8,004

Source: John Alvord, *Sixth Semi-Annual Report on Schools for Freedmen, July 1, 1868* (Washington, D.C.: Government Printing Office, 1868), 13–57, reprinted in John W. Alvord, *Semi-Annual Reports on Schools for Freedmen: Numbers 1–10, January 1866–July 1870* (New York: AMS Press, 1980).

that northern freedmen's aid societies sent to work in Georgia between 1865 and 1873, for example, only 18 were black.[7] And in 1868, the largest of these organizations, the American Missionary Association, employed only 100 black missionaries and teachers in the South. Of that 100, many were southern black people whom AMA teachers employed as assistants.[8] Thus, when the Freedmen's Bureau counted black teachers, it primarily recorded the presence of local African Americans and possibly a small number of northern African Americans who had ventured south and worked on their own.

The table depicts the number of black and white teachers in fifteen states as provided by the Freedmen's Bureau Superintendents of Education. The superintendents included day schools that submitted official Freedmen's Bureau teacher reports, as well as those Sabbath schools about which superintendents had information. Some schools received assistance from the Freedmen's Bureau, others did not, but the bureau asked any school serving freedpeople to report on its activities. Often, the same teacher taught the day and Sabbath schools.

In the border states represented in the survey, Maryland, Delaware, Missouri, and Kentucky, black teachers outnumbered whites. Further, in states like South Carolina, Virginia, and Louisiana, parts of which came under Union control early in the war and where African Americans consequently got a head start on openly seeking education, there were more black than white teachers. Texas and Mississippi present a telling contrast. Not only did white teachers outnumber blacks, but the total number of teachers was also relatively small. In Texas, word of emancipation came to slaves late, thus excluding them from the benefits of freedom for a longer period of time.

Black participation in educating the freedpeople is unmistakably demonstrated in the government's statistics. Less transparent is who the teachers were, their qualifications for teaching, and the circumstances and substance of their work. John Alvord mentioned a few of the black teachers in his reports. Autobiographies and interviews provide more material. However, a bureaucratic fluke in Georgia provides the most promising possibility for reconstructing the work of these early black teachers. In 1865, when Gilbert L. Eberhart became Superintendent for Freedmen's Education in Georgia, he "took steps to ascertain if anything and how much had been done in establishing schools for the freedmen." To accomplish this task, Eberhart designed "a circular of interrogatories" that the Freedmen's Bureau distributed to all schools known to the assistant superintendents. Other states also gathered information from freedpeople's schools, but the Georgia effort appears to have been unique in that, from December 1865 to March 1866, the form asked teachers to identify their race. Circular No. 8 asked teachers, "Are you white or colored?" In other states, and in subsequent years in Georgia, the bureau issued several different versions of teacher reports, none of which asked teachers to identify their race. The Georgia reports make it possible to identify a relatively large group of black teachers during a concentrated period of time.[9]

Of the sixty-six Georgia teachers who completed school reports, thirty-seven said they were "white," twenty-eight said they were "colored," and one did not identify her race. Evidently, schools either had white teachers or black teachers. In instances where a teacher prepared a report for a school with more than one teacher, only one white teacher reported that there was a black teacher in the school, but that teacher also filed a separate school report.[10] In each case where a black teacher completed the form, all the other teachers were also black. A total of twenty-eight black teachers completed school reports, and those schools employed fifty-three black teachers altogether.[11] With teachers reporting from both urban and rural locations, it is reasonable to believe that their experiences and the conditions of schools were similar to those in other southern states. The teachers' reports provide important information about tuition, sex of students and teachers, curriculum, books, as well as ownership and physical condition of sites used as schools.

The school reports and several follow-up letters from a school in Griffin, Georgia, offer an instructive overview of the challenges that some African American teachers faced. Three black men—Marshall Matthews, Bartley H. Townsley, and a third, unnamed man—organized the school in Griffin in July 1865. All had been enslaved "until made free by the goodness of God and by President Lincoln Emancipation Proclamation." Of the 111 pupils on the register, 57 were male and 54 female. None of the students, who ranged in age from five to twenty-one, had attended school before, and only two could read when they entered school. In an old, drafty, government-owned building with no stove for heat in the winter, the students studied spelling, reading, arithmetic, and penmanship. They used any books they could obtain: *New York Readers*, *Smith's Arithmetic*, and *Webster's Spelling Books*. The number of students in attendance fluctuated daily, and most were too poor to pay tuition regularly.[12]

Generations of enslavement, persistent poverty, and racism haunted the freedpeople of Griffin and threatened to thwart their attempts to educate themselves and their children. In a letter to Gilbert L. Eberhart, Townsley, who described himself variously as "teacher of the school" and "president of the school," delineated nearly every problem that freedpeople's schools confronted. "We are laboring under many difficulties in carrying on the school," Townsley confessed. "Our education is limited, our means amounts to almoust nothing with but little prospect of improvement and we have not sufficient accomodation to render our school as efficient as we desire." Then, he pointed to external impediments: "the prejudices of the white people are also a drawback to us." And, finally, he asked for help: "If we had one white teacher of experience to aid us, we would be greatly benefited but we are not able to pay him anything. any assistance you can render us would be Thankfully and greatfully received. We need most of all Things a comfortable [school] house and a better selection of books."[13] Limited education, poverty, a decrepit schoolhouse, lack of books, and hostility from local whites circumscribed freedpeople's education in Griffin and elsewhere.

It is not possible to determine with certainty the educational background of most of the African American teachers, but we can surmise that their educational training ranged from the "stolen" education of the enslaved, to formal, comprehensive schooling for some who had been free before emancipation. Handwriting on the reports ranged from the thick-lettered scrawl of a self-taught or new writer to a poised penmanship perfected over many years. Spelling and grammar provide other hints. Some teachers spelled simple words incorrectly and omitted punctuation, suggesting that they had not had much, if any, formal educational training. Two teachers asked a third party to fill out the report, perhaps indicating a lack of confidence in their own writing skills. Samuel C. Hitchcock, a farmer who filled out the form for the school in Sparta, said he presumed the teacher, Smith Varser, could "write a little," but Varser had asked him to complete the report. Hitchcock promised that if the Freedmen's Bureau sponsored the school, he would continue to complete the reports until Varser became able to do so. Harrison Berry, writing on behalf of teacher Edward Petty in Covington, explained his role thusly: "I am not the teacher of the school, nor do I have anything to do with it, other than a sincere desire to see the cloud of gloom removed from the brow of my much oppressed race." He wrote to the superintendent of schools at the request of the teacher and the freedpeople of the town. Perhaps the teacher in Covington, like Varser in Sparta, could only "write a little." From Marietta, Reverend Ephraim Rucker added a note of apology to his school report: "if this reporte is not right or defected for the want of education you will pleas look over that and forgive this is a privet school."[14]

Communities pressed even minimally literate African Americans into service to teach children and adults. In Greensboro, Georgia, for example, twenty African Americans, knowing that some freedpeople could not afford to pay for school, formed a board of trustees and contributed money to establish a "free institution so as to accommadate every class." In October 1865 Abraham Colby informed the Freedmen's Bureau that the board had hired a man as an assistant teacher "on account of him being disabled, and we felt it our duty to help him all that we could." The teacher performed his duties well, but Colby requested that the bureau send an additional teacher "as we will be soon over-run with pupils and will have more than we can properly contend with." Within four months, Edward Powell, president of the board of trustees in Greensboro, admitted that "our present teacher is not considered fully competent to fill the position, but it is the best we have been able to do as yet." He added that the board retained the teacher in part out of sympathy as one of his legs had been amputated. Not only was the board concerned with the large number of students, it also worried about the teacher's knowledge and ability to teach students who quickly learned everything he knew. At about the same time as Powell's letter, Colby wrote again to the Freedmen's Bureau Superintendent of Education for Georgia. The need for a qualified teacher had become more pressing. He offered to pay fifteen dollars per month to rent a home for a teacher. Colby implored the superintendent, "I want a teacher to come rite away as I want the school taken charge of. I want you to come immediately to see about the school." Colby and other members of the freed community in Greensboro had pooled their resources and taken the initiative to launch a school, yet they struggled with the reality of their limited educational backgrounds and appealed to Eberhart and others to send them help.[15]

Interestingly, Abraham Colby, who represented the education association that freedpeople formed in Greensboro, could neither read nor write; nonetheless, several well-written letters bore his name. Colby apologized in one letter for his lack of training: "The want of learning or qualifications prohibits me from rendering this Report as full and satisfactory as it should be," but he never let on that he was in fact illiterate. In 1871 Colby, who was also a minister and barber and who by that time had served in the Georgia legislature, testified before the congressional committee investigating Ku Klux Klan (KKK) violence. A committee member asked Colby how much education he had. Colby replied, "None." The member wanted to know how he was able to discharge his duties. "I have a son I sent to school when he was small," Colby testified; "I make him read all my letters and do all my writing. I keep him with me all the time." Colby's amanuensis, William, was fifteen years old when he penned his father's letters to the Freedmen's Bureau on behalf of black education in Greensboro.[16]

Freedpeople with limited training who stepped in to teach were often cognizant of their limitations. As Elijah Marrs did, they doubted their capacity to teach but took on the task out of a sense of duty. Jacob Wade, who taught a day school with forty-one students and a night school with ten students in Thomasville, Georgia, did not feel competent "in the labors that is before me," yet he felt obliged to accede to parents' requests that he teach their children to spell and read. Jacob Wade, Elijah Marrs, and Abraham Colby would doubtless have agreed with the diplomatic assessment of Thurston Chase, the Superintendent of Education for Florida, who praised the schools established by trained, northern black teachers but expressed concern for the long-term sufficiency of those students taught by barely literate freedpeople. According to Chase, nearly half of the freedpeople's teachers in Florida had acquired a little learning while enslaved. "Without questioning their zeal or desire to elevate their race," he wrote, "it must be manifest that their qualifications only enable them to impart the rudiments of learning, and these in many cases but very imperfectly. They can read, spell, and write a little. Their pupils can do as much, and need teachers of higher qualifications." Chase was correct, of course, in his call for more qualified teachers, but *he* would certainly have agreed that even teachers with few skills provided an important service to freedpeople who had never before been able to acquire even the rudiments of literacy. As another superintendent of schools in Texas remarked, these teachers with limited skills were of "great use, for they are content with scanty support, and penetrate the country where white teachers cannot go." As anxious as Powell and Colby were to have qualified teachers in the school in Greensboro, Georgia, they were able at least to offer students an opportunity to acquire basic literacy.[17]

At the other end of the spectrum, Jane Deveaux had good reason to be confident about her abilities as a teacher. While the vast majority of freedpeople's schools had only been in existence for a few months, Deveaux could boldly respond to the Freedmen's Bureau inquiry that she had operated her school in Savannah for thirty years. Deveaux was the daughter of John Benjamin Deveaux, who was born into slavery, and Catherine Deveaux, a free woman from Antigua. Jane and her mother secretly taught black children to read the Bible, probably in the Third African Church, which John Deveaux pastored. Jane Deveaux began her school in her home in the 1830s despite city and state prohibitions. This fact caught John Alvord's attention when he met her in Savannah more than thirty years later. Alvord noted, "Although quite advanced in life, she labors with earnestness and zeal. It is especially interesting to hear her relate how her work was carried on in secret, eluding, for more than a quarter of a century the most lynx-eyed vigilance of the slaveholders of her native city." She had been "instrumental under God," Alvord continued, "of aiding in the education of many colored persons, who, scattered here and there through the south, are now able to contribute somewhat towards the general elevation of the newly emancipated race."[18]

Alvord observed that due to Deveaux's good reputation, children of "the better class of colored people" in Savannah attended her school. Deveaux's monthly reports suggest, however, that she did not operate a school exclusively for the middle class. In the first place, the fact that she submitted monthly reports to the agency that solicited information from schools for freedpeople indicates that at least some of her students had only recently become free. Further, the tuition she charged suggests that she had a mixture of social classes within the school. Whereas most schools charged $1.00 per month, Deveaux charged on a scale from $1.00 to $2.50, presumably based on a student's ability to pay. It is likely that a substantial number of her students fell at the lower end of the scale; if even one-half of her thirty-nine students had paid the higher tuition, Deveaux could have nearly doubled the $45.00 monthly salary that she reported.[19]

James Porter, who headed another school in Savannah, would also have been rightly confident in his qualifications to teach. Born to free parents in Charleston, South Carolina, Porter received an education that included training in ancient and modern languages. As an adult, he helped enslaved people escape via the underground railroad. He also held a secret school in his home in a room with a trap door so that students might flee in case of a raid. In 1856 he moved to Savannah to direct the black, middle-class, St. Stephen's Episcopal Church choir. He also established a music school where he taught violin, piano, organ, and voice. In 1872 Porter became the first African American principal of the public schools in Thomasville, Georgia. While there, he published a book entitled *English Grammar for Beginners*. Among southern black teachers, then, academic qualifications and teaching experience varied quite widely. Although some teachers quickly exhausted their learning, Porter, Deveaux, and some of the other Georgia teachers were qualified by any standards to teach freedpeople.[20]

Many African American teachers barely eked out a living. Most of the Georgia schools relied on tuition for support, charging a monthly fee that ranged from a low of fifty cents to a high of three dollars per month. The usual fee was one dollar per child per month. In addition to tuition, some parents also paid for the school's fuel, providing wood for stoves. In lieu of tuition, some schools relied on sponsoring organizations for support. The black-controlled Savannah Educational Association, for example, operated two schools that filed reports with the Freedmen's Bureau. These schools charged no tuition, and the association paid each of the fifteen teachers between fifteen and forty-five dollars per month, presumably based on qualifications or experience. Likewise, Abraham Colby in Greensboro wrote that the school there was in considerable debt as it charged no tuition. African American school associations collected subscriptions from community members who could afford to give in order to support the education of all interested members of the community. As a result, these schools and their teachers often operated with very limited funds.[21]

Five of the Georgia schools with black teachers received support from northern benevolent societies, namely, the New England Freedmen's Aid Society, the New York Society of Friends, and the Western Freedmen's Aid Society. However, even in some of those northern-sponsored schools, teachers lived on the brink of poverty when anticipated funds did not materialize. In Macon, for example, William Cole and Lewis Smith taught in separate schools established by John Ogden, a Freedmen's Bureau employee. Ogden had promised the teachers that the Western Freedmen's Aid Society would support their work, but the teachers complained that the organization did not live up to its financial commitments. According to the teachers, Ogden had agreed that each of the two teachers in Cole's school and the four in Smith's school would be paid twenty-five dollars per month. In addition, each teacher expected to receive thirty cents per day for rations from the government, the equivalent of rations given to commissioned officers. However, in the four months since establishing the schools in July 1865, none of the teachers had received rations and they had received only a fraction of the promised salary.[22]

In another instance of economic hardship, Isaac Primus, a teacher in Macon, reported that he had been assured a monthly salary of twenty-five dollars from an army lieutenant, but the payment was late. "Owing to the pressure of the times," the teacher asked parents for a donation. Presumably the parents helped out because the school remained open. At the time of the report, Primus's school had been in existence for only three months so it is not clear whether payment by the lieutenant was to be a long-term arrangement. Nor is it clear if the lieutenant, his regiment, or perhaps the government was to provide the funds. Two teachers in the Georgia sample reported that they neither charged tuition nor received a salary for teaching.[23]

Most of the Georgia teachers who charged tuition did not report difficulty collecting payment. Jack Mallard from Albany found that parents were "very prompt in paying for their children." Some teachers did, however, have a hard time collecting from parents. In one of several letters to the Freedmen's Bureau, Bartley Townsley wrote that parents had "not paid us one third of that amount, for the reason that they are too poor, but we think they will pay, if they ever get ebble to do so. We do not make a living at the present time, but hoping to do something for our emancipated race, we are willing to labor and to wate." Lewis Smith, who complained about the Western Freedmen's Aid Society's failure to keep its bargain, empathetically reported that he and the other teachers could not rely on tuition as an alternative because the freedpeople "are not able to pay to have their children taught, the rents being very high and provisions also." Still, Smith expressed optimism. "Notwithstanding," he wrote, "we have tolerable success."[24]

Black teachers in Georgia, like many others—black and white—in other southern states, taught under challenging physical conditions. With few material resources, freedpeople did not have ready access to buildings that could comfortably accommodate schools, and hostile whites regularly refused to rent property either to house northern teachers or the schools themselves.[25] In many communities, freedpeople pooled funds to build schoolhouses; sometimes, once the freedpeople had obtained title in a property, the Freedmen's Bureau funded the actual building of the school.[26] As they raised funds to purchase land and or lumber to build a school, or contended with hostile whites who refused to permit them to rent tools when they realized that the building would be a schoolhouse, freedpeople established schools in the meantime wherever they could find a space: in old sheds, a former mule stable, a hole in the ground that was an excavation under a house, private homes, and of course, churches.[27]

Perhaps most dramatic was the school that met in Bryan's slave mart in Savannah. In 1859 slave trader Joseph Bryan placed a newspaper advertisement for the sale of numerous people including a "likely country raised girl, 17 years old, capable servant; likely intelligent yellow girl child, 5 years, country raised; one man and his wife, and 2 girl children 8 and 4 years old,

fieldhands; 2 likely girls, 8 and 11 years old; 2 boys, capable to saddl
harness, making intelligent good workmen; 2 men, 24 and 26 year
several old men and women; 1 woman and 2 girl children, woman
cook; several other families."[28] As was his custom, Bryan would hav
locked these enslaved children and adults in cells, then paraded them
auction blocks in a room filled with the chatter of white men examining
human property and negotiating prices. Five years later, following the Union
victory in Savannah in 1864, African Americans established two schools in
this profane space, and students' recitation of the alphabet drowned out ves-
tigial echoes of the banter between traders and buyers. In a three-story brick
building fronting onto Market Street, in full view of the "strongly grated
windows" that had once penned them, freedpeople could now prepare themselves for a self-sufficient future rather than "perform their own commodi-
fication" in hopes of enticing a "kind" master, or subverting sale to a cruel
one.[29] The appropriation of Bryan's slave mart symbolized freedpeople's hope
that education would help them to throw off both the memory and reality of
exploitation.

An assortment of people and organizations controlled the other buildings
in which the Georgia schools met. Sites for schools fell into four primary
categories: buildings with private owners, African American churches, the
teacher's home, and government-owned property. Private persons owned
nine of the buildings and presumably rented them out for use as schools.
Reports did not indicate the race of the owners or the financial arrangements
involved. Seven schools met in African American churches; four teachers
held school in their own homes; one school was owned by "the colored
people;" the rest of the schools either belonged to the government or did not
provide ownership information.

African American churches doubled as schoolhouses throughout southern
states, whether the teachers were local people or northerners, as the buildings
were among the few places outside the financial control of local whites.
Operating a school in a church also eliminated the expense of rent. Black
churches, after all, belonged to and served the same population of freedpeople
who attended the schools. In the emancipation period, churches served as
sanctuaries, as sites for political meetings, and as classrooms. Many southern
towns had at least two black churches, one Methodist and one Baptist, that
were both transformed into classrooms for adults and children on weekdays;
on Sundays they housed Sabbath schools. Macon surpassed that figure; all
three schools that filled out reports met in churches, two Baptist and one
Methodist. William Cole, one of the Macon teachers, reported: "the Building that We are Teacher in is Belong to the first Baptist Denomination of
Colored People of this Place and have not bin any Expense to us." While

freedpeople worked to raise funds to build schoolhouses, they used the most substantial property they already had access to.[30]

But, as with much else associated with freedpeople's educational endeavors, the use of African American churches as schools stimulated conflict between whites and blacks in some communities. Potential for strife existed in at least two scenarios that could erupt into full-blown conflict. In the first, law or local custom required antebellum black churches to have white trustees with whom title to church property rested, even when funds for the purchase came from black congregants.[31] In this way whites maintained at least a modicum of control over black church activity. After emancipation, once freedpeople established schools in the church, white trustees surfaced to claim ownership, enforcing clauses that they claimed designated the building for church use only. Such a conflict in Jackson, Mississippi, ripened into a lawsuit and even reached the attention of the governor of the state in the fall of 1865. A white Methodist Episcopal church in Jackson held a deed in trust for a black Methodist Episcopal church. The land had apparently been granted to the Methodist Episcopal Church, South by the state of Mississippi, and the black and white churches built houses of worship on adjoining lots. According to the Freedmen's Bureau agent who investigated the matter, a committee of black men informed him that the church had been built before the war "by subscription among the colored people" with a "few white people contributing." "One old lady told me," the agent reported, "that she gave over one hundred dollars in gold and silver to help erect the structure."[32]

The white church did not interfere until the black congregation established a school in the building. At that point, the trustees ordered the teacher, Mrs. M. J. Ringler, to vacate the premises. We "have just learned that you have opened a male and female coloured school in the building erected by said church for the *public worship* of the coloured membership *only* of said church," they wrote. "The undersigned trustees have the sole controll of all the property in this c[oun]ty belonging to said conference, and are not willing that this church should be used for the purpose of a school therefore forbid it and request that you vacate the premises forthwith." Ringler was defiant. "I know of no good reason why the church built expressly for the use of the colored citizens of this place may not be used for school purposes, especially as the church on the adjoining lot, built we presume for the benefit of the whites is now used for similar purposes." When she refused to vacate, the trustees filed a petition with the county sheriff to enforce their right of possession. In official documents the white trustees based their argument on law. In other forums, they revealed their prejudice: they would soon be starting a school in the white church next door for white children and claimed to be concerned that the two sets of children would quarrel. Rejecting this flimsy excuse, the frustrated Freedmen's Bureau official remarked, "Whether they do so [object to the school] because they are opposed to educating the young colored children or not I cannot say. But I must confess I see no other grounds." Quite likely the white congregation had been inspired by the presence of the school for black children to open their own school, and this fact would now work to the disadvantage of the black community. The Freedmen's Bureau agent took the matter to the governor, who sided with the white trustees, saying that they had the right to appropriate property to which they had title.[33]

In a second scenario, white congregations "handed down" outgrown churches to blacks when they built new ones. When blacks established schools in these churches, the former occupants asserted a right to veto the building's use to educate freedpeople. Or, in a twist, whites attempted to extort from freed communities a promise to remain in the southern branch of the church. Continued use of the building for church or school purposes became contingent on the congregation's loyalty to the Southern Conference of the Methodist Church, for example, which faced great competition for African American church membership in the emancipation period. When African Methodist Episcopal ministers ventured into southern states, they made it a priority to "take out" local Methodist churches, meaning, to remove them from the watchful eye of the Methodist Episcopal Church, South, and initiate affiliation with the African Methodists. Further, the Northern Methodist Conference also went south with appeals for black membership, stressing the conference's anticaste and antislavery traditions. These proposed shifts of alignment met with resistance, as white southerners attempted to maintain "watch-care" over black churches.[34]

Freedpeople's schools represented in the Georgia monthly reports contended with both scenarios. In Covington, Georgia, Edward Petty taught school in the "colored church owned by the colored people through a verbal gift of the white people, the validity of which seems to have been based upon a continuance in the Southern Conference." The black congregation was evidently considering a change in affiliation because the teacher expressed concern that although whites readily gave permission to use the church as a school, use of the building might be revoked altogether if the "colored church should secede from the Southern and join the Northern Conference."[35] In Macon, Georgia, a similar dispute found its way into court. The judge ruled that the white Methodist Church that held title to the land and had built the church for the black people had the right to decide if the church should belong to the Southern or Northern Conference. That night the church burned down. Witnesses identified a black man as the arsonist. They reasoned that he had destroyed the church because the black people no longer had use of it.[36]

The whims of a white church also threatened the freedpeople's school in Greensboro, Georgia. The school met in a black church formerly owned by a white congregation. When the whites built a brick church for themselves, they offered to give the old church to the black people if they would pay the expense of moving it fifty yards behind the new church. The black people agreed to this arrangement. They worshipped in the church without interference for some time. However, three months after the black congregation opened a school in the church, the Quarterly Conference to which the white church belonged ordered the church removed. The African American church had no funds to remove the church. They had opened the school as a free institution, purchased a lot of land, and started building a new schoolhouse, then ran out of money. Without help from the Freedmen's Bureau they might be left without a school.[37]

Whether held in churches or elsewhere, freedpeople's schools were frequently in bad condition and poorly equipped. The Georgia monthly report question, "What is needed to render your school room convenient and comfortable?" elicited a range of responses. Jane Deveaux, who taught in her own home in Savannah, and Edward Howard, teaching in a government-owned building on St. Catherine's Island, threw up their hands and responded "Everything," while Simeon Beard serenely responded, "Nothing important." Between these extremes, teachers expressed concern about warmth in wintertime, ventilation, furniture, and supplies, including books. The Thomasville, Georgia, school needed seats and writing desks. The freedpeople built the school themselves, but they ran out of money to buy a stove or furniture. Likewise, James Porter reported that his classroom needed desks and seats. He also needed a clock, one of the items that Lucinda Jackson may have had in mind when she commented, "more space and every convenience of a good schoolroom is wanting." Several teachers used the bureau's question as an opportunity to reiterate their principal concern, the need for books.[38] The report from one school poignantly declared that its most important need was "A Good Teacher."[39]

In the places where schools met, cold seeped in between the logs or boards, and some buildings did not even have windows. The school in Thomasville needed two good stoves, and the one headed by Louis B. Toomer in Savannah needed repairs and fuel.[40] Bartley Townsley explained to the Freedmen's Bureau, "I am willing to do what is rite yet we collard people is very poor in deed and our school house is verry sorry. no stoves, no winder glass or nothing of that kine for the winter." In subsequent communications, Townsley reemphasized the inadequacy of the government-owned hospital building where the Griffin teachers held school. "We can use it in the warm season of the year," he wrote, "but for the winter it is too open. The floor is not close. The sides are open between the plank and there are no stoves or windows."[41] Townsley said that the freedpeople had not made repairs because with so little money, they did not want to invest in a building they were not certain they could keep. Their concerns were realized when the army moved out of Griffin and tore down the building in which the school had been meeting.[42]

Some of the Georgia communities, as well as other freed communities in the South, did build and undertake improvements on their own. According to Simon Ryall, the school in which he taught was built by freedpeople at a cost of one hundred dollars, but they were having a difficult time paying off their debt. Lewis Smith reported that the freedpeople had "been to the expense of fitting up one room" in the basement of the church for a school. It cost them eighty dollars. In Virginia, school superintendent R. M. Manly reported that "in more than a score of places the colored people have erected school houses with their own hands, and employed either some poor white person, or some one of their own people, who has some small attainment as a teacher." And a teacher in Carsville, Virginia, reported that the black people had built a new schoolhouse. "The colored people finished it, all but the floor, in four days. Twenty-nine men were at work on it one day," he said.[43]

The Georgia school reports suggest that at this moment of emancipation freedpeople valued and encouraged education equally for males and females. The percentage of male and female students varied from school to school, but overall there was no significant difference. The twenty-six schools that reported the sex of their students registered 1,360 females and 1,364 males. Evidently many freedpeople believed that both males and females had important roles to play in building black communities. In this they agreed with Uncle Job, who wrote to a black newspaper to encourage African American boys and girls to become serious about education, and Harry McMillan, who in his testimony before the Freedmen's Inquiry Commission expressed confidence that black children now in school would soon be able to manage black communities without white assistance.[44]

With so much faith invested in the empowering potential of education, freedpeople identified teaching as a critical job for building self-sufficient communities and called both men and women into service. Of the forty-six teachers whose sex can be identified, there were twenty-nine men and seventeen women. For freedpeople in Georgia in 1866, teaching was definitely not only women's work. In this regard black southerners were not so different from white. The nineteenth-century northern phenomenon of the feminization of teaching at the primary level had not yet taken place among white southerners.[45]

Students with teacher, James Heywood Blackwell. Courtesy Valentine Richmond History Center.

It is somewhat easier to construct even minimal histories of the male black teachers in Georgia than of the women, in part because the women provided far less information than did the men. None of the women appended a note to her report, nor did any write to the superintendent of education, as several of the men did. Women therefore did not leave as much of a record of their backgrounds, desires, or frustrations. In contrast, Bartley Townsley, who kept up a persistent correspondence with the Freedmen's Bureau, or Abraham Colby and Tunis Campbell, who each sent at least one long letter, permit a deeper understanding of the issues they faced. Further, some of the men appear in histories of Savannah and Georgia because they also participated in political activity during Reconstruction. With the exception of Jane Deveaux, the women teachers do not appear in these histories, and even then, her husband, John Deveaux, a minister and politician, appears with far more frequency and detail. Louisa Jacobs, who taught in a school in Savannah sponsored by the New York Society of Friends, surfaced in a study of northern African American teachers of freedpeople. The daughter of a nursemaid, she was a thirty-year-old single New Yorker who had received her education at a boarding school. Jacobs taught freedpeople for seven years.[46]

Some male teachers represented in the Georgia school reports were advocates and political activists as well. Lewis Smith and Tunis Campbell attended the founding meeting of the Georgia Equal Rights and Educational Association in Macon in 1866.[47] Jack Mallard and Edward Anthony of Albany also identified themselves as Equal Rights men. Louis B. Toomer became involved in Republican politics in the 1870s and received a political appointment to the post office.[48] Several were ministers or otherwise active in their churches: Ephraim Rucker and Simeon Beard were ministers; William Rose, a teacher in one of the Savannah schools, served as a deacon in the Second African Baptist Church; and James Porter was chairman of the board of vestry and wardens of St. Stephen's Episcopal Church and was active in Republican politics.[49] Ministers' double duty as spiritual leaders and teachers was consistent with an observation that Superintendent Eberhart made about freedpeople in Georgia: "I am unable to discover among them the least disposition to receive spiritual instruction from any who refuse or fail to provide for their intellectual training." Eberhart was specifically referring to African American expectations of white religious organizations, but freedpeople would certainly have held their own ministers to just as high a standard.[50]

Harriet Campbell and her sons Tunis Campbell Jr. and Edward Howard taught school on St. Catherine's Island, where their husband and father, Tunis Campbell Sr., was appointed superintendent by General Rufus Saxton. The younger Campbell and Howard also served in their father's government. Campbell Sr. completed the monthly reports for the school and wrote several letters to the state superintendent of education requesting books and an adequate building for the school on the north end of the island. He also served as administrator and benefactor of the school, paying for teachers as well as books and supplies out of his own funds.[51]

Most of the Georgia teachers worked alone, teaching from 18 to 146 students in one classroom. In a few places, however, several teachers worked together in one school. In Marietta, for instance, Ephraim Rucker was assisted by George Daniels and Mrs. M. Johnson. They taught 100 students in a church owned by "the colored people." The freedpeople of Marietta had formed an association to fund the school but soon ran out of money. Rucker subsequently carried on the school alone.[52] Some teachers created partnerships. In Savannah Jane Deveaux and Lucinda Jackson belonged to a fluctuating group of teachers who filed joint monthly reports. In her first report, dated January 1866, Deveaux was teaching thirty-nine students in her private residence. At that time, Jackson, who had a school of twenty-eight students in her home, also filed an individual report. In May 1866, however, the two women filed a joint monthly report with three other teachers, James Wilkie, King Thomas, and Ernestine Truchelot. By the June report the group had changed again to include only Deveaux, Jackson, and Wilkie. The nature or purpose of the partnership is not clear, as the reports suggest that each teacher continued to consider his or her school a separate entity.[53]

The Georgia teachers represent a microcosm of the spectrum of African American teachers in the emancipation South. They taught in rural and urban areas. They were freedpeople and people free before the war. They were minimally self-educated, and they had formal, even classical training. They were men and women. Some of the teachers operated independently. Most relied on tuition, but they also received sustenance from community organizations committed to making schooling a reality for freedpeople. They held schools in places that had never been intended for recitations, as well as in log buildings that freedpeople built specifically as schoolhouses. While some of them appealed to northern organizations to send more qualified teachers or additional resources, they carried on teaching with whatever they knew and had.

Most of the African American teachers in Georgia schools were southerners who came from the areas where they taught. A few, though, were northerners affiliated with missionary associations. Like the freedpeople themselves, many northern black teachers had high expectations of education; it was a tool to overcome the effects of oppression and perhaps even the oppression itself. Some African Americans from the North believed that their special affinity with former slaves better suited them than whites to teach freedpeople. Their invocation of character and education also competed with white benevolent associations' contention that white northern teachers brought something unique to freedpeople. James Lynch, the AME minister who helped to launch the Savannah Educational Association, believed that it was northern African Americans who possessed unique gifts to offer freedpeople. He was one of the first of nearly eighty AME missionaries to go south between 1863 and 1870.[54] In February 1864 he wrote from Beaufort, South Carolina, to urge the AME Church to send black teachers. "There is now a fine opportunity for this Society to send a teacher into this department," he told readers of the *Christian Recorder*. "You of the North, perhaps under-estimate the influence and power that can be wielded by colored men and women of character, intelligence and education, in military departments." The work of teaching, he argued, was of utmost importance to the elevation of the race. Lynch highly praised the work being done by whites in the educational mission, but he suggested there was a special role, as well as a special obligation, for African Americans. "I would no more let the color of a man's skin determine my estimate of him than the color of his coat," he wrote, "but I cannot see the entire work of the education of thousands of our black brethren being carried on entirely by the whites, without appealing to my colored friends to be up and doing, and have a lot and part in the matter."[55]

R. H. Cain, another AME minister working with freedpeople in South Carolina, was even more direct about his preference for black teachers. "None are so eminently qualified for this work as our ministry," he wrote in a letter published in the *Christian Recorder*. While also praising the work of white teachers in "this glorious work of instruction," Cain asserted that black northerners had a special bond with and understanding of the freedpeople. "We can feel and enter into all the sympathies of our poor down-trodden brethren," he contended; "Other teachers and preachers have feelings, but not as we feel for our kindred."[56]

Even with such a strong convictions, it was not a simple matter for African Americans to make it south to teach. The AME church was only one black organization among several white-controlled ones. Most African American teachers who went to the South were therefore not sponsored by the black denomination. Further, white missionary associations' biases against black teachers made it difficult for them to receive sponsorship from such associations. The AMA, for example, used a double standard to exclude blacks. It routinely rejected black women with children while it accepted white women with children as teachers and matrons of institutions. Moreover, even when it sponsored black teachers, the AMA often assigned even highly trained black professionals to undesirable locations.[57] Indeed, one reason the AMA and the Freedmen's Bureau wanted black teachers at all was to be able to send them to locations where white teachers would not be readily accepted by local whites and into rural, rugged areas where northern white teachers did not want to live.[58]

African Americans who applied to missionary associations for teaching positions often articulated a racially motivated commitment to working on behalf of freedpeople. Sara Stanley, a third-generation free black woman, a North Carolina–born descendant of both white and black slave owners, and an Oberlin College–trained teacher, applied to the AMA to work in the South. She described herself as "a colored woman, having a slight admixture of negro blood in my veins," and grounded her desire to go south in an affinity that she felt with the former slaves. "My reasons for asking to engage in the work of instructing the Freed people of the South," she explained, "are few and simple. I am myself a colored woman, bound to that ignorant, degraded, long enslaved race, by the ties of love and consanguinity; they are socially, and politically, 'my people,' and I have an earnest and abiding conviction that the All-Father, whose loving kindness give to me advantages which his divine wisdom withheld from them, requires me to devote every power with which he has endowed me to the work of ameliorating their condition." Stanley asserted her certainty that although they had been brutally oppressed for many years, freedpeople were nonetheless "susceptible of high cultivation" and that God had a plan of "spiritual greatness" for them. She believed that she had an obligation to take her Oberlin training and the preparation that eight years' teaching experience provided to the people she thought of as her own.[59]

Charlotte Forten's lot had also been radically different from the freedpeople she wanted to teach. She was born into a wealthy and prominent family, the fourth generation born free in America. Forten's grandfather, businessman and abolitionist James Forten, played a leading role in organizing the first Colored Convention in Philadelphia in 1817. Her father, Robert Bridges Forten, like many of her male and female relatives, was also an active abolitionist, and her mother, Mary Forten, who died when Charlotte was only three, came from an abolitionist family as well. Until age sixteen Charlotte had private tutors, as her father refused to send her to inadequate, segregated Philadelphia public schools. In 1854 the family sent her to Salem, Massachusetts, to attend integrated public schools. There she lived with the Remonds, a black family active in abolitionist circles. While in Salem, Forten attended normal school and frequented abolitionist lectures, where she mingled with prominent black and white agitators for freedom including William Lloyd Garrison, John Whittier, Lydia Maria Child, and William Wells Brown.[60]

Forten frequently wrote in her journals about slavery, the abolition movement, and their impact on her. When, pursuant to the provisions of the Fugitive Slave Act, a Boston court ordered Anthony Burns returned to slavery, Forten's entry read: "To-day Massachusetts has again been disgraced; again has she showed her submissions to the Slave Power; and Oh! with what deep sorrow do we think of what will doubtless be the fate of that poor man, when he is again consigned to the horrors of slavery." She regarded with scorn a government that would assemble thousands of soldiers to "satisfy the demands of slaveholders; to deprive of his freedom a man, created in God's own image, whose sole offense is the color of his skin!" She condemned the hypocrisy of a country that would boast of being the freest in the world but still order shot anyone who dared come to the rescue of the enslaved man.[61] And while she celebrated British Emancipation Day with other abolitionists, she considered America's Independence Day a mockery and dubbed fools the patriots who celebrated their "vaunted *independence*."[62]

Forten's anger came from her outrage at the enslavement of fellow blacks. She was enraged, as well, by the indignities that northern blacks often endured. When a museum denied her friends admission "solely on account of their complexion," she dreamed of a day of retribution. After a visit from escaped slave and abolitionist William Wells Brown, Forten's journal reflected her sense of identification with other blacks, free and enslaved, despite her own privileged class position. "At times I feel it almost impossible not to despond entirely," she wrote, "of there ever being a better, brighter day for us. None but those who experience it can know what it is—this constant, falling sense of cruel injustice and wrong. I cannot help feeling it very often, it intrudes upon my happiest moments, and spreads a dark, deep gloom over everything." Although Forten acknowledged that the racially motivated snubs she personally experienced from white classmates were but "trifles" compared to the public insults that other northern blacks experienced and to the daily oppression of slavery, she nonetheless articulated a deep sense of identification with others of her race in both northern and southern states.[63]

The Civil War brought the possibility that African Americans might finally achieve justice. In the summer of 1862, Forten took John Whittier up on his suggestion that she apply to the Boston Educational Commission for sponsorship to teach in South Carolina. The commission, however, had no interest in sending Forten to represent it in the South, even with Whittier's letter of recommendation and even though she had several years of teaching experience. The commission was not, its representatives said, sending women at the moment. Disappointed, Forten left Boston for Philadelphia, where her family's reputation was well known. She received approval from the Port Royal Relief Association and soon sailed for Port Royal, South Carolina. Forten had found a way to make good on her years of yearning to make a difference in the lives of her "persecuted race."[64]

Sara Stanley, Charlotte Forten, and other black northern teachers may have expressed themselves with more than a little rhetorical flourish—"No thought of suffering, and privation, nor even death, should deter me from making every effort possible, for the moral and intellectual elevation of these ignorant and degraded people," Stanley told the AMA—but their commitment to the educational effort was neither frivolous nor fickle. One study of teachers from New York State concluded that although the total number of black teachers was small in contrast to whites, New York blacks entered the educational mission at a rate proportionally higher than their presence in the population. While African Americans accounted for just over 1 percent of the state's population, they accounted for more than 14 percent of its total teaching force among the freedpeople. This meant that blacks participated in freedpeople's education at a rate ten times higher than whites. Second, African American teachers remained in the South on average longer than their white counterparts. Among teachers from all states, blacks averaged 2.25 terms, while all whites averaged 1.95 terms. Black teachers from New York had an even higher average of 3.13 terms. Among the black teachers, a higher percentage of women went south than men, though the numbers of men and women in the population were roughly equal.[65]

Race motivated many black teachers to teach freedpeople, and race mattered in missionary association's decisions about whom they would sponsor. Not surprisingly, race also played heavily in black teachers' experiences in their new southern homes. While white northern missionaries sometimes deferred to southern conventions of racial etiquette in order to keep the peace, it was also true that some whites from the North harbored their own beliefs in caste that did not permit blacks and whites to interact in a way that might suggest social equality. Blanche Harris, an African American Oberlin College graduate and AMA teacher, complained that the AMA minister in charge in Natchez, Mississippi, moved her from a black boarding house where she had been quite comfortable and placed her in the AMA mission house. The boarding house, he claimed, was too expensive. Harris was even more upset, and local black people were outraged, when she learned that she was expected to room with two black domestic servants in the mission. Further, Harris would not be allowed to eat meals at "the first table" but would be relegated to "the second table." When Harris and members of the black community protested her treatment, the minister explained that such segregation was necessary to avoid being mobbed by local whites. However, other comments made by the two white missionaries involved suggest that their own prejudices existed independently of southern customs and expectations. Black teachers in Norfolk, Virginia, including Sara Stanley, also complained of discrimination by AMA staff.[66] As Blanche Harris had hoped to do, some teachers, including Hartford, Connecticut–born Rebecca Primus, who taught on Maryland's Eastern Shore, avoided these problems by boarding with black families.[67]

Aware of these prejudices, the AMA's John Fee attempted to challenge fellow white northerners at Camp Nelson, Kentucky, where he ran a school for black soldiers and civilians. The episode illustrates the convergence of many of the character types and salient issues in the story of freedpeople's education. Fee, a native of Kentucky and president of Berea College, had served many years as a missionary to that state's white citizens in the 1850s. In 1860 Kentucky slave owners became so hostile to his abolitionist ministry, alleged to be "of the John Brown stripe," that they ordered him to leave the state. Mobs tarred some of his colleagues and drove them out of the state as well.[68] Yet, the Civil War found Fee more committed than ever to principles of equality and integration. In May 1865 Fee wrote to AMA officials about his school at Camp Nelson: "we should avoid making a 'nigger' school—avoid the idea that there must be separation. I believe we ought to make this a school for humanity—make efforts to have in here a due measure of white faces." Fee feared that his lofty goal would have to wait a generation to become reality. If not an integrated student body, then the school for freedpeople should have an integrated teaching staff, he argued. "We ought to have here some colored teachers that these people may *see* what they *can* be and that by *example* we may help put down the spirit of cast."[69] A few months later, Fee decided to implement his ideal of integration. It was a decision that would once again place him at the center of controversy.

In August 1865 Fee and another AMA employee, W. W. Wheeler, hired a "slightly colored" schoolteacher named E. Belle Mitchell from Danville, Kentucky. Mitchell had trained in Xenia, Ohio, as a teacher, and when the two men learned of her "correct Christian deportment, and unexceptionable personal habits," they hired her to teach in the school at Camp Nelson. In addition to training, character, and morality, Mitchell's appearance played an important role in her employment. Perhaps anticipating objection from other whites in the mission, Fee and Wheeler paid close attention to phenotype. Both men referred to her as being "slightly colored," hoping, it seems, that the slightness of her coloration would ameliorate objections. And, in a letter to the AMA, Wheeler wrote, "I might mention here (though I know it would make no difference with you) that her features are good European her complexion but little darker than yours or mine and her hair [faultless-crossed out] of the 'most straightest sect.' So that I think Bro Fee was fortunate in chancing on one so faultless in all these respects."[70]

Although Fee and Wheeler chose to integrate the AMA staff with a woman so nearly perfectly European in both character and appearance, Mitchell faced immediate rejection when she reported for work. "The lady teachers soon began to absent themselves" from the dinner table, and two male AMA missionaries suggested that Fee send Mitchell to the Soldiers Home to live with other black people. When Fee declined, all whites, except Fee and Wheeler, refused to eat with Mitchell and signed a petition alleging that Fee's "introduction into this house and to the table, of a woman of color without the consent of the occupants of it, and of those who conduct the mess, excites much comment and just repugnance to the act." The petition requested that Fee "withdraw from the table and the house at once the above mentioned person."[71]

Introduction of this woman of color into the missionary residence without prior consent became the residents' defense against charges of prejudice. One resident, Joseph C. Chapin, asserted that he had only signed the petition to maintain peace in the house since Mitchell's presence at the table had caused "unpleasant feelings" among many of the residents. "Her color was no objection to any one so far as I can learn," Chapin reported; "Her conduct (which was exemplary so far as I know) was no objection, simply the manner in which she was thrust into the family."[72] Likewise, Caroline Damon, a teacher whom John Fee described as the best they had, insisted that she had not refused to sit with Mitchell because of her race. "I had no ill feelings towards Miss Belle Mitchell on account of her color or position as teacher," she wrote. "Compulsion in acknowledging Miss Mitchell as an equal, was the only reason I did as I did."[73] Damon was honest, if not quite sincere. She did not object to Mitchell's race. Mitchell and anyone else could feel perfectly free to be black, so long as they were black somewhere else. They could not be black and equal to whites. The AMA petitioners certainly would not have objected if a new white person had been hired without their consent, as they would have presumed him or her to be equal to them. But Fee was attempting to force them to accept Mitchell's equality, something they certainly did not presume. If their own argument is accepted at face value, these white AMA employees seemed to say that they had a right to decide on a black person's equality. By bringing Mitchell in without prior consultation, Fee had usurped that right.

The AMA advised its employees at Camp Nelson that the organization's rules did not permit the continued employment of teachers who "refuse proper respect to others."[74] It also sent a team of investigators who required the white teachers to sign an agreement declaring that they would not make complexion a condition of association with other teachers.[75] Caroline Damon, offended by the AMA's reprimand, which she thought exceeded any she had ever received, even in her days as a student, and believing that the AMA had "lost confidence in [her] uprightness," resigned.[76] The AMA fired another teacher, Mrs. L. Williams, as a result of the incident. It is not clear what became of her husband, whom Wheeler described as the champion of the anti-Mitchell faction.[77]

Belle Mitchell lasted only three weeks at Camp Nelson. During Fee's absence, an army employee closely affiliated with the AMA house sent her away. She was gone before the AMA investigators arrived.[78] She returned to her home in Danville but was soon called into service again. During a tour of Kentucky, Reverend E. W. P. Smith, an AMA representative from Chicago, met with a group of African Americans who wanted a black teacher for a new school. There were several pay schools in Lexington, but the monthly fee of $1.25 precluded many, including soldiers' children, from attending. A black Baptist minister told Smith that the black people had held a convention at which they "appointed a committee to take measures to open a free school for these poor children—He says they will find a room for the school if a teacher can be procured—wants a colored teacher on account of the noise that might be raised if a white teacher should come." Smith thought immediately of Belle Mitchell. Since arriving in Kentucky, he had heard much about Mitchell and the "negrophobic" teachers and army officers who ha͜ driven her away from Camp Nelson. He asked if she would take over the new Lexington school. Mitchell, "feeling it [her] duty to engage in anything that would advance the Colored Race," consented. She opened the school with twenty-eight students.[79] Mitchell's new position held multiple ironies. The very factor that had led whites at Camp Nelson to reject her made her desirable to the black school organizers in Lexington. Even in that, however, white racism proved to be the determining element. The black organizers in Lexington wanted a black teacher precisely because they knew that local whites would not tolerate white northerners teaching freedpeople. African American teachers working for northern missionary associations contended with severe shortages of supplies, inadequate classrooms, and local white hostility as almost all freedpeople's teachers did. In addition, they had to withstand the very personal stings of racial prejudice from their own colleagues.

Among the many challenges to freedpeople's schools was hostility from some white southerners to the radical idea of educating former slaves. Aggressive whites employed many means to discourage black education. They refused to board white teachers in their homes, then they accused those teachers willing to board with black families of violating southern mores by advocating social equality.[80] They vetoed the use of formerly white churches as schoolhouses, and they intimidated teachers and students with threats, arson, and physical violence. Such antagonistic behavior was not bound by state or regional lines. Whites in both the upper and lower South evinced great hostility toward schools for black people and frequently used violence to attempt to stop the work. In January 1866 John Alvord commented on this phenomenon. "The educational work in Maryland," he observed, "has had much opposition, such as stoning children and teachers at Easton, rough handling and blackening the teacher at Cambridge." Moreover, intolerant whites burned a church and school in Kent County, and a guard had to be placed at the school in Annapolis. According to Alvord, "Colored churches have been burned in Cecil, Queen Ann, and Somerset counties, to prevent schools being opened in them, all showing that negro hate is not by any means confined to the low south." Rebecca Primus wrote to her family in Connecticut that her colleague, who was teaching in Trappe, Maryland, was ill treated by local whites. "She is stoned by white children, and repeatedly subjected to insults from white men, in passing they have brushed by her so rudely she says as to almost dislocate her shoulders."[81]

As African Americans gained political power and asserted social and political rights during Reconstruction, the hostility and violence escalated. John Alvord and R. M. Manly in Virginia may have believed that black teachers

netrate rural areas where white teachers would never be accepted,
teachers were actually even more vulnerable than whites.[82] Whereas
uthern whites scorned, intimidated, threatened, and harassed white
they threatened, whipped, shot at, and murdered black people in-
the educational effort. Whipping was an especially commonplace
black male and female bodies, an invocation of the memory of the
slave master's power to whip his slaves.

In Simpsonville, Kentucky, in the dead of night, the Ku Klux Klan rode
into the yard where Elijah Marrs boarded. As was often its practice, the mob
announced itself with a loud din of horns, drums, bells, and old tin pans.
Marrs grabbed his army pistol, and, hiding in a corner near the chimney, he
watched as the Klansmen picked switches from the trees as if "preparing to
come into the house to administer a flogging to every one of us." After
making some threats that Marrs could not quite decipher, they rode off into
the night. On another occasion, while Marrs's students played during recess, a
white man fired a shot into the crowd of children. Marrs attributed this action
to the KKK as well.[83]

Marrs and his students escaped injury, but other African Americans were
not so fortunate. The congressional committee that investigated conditions in
the former Confederacy in 1871 heard testimony of numerous attacks upon
African Americans in the years following emancipation. Witnesses described
groups of white men, among them professionals and large property owners,
on rampages in which they assaulted and threatened men and women whom
they believed challenged their economic and social status. Targets included
political activists, ministers, and teachers. In Mashulaville, Mississippi, African American teacher and minister Nathan Campbell was whipped for teaching school. In Winston County, Mississippi, Klan members burst into the
home of black teacher Peter Cooper while he was away. They stole his money
and set fire to his clothing, shoemaker's tools, and a trunk full of books. They
clearly intended to curtail both his economic and intellectual pursuits. At
around the same time, the Klan whipped Nathan Cannon, a black man in
Winston County, whom freedpeople paid to teach school. In Meridian, a
black teacher named Ritter was "taken out of his school-house and pretty
severely flogged." And in Noxubee County, a group of disguised men killed
George Chestnut. A schoolteacher, Chestnut had also begun electioneering
for the Republican Party. The white men threw his body into a well. When
witnesses testified in 1871 they usually could not recall the exact dates of these
attacks, but they knew that they had occurred within recent memory.[84]

When mobs of white men broke into African American homes at night,
they asserted that for freedpeople there could be no privacy, no safety, no
control over space or person or property. They dragged men and women out

of their homes, raised the women's clothing to expose their bodies, and whipped them for "sassing" white ladies, for supporting the Republican ticket, or for teaching.[85] Thirty-five-year-old Aury Jeter lived through such an invasion of her home and her person in the spring of 1870 in Douglas County, Georgia. While enslaved, Jeter had learned her letters from "a colored man who knew how to spell a little." When slavery ended, she studied geography, arithmetic, grammar, reading, and spelling for a short while at a school in Knoxville, Tennessee. She taught her husband to read and spell, but writing remained a challenge for her as it took a long time to form each letter. Jeter taught a day school, and her husband, Columbus Jeter, a preacher, taught night school in their home. Although Aury Jeter was aware that Herbert Morris, a white landowner in the area, was displeased with her teaching freedpeople (all potential laborers to his thinking), she chose not to pay any attention to his complaints and name-calling. Morris had made his disapproval clear to Columbus Jeter, remarking, "Your wife, the damned bitch, is teaching a colored school," to which Jeter reportedly responded, "I work for her and maintain her; why should she not teach school. The laws of the country permit her to do it."[86]

The Jeters' insistence on teaching other freedpeople, as well as their decision to attend a church some miles away from their neighborhood, brought down the wrath of Morris and other white men. Between eleven and twelve o'clock one night, as Aury Jeter and her husband prepared for bed, they heard an awful noise in the road. The dog began to bark, and then they heard a pistol fire. From the dark a man called out, "Open the door, God damn you; I will kill you if you don't open the door." Leaving his own shotgun on its rack, Columbus climbed into the chimney just as a group of men broke the door down with an ax, demanding to know where that "God-damn preacher" was. The men, including landowner Morris and a Dr. McClarty, grabbed Aury by the hair, threatened to set the house on fire, and put a pistol to her breast, threatening to shoot. She finally told them that her husband was in the chimney. One of the men fired his pistol into it. The men pulled Aury's clothing up to her waist and beat her with a hickory whip. They also dragged her twelve-year-old daughter out of bed by the nape of her neck, but they did not assault her. When they had finished whipping Aury Jeter, they blindfolded Columbus Jeter with an apron and carried him off into the woods. His wife found him the following day, two miles from their home, his clothing black and bloody from the soot of the chimney and his wounds.[87]

Arson was also a frequent and particularly insidious form of assault. Constructed from wood, African American churches and schoolhouses were veritable tinderboxes, and white southerners knew it. They could incinerate months of saving and building in just a matter of minutes. In perhaps the most egregious attack, white rioters in Memphis, Tennessee, burned down eight schoolhouses in May 1866.[88] In August 1866, during the New Orleans massacre, rioters burned down four black churches in which schools met and attempted to burn several other buildings also used as schoolhouses. Additionally, they demolished a new church in which a school was scheduled to open within a few days.[89]

As with other forms of violence, arson was not limited to one region or to rural or urban areas. Bartley Townsley and the three other black teachers in Griffin, Georgia, taught in a dilapidated, government hospital because their schoolhouse had burned down three days after it opened in July 1865.[90] According to the Freedmen's Bureau, three other schools in Griffin also burned down in the first half of 1866.[91] In Chattooga County, Georgia, freedpeople living and working on the plantation of Wesley Shropshire, a devout Union man, became targets of white violence when they began building a school. According to Shropshire, "there had been a little schoolhouse put up by the negroes on my place for the purpose of educating the children on the place, and carried on by a negro on the premises. About the time it was finished, these men came there and said that they controlled the country that I had no control over my land; that they would have schoolhouses put up when and where they pleased." The men whipped the black teacher and left him "right smartly cut the next day." Furthermore, they left a note for Shropshire, signed "KKK," ordering him to close the school. The freedpeople partially heeded the warning. They stopped building the schoolhouse but moved the school into a church that they had far off on the property. At about ten o'clock one night, the church burned down.[92]

Sometimes arson and other forms of violence had the desired result of impeding African Americans' attempts to get an education. Sometimes though, like Aury Jeter, freedpeople faced down complaints, warnings, and violence in their determination to make schooling available. An incident in Virginia demonstrates the tenacity required of African Americans to obtain even the rudiments of education. In January 1866 freedpeople built a schoolhouse near the Friends Meeting House. A Quaker teacher would staff the school. On the night of March 5 both buildings were set afire and burned to the ground. The following morning, John Alvord reported, "forty-five colored men met in the ashes of their school-house, sent for the teacher and assured her that if she would stay with them they would build her a larger and better house of lumber so green that it could not burn and would keep her supplied with green school-houses as long as she would stay." In the meantime, Alvord said, "the school assembled in the pine woods with only rails for benches and during the whole chilly month was only twice dismissed early on account of rain." The men lived up to their pledge, "and on the 1st of April, a hundred and fifty people assembled in and around the new house for a Sabbath school." In Memphis, where freedpeople began rebuilding burned-out schools immediately after the 1866 riots, they fittingly named one of the new schools "Phoenix."[93]

Teaching was one of many political acts in which freedpeople and other African Americans engaged during the emancipation period. When they entered classrooms, African Americans effectively extended the explicitly political work of black convention delegates by beginning to prepare former slaves to achieve civic and economic equality. Their decision to teach freed-people asserted that education was a valuable commodity and argued for African American access to it.

Although both black and white teachers encountered hostility from some southern whites, race came into play differently for each group. Whiteness marked northern teachers as representatives of the conquering Yankee force that threatened to overthrow white southern practices and values. A black teacher, on the other hand, signaled that perhaps it was too late; the status quo had already been overthrown. That is one reason why southern whites who opposed black education directed more violence against black teachers than against white. By chasing away white teachers, angry white southerners might curtail teaching. Black teachers, though, embodied change: their public presence proclaimed that African Americans were free, that some of them were educated, and that many more would soon be. White people in Simpsonville and La Grange, Kentucky, were astonished that Elijah Marrs was a teacher, and a literate one at that, because it was difficult for them to reconcile his blackness and his status as a former slave with qualities that had previously resided only in a particular class of whites. Southern whites received daily missives that a new world was taking shape. Black teachers were not only the messenger; they were also the message.

CHAPTER 7 ■ ■ ■ ■ ■ ■ ■ ■ ■ ■ ■ ■ ■ ■

A Long and Tedious Road to Travel for Knowledge

Textbooks and Freedpeople's Schools

Considering that we had to purchase all our books at a very high price and still labor under the disadvantage of not being able to obtain a sufficient number of different kinds of which to make our class uniform we are endeavoring to do the best we can under circumstances.

Lewis Smith, Macon, Georgia

But why have a *Freedman's* Primer any more than a Dutchman's Primer or an Irishman's Primer? Are not the so-called Freedmen to learn the same language, spell the same words, and read the same literature as the rest of us?

American Freedmen's Union Commission

Books were of course essential to teaching. These were the aids that teachers customarily relied on to provide common reference points. Setting individual lessons for large numbers of students could be tedious and exhausting. But books were scarce commodities within freed communities. James Yeatman reported seeing the young man in Arkansas with a worn book of poems by Tennyson. Henry McNeal Turner tried to barter with the government for books for his regiment, and Emanuel Smith in Apalachicola, Florida imported books from the American Missionary Association in New York to pass on to freedpeople who could hardly afford to pay for them.[1] At the same time, books with competing ideologies floated around the South: those that supporters of the Confederacy designed to inculcate values such as the morality of slavery and the inferiority of African Americans, and those that white abolitionists produced to advise black people how to carry out their new roles as free people.

Predictably, African American teachers in Georgia had to struggle to find the resources they needed in the classroom. Books cost money that many freedpeople did not have; thus teachers used what they could find. In response to the Freedmen's Bureau question, "What books do you use?" one Georgia teacher replied, "Any I can get."[2] His response underscored the overwhelming poverty of freedpeople and the challenge involved in establishing effective schools. Lewis Smith, who, with three other black teachers, taught over two hundred students in a Methodist church in Macon, expressed the problem well: "Considering that we had to purchase all our books at a very high price and still labor under the disadvantage of not being able to obtain a sufficient number of different kinds of which to make our class uniform we are endeavoring to do the best we can under circumstances."[3] Smith and the other teachers in his school used *Webster's Spelling Book, Davies' and Ray's Arithmetic,* and a "mixture" of other books. He asked the Freedmen's Bureau to send 150 copies of each of these books, and he also requested charts and a blackboard, which he believed would be of great help in teaching the alphabet.[4]

Edward Anthony, who taught sixteen students in his day school and thirty adults in his night school in Albany, Georgia, also needed spelling books. He told the Freedmen's Bureau that most of the freedpeople were "destitute and not able to buy books for their children." "It is very necessary," he reported, "that they should be educated but they are not able [to] buy their own books, therefore I Desire you to Furnish them if you can do it." Writing from the northern end of St. Catherine's Island, school administrator Tunis Campbell, who said he used any books he could find, also reported that he had no books to teach arithmetic, geography, grammar, or writing. He was therefore limited to teaching only spelling and reading. "The students would progress faster if they had proper books and slates," he suggested to the Superintendent of Education. Jack Mallard in Albany also needed books for his students to advance. He wrote, "Some of my scholars are ready for writing and I should like for you to send me twenty three or 4 books. Send me the first Reader and Second Reader and Third Reader Geography and Arithmetic."[5]

Campbell and Mallard honed in on a difficulty that plagued many freedpeople's schools beyond Georgia: student progress was hindered by a lack of books and other classroom necessities. Reverend Joseph Warren, the Freedmen's Bureau Superintendent of Education for Mississippi, echoed these teachers' concern in an 1866 report, when he noted, "Not more than two of the school-houses have been properly fitted up with writing-desks, even of the most primitive kind. Some others have very little accommodation for writing; most of them none at all. This is owing to the poverty of the people, and to the large demands upon the funds of the benevolent societies." As "nearly all had to begin with the alphabet and spelling," initially the lack of supplies and equipment "was not so great an evil." "But now," Warren concluded, "unless better apparatus can be provided in our schools, justice cannot be done to the pupils. Thousands of them have reached that point where to learn to write is the next important thing." Not only did the limited skills of some of the teachers inhibit students' growth, lack of books and furniture threatened to hold them back as well.[6]

As Lewis Smith pointed out, teachers relied on a mixture of textbooks. To teach spelling or orthography, reading, and grammar, some relied on *Webster's Spelling Book, Walker's Dictionary, McGuffey's Readers, Wilson's First and Second Reader, Sanders' Reader and Spellers, New York Reader, Smith's Grammar, Pinneo's Grammar,* and *Freedmen's Primers.* Teachers used *Quackenbo's United States History, Cornell's Geographics, Monteith's Geography* to teach geography and history. For arithmetic they used *Davies' Arithmetic* and *Ray's Arithmetic.* Teachers in nearly every Georgia school that employed African American teachers reported that they read the Bible or New Testament in class.

Resources were uneven from school to school. The two "colored freedmen" who taught a school in Calhoun County only had access to elementary spelling books. They therefore focused on teaching spelling and reading. Only one student was able to read when they filed their report with the Freedmen's Bureau, and none had studied arithmetic, geography, grammar, or writing. Lynch Lamar, teaching in his private residence in Columbus, used *Webster's Spelling Book* and *McGuffey's Readers.* Like the Calhoun County teachers, he taught only spelling and reading. At the time of his report, fifteen of fifty students could read. Jacob Wade used *Webster's Spelling Book* to teach spelling and reading. He reported that ten of his forty-one students could read. Simon Ryall also relied on the spelling book and had taught six of his twenty-five students to read. Even with these severely limited resources, teachers and their students managed to make some progress; but, as Ephraim Rucker, a minister who taught in a church owned by freedpeople in Marietta, so poignantly put it, "you will see from my report that I am useing the Elementary Spelling book which is a long and tedious road to travel for knowledge but it is a shew [sure] one and better than none."[7]

Simeon Beard, a minister in Augusta, stood out among the other teachers as having a relatively large number of textbooks for his forty-four students. He used *Sander's Readers, Davies' Arithmetic, Cornell's Geographics, Pinneo's Grammar, Quackenbo's United States History,* and *Walker's Dictionary.* Beard may have served a particularly well off population of freedpeople, for not only did he have a larger number of texts available than any other teacher, most of his students were writing on slates and in books. Beard also charged the highest tuition of all the Georgia teachers—three dollars per month—and students supplied fuel for the school as well. Even Jane Deveaux, teaching in urban Savannah with thirty years' experience, charged less than Beard. It is noteworthy, too, that although he was a minister, Beard taught not in a church but in a "comfortable" building owned by a Jacob Danforth, Esq. Not surprisingly, Beard was one of only a few teachers who had no complaints about the condition of his school.[8]

A few other teachers, including Jane Deveaux, Lucinda Jackson, and K. Saul Thomas, who taught in their homes in Savannah, and John Bentley and Isaac Primus, who taught in the African Baptist Church in Macon, had books that enabled them to teach a range of subjects including reading, arithmetic, and geography. Some were fortunate enough to receive donations of one or two types of books from northern organizations. Louisa Jacobs and a fellow teacher in Savannah relied primarily on a donation of one hundred *Freedmen's First and Second Primers* from the American Tract Society based in Boston. Jacobs was employed by the New York Society of Friends, which may have provided her with greater access to northern philanthropy. Likewise, Jane Ann Vattal received primers from her employer, the New England Freedmen's Aid Society. Two schools operating under the Savannah Educational Association received book donations from the American Tract Society. John Alvord likely helped to procure the donation, as he worked for the American Tract Society prior to heading up the educational arm of the Freedmen's Bureau and was present when the Savannah Educational Association was established.[9]

Local teachers without northern connections encountered more difficulty. Abraham Colby's school in Greensboro raised ninety-three dollars in gifts from a black regiment from New York and spent some of the funds on readers and spelling books. However, with nearly 150 students, the school needed even more books. Colby requested fifty *Elementary Spelling Books*, fifty *McGuffey's First Readers*, two dozen "Child's Primers," one dozen *Mental Arithmetics*, twenty-five copy books, and pens and holders, plus a dozen slates and pencils. The records do not indicate whether he received the requested supplies. The teachers in Griffin did reap benefits from their persistent requests for supplies. After writing several letters to G. L. Eberhart, the Superintendent of Education, Bartley Townsley received a donation of *Freedmen's Writing Lessons*. To express his gratitude to Eberhart, Townsley related that he and his students "highly praise" the books.[10]

The tool that African Americans used most frequently to decode written English was Noah Webster's *Elementary Spelling Book*, popularly called "the blue-back speller." This book, which insisted on an American pronunciation distinct from the English, was Webster's contribution to the American Revolution. Having "thrown off the shackles" of English rule, Americans, Webster believed, should also renounce the language. Instead of "honour," Americans would spell "honor"; instead of "publick," "public." In 1784 Webster printed the first edition at his own cost because he could not convince a publisher to challenge the popular *New Guide to the English Tongue* by Thomas Dilworth. By 1818 Webster's book had sold 5 million copies.[11] It was this little book that Frederick Douglass and countless other enslaved people used in their first steps toward literacy.[12] And when slavery ended, adults and children, many of whom could not attend school, got hold of the blue-back speller and slowly taught themselves to read. The speller accrued emotional significance as the guide that helped individuals to decipher written language. At eighty-seven years of age, John Walton expressed his sentimental attachment when he told an interviewer, "I learned to read and write a little just since freedom Us used Websters old blue back speller and I has one in de house to dis day and I wouldn't take nothing for it."[13]

Measuring only about six by five inches, the blue-back speller also demonstrated the portability of learning. Enslaved people hid it in their bosom or under their hats; freedpeople publicly displayed it on roadsides or in fields as they studied while resting from work. Lorenzo Ezel told an interviewer, "I ain't never been to school but I jes' picked up readin'. With some of my first money I ever earn I buy me a old blue-back Webster. I carry dat book wherever I goes. When I plows down a row I stop at de end to rest and den I overlook de lesson. I 'member one de very first lessons was, 'Evil communication 'rupts good morals.' I knowed de words 'evil' and 'good' and a white man 'splain de others. I been done use dat lesson all my life."[14]

African American teachers' scramble to obtain even the most elementary spelling books to teach the most rudimentary lessons took place within a broader context of contestation for control over what stories textbooks would tell and who would tell them. Textbooks are political tools aimed at transmitting particular ways of looking at the world, and some mid-nineteenth-century textbook writers carried out ideological struggles even in seemingly politically inconsequential elementary spelling and reading books. Both northern and southern white politicians and educators realized that even simple statements inserted into elementary spelling lessons could influence a new generation of readers and thinkers.[15]

In the antebellum period some white southerners came to believe that the northern textbooks and teachers in southern classrooms disapproved of and thus challenged the southern way of life. In the late 1850s, as regional tensions heightened, southern white politicians and educators moved to take control of what their children learned in school. Long dependent on northern teachers and texts, they began a campaign to remove both from the schools of the coming Confederacy. White southerners began publishing books that would introduce into the classroom values that they held dear. A defense of slavery, the institution and ideology that lay at the heart of sectional political disagreements, and which to some northerners rendered the South a pariah, naturally became an important insertion into children's textbooks. Southern white children would learn at home as well as in school that perpetuating slavery was their right and, just as important, that African Americans were better off and happier as slaves.[16]

Consistent with this shift, a conference of teachers in Raleigh, North Carolina, in 1861 resolved that the struggle for "national existence" being waged between North and South had to be maintained in the legislature, on the battlefield, in the home, and in the schoolroom. Calvin H. Wiley, Superintendent of Common Schools for the state, headed up a committee that issued a statement on behalf of the conference. Committee members thought it was incumbent on white southerners to break the dependence on books and teachers that sought to subjugate them, and thus the committee urged the conference to "encourage and foster a spirit of home enterprise and self-reliance." As a result, it called for the withdrawal of North Carolina children from schools in the North and for expansion of the state's own school system. It further affirmed that any independent nation must produce its own textbooks. This was certainly so for the southern United States, distinguished as it was by a "peculiar social system." The conference made its meaning even more explicit when it stated: "conscious that we are not, in any sense, an inferior people, and firmly convinced that our own position on the subject of slavery is the right one, we contend that it is but strict justice to ourselves to think and write on some subjects for other nations." This group of teachers not only wanted to insert the white southern paternalistic view of slavery into its classrooms, it also wanted to export its proslavery doctrine to northern states and to European countries it pursued as allies.[17]

Several authors and publishers took up the mandate to produce textbooks more in keeping with white southern values. In April 1863, two years into the war and months after the Emancipation Proclamation, the newly formed Educational Association of the Confederate States of America, comprised of male teachers and other men interested in education, released a two-page list of southern textbooks already available or in press. These included a series from a publisher in Greensboro, North Carolina, with titles like *Our Own Primer*, *Our Own Spelling Book*, and so on. Also from North Carolina came *The Dixie Primer*. The South Carolina list included *The Bucolics and Aeneid of Virgil* and *A Series of Confederate Readers*. Confederate textbooks set out to replicate traditional lessons on traditional texts like the *Aeneid*. Additionally, they interposed lessons deemed appropriate for a slave society into elementary reading and spelling books. In addition to the values of politeness, honesty, and hard work that northern spelling books included, the elementary texts set out to convince young, white, southern readers that black slaves were better off than poor whites, that slavery was a biblically approved institution, and that northerners, including the despot Abraham Lincoln, sought to deprive white southerners of their God-given rights. In a letter to the convention, Jefferson Davis, president of the Confederacy, encouraged the group's effort to produce southern textbooks for southern youth.[18]

Marinda Branson Moore, one of the more prolific authors of Confederate textbooks, was intent on conveying to her young readers that preserving the status quo would be the best option for black people. In a book that began its lessons with the spelling of monosyllabic words such as "cat" and "bat," Moore introduced reading lessons like this one to support her philosophy that freedom was worse than slavery:

1. Here comes old aunt Ann. She is quite old. See how she leans on her stick.
2. When she was young she did good work, but now she can not work much. But she is not like a poor white wo-man.
3. Aunt Ann knows that her young Miss, as she calls her, will take care as long as she lives.
4. Ma-ny poor white folks would be glad to live in her house and eat what Miss Kate sends out for din-ner.[19]

In another of Moore's lessons, Uncle Ned found out the hard way that he could not trust the Union. Ned, "a good old dar-key" who loved his master well, was convinced by the Yankee army to run off with his wife and children. "They told Ned that he should be free, and live like white folks, but he soon found they had not told him the truth." So Ned crept away one dark night, leaving his wife and children, and returned alone to his master. He explained to his master, "Ah mas-sa, dem Yan-kee no be no good to poor nig-ger, can't stay wid him. Ned lib wid you all his life." Thereafter, Ned and his master were both glad. Ned went back to work and prayed every day that his wife and children would return.[20]

Moore also spiced her elementary geographical reader with judgments of black inferiority.[21] In the torrid zones of the earth (that is, Africa), she told her readers, "the people are tall, dark complected, indolent and warlike. As a matter of course with lazy people, they are very ignorant." At the other extreme, in the frigid zones (that is, at the North and South Poles), the people were as contented and happy as white southern children. They were industrious and peaceful and had some education. In the temperate zones, including the United States, the "people are mostly white, of common stature and of milder disposition than those of hotter climate; but much more warlike than those of the Frigid Zones. They are generally industrious and intelligent." By intelligent, Moore said she meant that they "have good schools, and all who labor can get a good education." She reminded her young readers that in every zone there were some lazy people and hoped that her readers would not be among them.[22]

Moore denoted clear distinctions among the "Races of men." Europeans and Americans, mostly white or Caucasian, were more civilized and ranked far above the rest. They had churches, schools, and systems of government, and they treated women with respect. In fact, women's wishes were often law among their male friends. In Asia, the yellow people, a quiet, plodding race, were sensible and shrewd when educated. Their great downfall was that they were heathens who did not know Jesus. However, once converted they were faithful followers, not fickle like some other races. For their part, American Indians went nearly naked and had been very cruel and warlike when white people arrived in America. Now, however, they had books, schools, and churches, and many had learned about Jesus.[23] For Moore, the African or Negro race from Africa had no redeeming qualities. They were slothful, vicious, dull, and cruel to each other, selling their prisoners to white people as slaves. In Africa they knew nothing of Jesus, and the climate was so unhealthy that white men could not go there to convert them. As a result, "the slaves who are found in America are in much better condition." They were better clothed, fed, and instructed. Moore intentionally did not use the words "education" or "educated" in the African American context as she had for the others because relative educability was for her an important point of demarcation in the hierarchy of races. Not only were blacks uneducable, but as the cursed descendants of Ham, they had to serve their brethren forever. Although she made no attempts to explain the phenotype of any other group, Moore said she was at a loss to explain "how they came to be black, and have wool on their heads."[24] This is what the white children in the new schools of the southern Confederacy learned—lessons well designed to perpetuate slavery and white supremacy.

With freedpeople's schools opening just as these books reached the market, one can well imagine them falling into the hands of eager new black readers, transmitting the very lessons that the existence of freedpeople's schools meant to counteract. However, not one African American teacher in the Georgia sample reported using a recognized Confederate textbook. Even though they were desperate for books, black teachers, too, may have made political choices about what they would use in the classroom.

Following emancipation, abolitionists undertook a corresponding enterprise to produce textbooks for the freedpeople. Missionary associations that spent their resources on sending teachers to the freedpeople saw northern white teachers and the New Testaments they distributed as the most effective vehicles for transmitting their values. Several northern whites also produced books aimed at inculcating "northern values" into freed African Americans. In 1865 and 1866 the American Tract Society, a Boston-based, Congregational Church affiliate, published *The Freedman's Spelling Book* and *The Freedman's Second and Third Readers*. The publishers said that the books were prepared with special reference to the freedpeople. The books aimed to explain rules very simply and to introduce words that related to "important practical subjects; as occupations, domestic life, civil institutions, morals, education, and natural science." While teaching spelling and reading were of utmost priority, the publishers also wanted to impart practical information that would be of use to the freedpeople "in the new condition into which Providence has raised them." In *The American Freedman*, the organ of the American Freedmen's Union Commission, a missionary association that sent teachers to the South, a review of the new American Tract Society books praised their content but took issue with the decision to call them "Freedman's" books. "But why have a *Freedman's* Primer any more than a Dutchman's Primer or an Irishman's Primer?" asked the editor. The reviewer continued: "Are not the so-called Freedmen to learn the same language, spell the same words, and read the same literature as the rest of us? Then why in the name of common sense not learn out of the same primers? If we wish to abolish these odious caste distinctions from our laws, why ingrain it in our educational systems by the very titles of our books?" "Suppose the child was a slave," the reviewer posited, "is that any reason why this odious recollection should be thrust in his face for ever after? We hold that the emancipated are *men*; that they are entitled to the best literature which American authorship can produce, and to nothing inferior or different from that used by the rest of us."[25]

R. M. Manly, the white Freedmen's Bureau Superintendent of Education for Virginia, voiced similar doubts about the limitations imposed by designing books specifically for freedpeople. While he considered the *Freedman's* series "excellent books," written with "professional skill," he was concerned that they would alienate potential readers who would not identify with the name "freedmen." He reasoned that since schools operated by northern missionary associations did not exclude students on account of race or color, it would not promote the educational mission for schools to use books that did so. The few white students who attended freedpeople's schools, as well as African Americans who were free before the war, might be put off by the books. Books that spoke directly to freedpeople, Manly thought, would "be offensive to both of these classes, exceedingly so to the whites, and hardly less so to those whose pride it is that though colored they were always free." Notwithstanding this criticism, Manly informed the American Tract Society that he would promote the use of the books in the schools in Virginia. The society would have to make its own arrangements with the various northern associations, but Manly welcomed his own supply so that he might "meet occasional calls from planters and freedmen for books with which to start schools in remote localities." His criticism of the books was "slight," directed not at their effectiveness for teaching, but at the possibility that they might turn potential students away from the schoolroom.[26]

Yet, aside from its name, at first glance the *Freedman's Spelling Book* did not appear to be so different from other contemporary, northern spelling books. It presented lessons of etiquette and morality among the vocabulary words. Occasionally it was explicit, as in lesson 173, where it urged freedpeople to be economical: "A freedman should be prov-i-dent; that is, he should pro-vide for the fu-ture, and not be neg-li-gent." Other messages tended to be more subtle and could be read to have mass appeal. However, when read simultaneously with another publication by the American Tract Society, Isaac W. Brinckerhoff's *Advice to Freedmen*, published in 1864 or 1865, it is easy to see how teachers, with similar sensibilities and beliefs, would have amplified the spelling books' lessons in the classroom.[27]

Brinckerhoff, a white Baptist minister from Ithaca, New York, served as a plantation superintendent and teacher in the South Carolina Sea Islands from 1862 to 1863, then as a missionary in St. Augustine, Florida. In his book he addressed freedpeople directly, always with the condescending tone of a wise elder, introducing himself to them "as a friend who is doing all that he can to promote your welfare and the welfare of your people." Brinckerhoff assured those who would read the book as well as those who would hear it read by literate friends that he saw human qualities in them. "Though you have for generations been a dependent and enslaved race, yet with many visible marks of degradation still upon you," he told them, "there is evidence of a God-given manhood within, which only needs to be properly developed and rightly cultivated to make you happy, prosperous, and useful." He hoped, with God's blessings, to aid in this development of manhood.[28]

Where the *Freedman's Spelling Book* was subtle in its references to freedpeople, Brinckerhoff was explicit in his messages. Both textbooks covered several topics in common, among them, vanity, temperance, industriousness, honesty, humility, the duties and responsibilities of freedom, frugality, education, punctuality, and family. Regarding temperance, for example, the spelling book offered in an early lesson, "It is a sin to sip rum," or in a more advanced lesson, "Strong drink not on-ly stim-u-lates: it stu-pe-fies the sens-es and the mind, and leads one to vi-o-late du-ty, and per-pe-trate hor-rid crimes."[29] In contrast, while Brinckerhoff first stated the general proposition that temperance in food and drink was a desirable attribute, he then tailored his advice specifically for freedpeople. "I would especially and earnestly warn you against the use of intoxicating drinks. This is a vice from which at present you are free," he told them. "Indeed, under the rule of strict military law, the means for indulgence cannot be obtained. The time will come when these restraints will be removed. I tremble for your people when that time does come." He warned them of all the dangers of alcohol that could result from taking even one drink and urged them to pledge never to taste anything that could intoxicate.[30]

Similarly, the spelling book said, "La-bor is a u-ni-ver-sal duty, and ben-e-fi-cial to all. Some la-bor with the hands, and others with the mind, but all must work." Brinckerhoff, the former plantation superintendent charged with getting freedpeople to work for the government, advised his audience that freedom did not discharge their obligation to work. "God never intended that a freeman should live without labor," he told them. In fact, God had placed the first man in a garden and told him to till the soil and eat of the fruit of the garden. Brinckerhoff acknowledged that the freedpeople's former owners had considered work dishonorable, but he condemned their scorn for work and urged freedpeople not to emulate them.[31]

Both the *Freedman's Spelling Book* and Brinckerhoff's *Advice to Freedmen* sought to instill African Americans with a sense of obligation and loyalty to northern white men. The spelling book paired an illustration of a white soldier being greeted by a small white girl with a story of five sentences. The man had just returned home from the war. He was glad to see his little daughter. "Let us be joyful that the war is at an end," the story continued; "It was sad to see men die in battle, but it was to make us free. We will not forget all that God did for us." This insistence to African Americans that white men had died to make them free neglected any mention that black men had also fought for their freedom. Brinckerhoff joined in this omission when he wrote, under the heading "How You Became Free": "Many thousand households at the north are clothed in mourning, and many tears are shed for the dead who have been slain. With treasure and precious blood your freedom has been purchased. Let these sufferings and sacrifices never be forgotten when you remember that you are not now a slave, but a freedman."[32]

In her lessons to white, southern children, Marinda Moore reinforced a proslavery ideology that insisted African Americans were contented slaves who, even after being lured away by northern whites, returned to serve their former masters as loyal servants. Brinckerhoff, the white northerner, also represented himself as paternalistic caretaker, handing out advice to a benighted people. As Moore did, he too made claims on African American loyalty. While Moore's textbooks influenced white boys and girls to believe that blacks belonged in slavery, Brinckerhoff's book surely made it into freedpeople's classrooms and into the spaces where freedpeople gathered to listen to the readers in their communities. We cannot be certain what freedpeople made of the messages of debt and loyalty to white northerners.[33]

At the end of the Civil War, African Americans were in no position to create their own textbooks to promote a worldview. Noah Webster created a book that renounced British conventions. Secessionist southerners declared their separateness from the rest of the nation with separate texts to indoctrinate their children. And white abolitionists celebrated the end of slavery while attempting to instill a sense of obligation in African Americans. Each of these actions signaled radical changes and underscored the political work that textbooks do. African Americans' decision and determination to become literate was arguably as radical. In some imagined world they might have rejected the language of their oppressors, but by the 1860s most black people in America were far removed from the original languages of their ancestors. They had blended African cultural memories and practices with European ones, and in some places, they developed and preserved tongues that allowed them to speak their secrets loudly in the presence of whites.[34] Still, English was the language of commerce and politics in the world their labor enriched. While some chose to leave America for Africa or Haiti, most remained in the United States determined to claim a share of the country's wealth and to participate in the institutional bodies that governed their lives. In the aftermath of slavery, African Americans used an odd collection of books to announce to the world that they wanted to be literate and could become literate. The men, women, and children who studied lessons in the blue-back speller placed their own radical imprint on the book that Noah Webster had designed in an earlier revolutionary moment.

CHAPTER 8 ■ ■ ■ ■ ■ ■ ■ ■ ■ ■ ■ ■ ■ ■ ■

If Anybody Wants an Education, It Is Me

Students in Freedpeople's Schools

Nearly all [parents] are awake to the possibility of *their children* becoming "something."

E. E. Johnson, Evansville, Indiana

I don't know much, but one thing I do know: I want edication, and we, as a people, want edication. We must learn to keep books and do our own business, for already the white man is marking and thinking how cheap he can hire us, and how easily he can cheat us out of our pay.

Freedman, Trent Camp, North Carolina

London R. Ferebee, normal school graduate and elder in the AME Zion Church, marked three significant dates in his life: the day he was born, the day he became free, and the day he learned the alphabet. Ferebee was twelve years old when he ran away to Union soldiers at Elizabeth City, North Carolina, in 1861. He was fourteen when Isaac Bishop, a black minister, taught him the alphabet on June 1, 1863, in the school that Bishop held in his New Bern church. A few months later, Ferebee's family moved to Roanoke Island to escape an outbreak of smallpox, and Ferebee's father and other freedpeople built a schoolhouse to accommodate their children and the northern schoolteachers they hoped would come. Ferebee did well in school, and teacher Ella Roper, a graduate of Mount Holyoke Seminary in Massachusetts, soon appointed him assistant teacher, even as he was learning to write his letters. In 1866, when, according to Ferebee, "it was understood by both races, learned and unlearned, that freedom was established," African Americans began leaving Roanoke Island for other parts of the state, and northern teachers returned home. Ferebee's family returned to Elizabeth City.[1]

Former slave Georgia Telfair also attributed great importance to her first exposure to formal education, and at seventy-four years old she still recalled the details of her first days attending school as an eight-year-old girl. "I toted my blue back speller in one han' and my dinner bucket in de other," she told an interviewer. "Us wore homespun dresses wid bonnets to match. De bonnets wuz all made in one piece an' had drawstrings on de back to make 'em fit, an slats in de brims to make 'em stiff an' straight. Our dresses wuz made long to keep our legs warm. When us warn't in school, me an' my brudder wukked in de fiel' wid pa."[2]

Ferebee's and Telfair's recollections contain many of the elements that characterized other freedpeople's early educational experiences. Some students clung to the blue-back speller, the name thousands of Americans gave to Noah Webster's spelling book. The small book had helped enslaved people learn to read, and the new generation placed high hopes in it as well. As Ferebee recalled, learning the alphabet and how to read and write were first sought-after goals, then exhilarating moments for both children and adults. Telfair's work in the fields alongside her father and brother was typical of the many freedchildren whose schooling was disrupted by the need to assist their families in the fields. Ferebee was part of a phenomenon that occurred frequently in classrooms throughout the South: as soon as he learned a lesson, he became responsible for teaching it to someone else. Finally, Telfair's description of her clothing telegraphed her excitement as she set out to school for the first time.

Yet, not all young people responded well to the prospect of attending school. Tom Morris's recollections captured the sense of anticipation and apprehension that accompanied some children out of their homes and into a new environment. "Afte' de war was ober I had to go to school," Morris told an interviewer, "an I had to go by de grave yard to git to dat school house. Ebery time I passed by dat graveyard de dead folks wud ri' and blow deir breath on me. I cud feel dat hot breath. I wud run. I wus skeered. I didn't love to go ter school. Afte' while when my brudder, Willie, got big nuff to go to school sum how I was not so skeered."[3]

Like passing the graveyard, attending school for the first time must have been mysterious and frightening for some students. Many were already adolescents when they enrolled. Sitting in a classroom called for significant adaptation not only to an unfamiliar setting but also to new figures of authority. Whether teachers were white or black, local or northern, they presented dramatically new experiences for these children. As enslaved children, some had accompanied young masters and mistresses to schoolhouses and were thus familiar with at least the physical layout of a school. Morris and others, though, left their families each morning to venture into a wholly alien experience alone. Their communities had sent out pleas for teachers, local African Americans and northern missionaries had responded, and the adventure of attending school began for thousands.

Freedpeople's initial exposure to formal schooling produced a rich, textured experience. African American children and adults entered classrooms, anxious to acquire literacy and numeracy. At great sacrifice of time and money, they journeyed long distances to reach the places where schools met.

Once there, they pushed teachers to teach more hours, and they prodded weak ones to improve their offerings. Just as students made their assessments of quality, teachers, of course, also measured and compared and sometimes gauged how far they believed these formerly enslaved African American students could progress academically. Outside of the classroom, students faced additional challenges as local whites violently acted out their opposition to black education.

African American parents often saw education as a commodity, making direct links between schooling and upward mobility. They therefore took steps to ensure that their children, male and female, would have access to schools. Freedpeople such as London Ferebee's father pooled their resources and built schools on the faith that teachers would come to occupy them. Once teachers arrived, parents urged them to allow their children into schools. Parents sometimes overwhelmed newcomers with their determination. An AMA teacher in Athens, Georgia, wrote that when her school numbered nearly one hundred students, she refused admission to two new applicants, saying that she would not be able to teach at all with so many students. The children soon returned with their father, who pleaded, "Do let them come if you please, ma'am, and if you can't teach them even a little, just let them sit and hear what the rest learn; they'll be sure to catch it." Unable to resist, the teacher admitted the two students, only to relent many more times to similar appeals.[4] African American Charlotte Forten reported that eager parents urged her to help their children: "Do, Miss, let de chi'en learn ebery-ting dey can. We nebber hab no chance to learn nuttin', but we wants de chil'en to learn." Parents, she said, willingly sacrificed so that their children could attend school.[5] One teacher similarly reported, "nearly all [parents] are awake to the possibility of *their children* becoming 'something.' "[6]

Some young people also understood education as a valuable commodity. Students pushed two teachers at the Stoney Plantation on Hilton Head Island, South Carolina, to open the school doors earlier than planned. Actually, there were no school doors for there was no school building on the plantation; classes met on the twelve-foot-wide piazza that surrounded three sides of the large house in which the teachers lived. Although classes were scheduled to begin at nine o'clock, children began arriving at half past six in the morning, before the teachers had even finished their breakfast. Teacher E. B. Eveleth observed that it was "really a pleasant sight to see them flocking toward the house from all directions." With over one hundred students waiting, the two women started school at eight o'clock. One of them commented that the "enthusiasm of the children to learn is intense. Their school-hours seem like one bright holiday, and their progress is remarkable."[7]

For all their zeal, African Americans contended with a host of oppositional forces when they attempted to attend school. Ardor vied with material insufficiency; hope struggled against intractable hostility; and self-confidence and ambition wrestled with historical perceptions of African Americans as socially degraded and intellectually deficient. Poverty was by far the most immediate and the most salient factor that threatened to thwart the educational effort. Still, thousands of freedpeople believed that becoming literate would potentially open up access to the riches of American society, and therefore many obstinately made education a priority despite the limitations of poverty. An AMA employee in Beaufort, North Carolina, advised the organization that it needed to add a thousand more teachers to its staff because freedpeople flooded him and other missionaries with applications for books and teachers. "All around us the Freedmen are struggling hard against poverty, some against actual starvation, yet they beg harder for school than for food or clothing," he observed.[8] John Alvord was similarly impressed by freedpeople's insistence on education despite their dire material conditions. The war had barely ended, he observed, southern society was still disorganized, "and yet here is a people long imbruted by slavery, and the most despised of any on earth, whose chains are no sooner broken that they spring to their feet and start up an exceeding great army, clothing themselves in intelligence. What other people on earth have ever shown, while in their ignorance, such a passion for education?"[9]

Having escaped slavery with few or no possessions, children who crowded into schools in Beaufort, North Carolina, Norfolk, Virginia, and numerous other towns and villages did so despite enormous obstacles. For example, they often went to school wearing torn or outgrown clothing. Of course some children were better off. Those whose parents were self-employed or whose fathers sent military pay home fared better than those whose families survived on rations or received low wages for work on plantations. For the most part, however, freedpeople struggled to find enough money to pay exorbitant rents, buy food and clothing, and meet medical expenses. As a measure of the standard of living, one northerner observed that in Newport News, Virginia, three freedmen who owned a cart, a mule, and a few pigs were considered rich, great men. Those who still had a little cornmeal and pork were considered well off.[10] A missionary in Wilmington, North, Carolina, described freedpeople's wages as "extortionate and distressing." Another, writing from Raleigh, described the freedpeople as living "from hand to mouth" and wanting for the very necessities of life. Some plantation hands received less than ten dollars per month. For some, precarious economic conditions were made worse by crop failures or by planters who fired them for organizing fellow workers or for participating in political activity. Many were victims of fraud, plain and simple. Planters drew up unreasonable contracts that workers could not understand. In many places, after a full year of work, planters turned workers away with no financial compensation.[11]

With such extreme levels of poverty, harsh winters in uninsulated homes or outbreaks of epidemics such as smallpox put even more pressure on already strained family finances. Parents and children who slept in wooden cabins with crevices that allowed cold winter temperatures to enter frequently suffered from pneumonia. As the teachers in Georgia attested, schoolhouses, too, were often flimsy, wooden structures that exposed children to the cold. And in the hot summer "sickness season," teachers and students alike became ill. In fact, many northern teachers closed schools and returned home from summer into early fall.[12] Under these conditions, physical nourishment and intellectual nourishment competed for scant resources. Sometimes the physical won out; sometimes the intellectual did. One student, when asked why he was not writing on his slate, told the teacher that he had sold his pencil for a piece of bread. His father had been ill all winter, and the family of nine had nothing to eat.[13] The contest ended differently when a ten-year-old girl in Charleston, South Carolina, chose to give up meals so that her grandmother's limited funds could pay school fees.[14]

Children like this boy and girl often arrived in school barefoot, wearing torn, ragged clothing. While enslaved, they had likely been inadequately clothed, and for many, matters got even worse during the war and in its immediate aftermath. Although there was some variation among antebellum slaves with regard to urban or rural locale, economic status, or treatment by owners, for the most part slaves owned very few garments.[15] On some large plantations slave owners issued annual or biannual rations of clothing for adults and children. Not yet fully productive laborers, children received fewer items of clothing than did adolescents and adults. For many boys and girls, the annual clothing issue consisted of one or two loose-fitting shifts cut from rough, undyed osnaburg, also called "Negro cloth," or equally coarse home-spun fabric that resembled burlap. Children frequently went naked when the annually dispensed clothing wore out. Some enslaved people also received a coat and a wool hat to last for two to three years. Shoes, when provided, consisted of "Negro brogans"—uncomfortable pieces of rawhide tacked onto a wooden or heavy leather sole and shaped like a club so that either the left or right foot could fit into the shoe. Many children received no shoes at all.[16]

Following emancipation some children went to school in the remnants of clothing they had already worn for a year or more. A teacher in South Carolina wrote north that "some of the children had been to school in ragged garments for a long time, and some of these, not having any proper fastenings, were *sewed* together in front." One of her students arrived at school wearing one boot and one shoe that he had picked up in the street. He had never owned a pair of shoes before in his fourteen years.[17] Teachers in Raleigh, North Carolina, reported "that a boy, who walks four miles to school, stays at home three days in the week to lend his shoes to his sister, so that she also may learn."[18] One teacher noted that children came to school barefooted when there was ice on the roads, in clothing that was so "worn and scant" that it offered no protection against wind and rain.[19]

Contemporary photographs depict enslaved or recently freed boys wearing ragged, ill-fitting clothing. One set of "before and after" photographs demonstrate a boy's transformation from an enslaved child working as a servant in the Confederate army to uniformed young man, serving as a drummer in a regiment of the United States Colored Troops. In the "before" photograph, the boy, Jackson, who appears to be between twelve and fourteen years of age, wears a shirt so shredded from wear that he could not possibly put it back on if he removed it. The right side of his chest is fully visible because an entire panel of the shirt has torn away. His pants end above his ankles. They are patched in some areas, torn in others, and threadbare in still others. In another image, the photographer seems to have surprised three boys as they walked through a wooded area. A twelve- or thirteen-year-old, the eldest of the three, carries a four- or five-year-old on his back. The third boy is about nine years old. The right pant leg of this last boy stops just below the knee, and the left leg is rolled up to match. He is wearing a jacket and a shirt, both of which are stained and torn. Shreds of cloth hang from the sleeves of his jacket. The older boy's clothing is in considerably better shape. Although his pants stop several inches above his ankles, they are in one piece. He wears suspenders over his long-sleeved, button-down shirt. The small boy's clothing is barely visible in the photograph. He wears a shirt under a jacket. It is not summer: the trees are bare; the two younger boys are wearing at least two layers of clothing; and all of the boys wear cloth or leather hats pulled snuggly over their heads. Yet, all three are barefoot.

While many children went to school in torn, dirty, or outgrown clothing, others remained at home precisely because they were inadequately clothed. One teacher surmised that many more children would attend his Sabbath school, which already had three hundred students, "if they could *fix up*, so as to look as neat as 'other people's children.'" Another intimated that warmth was more important to the freedpeople than appearance when he guessed that while hundreds of children already attended school, there were "one hundred children and adults who would be in the school if they had clothing sufficient to protect them." In Lynchburg, Virginia, school attendance fell off dramatically because the roads leading to the schoolhouse were in bad condition. It had also snowed, and according to the teacher, "insufficient supply of clothing prevents many from attending."[20]

Jackson as a slave and then as a drummer in the Union army. Courtesy Massachusetts Commandery, Military Order of the Loyal Legion and the U.S. Army Military History Institute.

Three boys. Courtesy Valentine Richmond History Center.

In contrast to these descriptions of children in shreds of clothing, Georgia Telfair was fortunate enough to have more than one homespun dress long enough to keep her legs warm in the winter. Sara Stanley had many students who dressed as well as Telfair. She commented on the "general cleanliness and appearance" of most of the students who attended her school in the church basement in St. Louis, Missouri. "The girls," she wrote, "come daily to school attired in neat print dresses and shaker hoods; the boys in garments, if patched, yet scrupulously clean." Many of the children who had been free before the war dressed as well as any children Stanley had seen in the North.[21] A Freedmen's Bureau Assistant Commissioner of Education reported that of the 180 students he saw in three schools in Tallahassee, only a single child did not have comfortable clothing, stockings, and shoes.[22]

Photographs also depict better-dressed children. A formally posed photograph taken at Laura Towne's Penn School on St. Helena's Island depicts five boys all dressed up. They have obviously been coiffed and polished for this shot. Despite the care given to their appearance, and perhaps because of that attention, their clothing nevertheless calls attention to their economic status. They seem to be overly dressed, in clothing that looks borrowed for the occasion. One child's jacket, though clean and in one piece, is too short and barely buttons across his chest. In fact, all the boys in the front row are wearing jackets that appear to be too short, and possibly too tight. Both older boys in the back row wear bow ties. The boys in front are wearing shoes.[23]

Wearing uncomfortable hand-me-downs, shivering in clothing that provided little protection from winter winds, or neatly dressed in carefully made dresses with matching bonnets, many African American children made their way to schools on plantations and in towns. Wearing matching shoes, mismatched boot and shoe, or barefooted, these children frequently walked long distances to get there. This was particularly the case in rural areas where a school on one plantation might draw children from several distant plantations. When Laura Towne ordered a bell for her school on St. Helena Island, she had to settle for one large enough to be heard three miles away, as she did not imagine that any bell could be heard from five or six miles away on the more distant plantations from which some of her students came to school each day.[24] Some students and parents devised methods to reduce the onerous walk to school and back home. In Hallettsville, Texas, for example, although some students walked distances of three to eight miles to get to school each day, those who lived farthest out in the country remained in town on weeknights. Likewise, in Oxford, North Carolina, students from as far as fifteen miles away stayed over during the week.[25]

The reward for such long journeys had to be significant indeed. For some, particularly adults, it lay in the promise that they would soon be able to read the Bible for themselves. Others wanted to be able to decipher contracts or leases and thus protect themselves from unscrupulous employers and landlords. For some children, of course, parental insistence provided the only impetus, while others were propelled by an intense personal desire to become literate. For some adults and youth, the motivation to trudge along muddy country roads or roads baked hard under their feet by the blazing sun lay in

Schoolboys at Laura Towne's Penn School, St. Helena Island, South Carolina. Courtesy Photographs and Prints Division, Schomburg Center for Research in Black Culture, The New York Public Library, Astor, Lenox and Tilden Foundations.

the hope that they would become literate enough to one day walk away from plantation life and its labors altogether.

As much as education was a priority, attending school was nevertheless a luxury that many freed children could only afford to indulge in for brief stints—when they were not needed to plant and harvest crops, to deliver clothes for mothers who took in washing, to gather wood, to catch crabs for dinner, to do domestic work for whites, or to care for siblings while parents worked. Missionary teachers generally kept schools open from October to May, but students often left during that time to go to work.[26] One teacher commented that "in the spring, every available hand is at work hoeing in the cotton fields. Little children, hardly big enough to 'pick up chips,' are flinging the heavy grubbing hoe with a will, all through the long, hot days."[27] Teachers in Alabama and Georgia reported that enrollments fell in March, April, and May, when older students left school to assist parents with planting. In October, as soon as school got underway, these students left again to harvest cotton.[28] Students left one Tennessee school in November to sow wheat."[29]

Brief exposure to freedpeople's schools might be the only opportunity in a lifetime to learn to read and write. Many former students recalled that they left school for good after short periods of attendance. John Harris attended school for three months each year until his mother hired him out in order to add twelve dollars to the family's annual income.[30] A woman identified only as Mandy was able to calculate the precise amount of time she spent in school: "I had three months a year for three years, and a extra month once that my mammy paid for. Dat make ten months for me I was de forwadest chile my mammy had," she boasted. "When dey was any reading to do my mammy sent for me."[31] Frank Wise attended school for about eight days, and Hannah Brooks Wright went for a week before her parents put her "in the field to plow." According to Wright, her father reasoned that he had to teach her how to work because he would not always be able to take care of her. Carrie Lucas left school in Manassas, Virginia, at the age of eleven to "nurse" a deaf-mute child in a white family in Baltimore, Maryland.[32]

White hostility could also impede school attendance. African American schoolchildren were often targets of racial violence. In many locations, stoning was the preferred method of attack employed by angry white children who resented the idea of black children attending school.[33] Samuel Spottford Clement recalled attending a summer school for freedpeople in Campbell County, Virginia. On his five mile walk to school, he passed several white schools, and he recalled, "it was almost like passing a lot of lions as the boys would beat and thump me and throw rocks as long as they could see me." His mother removed him from the school after only two months because of the attacks. Colonel Douglass Wilson, former slave and Civil War veteran, was a parent of children who attended school in New Orleans in 1866. "When we sent our children to school in the morning," he told an interviewer, "we had no idea that we should see them return home alive in the evening. Big white boys and half-grown men used to pelt them with stones and run them down with open knives, both to and from school. Sometimes they came home bruised, stabbed, beaten half to death, and sometimes quite dead." Wilson compared his own experiences fighting in the Civil War to the battle that children sometimes fought simply trying to get to school. "My own son himself was often thus beaten. He has on his forehead to-day a scar over his right eye which sadly tells the story of his trying experience in those days in his efforts to get an education. I was wounded in the war, trying to get my freedom, and he over the eye, trying to get an education. So we both call our scars marks of honor."[34]

Because the opportunity to attend school was so limited and so prized, students and parents discriminated among schools and teachers, choosing the ones they thought could best meet their educational goals. When a Georgia Freedmen's Bureau employee filed a monthly teacher's report for a failing school, he noted that the teacher, John Compton, "has had very little experience in teaching, and is a person of very limited culture. To this I think may be attributed part of the lack of interest manifested by the freedpeople."[35] At Natchez, Mississippi, the AMA noted that for a time, several missionary associations carried on an intense competition to attract students. With a surplus of teachers, freedpeople had the liberty of choosing which schools they would attend, and "not a few of the colored people came to think it a condescension on their part to patronize any [particular] school." Competition having driven all the other associations away, finally, freedpeople had no choice but to attend AMA schools.[36] When they had no choice, freedpeople sent their children to schools with minimally competent teachers. Given a choice, they exercised it.

On St. Helena Island, teacher Laura Towne claimed that students refused to attend a school that a Mrs. Wells taught because her school hours were so irregular. The students complained that after they had slogged across the creek to get to her school, Wells was often not prepared to teach them. Further, when she did hold class, she gave only abbreviated reading lessons; they wanted to learn writing and arithmetic as well. Students also refused to attend a school held by a Miss Ruggles on similar grounds. Sometimes class met for a week or two, they told Towne, then closed for a week or two. The students complained, too, that Miss Ruggles did not have copy books or slates for them to practice writing.[37]

Students pressed teachers far more dedicated and reliable than Ruggles and Wells to provide them with increased time in the classroom. They sometimes refused to leave school at closing time and appealed for shorter vacations. A teacher in Charleston contrasted her southern students' "appreciation of school privileges" with the indifference of students she had taught in the North. She reported that at the start of Christmas holidays, one of her students requested a shorter vacation, and another urged, "We want a few days, but not long. We like to read." Parents also testified to children's eagerness for school: "They needs no driving; they is always talkin' about their teacher."[38] When the school at Taylor Farm near Norfolk, Virginia, closed for summer vacation at the end of July, the teacher reported that several students came to her in tears and said, "Now, Miss Dodd, you ought not to stop school, for we are just beginning to learn."[39] As one teacher put it, freed children "appreciate their past deprivations, and present advantages, and mean to make the most of it."[40]

Students requested shorter summer vacations because they knew that teachers who went north to escape the heat and disease of the southern summer might not return. Those who did return generally did so in October, at just the time when families needed children to harvest crops. A teacher in Dallas County, Alabama, expressed what students and their parents likely thought when he told the Freedmen's Bureau, "I believe that if July, August and September were used as school months, in place of December, January and February, the colored children would be benefited, as they have more leasure [sic] time at that season."[41]

Both to thank them for teaching and to induce them to teach some more, parents and children plied teachers with gifts of eggs, flowers, bunches of holly, fruit, groundnuts, peas, rice, sweet potatoes, candy, and cake—all this in addition to paying tuition.[42] At Christmastime in 1865, a father gave two chickens to his son's teacher, saying, "I don't pay anything for my children's schooling, and I have the chickens to spare. It would give me pleasure to do a little, and show I thanks the people who provides school for us."[43] When Elijah Marrs started a school in New Castle, Kentucky, the people greeted him and his wife with enough meat, sugar, coffee, and other foodstuffs to last them three months. The community hoped to induce Marrs not to return to La Grange where he had taught before coming to New Castle. Laura Towne was certain that the eggs and chickens the local freedpeople frequently offered her and other teachers were meant to guarantee their continued service.[44]

The walk to school could span a cultural gap between North and South, black and white, between the playful freedom of childhood and the discipline of sitting quietly in a classroom, between furtively studying a smuggled spelling book and openly, loudly declaiming from a *Freedman's Spelling Book*, "The

Proclamation of Emancipation was a notification of freedom to millions. The administration of President Lincoln will always be remembered by it."[45] When they entered a missionary classroom, many African American children encountered northerners for the first time. A black, northern teacher may have been the first middle-class African American a recently freed child had ever seen. Students must have been transfixed by this person who in some ways resembled their own parents, but who in dress, behavior, and speech was vastly different. A white missionary teacher could stir up mixed and disquieting feelings as well. The white people in these students' lives had been owners, overseers, and more recently Confederate and Union soldiers—all of them figures of authority, even severity. To some students, the white teacher might not have appeared much different. Interacting with a white adult in the classroom would at least have been a novel—if not mystifying—experience.

Moreover, it was difficult for students to understand northern accents and expressions. At the same time, New England teachers were often baffled when trying to decipher the language of a Gullah- or Creole-speaking student. Laura Towne recalled that when she first arrived in South Carolina, the students "evidently did not understand me, and I could not understand them, and after two hours and a half of effort I was thoroughly exhausted."[46] African American teacher Edmonia Highgate used what little French she knew to help teach her French-Creole students in Louisiana.[47]

Some students were quick to exploit what they perceived as a teacher's weakness. Wayman Williams, who attended a school in Texas, recalled taking advantage of the communication and cultural gulf between southern black children and white northern teachers. "Some white school teachers from up North come to teach de chillen," Williams recounted, "but dey didn't talk like folks here and didn't understand our talk. Dey didn't know what us mean when us say 'titty' for sister, and 'brudder' for brother, and 'nanny' for mammy. Jes' fer fun us call ourselves big names to de teacher, some be named General Lee and some Stonewall Jackson. We be one name one day and 'nother name next day. Until she git to know us she couldn't tell de difference 'cause us all look alike to her." Students also capitalized on the teacher's unfamiliarity with their culture. As Williams remembered, "Us have good times tellin 'bout black magic and de conjure. Us tell her night birds full of magic and dere feathers roast in ashes work spells what kills evil conjure. De teacher from the North don't know what to think of all dat. But our missy, who live here all de time, know all 'bout it. She lets us believe our magic and conjure, 'cause she partly believe it too."[48] Williams and his classmates understood that, culturally, they had more in common with the white woman who had owned them than with the white woman from the North.

Adjusting to this new experience was clearly a two-way street. Even more than they remarked on the condition of schools or on freedpeople's dress, white northern teachers and ministers commented on their students' intelligence. Both implicitly and explicitly, these comments reflected the fact that although many northern missionaries and teachers had been committed to freedom for African Americans, they also believed that black people were intellectually inferior to whites. Many admitted to being shocked by how quickly students learned, not only because it undermined notions of racial inferiority, but also because it challenged the idea that slavery had so degraded blacks into a sort of benumbed mass. White northern teachers had come expecting it to take a very long time—a generation, perhaps—to unlock whatever intellect lay in the former slaves. They were amazed when children and adults learned quickly. Their correspondence and reports are replete with references to freedpeople exceeding long-held expectations of limited intellect.

Martha Kellog, for example, wrote from Hilton Head Island, South Carolina, that her eighty students, who ranged in age from five to fifty years old, "differ like others in mental capacity—but when their degradation is remembered—their success seems almost wonderful, and as a people, they are much more intelligent than I supposed."[49] From Missouri, Margaret Stalker wrote that she had never "had scholars advance more rapidly, and they are governed more easily than I anticipated."[50] From Virginia, Reverend J. B. Lowery wrote that the freedpeople "are not as degraded as I expected to find them. They are quite intelligent naturally." He buttressed his own conclusion with the opinion of a white southerner, who, he intimated, not only knew African Americans better than he, but would also be expected to think little of them. According to Lowery, this "pro-slavery man here, very much prejudiced against the African race, declares that, if there was any difference, so far as mind is concerned, between the colored population here and the native Virginians, the advantage is on the side of the colored people." And, Thomas Whitby confessed that the progress of his school "surpassed my most sanguine expectations."[51]

Frank H. Greene, a teacher in Baton Rouge, Louisiana, issued a challenge to those who doubted black intellectual capacity: "If any one thinks that the *negro* is not capable of being educated, let him visit any one of the schools in this Department, and I think he will be convinced that the color of the skin does not affect the mental capacity." To further sustain his assertion, Greene made a comparison that he knew would be meaningful to his readers in the northern states. "I have as intelligent children in my school," he wrote, "as I ever saw anywhere in the North. I never saw children show greater eagerness for learning."[52] A teacher in Norfolk, Virginia, was also glad to bear "testimony to [the freedpeople's] intelligence and capacity." She compared black southern children to the children with whom she was familiar from the "lower classes" of England and Ireland. She believed the black children were equal to these, and far superior to the children from agricultural areas in England. "I notice, too," she added, "that the mistakes they make are exactly the same as I have heard all my life from white children."[53]

Some teachers balanced their enthusiasm regarding this rapid progress by noting that not all children learned at the same remarkable pace. Mrs. A. T. Howard in Maryland informed her sponsors, "Many of my pupils are making marked progress, others are doing very well. There are, of course, some drones to be found in all hives; the more industrious present a good example for them to follow." Likewise, T. M. Kennedy reported from Clayton, Alabama, that while some students "show a disposition to learn and will be benefited—others as yet have made but little progress."[54]

Charlotte Forten folded her assessment of southern African American intellect into a tirade against presumed white superiority as well as white hypocrisy. Among her students, she said, there were of course "some stupid ones," but these were the minority. In her experience, most of the children in her St. Helena Island school learned quickly, and she was impressed that a large number of "grown people" also wanted to learn to read. "It is wonderful," Forten remarked, "how a people who have been so long crushed to the earth, so imbruted as these have been can have so great a desire for knowledge, and such a capability for attaining it." In this sentiment she kept company with many fellow northern teachers. As she continued, however, her criticism may have appeared harsh to well-meaning white colleagues. "One cannot believe that the haughty Anglo-Saxon race," she wrote for publication, "after centuries of such an experience as these people have had, would be very much superior to them. And one's indignation increases against those who, North as well as South, taunt the colored race with inferiority while they themselves use every means in their power to crush and degrade them, denying them every right and privilege, closing against them every avenue of elevation and improvement."[55]

Sara Stanley at first found marked intellectual differences between the freed children whom she taught in Virginia and St. Louis and the ones she taught in the basement of the Colored Methodist Church in Louisville, Kentucky. Whereas in St. Louis she was "encouraged by the interest manifested" by her students, in Louisville she thought her students suffered from "excessive dullness." She told the AMA, "There is but little of that quickness in learning, that ready comprehension of ideas, that facility of acquisition which I have almost invariably found in the schools of Freedmen with which I have previously been connected. They manifest a familiar eagerness to learn but the acquisition of knowledge is with them a slow and laborious process." Stanley believed this contrast was due to a lack of exposure to schooling in Louisville.[56] Within two months, however, she was complimenting her students and herself for their advancement. She had received school supplies, such as maps, globes, and charts, and reported that several visitors, including some former Confederates, praised the "decorum and general proficiency" of the school.[57] She was pleased when her students passed examinations in history, geometry, grammar, and arithmetic at the end of the school year. After a month of review, she wrote, her students had "become so thoroughly familiar with the branches pursued as to cause the knowledge acquired to seem a part of themselves, and capable of practical application in everyday life: they have learned to have confidence in their own powers and properly to estimate their capability for improvement."[58] Stanley's "dull" students needed only the skills of an experienced teacher. She, in turn, seemed particularly pleased with the confidence they had gained in their own abilities.

Missionary organizations that sponsored northern teachers in the South received hundreds of letters attesting to the rapidity with which black students learned. Apparently convinced of black intelligence, the AMA sought data that might lead to a more fine-tuned assessment. The association asked teachers to respond to the following question: "Do the mulattoes show any more capacity than the blacks?" The wording of the question begs to be interrogated: What did the AMA mean by "capacity"? What did the organization think it meant to be "mulatto" as opposed to "black"? Did the question seek to get at social factors that might have affected how black children learned in comparison to mulatto children? The AMA did not specify its intentions; however, the question's wording renders transparent some of the association's presumptions. The organization did not ask, for example, if black students showed any more "capacity" than mulattoes because the AMA did not consider that a possibility. It did not ask if children who were free before the war had any more skills than newly freed children. It also did not ask if mulatto children arrived in school with more preparation or exposure to literacy than black children. Instead, the question asked about capacity, or ability—something that the AMA linked directly to race. It was perfectly conceivable to these abolitionists that mulattoes, by virtue of being partially white, would have a higher capacity to learn.

Although scientific notions of black inferiority had held sway in intellectual circles since the 1840s, the AMA's presumptions were not an inevitable consequence of contemporary ethnological thinking about race. The organization might have taken the tack of the Emancipation League, for example, which, in a survey sent to superintendents of contrabands, asked the following questions regarding freedpeople's intellectual abilities: "What are the facts as to their capacity and desire to learn? How many could read when they first came within our lines? How many can read now? How does their capacity to learn compare with that of others in similar ignorance, and with the same means of education?" These questions based potential distinctions on social and economic conditions rather than on race.[59]

Indeed, some of the AMA's own teachers found it more useful to compare students who had been free before the war to those who had only recently become free, than to make comparisons based on race. Francis Cardozo, the African American principal of the Saxton School in Charleston, acknowledged the existence of racial groupings, noting that large numbers of the students were "pure Africans," but he chose a different category of assessment. Half of the students were freeborn; the other half had been slaves. Cardozo could find "no difference in the capacity of *freemen* and *freedmen*; indeed the difference between them would not be known if it were not for the more advanced condition of the former on account of previous advantages." In other words, Cardozo linked any greater knowledge by free people to their earlier academic advantage. He did not speak in terms of racial distinctions such as mulatto or colored, but about prior status as slave or free. Likewise, A. Sumner, principal of the Morris Street School (also in Charleston), reported that half of his pupils were of "unmixed African blood" and 10 percent of the students were freeborn. Sumner did not distinguish between the capacity of the mixed and unmixed students; instead, he based his observations on their former legal status. He found it interesting that among the most distinguished scholars in the most advanced classes, "those who were formerly slaves rank equally well with those who were free and had received some instruction before and during the war."[60]

In response to the AMA's question as to whether mulattoes showed greater capacity than blacks, many teachers simply replied, "They do not." Others made more extensive comments. Palmer Litts, teaching at Fortress Monroe, Virginia, admitted that experience had challenged his own preconceptions that blacks were less intelligent than whites. "I must frankly say," he wrote, "that their rapid progress has entirely robbed me of the vague idea of the inability of the colored race to become an educated people." His experiences also challenged the notion, implied in the AMA's query, that mixed-race freedpeople learned more quickly than others. "The question is often asked, do you find those who are partially white, more apt to learn?" Litts thought it a difficult question to answer scientifically because, in his estimation, so few of the freedpeople were unmixed Africans. Even so, he wrote, "I can say that some of the blackest are among those who make the most rapid progress." He further offered some examples from among his students to rebut any belief that mixed-race people were more intelligent. One boy and girl, "as much African as any in my school," had rapidly learned the alphabet and were quickly progressing through the first reader. "These cases," Litts insisted, "can by no means be called isolated ones, as I have heard other teachers speak of the same aptness in their pupils."[61]

If white teachers denied that skin color affected intelligence, they were nonetheless very much aware of their students' complexions. Teachers referred to the "dusky faces and glistening eyes" of their students.[62] Their words sometimes betrayed prejudice and condescension, as when Lydia Hess, from St. Louis, Missouri, commented that the "schollars meet me at the door with bright eyes and smiling faces which make them look very attractive to my eyes, although they are very black and many times not as clean as I would wish to see, although they are improving rapidly in that respect as well as in others."[63] Mary F. Root wrote of her students in a plantation school in Beaufort, South Carolina, "A pretty class of little boys and girls they are too, *though* their heads are wool, and their faces more or less dark. I don't see the difference between them and so many white children in school, except that the older ones learn faster, because they try so earnestly."[64] Some teachers found the children who were nearly white far more attractive than darker ones. In her early days in Beaufort, Laura Towne, drawing on her medical background, used the language of eugenics and phrenology to describe and compare students. Noting that there were several very light children at the schools, she singled out one boy with straight hair, whose "remarkably developed" head reminded her of Andrew Jackson. She contrasted the presidential look-alike with most of the other children, who were "the real bullet-headed negroes."[65] Three teachers writing from Raleigh about their students' exhibition at the end of the school year remarked, "The pupils were tastefully dressed in white, with wreaths of flowers, and as the Anglo-Saxon blood predominates in many of them, were by no means unattractive in appearance. They went through the recitations and dialogues and declamations with great credit to themselves."[66]

Dedicated as they were to teaching former slaves, northern white teachers carried with them deeply internalized beliefs of racial hierarchy based on skin color. Some teachers empathized with light-skinned, mixed-race children who had been enslaved. Slavery seemed to them an even more grievous offense when the victims were nearly white. In Little Rock, Joanna Moore, an Indiana Quaker, and another teacher "went to the Home Farm and gathered up 18 little ones from the dark, filthy hovels of ignorance and want, brought them home, and after considerable scrubbing, washing, shearing, and combing, they looked nice and clean and *black*, all except one who *would* be white, do our best." This child, she wrote, "has pretty blue eyes, straight light hair, and very white skin. Poor, unfortunate child! He must still endure the withering blight of slavery."[67] Although as a Quaker Moore would have strongly opposed the enslavement of African Americans, she nonetheless harbored a sense that enslavement of a white person was even more reprehensible, thus enabling her to single out the young boy with blue eyes, straight light hair, and very white skin for special compassion. AMA minister David Todd also expressed empathy with visibly mixed-raced people. He wrote from Pine Bluff, Arkansas, "I confidently believe in my school, the blacks are intellectually equal to the mulattoes." However, Todd confessed that he looked with a "kind of extra pity on those partly white." He, admittedly, loved them more.[68]

Some northern white teachers went beyond empathy; they singled out light-skinned blacks for special access to limited higher education. By so doing, teachers made critical choices about who should enter the middle class, thus helping to shore up and exacerbate racially tinged socioeconomic hierarchies that already existed within freed communities. When, for example, Mary S. Battey wrote to the AMA that "some cases in the day school are worthy of mention," she chose two children of mixed-race for comment. The first, a fourteen-year-old girl, had only recently learned the alphabet but had already advanced to the second reader. She was doing arithmetic and could write quite legibly. Battey endorsed this student's ambition to become a teacher and was already working to make it a reality. The Freedmen's Bureau, she wrote, had agreed to pay for the student's transportation to a normal school if a donor from the North would pay for her education. Immediately after requesting financial support, Battey hastened to add that the student is "nearly a quadroon, her father being a *professional* man of the vicinity." Battey's second case worthy of mention was also a mulatto girl who had made rapid progress. The very mention of these students' racial composition suggests that Battey considered their mixed heritage appealing to white northern sponsors. By highlighting these particular students, Battey hoped to attract the attention of benefactors who might underwrite the students' advanced education.[69] Similarly, when teacher Carrie L. Guild recommended Leafy Jackson for admission to Hampton Institute, she described her as a "most deserving girl and very promising." She also pointed out that "Leafy is nearly white," very much like her sister Eliza, who was already a student at Hampton.[70]

When white northern Freedmen's Bureau agent John De Forest wrote to the American Freedmen's Union Commission to urge the organization to continue supporting a school in Greenville, South Carolina, he reported: "I have just visited the school. I assure you that it is an extremely interesting sight, whether considered as a moral or intellectual, or even physical spectacle. There is good order, eagerness to learn, rapid progress in learning, and there is a great deal more. There is such a new hope in their childish faces, such a sunrise of difference of expression between them and the densely ignorant men and women of their race, such a near possibility of moral elevation, that failure would be shocking." De Forest obviously did not think highly of the intellect of African Americans, and he was just becoming convinced of their humanity. Yet he, too, made special mention of the light-skinned children. He was enthralled with them and seemed to suggest that their presence in the school made it particularly worthy of support: "I have seen such bright eyes and sweet looks that I longed to get the portraits of some of them to send North. Then, too, my own race—the blood of the Caucasian—appealed to my sympathy. Boys and girls with rosy cheeks, blue eyes, auburn and flaxen hair, persons whiter than myself, though lately slaves, were mingled with the black and brown faces. Can nothing be done for them? Must they stop learning and thus lose their only ladder?" De Forest may have included the black and brown children in his appeal, but it was those with the rosy cheeks and flaxen hair that fueled his passion for the continued support of the school.[71]

Darker-skinned students noticed and resented their teachers' biases and preferential treatment. London Ferebee and thirty-four other young men attended a normal school in North Carolina to prepare for admission to Howard University. They needed financial assistance from northerners to make advanced education a reality, but, Ferebee complained, their teacher, a white man from New York City, focused his fund-raising efforts on three of the students because of their complexion. "Prof. Cardozo only appeared to look out for those of a light hue, or mulatto—none of the dark ones could get any assistance," Ferebee recalled.[72]

Even when mixed-race and dark-skinned students started school with similar backgrounds of servitude and poverty, some lighter-skinned children acquired an advantage from teachers' preferences. Some white northern teachers caught glimpses of themselves in light-skinned mulatto children's eyes and were saddened and appalled that people who so closely resembled themselves could have been reduced to bondage. Teachers imagined these children as doubly oppressed because, although almost white, they had been denied the privileges of whiteness. When teachers mentioned a student's light skin color, they counted on stimulating similar feelings of empathy within white northerners who could fund that student's education and thus help him or her to climb that ladder out of poverty. In the antebellum South white slave owners had similarly provided enslaved mulatto men enhanced opportunities to become skilled workers. The men then passed these skills down to their sons, thus in the minds of southern white elites naturalizing a correlation between skin color and proficiency. In the aftermath of slavery, white northern teachers, who claimed a higher degree of enlightenment than white southerners, replicated antebellum practices when they singled out light-skinned mulatto students for special privileges and thus perpetuated hierarchies of color.[73]

African American students encountered still another challenge to their intellect, one that students considered mulatto and black both faced: some white northerners marveled at their elementary scholastic aptitude but wondered about their capacity for higher-order thinking. Augustus Stickler, a teacher in Arkansas, reported, for example, that more than one hundred of his students had learned the alphabet in one month. "I never saw people learn so fast," he exclaimed. "It generally took me three months to teach white children what these will learn in ten or fifteen days. But I am satisfied the difference is caused by more intense application. How far in the higher branches this will continue to be the case experience must determine."[74]

Stickler's concern as to whether the freedpeople would continue to master their studies as they progressed into the higher levels of material, however, was rather unusual. Most missionary teachers, according to their letters and reports, rarely considered the issue. Such questions were raised more frequently by northern white men who heard of or witnessed the rapid progress that some students made, yet who sought to impose limits on these students' intellectual potential. Mathematics was particularly troublesome for those who thought African American intellect had limits. Teacher M. E. Watson heard this concern expressed frequently enough to prompt her to write disdainfully of the "oft repeated assertion of the incapacity of the negro to acquire a knowledge of arithmetic." She was particularly pleased when white Marylanders who attended a public examination of her students were impressed with the manner in which even young children excelled at arithmetic.[75]

Even John Alvord, advocate for freedpeople's education, suspected that black people were innately inferior to whites. Early in his tenure as Superintendent of Freedmen's Education, Alvord questioned how quickly African Americans would be able to grasp higher intellectual skills, though he seemed to believe they eventually would. Despite his observations that the majority of black children exhibited the "same brightness, the same quick ambition as with children of the more favored color," Alvord found it difficult to believe unequivocally in continued academic advancement by black students. He held on to the notion that their race would somehow impede their intellectual development. "It is probable that the tastes and temperament of the race, which are peculiar, certainly, will lead in special directions. They may not at first excel in the inventive power, or abstract science, perhaps not in mathematics, though we have seen very commendable ciphering in the colored schools," Alvord offered. "But they certainly are emotional, imitative, and affectionate; are graphic and figurative in language; have conceptions of beauty and song, and already become teachers, skilled mechanics and even artists." Alvord had difficulty reconciling objective observations with long-held expectations about characteristics thought to be essentially black. He concluded that, on balance, there was nothing to keep African Americans from adding "important elements to the more perfect civilization of the coming time." Nevertheless, Alvord suspected, the elements that African Americans contributed would be racially based and reflect peculiarly African American characteristics.[76]

John Alvord and other white missionary men from northern states may have been avid abolitionists or at the least antislavery men, yet their tendency to believe that African Americans did not measure up intellectually to Europeans and Americans of European descent had deep roots in an American ethnological movement that had been used to shore up proslavery arguments in the 1840s and 1850s. The missionaries' willingness to believe in limited black intellectual capacity was certainly not as vicious as ethnologist Josiah Nott's assertion that African Americans could achieve no greater level of "civilization" than they had attained after one or two generations of "domestication" under slavery.[77] However, in the 1860s, as African Americans liberated themselves from slavery and established schools throughout the South, the questions, the arguments, and the doubts about black intellect that erstwhile white allies uttered had substantive consequences. These were the white men, who from positions of power endowed by their whiteness, their northern-ness, and their education would help to shape higher education in the South for African Americans. They would be influential in making the choices between liberal arts and agricultural training, between academic work and manual labor. Their unwillingness to acknowledge black intellectual equality with whites would have ramifications for many years to come.[78]

When students and teachers met, structural and cultural factors came together to produce potentially troublesome interactions. Any teacher had the challenge of creating order when children of varying ages, unfamiliar with school's rigid behavioral requirements, gathered in small, overcrowded classrooms. Teachers' language betrayed a struggle to gain control in the classroom. They spoke of teaching self-control, bringing students under proper discipline, establishing good order, subordinating students to the teachers' will, harnessing children who were otherwise too playful, and placing children under restraint.[79] William B. Cole, who taught with another black teacher, Livina Martin, in Macon, Georgia, spoke of "civilizing" the students. Cole informed the Freedmen's Bureau in a monthly report, "the Deportment of the pupil is very good at this time but Sir I will assure you that I had a pile of truble to sivilize them to order of sivilization. Sir I can safely say that I have as good order as can be expected for the time the school was organized."[80] This pedagogical desire to control the learning environment existed in any school setting.

Both children and teachers in freedpeople's schools faced additional challenges caused by the newness of this particular situation in which thousands of youngsters, many of them adolescents, found themselves. Caroline Walker Walton was so small when she started school that her feet could not reach the ground. She recalled falling out of her seat in the classroom more than once.[81] Caroline's seat, was probably a roughly hewn bench made by local freedpeople. It certainly had not been designed with the special needs of young children in mind. Laura Towne recalled that her first students on St. Helena Island "had no idea of sitting still, of giving attention, of ceasing to talk aloud." "They lay down and went to sleep, they scuffled and struck each other," she recalled; "They got up by the dozen, made their curtsies, and walked off to the neighboring field for blackberries, coming back to their seats with a curtsy when they were ready."[82] Another teacher confessed that some children "try our faith and patience," and Charlotte Forten was convinced that some of her youngest pupils had "discovered the secret of perpetual motion." The children to whom Forten referred were too young to learn the alphabet, but they accompanied older siblings to school, since it was the only way that the older children could attend.[83]

The inadequacy of the physical spaces in which schools were held contributed to the difficulty of maintaining order in the classroom. Maria King admitted that she and four assistants were having a hard time keeping as good order as they desired in the overcrowded church that served as the classroom for 145 students.[84] Sara Stanley understood that the lack of light and teaching equipment in her crowded, dark, subterranean classroom in St. Louis impinged on her students' ability to learn as well as on their behavior. "My experience in the classroom has taught me the subtile [sic], moral influence of material objects," she wrote. "Maps, globes, pictures, are disciplinary; the vase of fragrant flowers on the teacher[']s desk, the green foliage visible at the open window through which the sunshine pours its golden flood and the air comes purely and freshly, are more efficacious in preserving order, in calming turbulent spirits and keeping them attuned to the sweeter harmony of love, gentleness and truth, than any instrument of corporal punishment I have ever seen." Stanley's control over her students improved once she improvised better teaching tools.[85]

Sometimes teachers preferred to acknowledge disciplinary problems in the classroom only after they had been resolved.[86] A teacher in Wilmington, North Carolina, for example, hoped that he would not be adjudged vain for his pride in the great progress he reported from his school. "My school has reached a state of discipline," he wrote, "for which I had scarce a faint hope when three months since, I assumed the (so-called) *command* of the most chaotic mob of children ever misnamed a school." This teacher boasted that he had used the wisdom of Solomon to bring about discipline and take "command" of the classroom.[87] Teachers understandably preferred to reflect on challenges overcome, than to admit to having difficulty managing students in the classroom, as sponsors could easily consider any such admission an indication of weakness. As one tired teacher wrote, "I found my school very easily governed; all that was necessary to secure the most perfect attention on the part of the pupils, was perfect attention on the part of the teacher, and this was absolutely necessary."[88]

Teachers were further motivated to tell only of improvements out of fear that any negative remarks would fuel opposition to black education. A teacher in Norfolk hinted at this concern when she disclosed her most effective tool for obtaining good behavior in the classroom: "I can see a decided improvement in many as regards deportment," she wrote; "Their pride seems very easily touched in that respect, as you remind them that they are being watched by those who are not their friends."[89] Also concerned about southern whites' opinions, J. E. Lazenby was pleased with the "general good behavior" of his students in Bedford County, Virginia. It "commends itself to the approval of all, even the prejudiced," he thought. "This is peculiarly gratifying to me, and I am led to believe that a very favorable impression is being made." Several local teachers had visited and expressed their surprise "that negroes can be taught." Lazenby believed that his school was "creating a very general feeling in favor of public schools, and the prospect is not far that our land will soon be blessed with a general system of public instruction."[90] These teachers were concerned that their students should make a good impression on observant local whites looking for any reason to criticize. This, of course, burdened students not only with pleasing their teachers, but also convincing local whites that schooling was not wasted on them.

To keep control in classrooms, some teachers applied corporal punishment, a fairly common practice in schools both in the North and South.[91] A progressive movement begun in the 1840s, led by Horace Mann, Walt Whitman, and Lyman Cobb, encouraged more cerebral means for disciplining students. Whitman decried "the flogging plan" as the "most wretched item yet left of the ignorance and inefficiency of school-keeping."[92] Drawing on that movement, an 1865 article in the AMA's organ, *American Missionary*, adopted Enlightenment views of human perfectibility and urged teachers to use love to guide students. "The heart of a child is easily won," the article reasoned. "It needs no besieging, no formidable preparation for a grand assault, no advancing by regular approaches. You have only to go in the name of love and demand a surrender; and without parleying the prize is yours."[93] Some missionary organizations particularly objected to corporal punishment for children who had been enslaved and subjected to beatings by owners and overseers.[94]

Pronouncements against corporal punishment notwithstanding, teachers and students in freedpeople's schools revealed that both northern white teachers, local white teachers, and local black teachers used corporal punishment.[95] Laura Towne scornfully reported that the white southerners who taught black children in Beaufort, South Carolina, "whip the children in their school and make them call them 'massa' and 'missus,' as in the old time." Reverend S. G. Wright, an AMA teacher in Natchez, Mississippi, admitted that "the rod has only been used in extreme cases" in his school, and he claimed that the teachers in other local AMA schools had "discarded corporal punishment as far as possible."[96]

Some former students mentioned punishment as a matter of course, something to be expected in the exchange between teacher and student. Punishment might involve staying after school, public humiliation, or physical beatings. Neglect of school work, stubbornness, impudence, lateness, and talking in class could all trigger corporal punishment. Nancy Smith recalled that her teacher, a black man, was a strict taskmaster: "You had better know dem lessons, or you was gwine to get fanned out and have to stay in after school." Nellie Smith had a "Yankee man" as a teacher and was surprised to discover that the students had to do "something real bad to get a whippin', but when we talked or was late gettin' to school we had to stand up in the back of the schoolroom and hold up one hand."[97] Mary Ann Gibson was a good student with a supportive teacher, but even she did not escape punishment. According to Gibson, "I kin read and write. I went to school after slavery fo' three winter terms. De teachah, Isabella Shaw—a light colored woman, said dat I was swift. I learned fast. I never got no whoopins fo' not studying, but 'cause I was stubborn at times."[98] Aleck Trimble recalled being beaten by his white teacher for half a day because he could not spell the word "gangrene." "She whip me 'till I learn how to spell it and I ain't never forgit. I kin spell dat word yit."[99] Some students perceived teachers as always armed and ready to strike. Henry Hence Smith's teacher, a white man, "was [pretty] rough wid us chillun sometimes. He always carried a switch under his arm, and if a child acted ugly, he'd call him and make him roll up his pant's leg, and den whoop him across de knee."[100] Ninety-two-year-old William Smith remembered that his teacher, a white man from the North, "would watch us and if we talked too loud, he'd git us fo' it. If a boy didn't mind, dat teacher would make him stay after school, and make dat boy go and cut his own switch."[101]

Although some black parents encouraged teachers to use corporal punishment, teachers sometimes exceeded acceptable limits.[102] Mollie Hatfield recalled attending a school taught by a "white man named Lake, an ole Yankee what whipped me—jes tore my back all to pieces." Hatfield claimed that her mother complained to a colonel in the Union army who "made dat white man pay for beating me up." The beating must have been harsh indeed for Hatfield's mother and the colonel to take such steps.[103]

In lieu of corporal punishment, teachers implemented several strategies to punish students. Miss E. P. Bennett sent a boy home for a week and made several others stand on benches. She was proud that she was able to discipline the other students by appealing to reason.[104] Rebecca Primus, in Royal Oak, Maryland, reported: "I suspended two boys from school for fighting, one went home and received a severe whipping, and I've not yet learned what was bestowed upon the other." "As a general thing," she wrote, "my pupils behave very well, but now and then an evil spirit rises up among them and I introduce different methods of punishment to quell it." In this instance, the boy's mother relieved Primus from inflicting corporal punishment herself.[105] Esther Pinkney, an African American teacher in Washington, Georgia, also called in assistance to get some of her students under control. She had difficulty with some of her "large female pupils" and transferred them to a classroom "under the control of a male teacher."[106] And Hattie E. Sabattie, another African American teacher in Darien, Georgia, actually closed her school because there were too many students, including a "great many large boys and girls who I think need a man to controle [sic] them."[107]

Some young people could not be easily subdued, leading even male teachers and administrators to call for state-invested authority to exert control over them. Simon Ryall from Thomasville, Georgia, asked the Freedmen's Bureau to permit him to take charge of delinquent children. "There are in my neighborhood," Ryall wrote, "some children that are roaming the country at large stealing from the white folks and committing other depredations. These children are fatherless and with your permission I desire to take them in charge and make them worke half the time & go to school the other." Ryall did not indicate how he intended to make the children obey him, but he was ready to step in as a parent. He wanted the government to empower him with the discretion to make these young people work and attend school.[108]

In July 1866 John Alvord recommended establishing reform schools at a number of central locations for the most serious offenders. Unlike Ryall, however, Alvord's argument seemed anticipatory rather than grounded in concrete disruptive incidents. "While the great majority now at study will become far more virtuous by being educated, a small portion, as is always true, will, by increased knowledge, become increasingly vicious," he wrote to Freedmen's Bureau headquarters. "These need the rigid, though humane, discipline of this kind of school. By its influence such children often develop the highest talent, and at length become the most useful class of men. If, however, they are permitted to break away, as they soon will, from our ordinary schools, they are sure to be the pests of society, a marked disgrace to their color, and an ever present scandal on our attempts to educate the race." Here again, in Alvord's view, student misbehavior was not only serious on its own merits, but had the power to tarnish the image of all black people and damage efforts to establish black schools.[109]

One year later, Alvord repeated his call for reform schools, now based more on actual incidents than on predictions of misbehavior. "A reform school for bad boys, to which the attention of the Commissioner has heretofore been called, is needed in or near this city," he wrote from Washington, D.C. "Its necessity is daily forced upon us as we witness the contaminating influence of such boys upon society at large, and especially upon the schools." To support his proposal, Alvord presented the comments of A. E. Newton, a local superintendent of education, who said that he received complaints each week about past and present students who were proper subjects for reform schools. These children disrupted school activities, and neither suspension nor expulsion succeeded in ridding the school of them as "they hang round the schoolhouse, to the constant annoyance of the teacher and the demoralization of the school." Nor did involving the police help because "the result is the imposition of a fine, the payment of which often distresses poor and well-meaning parents; or a brief term in the workhouse, the effects of which are seldom in the direction of reform."[110]

Two elements of these calls for forced schooling or for reform schools are particularly noteworthy. First, although Alvord referred specifically to "bad boys," both Ryall and Newton used the gender-neutral children, or students, suggesting that both boys and girls may have been implicated in the disruptive behavior. Esther Pinkney and Hattie Sabattie certainly found that to be the case in their Georgia schools.[111] Second, Ryall, Alvord, and Newton were able to express concern about the young people's needs, while disapproving of their actions. Ryall seemed to locate the children's misbehavior in the fact that they were fatherless and lacking a male authority figure. He sought permission from the Freedmen's Bureau to insert himself into that role. None of the men was interested in simply punishing the children; rather they spoke in terms of reform, and Ryall suggested putting them to work part-time, no doubt as a means of discipline as well as a means of providing income for their families.

The men's proposal had roots in the reform movement of the 1820s, which instituted the first custodial institutions for juvenile offenders in New York, Philadelphia, and Boston. One sociologist has argued that Jacksonian-era reformers were motivated to establish "Houses of Refuge" for juveniles by "a profound fear" brought on by the impact of industrialization, immigration, poverty, and crime.[112] Alvord, Newton, and Ryall expressed a more focused fear, but one no less profound than that experienced earlier in the century. They feared not a general societal disorder, but disorder caused by freed black adolescents in a rapidly transforming society, who should instead have been proving that they were worthy of freedom. Slave owners had previously been responsible for disciplining black youth; now would-be reformers appealed to the government to take on the part. As with the early attempts at reform, not only lawbreakers, but also incorrigible children, would fall under supervision. These men, friends of the freedpeople (Ryall being one himself), wanted to rein in disruptive boys and girls before their enemies did. Earlier efforts at reforming juveniles were motivated in part by changes brought about by immigration. Following emancipation, freedpeople may have appeared similar to the European immigrants in northeastern cities as they, too, moved from one state of being to another. Freedpeople had to become Americans, had to prove themselves worthy of the benefits of being American, even though they had always been here.

It is well known that African American adults attended freedpeople's schools along with their children; what is less well known is the fact that freedpeople initiated this adult education movement. Southern black teachers would not have been surprised by adults who wanted to become literate, but northern teachers were shocked to find that not only did parents want education for their children, but that many also insisted on becoming literate themselves. Mary F. Root in Beaufort, South Carolina, charted the establishment of an evening school. The adults, she said, "came first without invitation, and begged me to tell them just two or three words. I assured them that I would like to have them come often, and now, every day, after they have finished their tasks in the field, (they are now preparing the ground for cotton) all the men and women on the place, except some quite old, are gathered round me spelling out their lessons." "I am astonished, really, to see the progress they make," Root confessed; "I had supposed teaching the grown people would amount to little."[113] Rather than amounting to little, adult education became an important part of teachers' work, adding hours to the time they spent teaching each day.

Northern teachers went south expecting the ages represented in their classrooms to resemble what they were accustomed to in the North; freedpeople who had for years wanted to learn to read and write had something else in mind. A teacher in Wilmington said that his evening classes for adults had been "instituted at the suggestion, indeed at the urgent request of its members." His students paid for their lessons, believing that a pay school would limit enrollment and thus ensure them swifter progress.[114] Teachers in Columbia, South Carolina, were surprised when adults arrived at school for lessons, and thinking it "seemed unsuitable" to place them in the same classes with small children, the teachers created a separate class for them.[115] As one teacher wrote of the adults who attended her night school, "they come in crowds and are eager to learn."[116] Harriet Greely's adult class was so eager to learn that she cancelled her summer vacation to remain in Florida to teach them.[117]

Teachers soon held classes with students many years their senior. Sometimes adults attended class alongside their children. One teacher wrote that it was not uncommon to see "the white-headed old man or woman, with great brass-bowed spectacles, sitting among their grand perhaps great grand-children, spelling out the words; turning the book, now this way, now that, so that the outline of the not very clearly perceived word might be a little more distinct." F. A. Fiske, Superintendent of Freedpeople's Education for North Carolina, reported that in one school, "side by side, sat representatives of four generations in a direct line, viz: a child six years old, her mother, grandmother and great-grandmother, the latter over seventy-five years of age. All commenced their alphabet together, and now each can read the Bible fluently."[118] Other times adults attended special night schools intended just for them. One such school had five students ranging in age from forty-five to fifty-six.[119] In another example, approximately forty adults went to school on Dawfuskie Island, South Carolina, four nights each week after working in the cotton fields all day. One woman took her baby with her to class. The students' commitment caused their teacher to wonder how many of those who "call the Freedmen 'lazy niggers' would walk five and six miles, after working hard all day, for the sake of learning to read!"[120]

As with their younger pupils, some teachers marveled at the progress adult students made in achieving literacy. Those who had harbored doubts soon realized that black adults were capable of learning, and that many did so rapidly. Teachers expressed admiration for students' diligence, earnestness, and perseverance.[121] "Where, but in colored schools," one teacher asked, "were people ever known to learn their letters, and then to read, after they were seventy years of age, only that they might study for themselves in the Word of God?"[122] Another teacher whose adult students learned to read in one month concluded that white notions of black intellectual inferiority could only be attributed to white ignorance or prejudice. "I reckon," he asserted, "that those who tell us that the African cannot *learn* and *know*, like the whites, are either ignorant of their *real* ability, or are *haters* of their intellectual progress."[123]

As would be expected, adult classes focused on literacy, but these students also studied geography, history, grammar, and arithmetic.[124] The Bible served as a seminal text in many classrooms. and some teachers used the American Tract Society's books for freedmen. One teacher read a chapter of *Uncle Tom's Cabin* to her students each night because she thought it would encourage them to learn to read and would "also show them how much we previously knew of their condition, and sympathized with them."[125]

Literacy and numeracy were urgently needed for progress. Adults studied so that they would be able to read the Bible for themselves, to prepare themselves to exercise the vote, to become candidates in elections, to make it more difficult for whites to cheat them in business transactions, and to satisfy a longing that they had nurtured for many years.[126] A freedman in Trent Camp near New Bern, North Carolina, told a group of men, women, and children who had gathered to establish an educational society, "I don't know much, but one thing I do know: I want edication, and we, as a people, want edication. We must learn to keep books and do our own business, for already the white man is marking and thinking how cheap he can hire us, and how easily he can cheat us out of our pay."[127] When a Georgia plantation owner drove teachers away, some of the freedpeople concluded that he was afraid they were learning so much that he would not be able to cheat them in the next contract. They threatened not to work for him in the future, but he was unyielding in his decision.[128] These and other freedpeople used schooling as one method to mark the shift in status from slaves to free people.

Yet, as one teacher realized after interacting with adults in his school, illiteracy did not diminish intellect. "Everywhere among the Freedmen here, there is much anxiety to learn," he wrote. "The judgment of the adults is better developed than I supposed. Many of them have clear intelligent ideas on a great variety of subjects. They need only the power of letters, to clothe those ideas with taste and beauty."[129] Adults had spent a lifetime developing ideas and debating issues among themselves when they met at night and on weekends. They had formulated plans and had distinct notions about how they would choose to live when freedom came. They did not by any means arrive in school as blank slates; rather, they made a choice to pursue literacy and numeracy as one important strategy for advancement.

Adult school attendance can tell us quite a bit about class, gender, and age arrangements within communities of freedpeople. Many elderly people attended school during the day, alongside their grandchildren, because they had reached an age when they could no longer be expected to work. Apparently a relative or other member of the community supported them. Numerous teachers told of gray-haired men and women, as old as 108 years of age, who were determined to learn to read the Bible before dying. Ministers comprised another interesting group of students. Anxious to hold on to leadership roles within communities intent on becoming literate, they attended day schools and formed separate night classes, precursors of a sort to theological seminaries for African Americans.[130]

Of particular significance is what school attendance reveals about the practices of freedwomen. Following emancipation, some African American women withdrew themselves from the labor market to the chagrin of southern whites, who complained bitterly that the women they had relied on to perform agricultural and domestic labor were instead "playing the lady." Historians have refined our understanding of the conditions of this withdrawal, demonstrating that freedwomen did not remove themselves from the labor force fully; instead, many continued to work but significantly reduced the amount of time spent at agricultural labor for planters. Women in domestic service also attempted to cut back the tasks required of them. These historians have believed that the wives and daughters of men who earned enough to enable them to pull out partially or completely from the labor force turned their full attention to home, garden, husband, and children.[131]

However, freedwomen who did not have to work full-time did not focus their attention solely on domestic matters; they counted education among their priorities and took time during the day to attend school. Sometimes women sat in classrooms with younger students, and sometimes they attended classes devoted to women. A teacher in Kentucky reported that "adult females begin to come in and this number will probably increase. Seven new ones of this class came in this morning." Another teacher noted, "This month has ushered into school a number of married people. Mothers leave their infants with their neighbors and come."[132] A teacher in Jacksonville, Florida, held a class at two o'clock in the afternoon for women and another at seven o'clock in the evening for the men.[133] A freedman approached a teacher in Savannah to inquire if "*he* and *his wife* (not now especially occupied,) may come into our day school with the children."[134] The opportunity to attend school during the day designated these women as being of higher status than those who had to work all day. H. S. Beals wrote from Beaufort, North Carolina, that his wife's afternoon school for married women "was composed of representative women. Neat in person, chaste in their language, [C]hristian in their deportment, and intensely earnest in their studies." These women left their children for an hour during the day to attend school.[135] This select group of women signaled class stratification among communities of freedpeople.

Women frequently went to class with infants in their arms. Charlotte Forten rhapsodized about such an infant who accompanied his mother to school each day. "It happened to be one of the best babies in the world," Forten wrote, "a perfect little 'model of deportment,' and allowed its mother to pursue her studies without interruption."[136] Another teacher was not so generous in describing an infant in her classroom. "A married woman 16 years of age," she wrote, "occupied a part of one of the benches, by her side was a pillow, and a little 'weebit' specimen of a darkey, 3 months old, lying upon it covered with a quilt." The infant was quite troublesome, but the mother managed to learn her lessons.[137] A teacher in Mississippi wrote that he had several mothers in his class whom he had to "excuse, at intervals, to nurse their children."[138] To accommodate women's schedules, a teacher at Fortress Monroe held two small private classes at noon for "mothers who have babies in arms."[139] These women were able to attend school during the day only because they were not employed outside of their homes full-time. This was a dramatic shift for women who had been accustomed to performing tasks alongside men, and who had been expected to return to work soon after delivering a child. One of the freedoms that emancipation afforded some women was the chance to take their children along with them, or leave children for a few hours while they went off to class.

Still, most black women who attended school did so at night, and most sat in classes with men. But here, too, gender distinctions began to appear. Although it was by no means the norm, some adult evening schools, unlike the day schools that children attended, were separated by sex. A teacher in Norfolk, Virginia, spent four evenings each week with a night school class of women. Another teacher in Norfolk taught a night school with twenty women, and a teacher in Wilmington, North Carolina, taught a group of women two times each week and a group of men three times each week. The Wilmington teacher had been besieged by a group of twelve men to teach night school, and according to him, the men had "no thought of leaving in their untutored ignorance the wives who stand with them in whatever else of blessing fall to their lot, and hence came the application that the women might take their places in the class."[140] Miss W. Webster in Petersburg, Virginia, taught an "interesting" evening class of twenty-six young men aged twenty-one or twenty-two. She intended to keep class through the Christmas holidays because "they are all anxious that no time should be lost."[141] It is not clear whether teachers or the freedpeople chose to separate adult students by sex.

As soon as they mastered the rudiments of reading and writing, adult and younger students began teaching others. Education was not a commodity to be selfishly hoarded. Rather, many freedpeople considered it an asset that should be spread around communities. In formal and informal settings, students attempted to supplement the scant supply of trained teachers. One freedman reportedly traveled forty miles to attend school. When he learned to read, he returned home and organized a school.[142] African American teacher Robert Harris, who taught writer Charles W. Chesnutt in Fayetteville, North Carolina, responded to the call from freedpeople in surrounding communities for more schools by sending three of his students to teach in three schools. H. S. Beals noted that even his mediocre students quickly began to teach. "It is impossible," he remarked, "for those who have mastered the Alphabet to go any where in the country and not have every leisure hour taken up by an eager multitude clamoring for help to learn 'the book.' "[143] Teachers in overcrowded classrooms eagerly appointed promising students such as London Ferebee to serve as assistant teachers.[144] Teacher J. Silsby, who was forced to turn away children under six years old from his school for want of teachers, was "assisted nicely by inexperienced and very poorly educated colored young men" in his schoolhouse. Although lacking in both education and experience, the young men were energetic, and Silsby was satisfied that by giving them special instruction after school each day, he and they served the students nearly as well as if he had more knowledgeable help.[145]

The classroom, then, was just the central point of an educational sphere, as lessons quickly spread out from the center to other points in the community. Some children accompanied parents to night school to help them with their lessons, while others, "as soon as taught," became "teachers at home."[146] State superintendents of education also reported on the pervasive practice of children teaching parents, pleased that it enabled many who could not attend school to receive enough instruction to learn to read and write.[147]

Communities made use of children's recently acquired academic skills in other ways as well. Caroline Walker Walton's family regularly sent her to "read the texts from the Bible to the negro preachers, so they could remember them and preach the next Sunday." According to Walton, "most of the negro preachers, that started out at that time, didn't even know how to read. It was my job to help them to read."[148] This system of beginning to teach as soon as a student acquired basic skills led one Freedmen's Bureau employee to remark, "The fact of the Freedmen's interest in education is ever appearing in new forms. Old men and women are students, and children are leading them. One boy, near Tallahassee, but thirteen years of age is teaching at night a dozen or more grown persons at fifty cents per month, and has already deposited a portion of his earnings in the savings bank."[149]

White northern observers noted with surprise that there was no abatement in African Americans' desire to become educated. The passage of time did not quell what some had suspected might be a short-lived fascination with books. Motivated students wanted to acquire more education than any one teacher in a freedpeople's school could provide, and they wanted much more than short-term, intermittent school attendance could offer. Students like William Henry Heard, whose "patchwork" education consisted of self-teaching from a Webster's blue-back speller, teaching by a "poor white boy," and three-month morsels of school attendance between crops, were not satisfied to rest with the knowledge that they had managed to acquire much more education than their parents ever had.[150] After attending examinations of students in schools in Hampton, Virginia, General Samuel C. Armstrong declared that he could "bear witness to a steady growth in knowledge, and interest; the more advanced pupils seem to have a healthy ambition." "It is clear," he said, "that freed children do not get tired of going to school; the more they know the more they wish to know."[151] The Superintendent of Education for North Carolina joined in this assessment that the freedpeople's interest in education was "constantly deepening and widening."[152]

CHAPTER 9 ■ ■ ■ ■ ■ ■ ■ ■ ■ ■ ■ ■ ■ ■

First Movings of the Waters

The Creation of Common School Systems for Black and White Students

The "poor" whites are provoked by hearing Negroes read, while they are ignorant; and it is my belief that they will now receive schools, if furnished them, as never before. The educated class are not slow to perceive that their schools must be reopened or fall behind humiliated, and that new schools must now be organized on a more popular plan than heretofore.

John Alvord, Washington, D.C.

These so-called Carpet Bag governments established the public school systems of the South.

W. E. B. Du Bois, *The Negro Common School*

Freedpeople's commitment to education took both white southerners and northerners by surprise, but it was particularly stunning to those from the South who thought they knew the black people who lived among them. John Alvord recounted the following experience with a member of the Louisiana legislature in New Orleans in 1866. The two men were walking past a schoolyard at recess when the legislator stopped, stared, and asked:

> "Is this a school?"
> "Yes," I replied.
> "What! Of niggers?"
> "These are colored children, evidently," I answered.
> "Well! well!" said he, and raising his hands, "I have seen many an absurdity in my lifetime, but *this is the climax of absurdities!*"

With that, the astounded and repulsed legislator abruptly turned and hurried away.[1]

African Americans' insistence on establishing schools transformed education throughout the southern states. Absurd as it may have first appeared to many white southerners, over time the sight of black children in school became an inescapable fact. In the decade of the 1860s, freedpeople attended schools by the thousands. They rebuilt burned-out schoolhouses, armed themselves to protect threatened teachers, and persisted in the effort to become literate, self-sufficient participants in the larger American society. The impact was palpable. White planters began to provide schoolhouses to attract and retain black laborers. Newspaper editors who visited freedpeople's schools toned down their virulent rhetoric against black education. And both elite and poor whites worried that blacks would outpace poor whites in educational achievement. Following freedpeople's example, poor whites in the South began attending school, and northern missionaries and state legislatures took action to establish educational facilities for large numbers of poor whites who had previously gone unschooled.

The continuing and expanding interest in education was certainly not lost on southern whites who understood the implications of black people's continued pursuit of formal education. A Freedmen's Bureau official observed, for example, that in the university town of Athens, Georgia, it pained the young white male students exceedingly to see young black men going to school instead of waiting on them as in the past. The official further recounted that a professor at the University of Georgia "expressed the fear that 'the Niggers will soon be thundering at the gates of our Universities.' "[2] The professor had reason to be concerned because he, of all people, had to know that the quest for education could not be turned back. Indeed, he uttered his fearful and prophetic words in 1868, after black students had already begun to leave small, overcrowded freedpeople's schools to enter newly established normal schools and colleges.[3]

Students eagerly sought entry to the new schools, among them Hampton Institute in Virginia, Fisk University in Tennessee, and Howard University in Washington, D.C.[4] They, their teachers, and family members besieged administrators for admission and scraped together resources to make higher education possible. In April 1866, when Fisk University was barely more than a rumor, members of the Fifty-sixth Colored Regiment stationed in Helena, Arkansas, sought admission to the three-month-old institution.[5] From Smyrna, Tennessee, a teacher wrote to Fisk on behalf of the father of a thirteen-year-old girl in her school. Though not a brilliant scholar, the girl had made good progress in reading, arithmetic, and geography. The teacher said she seemed to have "a very pure character, and is modest and pleasing in her manners. Her father is poor, but she being an only daughter, he is willing to make extra exertions to give her a good chance in life."[6] The Superintendent of Public Instruction in Sparta, Tennessee, also wrote to John Ogden, head of the school, on behalf of "four young colored men in this county who are very anxious to attend your school, but are not able to pay you anything." He said that the people of the county were so poor that the tuition could not even be paid by taking up a subscription. Two of the young men had attended school in the Union army.[7]

In letters of application, students attempted to impress school administrators with their qualifications. Given sporadic and brief school attendance, academic skills varied greatly, but students and the teachers who wrote on their behalf used what they had. Landon Deskins from Christiansburg, Virginia, was able to read and write and had been teaching for several months at a school for freedpeople. A "bright, steady, sober, Christian young man," he was "willing and ready to work his way as far as he can."[8] A. Jared Montgomery had attended college in Pennsylvania before returning to his home in Williamsburg, South Carolina, to teach. His students were so poor, however, that he was not able to earn enough money to continue his studies. He was attracted to Hampton Institute's manual labor program because it would enable him to work his way through school. Montgomery had been raised on a farm and, at twenty years old, was healthy and willing to work hard to pay for his education.[9] Brooks Turner also considered his farming experience a high recommendation for admission to Hampton Institute. "I am a farmer only," he wrote; "My father is a farmer and thus he learned me the identical trade." Turner had attended school for three sessions—a total of seventeen months—and had progressed to the fifth reader. He had also studied geography, grammar, and arithmetic. He included an example of his skill with fractions in his letter, and he assured the school that his letter of application was in his own handwriting. James and Mary Eliza Dungey relied on their father's activism to recommend them. Jefree Dungey had given land, labor, and about two-thirds of the material provided by the freedpeople for building a school in King William Courthouse, Virginia. He was eager for his children to attend Hampton as a reward for his generous assistance in his hometown. Hampton accepted both students.[10] Finally, seventeen-year-old Caleb Nelson, a former soldier in the Union army, had attended school for one year. His teacher considered him a peculiar boy who rarely spoke in class. Nelson was, however, determined to have an education: although he walked 7½ miles to school, he was there first thing each morning. He was just learning to write on paper, having had to use a slate for want of desks. He knew a little about figures. His father, the teacher said, "is willing to work the harder, to give him an education."[11]

For poor students, who already had overcome particular challenges to attend local freedpeople's schools, the prospect of studying at a college or normal school raised additional complex problems such as how to obtain the best recommendation and complete a successful application, how to come up with the money for tuition, room, and board, and how to travel to a school that might be a hundred miles away. In July 1868, when E. D. Tilghman wrote from Richmond, Virginia, seeking admission to the newly established Hampton Institute, he could not contain his excitement. "I cannot stop writing to you about that scholl [*sic*]. I would like very much to find out all the particulars concerning the school."[12] Tilghman already knew some of the particulars. He was aware, for example, of Hampton's requirement that testimonials of good character be submitted and that students remain through the course of three years. In search of a testimonial, he approached R. M. Manly, the Freedmen's Bureau Superintendent of Education. Although Manly said that he would like Tilghman to get an education, and would do anything in his power to help black education in general, he declined to write a recommendation because he was not familiar with Tilghman's character personally. Instead, Manly suggested that Tilghman get recommendations from his pastor and from his former master. The idea of soliciting a recommendation from his former master must have struck Tilghman as ironic, even inappropriate. Nevertheless, without better options, Tilghman hoped such a recommendation would suffice. Twice in one letter he pointedly asked whether the school would accept a letter from a former slave owner. He seemed to want to convince school officials to do so, telling them that his former owners knew more about his character than anyone else. As to his academic credentials, Tilghman admitted that he had only attended a school for a short time before it closed and that he was behind in arithmetic, but he was confident that he would be able to learn. Finally, aware of Hampton's desire to have students who were committed to completing the course of study, Tilghman sought to establish his earnestness. "I don't want to come to school to stay one month and leave in two or three," he assured them. "But I do want to stay as long as I can if it is five years if I should live that long for if any body wants an education, it is me."[13]

Tilghman made his case. Hampton Institute invited him to come. "I am very glad of the opportunity," he wrote in response. "When I received your letter I jumped for joy." Now having received the chance he had dreamed of, Tilghman shifted his focus from seeking the goal to considering the conditions that could impede its attainment. He had no clothing. He earned only $5.50 per week. He begged the school to wait for him until he could get a suit of clothes, and he again tried to assure them of his earnestness. "You may relie on my coming for I am coming without I dies or sickness prevents, as soon as I get my clothes look out for me." Sadly, Tilghman does not appear to have made the trip from Richmond to Hampton. His enthusiasm was not enough to get him there.[14]

For those who did make it to normal schools, a term or two readied them to head back to local communities to teach summer schools. The first students who went to the normal school at Talladega, Alabama, for example, returned that first summer to teach "bush" schools in the communities that had sent them off to college with sacks of corn and bacon. Talladega had been established in 1865 on the initiative of two African American men, after they attended the "Convention of the Colored People of Alabama" in Mobile in 1865. Those first students learned the alphabet at Talladega. Within six months they had progressed through the second and third readers, and they learned how to teach reading.[15] Many students from Fisk also went out to teach when they returned home. In the summer of 1868, after a year in school, Fred Hunt wrote to John Ogden to say that he had arrived home safely and would start a school on the following Monday. Alice Allen similarly informed Ogden that she was now teaching a class of little boys in Sabbath school. "I like them very much I am going to try to teach them the best I can although I dont know very much," she wrote. She hoped to be able to return to Fisk in the fall, but she was not certain that her sick mother would be able to spare her. John Burrows notified Ogden that had not been able to "get up a school" in Murfreesboro, Tennessee, but that he was heading to Woodberry, where he had heard that "the prospect of two schools are very good."[16] This practice of "getting up a school" supplemented black public education until the turn of the century. W. E. B. Du Bois, Charles W. Chesnutt, and Anna Julia Cooper all taught in country schools during summer vacations from college.[17]

These students who attended Fisk, Hampton, Talladega, and other institutions constituted part of the first generation of "formally" trained, southern African American teachers. They were the new "native" teachers who went into southern communities to teach in freedpeople's schools that would soon be incorporated into systems of separate, state-funded schools for black children. Many spent decades inside classrooms working with limited resources in order to enable African American students to reach their highest potential.[18] As this new generation of teachers took its place inside classrooms, southern whites continued to challenge the existence of freedpeople's schools, even as African American education deeply influenced the development of public education in the South for both black and white children.

White southern responses to African American education, both elementary and advanced, proved complex and shifting. Initial shock gave way to envy, anger, and resentment as education threatened the remnants of the antebellum social structure. Indeed, one sympathetic historian defended white southerners' hostile reactions by explaining that they believed the "underlying purpose of the schools was nothing less than the establishment of the political and social dominance of the Negro race."[19] Whites worried that blacks would rise out of their traditional subservient place and, as a result, that many whites would be left behind. Poor whites, for whom southern states provided little or no education, stood to fall far behind former slaves who insisted on attending school. This prospect was more than many white south-erners could tolerate. Such threats to the supremacy of whiteness endangered not only those on the lowest economic rungs, but also those wealthier whites whose class position depended, in part, on poor whites' finding solace in the psychological compensation they received from being white.[20]

Both elite and poor whites, then, perceived a threat. Poor whites could see themselves becoming even poorer culturally and materially, and slipping in status below blacks. How long could they expect to rely on mere whiteness to elevate them above better-educated black people? Lieutenant Governor Ridgely C. Powers of Mississippi testified in 1871 that "the opposition to the free schools—the colored schools—comes from the men who were formerly overseers, and the lower class—those who themselves most need education here in the State." These lower classes, Powers said, believed blacks to be inferior to them and thought there was no use trying to bring them up to equality with whites. "There seems to be a jealousy on the part of the poor class against the colored people, very much the same kind of jealousy felt by the Irishmen all over the United States against the colored people."[21]

At the same time, white elites worried that disgruntled poor whites might agitate for more concrete, material signs of social status and thus disrupt existing class divisions. As a result, some elites made paternalistic gestures on behalf of poor whites, articulating concern for their well-being. An Athens, Georgia, newspaper thus expressed bitter sarcasm in its columns in 1867: "We also learn that two more missionaries will soon be here, and that the F.B.[Freedmen's Bureau] will build a school house for their express accom-modation—at the expense of the 'poor white trash' of the country, of course. All of which is very pleasant news, and calculated to make southern 'barbar-ians' feel good all over."[22]

In December 1866 a newspaper in Wilmington, North Carolina, took an equally contemptuous stance toward freedpeople's insistence on having access to education. The editors sadly acknowledged that black people appeared unwilling to abandon the South for northern states and concluded that there-fore southern whites would have blacks in their midst until "by the mandate of that great natural law which forbids the co-existence of superior and inferior races in a condition of freedom, they shall become extinct." The burden thus fell to southern whites to render African Americans "industrious and worthy people." The editors claimed not to object to black people being taught, but they thought it important that southern whites "endeavor to direct their education." Books would be of little use to these people in their "primitive condition." Rather, blacks should be taught first and foremost that work was their most important duty. The editors believed that freedpeople should learn that "their children will become much more useful, and will be much more highly esteemed if they are instructed as to their duty in this respect, instead of being the recipients of a smattering of an education, which they can not appreciate and which will only render them unhappy and disappointed because of the social status to which their flat noses, kinky hair, and thick lips have consigned them." According to the newspaper, freedpeople needed to realize that their race would never reach a social position in which "polite education" would be of any use. It was best for them to "believe that through labor they may become in their own peculiar sphere a worthy and respected people."[23] This caustic view of African American's position in southern society was not uncommon; for as determined as freedpeople were to use schooling to get access to power, many southern whites were equally determined to hold on to their own power and to "teach" black people that emancipation had not freed them from perpetual roles as laborers.

The actions of delegates to the black conventions, black teachers, parents, and students convinced some elite whites, however, of the inevitability of education for freedpeople and of the benefits that could flow to whites. Some whites also thought it important to project a more tolerant, more sophisticated image from the South. Ridgely Powers testified that "liberal men, the best men, the most intelligent men in the community, are in favor of free schools and the education of the colored people."[24] Prominent white citizens who visited freedpeople's schools in many cities did indeed have conversion experiences, becoming convinced that their former slaves could learn.[25] In 1866 African American principal Francis Cardozo proudly reported that his Charleston, South Carolina, school had finally received its first visit from white southerners. The three visitors, all prominent Episcopalian ministers, one of them the former secretary of the Confederate treasury, found in the school's efficient teaching methods and students' good behavior a model for schools they hoped to establish throughout the state. Shortly after the visit, a prominent attorney expressed "liberal ideas" regarding black education and informed Cardozo that he and his friend, South Carolina governor James L. Orr, supported a common school system for black and white children. Cardozo enthusiastically reported these developments to the AMA: "I think such things are the first movings of the waters in the formation of a public opinion in favor of educating the colored people, and giving them their rights."[26]

Freedpeople turned their desire for education into an economic factor with which potential employers had to contend. Motivated by their own pecuniary interests, planters, many of them members of the ruling elite, were often among the first to accept schools for freedpeople. In many places planters began to realize that they could better retain a workforce if they provided schools on their property. (Often planters simply provided the land on which freedpeople built schools. The freedpeople generally paid for teachers.) John H. Wager, an employee of the Freedmen's Bureau, testified before a congressional committee in Huntsville, Alabama, that at first many local whites objected to black education, "but they begin to see the advantage it is to them. The negroes rather prefer to work when their children can go to school. I think that has changed the sentiment." A few planters, Wager said, had applied to the bureau for funds to establish schools on their plantations.[27] John Alvord, too, remarked on planters' eagerness to provide schools as a means of holding on to black workers. "Negroes now crowd into large towns where their children can have learning," he wrote. "If they are to be retained as laborers in the rural districts, similar opportunities must be furnished on the plantations. More than one instance could be already given where a school in the interior has been started from this motive," he said. "This is now being stipulated in the contracts. Liberal minded and northern men, who are preparing for crops, are earnestly asking that schools be established, knowing that they concentrate and keep the people contented, greatly stimulating industry, and especially that labor is valuable just as it becomes intelligent."[28] In Louisiana, labor contracts even specified a government-imposed 5 percent tax on planters to educate workers' children.[29] At the same time, however, the realization that black laborers insisted on schooling for their children led some planters to hire workers with as few children as possible.[30] Some planters were beginning to bow under freedpeople's pressure to provide schools, but they were far from capitulating to black demands for education.

Adult black scholars found themselves under assault from white employers for attending school. Although some planters may have felt compelled into accepting schools for black children, they had no intention of losing adult workers to the classroom. Landowners who realized that they needed schools to retain black laborers also foresaw that literacy would provide African Americans with increased mobility that might very well take them away from plantations. When Jasper Carter, a twenty-five-year-old from Haralson County, Georgia, received a visit from the Ku Klux Klan late one night, he recognized his employer, a planter named Monroe, among the men who forced him to the ground, pulled his pants down, and beat him, leaving "welts as wide as a grown man's finger." Carter had worked for Monroe for a year and a half without pay. Frustrated, he had decided to stop working and instead attend school. An infuriated Monroe threatened that if Carter ever went to school with the other black people, "the KKK would have him." Carter never did go to school. His brother, who did, also had an encounter with the Klan. According to Carter, they "took him off and told him to stay at home, and not go [to school] any more, and to serve the master and mistresses, and to do everything that white people told him to do; that he was not free yet, and should not vote for such and such a man."[31]

If African Americans made it impossible for hostile whites to impede black education, whites sometimes insisted on the prerogative of choosing teachers for the former slaves. A few white southerners expressed a preference for white southern teachers who would teach blacks appropriate lessons of docility, loyalty, and hard work for low pay. Much as slave owners had retained the right to select preachers who would hammer in repetitive biblical lessons of obedience to masters, so too after emancipation, some southern whites hoped to choose teachers who would instill lessons of subservience. By controlling freedpeople's teachers, these whites hoped to excise offensive political lessons as well as diminish competence. In testimony before the congressional subcommittee investigating the Ku Klux Klan, Thompson C. Hawkins of Greene County, Alabama, offered that some whites did not object to a black school so long as it was "taught by a man that we are acquainted with, and know his principles, and about what he will instruct them; a man outside of them, that we don't know how he is going to instruct—I do think they are opposed to that, though."[32] A Virginia newspaper bitterly asserted this preference in the summer of 1866, when editors congratulated themselves on being rid of the northern "schoolmarms," whom they considered "ignorant, narrow-minded, bigoted fanatics" who had done "incalculable mischief" by demoralizing the South's "peasantry and laboring population." The editors hoped that the teachers had made their way to hell. However, in an apparent submission to the reality that black education had become a permanent feature of the southern landscape, the newspaper also put forth its own ideas of who the freedpeople's teachers should be. "We have plenty of material, native of the south and to the manor born, to make teachers for those colored schools, and who can instruct them aright, too, in the duties of their station as well as in the less important rules of English syntax and natural philosophy."[33] As clearly scornful as the editors were of the idea of African Americans studying syntax and philosophy, they were deadly serious about teaching blacks to keep their place.

If southern white teachers could not be found, some whites preferred local black teachers "who were born and raised up among us," believing it would be easier to control such people.[34] Some also assumed that black teachers would not be qualified to teach much of anything. The Freedmen's Bureau Superintendent of Education in Louisiana reported that many of the freedpeople "make it a special clause in their contract this year, that they have the benefit of schools. But the planter was only willing to have colored teachers employed, thinking that such schools would amount to little or nothing. In this they are mistaken, as many of the most prosperous schools in the State are taught by competent colored teachers."[35] Although African Americans now attended colleges and normal schools, the concept of competent black teachers still lay beyond the grasp of many southern whites. Freedpeople and their teachers had, however, already begun to transform the face of southern education. What had once been forbidden, underground activity had not only surfaced and multiplied, it was having a marked influence on white people in the South.

It took several more years for whites to demand public education, but early signs appeared that the sight of black adults and children filing into schoolhouses and poring over spelling books inspired some southern whites to seek education for themselves.[36] Several factors no doubt motivated this emulation. Some whites may long have harbored the same desires to learn to read and write as so many enslaved African Americans had. Poverty plus the absence of routes to upward mobility may have subverted their desires. It may be that when freedpeople built schools and began to transform their own dreams into reality, some poor whites came to believe that they too could cast aside the restraints that had kept most of them from attending school in the antebellum period. To be sure, racism was also a factor. The prospect of African Americans utilizing education to move out of what had once seemed permanent positions of subjection motivated some whites to compete and thus seek to hold on to the superior social position that their whiteness alone seemed no longer able to guarantee.

To white elites' concern about disruptions of the social order, and poor whites' desire to break free from their constraints, add white northern missionaries' interest in exposing poor white southerners to northern culture and values. White northern commentary on the debasement of poor southern whites was nearly as common as their diametric assessment of freedpeople's interest in education. Many white missionaries went south intending to elevate both blacks and whites to what they perceived as the superior intellectual, cultural, and moral position held by white northerners of a particular class and training. If missionaries held on to any sense of an innate superiority in whiteness, such beliefs seemed to give way to their experiences in the South. Interactions with poor whites convinced them that whiteness was not supreme—it did not universally guarantee ambition or energy or any of the values that they held dear. Northern whites who distinguished themselves morally from elite southern slave owners identified even less with poor southern whites.

For some white northern observers, ambition trumped race when it came to comparisons of freedpeople and poor whites; they frequently bemoaned what they interpreted as poor whites' lack of interest in education. Some thought freedpeople had "superior intelligence to the lower order of white people" of the South and believed freedpeople would soon outpace poor whites economically and intellectually.[37] One New Jersey journalist likened the condition of antebellum poor whites to enslavement and opined that the now emancipated whites showed "no opinion to rise, no aspirations for learning, or for any of the means for attaining a higher level."[38] Union general Rufus Saxton contended that poor whites had suffered "wrong and oppression scarcely less than that of the negro," and, as a result, he thought the government had an obligation to help poor whites as well as former slaves.[39] *American Missionary* reported on the complaints of a teacher in Harpers Ferry, West Virginia, that while "the colored children (lately slaves) were studying with all their might, idle and vicious white boys no more than seven years old, sat outside the schoolhouse swearing and playing cards." The AMA editors urged northern children to be grateful that they had not been born and brought up in the slave states and had therefore escaped a fate of ignorance and wickedness. The article concluded with the hope that all white and black children of the South would soon be able to attend school.[40]

White northerners who anticipated that nothing could surpass the deprivations of slavery were surprised when they found poor whites who appeared to be even worse off than recently enslaved people. Emma Eveleth, a missionary teacher in Jacksonville, Florida, was stupefied when she encountered a white woman living near freedpeople in conditions worse than theirs. The woman lived in a "car" that was as untidy as she was. She kept a fire in an iron basin with no chimney through which smoke could escape. Eveleth encouraged her to clean herself up and to come to the school to "learn to live like other folks." Although the woman promised that she would attend, she never appeared. When the teacher returned to urge her to go to school, the woman said that it was too cold. Over time, Eveleth came to consider the poor white people of Jacksonville "more degraded and in need than the colored people for the latter are not afraid to work, the others have always thought work degrading; and even now it seems as if they would starve rather than work." She hoped that once slavery was truly dead, and the spirit of caste banished, poor whites would "arise and be equal to the colored people."[41]

Freedpeople across the South seemed poised to quickly outdistance poor white southerners in education and industry. In one of the many comparisons that northern whites made between freedpeople and poor southern whites, Horace James, Superintendent of Negro Affairs in North Carolina, concluded that the freedpeople he observed were far more industrious and independent than whites. According to James, large numbers of white women and children whose husbands and fathers were soldiers in the Union army came under the care of the federal government. In his estimation, the " 'piney woods' people, the 'clay eaters,' or whatever name be given to the poor whites of the South, are a more helpless and spiritless race than the negroes of the same section, and indeed naturally inferior to them. They have more pride, but less activity; they make more pretensions, but possess fewer mental resources." "Being unused to labor," James suggested, "they know nothing of its processes, and are therefore incapable of self-support." Horace James concluded that among those in equally destitute conditions, "the white person will be the one to sit down in forlorn and languid helplessness, and eat the bread of charity, while the negro will be tinkering at something, in his rude way, to hammer out a living."[42]

Like Horace James, the Freedmen's Inquiry Commission also concluded that African American refugees from slavery and the Civil War were more self-reliant and less dependent upon the government for assistance than were whites. In New Orleans in 1863, for example, the commission found that the government supported many more whites than blacks.[43] Similarly, O. O. Howard, head of the Freedmen's Bureau, pitied the "Georgia crackers" or South Carolina "sand-hillers," who were generally lethargic and stupid.[44] John Alvord made an unsuccessful attempt to refrain from such evaluations. "We make no invidious comparison of the freedman and the ignorant Anglo-Saxon of the south," he wrote; "We only say the former has most creditably won his present position; and he has done it by good conduct and rapid improvement under that instruction we are now reporting." Alvord may have considered it uncharitable to compare poor whites and freedpeople publicly, but his words betrayed his true sentiments.[45]

These negative characterizations of poor white southerners notwithstanding, a phenomenal thing had begun to happen. Some southern whites were so anxious to become educated that they attended freedpeople's schools. The numbers were small but remarkable nonetheless, on at least three levels. First, that these schools existed at all was a tremendous achievement for people who had recently been enslaved. Second, it must have been evident to whites that freedpeople were learning valuable skills worthy of their own attention. Third, when white children sat in classrooms with black people, they often contravened their communities' taboos against racial mixing.

In January 1867 the Freedmen's Bureau recorded 470 white pupils attending freedpeople's schools in thirteen states. Seventy-eight thousand black students attended those schools.[46] Missionary workers and teachers also noted the presence, here and there, of white children in black classrooms. The American Freedmen's Union Commission (AFUC) noted in August 1866, "the children of the poor whites have already come into the schools in Virginia and North Carolina to a small extent. Say in a dozen schools about one white to fifty colored. These have been admitted at the request of their mothers, who said they could not give them an education, being too poor to do so."[47] From Norfolk, Virginia, a teacher of a freedpeople's school reported, "I have two white boys in my class." One, she said, was formerly a drummer in the Confederate army. He told her that he had heard they were missionaries and came to see if they would be willing to teach him. The teacher described him as "a noble boy, and very anxious to learn."[48] In South Carolina, among the 10,300 students in freedpeople's schools in 1866 were 24 "purely white children." AFUC described its school in Summerville, South Carolina, as the "mixed school," where black and white children attended and studied together.[49]

In Morehead City, North Carolina, a widowed white woman, whose husband had served in the Union army, sent her six children to the freedpeople's school after learning that there was no school for white children. Interestingly, she told the teacher that as a child she had attended a pay school in North Carolina along with black children. She had no prejudice against color, she said. When she visited the freedpeople's school, she confessed to the teacher that she was ashamed to send her children there "among such smart students."[50]

Such liberal sentiments did not always prevail, of course. Indeed, whites who sent their children to black schools constituted a rare exception. Most southern whites, whatever their interest in education, preferred to deprive their children than to have them associate with black children in classrooms. As a teacher wrote from Raleigh, North Carolina, "I have been disappointed, by seeing all the white children leave us. The most of them go without any schooling at all, rather than bear up against the ridicule that meets them for going to a Freedmen's school." Although the teacher believed their deprivation was in part self-imposed, his compassion for them led him to request that the AMA send a teacher to serve their needs.[51]

In some instances, black pupils became teachers of white students. Some white students were too proud or too afraid of harassment from other whites to sit with black students in public, but they were shrewd enough to take advantage of the black children's knowledge. A teacher from southern Virginia reported, "We are satisfied that we have a good field. Many of our pupils teach white children at home, who are too prejudiced to come to our school."[52] But it was not only misplaced pride that motivated white children to have black tutors outside of the classroom. In Washington, D.C., for example, a white mother approached a teacher to seek admission for her children to a freedpeople's school. They were attending a white private school, the mother said, but she judged the black school superior. However, the black school was overcrowded, and its teacher was too busy to give private lessons. Finally, the mother sought a black student who could offer her children private lessons. Pleased with this turn of events, the school's sponsoring organization boasted, "This colored pupil from our school is now teaching the children of this white family—in preference to sending them to the best educational institution for whites which the city affords."[53]

Middling and poor white people in southern states had to look to freed-people's schools to provide them with schooling because, for the most part, southern governments had failed to implement common school systems. In contrast to New England, Middle Atlantic, and midwestern states that had instituted tax-supported common school systems in the 1840s and 1850s, most states in the South relied on individuals to provide education for their own children.[54] North Carolina, which had implemented and funded a state-wide system in 1853, proved the only exception. Antebellum southern whites who received any formal education at all did so in a range of settings. Wealthy planters and professionals provided private tutors for their offspring and relied on schools in the North or in Europe for more advanced education. Middling whites sent their children to academies and to private, secondary schools. People in the lower economic classes or in rural areas supported subscription schools, also called "old field" schools, as they were often built on the old abandoned fields in a town. Finally, some states provided their only free schooling for the very poorest students whose parents could not possibly afford to contribute to subscription schools. In these states, only the poorest children had any guarantee of even minimal education.[55]

A number of factors explain the failure of southern states to create structured, publicly financed, common school systems: rural opposition to taxation, without which schools could not be properly funded; low population density, which made it difficult to build schools in locations convenient to everyone; and reliance on a single crop in many parts of the South, which created a vulnerability to weather, blights, and economic downturns that in turn tended to reduce citizens' willingness to commit to supporting school systems. Additionally, white southerners' antagonism toward the North in the 1850s may have contributed to the failure to develop common school systems, as some southerners denounced the adaptation of northern models of school organization. The southern states could best design their own approach to education, proponents argued.[56] Despite these claims, most white southerners went without any formal education.

Based on their experiences with African Americans, and motivated by compassion as well as by a desire to spread their conceptions of northern moral values to all southerners, some northern missionaries and institutions reached out to poor whites. Like Emma Eveleth, they wanted to clean them up, both by washing the soot and grime from their skin and by inculcating them with values and education from the North. "True, they're white; but it's not their fault," wrote the Freedmen's Bureau Superintendent of Education in Jacksonville, Florida, as he pleaded with the AMA to send a teacher to a settlement of loyal whites, whose men had deserted from the Confederacy and "laid out in the woods" until the Union army arrived. The men of the settlement agreed to build a schoolhouse and to allow black children to attend, if the Freedmen's Bureau could provide a teacher.[57] From Gadsden County, Alabama, teacher Charles Day inquired in his monthly report whether the Freedmen's Bureau or a missionary organization would support a school for poor whites. "We need here a public white school," he wrote. "There could be got together some 40 or 50 poor white children whose parents have been killed in the war. The wealthy whites have got up their schools—and as carefully exclude the poor white children as they do the negros [sic]." Day had in mind a very good teacher, a "Yankee schoolmarm" who had not found employment due to her northern origins.[58] As Day made clear, in the aftermath of the Civil War, whites with money still educated their children privately, while other whites were left to scrape for themselves.

The success of African American education posed a dilemma for northern missionary organizations and for the success of Reconstruction. White missionaries wanted to inculcate southern whites with their values, and some were convinced that the best way to influence southern ideology was to admit white children into schools with white northern teachers. In 1866 the AFUC published a letter articulating this strategy. The organization's agent in Raleigh, North Carolina, Fisk P. Brewer, wrote that white southern resentment of northern intrusion was still as deeply entrenched as it had ever been. "There are not a few who will put an evil construction on all that we may do or say," he reported. "But beside this opposition the work among the freedmen has awakened much jealousy among the poor whites. As they know that they are about equally poor and destitute, they feel hurt that the blacks should receive special help while they are neglected." Brewer offered a remedy: "admission to an equal share in the distribution of supplies, and in general, the showing of an equal interest in their welfare would entirely disarm their prejudice and win their favor. I think that it is highly important, if we have in view simply the performance of our labors among the blacks that we should diligently labor for the welfare of all the poor, without distinction of color." "They have all suffered from the cruel system of slavery," he concluded. Brewer imagined that education could be a bargaining chip with poor white people, much as Edward Pierce and other early northern arrivals in the South Carolina Sea Islands looked to education as a mechanism for controlling freedpeople.[59]

The dilemma for white northerners derived from their impetus to provide education for whites in an environment overwhelmingly hostile to including black and white students in the same classrooms. It would be problematic for northern organizations, ostensibly committed to treating blacks and whites without bias, to provide education for both groups without violating southern mores that demanded separation. But it would be equally troubling for organizations that articulated policies of nondiscrimination to operate segregated schools.[60]

The conflict played itself out in Beaufort, North Carolina, between 1865 and 1867. In November 1865 H. S. Beals arrived in Beaufort to represent the AMA. He opened a day school in the black Methodist church, and on the first day one hundred students enrolled. He also opened a night school with eighty-five adults, more than half of whom could already read and were eager to begin arithmetic and geography. In visits to over fifty homes of African American families, Beals found "most of them able to provide food and comfortably clothed," though a few people were infirm, aged, or destitute. In contrast, the poor white people were "deplorably wretched." Beals reported, "The children of poor whites are already applying to me for books and lessons, as well as something to cover their nakedness." He asked the AMA if it intended that its "charities shall extend beyond the immediate wants of Freedmen." Like Fisk P. Brewer in Raleigh, Beals wanted to be able to donate clothing and other goods sent from the North to poor whites as well as to freedpeople.[61]

In February 1866 Beals repeated his request for a teacher for white students, although several white students had already enrolled in the freedpeople's schools. According to Beals, a few white people had "pleaded so earnestly for these crumbs of knowledge though they should gather them at the Freedmen's table, that I had no heart to deny them." He wrote of white students ranging in age from nine to forty-five attending the freedpeople's schools, "sitting side by side with colored children, without seeming to know or care what is the complexion of their fellow students." Not all prospective white students would attend school alongside blacks, however, and Beals worried about the taunting that the white students endured. Beals also confessed that he "felt compelled to give [supplies from the North] to whites in some instances to preserve life at this inclement season." In addition, he and another teacher paid the monthly tuition for five orphaned white children at a white school, and Beals supplied the children with books that the AMA had sent for freedpeople.[62]

By May 1866 the freedpeople of Beaufort had begun construction of a building large enough to accommodate all of their schools. That fall Beals was eager to open a white school and in fact had discussed with a visiting AMA official the possibility of purchasing a building to house it. However, realizing how controversial such an action would be, he dared not go out on a limb; instead he asked the AMA to send "definite instructions so that I shall not be left to assume any responsibility *beyond* my instructions."[63] In November, when Washburn Institute—the new school for freedpeople—opened, local white officials rented a building to house the white school that Beals agreed to staff with an AMA teacher. "Behind the multitude of Freedmen clamoring for a higher life, intellectually and morally, the white race are pressing, with the same signs of mental starvation, and the same cry for help," Beals informed the AMA. He assigned a "thorough" teacher from the freedpeople's school to the white school, "to give character and success to the work." In January 1867 the teacher, Amy Chapman, reported attendance of ninety-eight students: one-half male, one-half female, all white. The AMA printed Beals's correspondence regarding the white school in the *American Missionary*, but it hastened to add an editorial note assuring readers that the organization would not open a school from which any person could be excluded on account of color.[64]

The AMA was playing it both ways. Officially it propounded a policy of nondiscrimination, but, quietly, some of its officers agreed with Beals that the organization might best modify the biases of white southerners by providing them with teachers.[65] Establishment of the white school ignited open conflict within the AMA between Beals and Samuel J. Whiton, another AMA employee in Beaufort, as well as between Beals and the freedpeople, who considered the separate school offensive. Whiton and Beals had a similar end in mind— changing the prejudices of southern whites—but they thought different means would best get them there. Beals believed teaching would change minds. "Shall we wait to convert them to our ideas, before we give them what alone will secure conversion? Is it our policy, or our principle, to hold this multitude clamoring for intellectual lights outside the benign influence of schools, till we force them to adopt our ideas?" he asked his AMA colleagues. Whiton, on the other hand, believed that southern whites would change their attitudes only if forced. "Last year," he argued, "there were a good number of white children who attended the colored schools, (they were not turned away when they came), and if the same policy had been pursued this year, I think there would have been more—and thus the barrier of prejudice would have been broken down."[66]

For their part, the freedpeople of Beaufort seemed to care less about changing white southern minds than about protecting their resources and their dignity. In March 1867 the "Colored Citizens of Beaufort" drafted a memorial to the American Missionary Association that challenged the AMA's support of a school that excluded black students. The AMA, the group charged, pretended to be a friend to black people but made distinctions based on race and drove them away from the door of the white school like dogs. "This school create a great deal of hurt feelings among the colored people both young and old. The cause of it they have been to that school and they were turn up at the door and by doing that it has been the instigation of white children thinking they are better than colored." Beals, they alleged, was building "up the wall of separation between the two races."[67]

Hyman Thompson, a freedman, followed up with his own letter to the AMA requesting that the white school be opened to black children. He reiterated the concern that the northern men who were supposed to be the friends of the freedpeople were helping to perpetuate the old prejudices of southern whites against blacks. "Mr. Beals says he makes no distinction on account of color," Thompson wrote, "yet he turns colored folks away from it [the white school]. The rebels frankly acknowledge that the reason we cant go is because we are black, and they openly boast that no nigger goes in there." He believed that having a separate school for whites "makes the poor white children feel above the colored and helps to build up the old prejudice." Thompson refuted Beals's assertions that the freedpeople had made no complaints about the school: "I hear that some have written you that the most of the colored people are satisfied about the school. This is false. We are not satisfied." Many people did not openly complain, he said, because they were afraid that Beals would deny them clothes or refuse to hire them if they did. Not only was Thompson concerned with the message of black inferiority that he believed the white school sent, he also accused Beals of diverting resources intended for freedpeople to whites. He alleged that many of the white students had attended pay schools previously and therefore did not need this AMA school. Clothing, sent from the North for freedpeople, was also being given to whites who could afford to purchase their own.[68]

In the midst of this controversy, Amy Chapman resigned her commission, foreseeing potential for a "strong collision between the local authorities and the Bureau Agent on one side, and the colored people on the other." Whiton also resigned, saying that he could not "sanction distinction on account of color in schools or churches." Beals kept the white school open for the remainder of the semester with help from teachers from the black school. In June the freedpeople once again wrote to the AMA: "We would be pleased to have Mr. Beals the next year, provided he made no discrimination in regards to color in the schools. We want new teachers and we would like to have such teachers as Miss Worthington of Morehead City." The letter was signed by Hyman Thompson and twenty-two other men.[69]

Two northern newspapers charged the AMA with operating schools that excluded people of color,[70] but county commissioners in Beaufort soon relieved the organization of further embarrassment by folding the white school into the state's educational system. Even so, it was no secret that the AMA had operated a whites-only school. When, for example, a white woman asked an AMA teacher in Morehead City, North Carolina, ten miles from Beaufort, if there would be a school in the city for whites, the teacher told her that the "Association did not support schools exclusively for whites, and that the one in Beaufort had already passed out of its hands."[71]

African Americans in Beaufort objected to the AMA's decision to establish a whites-only school because they found it demeaning to be summarily excluded from a school solely because of their race, even as whites had been permitted to attend the freedpeople's school. The goal of the Beaufort black community was not integration but equal access to facilities and resources. Some black people in another part of North Carolina were not as tolerant as those in Beaufort had been—they refused to welcome white students into their schools. In Smithfield, white parents, unable to pay tuition at the white school, placed their children in the freedpeople's school taught by an AMA teacher. According to the teacher, "some of the Freedmen did not like this 'spotting the school.'" As the teacher provided no further insight into the black parents' objections, we can only wonder if they sought to exclude white children because they did not like whites, or because they had built the school and resented whites' sharing the benefits, or if they were afraid of the wrath that a mixed school would almost certainly incur from some local whites. Whatever the source of their opposition, the teacher argued that admitting white students was calculated to break down the barriers that had long existed between whites and blacks, and, he reported, the black people acquiesced in his decision. The white children remained.[72]

However much freedpeople may have resented local whites' incursion into their classroom space and whites' use of resources sent to relieve freedpeople's poverty, the success of the schools beckoned to poor whites, and it inspired influential whites to emulate the programs. In April 1866 Francis Cardozo, who was successfully heading up the Saxton School for freedpeople in Charleston, received a message from the governor of South Carolina conveying an interest in establishing a common school system for blacks and whites.[73] The Howard School in Fayetteville, North Carolina, served as a model when whites finally decided to design common schools for white children. The school, built on land purchased by seven black parents, including Charles W. Chesnutt's father, was headed by Robert Harris, an African American who worked for the American Missionary Association. Whites in Fayetteville, embarrassed by a recent court trial in which several white boys had to sign their mark while black boys easily signed their names, decided to create a school for white children and set out to match the quality of the Howard School.[74] Likewise, when a North Carolina state senator and chair of the legislature's education committee wanted to propose legislation to establish a free school system in Wilmington, he turned to an AMA missionary to learn more about freedpeople's schools.[75] The Fayetteville and Wilmington examples are all the more significant when we consider that North Carolina had the best common school system for whites among the southern states. Yet clearly it was not adequately serving the needs of the population.

Schools that freedpeople established became a catalyst that would transform southern education. Reverend S. S. Ashley, an AMA missionary in Wilmington, presciently concluded that schools for freedpeople were "piloting the way for the inauguration of a thorough free school system through the entire South." He was jubilant at the prospect. "The free school(!) the new England free school, has commenced its march through the South(!)," he proclaimed. "Its progress will be irresistible and its track will not be like that of Sherman's army, marked by deserted farms, blackened ruins and a desolated country, a distressed and fugitive people. On the contrary, it will be marked by peace, plenty, prosperity, opulence and righteousness. So let it be."[76]

Public school systems for black and white students came into being while Reconstruction governments composed of African Americans and white northerners held sway in southern statehouses. Throughout the late 1860s and early 1870s, southern states enacted legislation establishing common school systems, most for the first time. As W. E. B. Du Bois put it, "These so-called Carpet Bag governments established the public school systems of the South."[77] African Americans greatly influenced the design of the states' educational agendas. For example, the message that Francis Cardozo received from the governor of South Carolina that indicated the state's interest in a common school system for blacks and whites was not idle talk. When the South Carolina constitutional convention met in Charleston in January 1868 to frame a civil government as required by the Reconstruction Acts, Cardozo was appointed chairman of the convention's education committee. There, he and a number of other African Americans proposed and debated, among other things, a provision for compulsory integrated education supported by taxation. The convention adopted a Cardozo-backed proposal for compulsory education for children between six and twenty-one for at least six months of the year, and it provided for a capitation tax instead of a property tax so that even citizens who did not own property would help to pay for schools. After much debate, the delegates also approved a constitutional amendment providing that all publicly funded schools should be open and free to all youth without regard to race or color. This was an expression of Cardozo's belief that the best method for eliminating prejudice was to permit children to interact in schools. Opponents argued that the provision would force whites who could not afford private schools to send their children to schools with blacks. Governor James Orr and his successor objected as well and repealed the attempt at state-supported integration.[78]

Public funding of education met with great resistance from some white southerners as the opposition to taxation that blocked the establishment of public schools in antebellum period resurfaced to rebuff Reconstruction legislative initiatives.[79] In some places, white response to taxation perverted Reverend Ashley's prediction that common schools would usher in "peace, plenty, prosperity, opulence and righteousness" into naive hyperbole. The violence against freedpeople's schools, teachers, and students, which had been a part of the southern landscape since the first schools began, only increased in some states after legislatures imposed school taxes. Furthermore, in a move that must have taken the air out of Ashley's jubilation, in some parts of the South, white people violently rejected the use of public funds to support education even for white children.

If there were moments when it seemed the South might establish free, even integrated public schools, black teachers and students more often found their very existence under attack from white southerners who questioned the federal government's control of Reconstruction. From the beginning of their education movement, African Americans observed reactions from southern whites ranging from shock, to repulsion, to outright violence. Over time, violent attacks declined in some areas, partly due to the presence of federal troops, but in others men donned the masks and horns of the Ku Klux Klan and whipped schoolteachers and burned school buildings to the ground.[80] This violence was particularly pronounced in Mississippi, where new legislation prescribed support of public schools through a school fund supported from the proceeds of license fees, fines, a two dollar poll tax, and the sale of state-owned property. The congressional committee that in 1871 investigated white violence against blacks in southern states remarked on this phenomenon in its report: "In addition, however, to the general characteristics of Ku-Klux proceedings elsewhere, those in Mississippi are marked by the development of most decided hostility to all free schools, and especially to free schools for colored children."[81]

Black people had begun the educational movement in the South, Reconstruction state legislatures that included African Americans instituted the first public school systems in several states, and now many southern whites associated blacks with public schooling and saw the concept as a sinister measure to give blacks advantages over whites. Since the new legislation provided schooling for all children, opponents set out to eliminate all public schooling, rather than see blacks included. G. Wiley Wells, the United States attorney for the northern district of Mississippi, testified that the Ku Klux Klan in

Winston County, Mississippi, ordered white, native Mississippian John Avery to close his school for white children. According to Wells, the Klan told Avery that the "free-school system could not be put in force in this State, and that no man should teach in that county, under this school system, as the Ku-Klux Klan had received orders from general headquarters to demolish the school-houses, and drive out the teachers." The Klansmen assured Avery that they were his friends and that they issued their warning in a friendly manner. Avery discontinued the school, and the Klan burned down the building. The Klan next visited a member of the school's board of trustees to reinforce the message. Klan members demanded of him the certificates from the school fund, built a bonfire, and burned them. Further, they advised the board member that the recently enacted public school system was a "scheme gotten up by the radicals of the State to educate the negroes so that they might be more than equal with the whites; that they might become superior to the whites, and then terrorize and rule over the whites." The KKK would not permit this shift of power.[82]

Klan members also made clear their objections to free schooling when they visited Colonel A. P. Huggins, a white veteran of the Union army and former Freedmen's Bureau employee, who rented a large plantation in Monroe County, Mississippi. Huggins also served as assistant assessor of internal revenue—he was a tax collector. Klan members ordered him to leave the county within ten days because, they said, he was "collecting obnoxious taxes from southern gentlemen to keep damned old radicals in office." They wanted no laws enforced that they had not made themselves. Huggins chal lenged the men. There was a black school and a white school in the neighbor-hood, and he knew that most of the men's children attended the white school that a Mr. Davis taught. He asked if they were dissatisfied with the school. They liked Davis well enough, the men said, but they were "opposed to the free-school system entirely; that the whites could do as they had always done before; that they could educate their own children; that so far as the negroes were concerned, they did not need educating, only to work." The Klansmen asserted that they could manage their own affairs and did not need the state or the United States government sending people like Huggins to educate either their children or black children. Perhaps due to his job as tax assessor, or perhaps because Huggins was more confrontational than most whites whom the Klan visited, the Klansmen took him from the yard and whipped him severely. Most whites got away with a warning.[83]

White resistance to school taxes was not limited to the South; indeed, citizens of northeastern and midwestern states also initially rejected the no-tion of being taxed to pay for education.[84] Two factors, however, exacerbated southern hostility. First, portions of the school tax would be used to educate African Americans. Second, Reconstruction governments, which many southern whites believed did not represent them, imposed numerous other taxes on citizens. Following the war, revenue systems in southern states were fundamentally restructured as states had to raise money for rebuilding as well as to fund new priorities, including education. As property values had fallen during the war, rates had to increase in order to collect significant revenues. This placed a heavy burden on potential taxpayers. In Mississippi one-fifth of the privately owned land in the state was forfeited to the government for failure to pay property taxes.[85]

The result was an outcry from whites who complained that since most blacks did not own property, they paid less than their share of the taxes. These arguments, of course, discounted the poll taxes and the property taxes that some African Americans paid, and they certainly failed to acknowledge the reasons why most blacks did not own property. As W. E. B. Du Bois argued as well, black people who leased the land on which they farmed paid taxes through their rents since plantation owners passed tax assessments on to tenants.[86] Southern gentry had lost the property they held in slaves, and the value of their real property had declined. Now new state governments over which they exercised little control sought to collect additional revenue from them, some of which would be used to educate their former slaves. Some southern whites opposed taxation for education on principle, and others felt its pinch in the economic hard times that followed the war. But their animosity toward black schools was more intense than toward the white ones that they sometimes allowed to continue operating if parents paid the fees.[87]

At its core, white opposition to black education lay in much more than hostility toward taxation; it was born of jealousy, fear, and insecurity in a radically shifting social order. Southern whites could not help but hear the positive comments of supportive whites and, indeed, view for themselves African Americans' public displays of newly acquired knowledge and skills. This phenomenon of African Americans outwardly proclaiming their access to education was everywhere. Mississippi attorney general Joshua Morris, a white southerner, testified to facts that had become common knowledge: "The children go to school, as do also many of the adults, and they learn rapidly. I have seen colored children learn as rapidly as I ever saw white children learn." Then Morris commented on the public nature of the learning: "Going along the street I have seen little fellows of an age at which you would hardly expect white children to read, spelling the signs on the doors; and I have seen them reading books and newspapers. I have occasionally visited their schools and heard them recite, and they show a great deal of improvement."[88] Morris claimed to be in favor of this turn of events, but the sight of black children performing their learning in the streets sent chills down the spines of many southern whites who shared the frustration, chagrin, and violent inclinations of a white woman who, upon hearing black children singing "John Brown's body lies a-mouldering in his grave," stepped into the doorway of the Charleston, South Carolina, school and exclaimed, "Oh, I wish I could put a torch to that building, the niggers."[89]

Black adults and children attending school constituted no innocent act to white people attempting to recover from humiliating defeat and trying to hold on to the power that their whiteness had previously either bestowed upon them or, at least, had enabled them to imagine. If African Americans saw in education the promise of political and social advancement, southern whites did, too, and dreaded just that outcome. James Rives, a white attorney and former Confederate soldier from Noxubee County, Mississippi, expressed his own fears and those of other whites when he testified before the congressional committee investigating Klan violence thusly: "The apprehension seems to be this; that the conferring of the right of suffrage on the negro, and his equality before the law, and his right to all the privileges of the free schools, will in process of time bring the two races together in the schoolroom as children, and that in that way the principles of their children and the rising generation will eventually be more or less affected." Committee members wondered how the intermingling of black and white children would be any different in postbellum schoolrooms than it had been in slavery, when black and white children played and grew up together. The difference, however, was vast and consequential to Rives. Freedom had changed everything. "When they mingled together heretofore," he informed the committee, "the white child recognized his own superiority; he was the child of the owner, and the negro or colored child was recognized as the child of the slave." Subordination of blacks to whites was critical to Rives's understanding of what he and other white people had lost and stood to lose. "The negro himself recognized that supposed superiority, and in recognizing it showed a proper deference. When you would see the negro child and the white child at play together around the plantation, the negro child invariably gave way to the white, and the white children were often domineering in consequence." Rives and many other southern whites feared the loss of this social system steeped in deference and domination. If black children no longer recognized themselves as inferior, and were in fact surpassing white children in measurable ways, and if white children, through intermingling with black children, had begun to doubt their own superiority, how long could white adults hope to hold on to power?[90]

African Americans well understood that white objections to their education directly related to a desire to relegate them to their pre-emancipation social status and to regulate black behavior. Caroline Smith, a thirty-five-year-old black woman in Walton County, Georgia, whose naked body the Klan whipped for allegedly sassing white women, articulated the connection between whites' desire to deny education and the intention to keep blacks subservient. She testified that the Ku Klux Klan threatened to whip numerous black people if they kept a school. When an investigator asked her why the Klan did not want blacks to have schools, she responded as though he must surely have understood their motivations as well as she. "School!" Smith exclaimed. "They would not let us have schools. They went to a colored man there, whose son had been teaching school, and they took every book they had and threw them into the fire; and they said they would just dare any other nigger to have a book in his house." According to Smith, before this incident members of the black community had vowed that they would have a school in each district. The black people had begun the schools. "But," she testified, "the Ku Klux said they would whip every man who sent a scholar there. There is a school-house there, but no scholars." Then, in the same breath Smith told investigators, "The colored people dare not dress up themselves and fix up, like they thought anything of themselves, for fear they would whip us. I have been humble and obedient to them, a heap more so than I was to my master, who raised me; and that is the way they serve us." It was all of one piece to her: denial of education and denial of self-assertion and self-determination. In Smith's estimation, by burning schools and humiliating her with a whipping, the KKK had set her and other African Americans farther back than they had been while enslaved. Release from slavery had not granted them the freedom to educate themselves, nor had it freed them from displaying deference to white people.[91]

Violence was not the only way to thwart African Americans' intentions to attend school and receive a quality education. Reconstruction legislatures frequently underfunded state school systems, and sometimes the monies provided were either redeployed to competing priorities or depleted by graft. But in the beginning, these failings tended to affect black and white children equally. As Reconstruction came to an end, however, and northerners relinquished their objections to white southern racism and pursued sectional reconciliation, provisions for black education took a decided turn for the worse.[92] White supremacist Redeemers who took power after federal withdrawal did not eliminate schools for African American children, but through disparities in funding, they set out to make clear distinctions between the quality of white education and black education.[93]

States did not immediately push back African American educational or political gains; retrenchment took place gradually. Institutionalization of segregation happened over a period of years as well.[94] Gradually, too, states either designed statutes that permitted them to treat blacks and whites unequally, or they gave local governments vast discretion to reduce funding for black schools. Local governments, in turn, devised all manner of methods to minimize spending for African American schools. An 1867 Mississippi law, for example, established separate schools for black and white students and provided that teachers could be paid differentially depending on the type of certification they held. This placed county superintendents in the position to determine teacher salaries. As disfranchisement removed African Americans from government offices and rendered them incapable of influencing electoral outcomes, African Americans also lost any authority to have input into educational policies and laws. As a result, per capita expenditures for black students fell below that for white children, and the length of school terms as well as teacher salaries for black schools lagged behind those of white schools.[95]

In his 1901 examination of black southern schools, W. E. B. Du Bois concluded that they had been severely neglected by the state. Whites, he said, had no interest in black schools, and teachers, particularly in country schools, were often inadequately trained. Higher wages, he suggested, would attract better-prepared teachers.[96] By 1911, when Du Bois and Fisk University published an updated study, every southern and some western states had enacted Jim Crow legislation. Separate but equal was the law. And though southern states paid close attention to enforcing separateness, equality was anathema. Du Bois and the Fisk University team of researchers studied school records from eighteen states and the District of Columbia. They reached nine conclusions. First, the majority of black children of school age did not attend school at all. Second, these children were out of school due to a lack of facilities, poverty, and the "ignorance" of parents. Third, many students in school had undertrained, underpaid teachers and school terms that varied between three and six months. Fourth, schoolhouses and the equipment in black schools were frequently "wretched and inadequate." Fifth, black schools received little attention from school superintendents and other authorities. Sixth, the result, and apparently one of the objectives of disfranchisement, had been to reduce school funds for black schools, lower the pay of teachers in the schools, and thus dissuade the most competent teachers. Seventh, the emphasis on manual and industrial training in black schools diminished the amount of time that teachers devoted to essential studies such as reading, writing, and arithmetic. Eighth, educational progress in the South in the preceding ten years had been almost entirely confined to white students. The movement for local school taxes, better high schools, consolidation of schools and facilities, and transportation had been undertaken on behalf of whites alone. Further, in some instances, African Americans were taxed for the improvement of white schools, yet their own schools continued to be inadequately funded. Ninth, the decline in elementary education was accompanied by a tendency to decry intellectual training for African Americans.[97]

The Fisk researchers summarized their findings with a statement that could have been uttered in 1861 when African American freedpeople first began to establish schools: "The Negroes themselves are making heroic efforts to remedy these evils thru a wide-spread system of private, self-supported schools."[98] In 1861 such a statement would have been hopeful, an acknowledgement of agency and a promise of empowerment. Fifty years later, it was sad and disheartening. What good emerged from neglected, underfunded southern black schools in the early twentieth century once again came only through the determination of black teachers and students.[99]

EPILOGUE

Elijah Marrs died in the summer of 1910, even as W. E. B. Du Bois and his Fisk University team conducted the research for *The Common School and the Negro American*.[1] At seventy years old, Marrs had lived through slavery, emancipation, Reconstruction, and redemption. He had been enfranchised and disfranchised. Marrs taught in Kentucky's "Colored Schools" for nearly thirty years, until 1892. Both as a teacher and, after retirement, an observer of the state's public schools, Marrs would have been mindful of the unequal system that the state had designed for black students. Unless his political sensibilities had mellowed considerably, he, like Du Bois, would have been chagrined at the glaring disparities between resources committed to white students and those grudgingly provided to black students. He would have been one of the black teachers who drew upon personal resources to countervail paltry school budgets.

Despite these frustrations, Marrs would likely also have recalled the days when as an enslaved boy, he had stolen his own education. He would have remembered that the markings he left around the plantation as he practiced his new writing skills could have earned him a whipping. As an adult, far removed from enslavement, there would have been moments, too, while teaching a lesson that he would have marveled at the rows of African American children seated before him in a government-funded school. At the same time, Marrs's anger would have flashed when he confronted the fact that despite freedpeople's deep desire for education, despite their labors to establish schools, and despite the impetus that African Americans provided for the establishment of southern public school systems, black students remained shut out from receiving the full benefits of the educational system that their parents and grandparents had helped to create.

After thirty-five years of freedom, southern African Americans still provided land and built their own schools, with a little help from northern philanthropists. They still trained their own teachers, in grotesquely underfunded normal schools and colleges. They still received a disproportionately meager share of state funds to support their schools. When Elijah Marrs died in 1910, southern African Americans remained, like Marrs, self-taught. They would remain so for another forty-five years.

African Americans invested great faith in the ability of literacy first to enable them to escape from slavery, and then to make freedom meaningful in the emancipation period. They went to extraordinary lengths to gain this literacy: in slavery, they defied laws and disobeyed owners; in freedom, they sacrificed scarce material resources and their personal safety. In the earliest moments of freedom, former slaves sought to carve out education and public schooling as rights to which their forced labor entitled them. Education, they believed, would make possible their independence and their full participation in civil society.

Slave owners feared black literacy, fully realizing that literacy rendered even more difficult the task of sublimating and controlling individuals and communities. When freedom came, some northern whites suggested that African Americans had limited intellectual ability, and many white southerners employed a host of strategies, including violence, to restrict black access to education. The shame of it is that this inclination to question black people's intellect survives. Further, many white people, including some influential ones, still fear the economic and social disruptions that could result if most black children had access to the highest quality education available in this country. Sadder yet is the fact that some black people, either unaware of the histories of African Americans' struggle for education or weary from the daily battles within classrooms, internalize negative assessments of both their abilities and their values and opt out of the fight. The dedication to education of the people within these pages—Mattie Jackson, Frederick Douglass, Harry McMillan, Rose Anna, John Sweney, John McCline, William Grey, Margaret Adams, Bartley Townsley, London Ferebee, and Aury Jeter—explodes any narrative that seeks to represent African Americans as people who do not value education.

APPENDIX

African Americans, Literacy, and the Law in the Antebellum South

This appendix contains, in the first section, the wording of southern state laws that prohibited teaching slaves and free people of color to read or write and, in the second section, the wording of other southern state laws that pertained to literacy.

State Antiliteracy Statutes

Alabama

Acts Passed at the Thirteenth Annual Session of the General Assembly of the State of Alabama, 1831

Section 10. *And be it further enacted*, that any person or persons who shall endeavor or attempt to teach any free person of color, or slave, to spell, read, or write, shall, upon conviction thereof by indictment, be fined in a sum not less than two hundred and fifty dollars nor more than five hundred dollars.

[Sections 11 and 12 further prohibit any free person of color or any slave from writing any "pass or free paper" for any slave.]

Source: Paul Finkelman, ed., *State Slavery Statutes* (microfiche; Frederick, Md.: University Publications of America, 1989).

Acts of the General Assembly of Alabama, 1856

AN ACT to prohibit the teaching of slaves to read and write.

Section 1. *Be it enacted by the Senate and House of Representatives of the State of Alabama in General Assembly convened*, That if any person or persons shall teach or be engaged in teaching, in this State, any slave or slaves to read or write, he, she, or they shall be liable to indictment therefor, and, on conviction, shall be fined not less than one hundred dollars and be imprisoned in the county jail not less than three months, one or both, at the discretion of the jury trying the case.

Source: Paul Finkelman, ed., *State Slavery Statutes* (microfiche; Frederick, Md.: University Publications of America, 1989).

Georgia

Georgia, 1829

An Act to be entitled an act, to amend the several laws now in force in this State, regulating quarantine in the several sea ports of this State, and to prevent the circulation of written or printed papers within this State calculated to excite disaffection among the coloured people of this state, and to prevent said people from being taught to read or write. . . .

Section 10. *And be it further enacted,* That if any slave, negro, mustizzo [*sic*], or free person of colour, or any other person, shall circulate, bring or cause to be circulated or brought into this state or aid or assist in any manner, or be instrumental in aiding or assisting in the circulation or bringing into this state, or in any manner concerned in any printed or written pamphlet, paper or circular, for the purposes of exciting to insurrection, conspiracy or resistance among the slaves, negroes, or free persons of colour, of this state, against their owners or the citizens of this state, the said person or persons offending against this section of this act, shall be punished with death.

Section 11. *And be it further enacted,* that if any slave, negro, or free person of colour or any white person shall teach any other slave, negro or free person of colour, to read or write either written or printed characters, the said free person of color, or slave, shall be punished by fine and whipping, or fine or shipping at the discretion of the court; and if a white person so offending, he, she or they shall be punished with fine, not exceeding five hundred dollars, and imprisonment, in the common jail at the discretion of the court before whom said offender is tried.

Source: Paul Finkelman, ed., *State Slavery Statutes* (microfiche; Frederick, Md.: University Publications of America, 1989).

Georgia Penal Code, 1833

Section 18. If any person shall teach any slave, negro, or free person of colour, to read or write, either written or printed characters, or shall procure, suffer, or permit, a slave, negro, or person of colour, to transact business for him in writing, such person so offending, shall be guilty of a misdemeanor, and on conviction, shall be punished by fine, or imprisonment in the common jail of the county, or both, at the discretion of the court.

Section 19. If any person, owning or having in his possession and under his control any printing press or types in this State, shall use or employ, or permit to be used or employed, any slave or free person of colour, in the setting up of types, or other labour about the office, requiring said slave or free person of colour, a knowledge of reading or writing, such person so offending, shall be guilty of a misdemeanor, and on conviction, shall be punished by a fine not exceeding one hundred dollars.

Source: Paul Finkelman, ed., *State Slavery Statutes* (microfiche; Frederick, Md.: University Publications of America, 1989).

Louisiana
Acts Passed at the Second Session of the Ninth Legislature of the State of Louisiana, January 4, 1830
An Act to punish the crimes therein mentioned and for other purposes.

Section 1. *Be it enacted by the senate and house of representatives of the state of Louisiana, in general assembly convened*; That whosoever shall write, print, publish or distribute, any thing having a tendency to produce discontent among the free coloured population of the state, or insubordination among the slaves therein, shall on conviction thereof, before any court of competent jurisdiction, be sentenced to imprisonment at hard labour for life or suffer death, at the discretion of the court.

Section 2. *Be it further enacted*; That whosoever shall make use of language, in any public discourse, from the bar, the bench, the stage, the pulpit, or in any place whatsoever; or whosoever shall make use of language in private discourses or conversations, or shall make use of signs or actions having a tendency to produce discontent among the free coloured population of this state, or to excite insubordination among the slaves therein, or whosoever shall knowingly be instrumental in bringing into this state, any paper, pamphlet or book, having such tendency as aforesaid, shall on conviction thereof, before any court of competent jurisdiction, suffer imprisonment at hard labour, not less than three years, nor more than twenty-one years, or death, at the discretion of the court.

Section 3. *Be it further enacted*; That all persons who shall teach, or permit or cause to be taught, any slave in this state, to read or write, shall, on conviction thereof, before any court of competent jurisdiction be imprisoned not less than one month nor more than twelve months.

Source: Paul Finkelman, ed., *State Slavery Statutes* (microfiche; Frederick, Md.: University Publications of America, 1989).

Mississippi
Code of Mississippi. Article 3, Section 2, 1823
Meetings of Slaves or Free Negroes with Slaves, above the number of Five, in places of Public Resort, by Night, or at Schools by Day or Night.

All meetings or assemblies of Slaves, or free negroes, or mulattoes, mixing and associating with such slaves, above the number of five, at any place of public resort, or at any meeting house or houses, in the night, or at any school or schools, for teaching them reading or writing, either in the day or night, under whatsoever pretext, shall be deemed and considered an unlawful assembly, and any Justice of the Peace of the county or corporation, wherein such assemblage shall be, either from his own knowledge, or the information of others, of such unlawful assemblage or meeting, may issue his warrant, directed to any sworn officer or officers, authorizing him or them to enter the house or houses where such unlawful assemblages or meetings may be, for the purpose of apprehending or dispersing such slaves, free negroes, or mulattoes, and to inflict corporal punishment on the offender or offenders, at the discretion of any such Justice of the Peace, not exceeding thirty-nine lashes, in the manner hereinafter directed.

Source: A. Hutchinson, comp., *Code of Mississippi: Being an Analytical Compilation of the Public and General Statutes of the Territory and State, with Tabular References to the Local and Private Acts, from 1798–1848* (Jackson, Miss., 1848).

Missouri
Laws of the State of Missouri Passed at the First Session of the Fourteenth General Assembly, 1847

AN ACT respecting slaves, free negroes and mulattoes, 1847

Be it enacted by the General Assembly of the State of Missouri, as follows:

1. No person shall keep or teach any school for the instruction of negroes or mulattoes, in reading or writing, in this State.

2. No meeting or assemblage of negroes or mulattoes, for the purpose of religious worship, or preaching, shall be held or permitted where the services are performed or conducted by negroes or mulattoes, unless some sheriff, constable, marshal, police officer, or justice of the peace, shall be present during all the time of such meeting or assemblage, in order to prevent all seditious speeches, and disorderly and unlawful conduct of every kind.

3. All meeting of negroes or mulattoes, for the purposes mentioned in the two preceding sections, shall be considered unlawful assemblages, and shall be suppressed by sheriffs, constables, and other public officers. . . .

5. If any person shall violate the provisions of this act, he shall, for every such offence, be indicted and punished by fine not exceeding five hundred dollars, or by imprisonment not exceeding six months, or by both such fine and imprisonment.

Source: Laws of the State of Missouri Passed at the First Session of the Fourteenth General Assembly, 1847 (Jefferson, Mo.: James Lusk Public Printer, 1847), 102–4.

North Carolina

Acts Passed by the General Assembly of the State of North Carolina, at the Session of 1830–31

Chapter VI. An act to prevent all persons from teaching slaves to read or write, the use of figures excepted.

Whereas the teaching of slaves to read and write, has a tendency to excite dissatisfaction in their minds, and to produce insurrection and rebellion, to the manifest injury of the citizens of the State: Therefore,

[I.] *Be it enacted by the General Assembly of the State of North Carolina, and it is hereby enacted by the authority of the same,* That any free person, who shall hereafter teach, or attempt to teach, any slave within this State to read or write, the use of figures excepted, or shall give or sell to such slave or slaves any books or pamphlets, shall be liable to indictment in any court of record in this State having jurisdiction thereof; and upon conviction, shall, at the discretion of the court, if a white man or woman, be fined not less than one hundred dollars, nor more than two hundred dollars, or imprisoned; and if a free person of color, shall be fined, imprisoned, or whipped, at the discretion of the court, not exceeding thirty-nine lashes, nor less than twenty lashes.

II. *Be it further enacted,* That if any slave shall hereafter teach, or attempt to teach, any other slave to read or write, the use of figures excepted, he or she may be carried before any justice of the peace, and on conviction thereof, shall be sentenced to receive thirty-nine lashes on his or her bare back.

III. *Be it further enacted,* That the judges of the Superior Courts and the justices of the County Courts shall give this act in charge to the grand jurors of their respective counties.

Source: Paul Finkelman, ed., *State Slavery Statutes* (microfiche; Frederick, Md.: University Publications of America, 1989).

South Carolina
Act of 1740

Whereas the having of slaves taught to write, or suffering them to be employed in writing, may be attended with great inconveniences, *Be it enacted*, That all and every person and persons whatsoever who shall hereafter teach or cause any slave or slaves to be taught to write, or shall use or employ any slave as a scribe in any manner of writing hereafter taught to write, every such person or persons shall for every such offence forfeit the sum of one hundred pounds current money.

Source: George M. Stroud, ed., *A Sketch of the Laws Relating to Slavery in the Several States of the United States of America* (1856; New York: Negro Universities Press, 1968).

Acts and Resolutions of the General Assembly of the State of South Carolina, December 1800

Whereas, the law heretofore enacted for the government of slaves, free Negroes, mulattoes, and mestizoes, have been found insufficient for the keeping them in due subordination:

Be it therefore enacted by the honorable the Senate and House of Representatives, of the state of South-Carolina, now met and sitting in General Assembly, and by the authority of the same, That from and after the passing of this law, all assemblies and congregations of slaves, free Negroes, mulattoes, and mestizoes, whether composed of all, or any of the above description of persons, or of all or any of the above described persons, and of a proportion of white persons, assembled or met together for the purpose of mental instruction, in a confined or secret place of meeting, or with the gates or doors of such place of meeting barred, bolted, or locked, so as to prevent the free ingress and egress to and from the same, shall be, and the same is hereby declared to be an unlawful meeting; and the magistrates, sheriffs, militia officers, and officers of the patrol, being commissioned, are hereby directed, required and empowered, to enter into such confined places where such unlawful assemblies are convened, and for that purpose, to break doors, gates, or windows, if resisted, and disperse such slaves, free Negroes, mulattoes, or mestizoes, as may be then and there found unlawfully met together, and convened, and such magistrates, sheriffs, constables, militia officers, or officers of the patrol, are hereby empowered and required to call unto their assistance, such force and assistance from the neighbourhood, as he or they may judge necessary for the dispersing of such unlawful assemblage of persons of colour as aforesaid . . . . [The punishment for this offense was not to exceed twenty lashes.]

And be it further enacted by the authority aforesaid, That from and after the passing of this act, it shall not be lawful for any number of slaves, free negroes, mulattoes, or mestizoes, even in company with white persons, to meet together and assemble, for the purpose of mental instruction, or religious worship, either before the rising of the sun, or after the going down of the same. And all magistrates, sheriffs, militia officers, and officers of the patrol, being commissioned, city or town guard, or watchmen, are hereby vested with all the powers and authority for dispersing such assemblies, before day, or after sunset, as is herein and hereby given to them in the first clause of this act. And the said officers are also empowered to impose on all such slaves, free negroes, mulattoes, or mestizoes, the same punishment as by the patrol law they are authorized to do in any case whatsoever.

Source: Paul Finkelman, ed., *State Slavery Statutes* (microfiche; Frederick, Md.: University Publications of America, 1989).

Acts and Resolutions of the General Assembly of the State of South Carolina, December 1834

Chapter 5—An Act to amend the Laws in relation to slaves and free persons of color.

Section 1. *Be it enacted by the Honorable the senate and House of Representatives, now met and sitting in General Assembly and by the authority of the same.* If any person shall hereafter teach any slave to read or write, or shall aid or assist in teaching any slave to read or write or cause or procure any slave to be taught to read or write; such person, if a free white person, upon conviction thereof, shall, for each and every offence against this act, be fined not exceeding one hundred dollars, and imprisoned not more than six months; of if a free person of color, shall be whipped not exceeding fifty lashes, and fined not exceeding fifty dollars, at the discretion of the court of magistrates, and free holders before which such free person of color is tried; and if a slave, shall be whipped at the discretion of the court, not exceeding fifty lashes; the informer to be entitled to one half of the fine, and to be a competent witness; and if any free person of color or slave, shall keep any school or other place of instruction, for teaching any slave or free person of color to read or write, such person of color or slave, shall be liable to the same fine, imprisonment and corporal punishment, as are by this section, imposed and inflicted on free persons of color and slaves, for teaching slaves to read or write.

Source: Paul Finkelman, *State Slavery Statutes* (microfiche; Frederick, Md.: University Publications of America, 1989).

Virginia
Revised Code of 1819

That all meetings or assemblages of slaves, or free negroes or mulattoes mixing and associating with such slaves at any *meeting-house* or houses, &c., in the night; or any SCHOOL *for teaching them* READING OR WRITING, *either in the day or night*, under whatsoever pretext, shall be deemed and considered an UNLAWFUL ASSEMBLY; and any justice of a county, &c., wherein such assemblage shall be, either from his own knowledge or the information of others, of such unlawful assemblage &c., may issue his warrant directed to any sworn officer or officers, authorizing him or them to enter the house or houses where such unlawful assemblances &c., may be, for the purpose of *apprehending or dispersing* such slaves, and *to inflict corporal punishment on the offender or offenders*, at the discretion of any justice of the peace, *not exceeding twenty lashes.*

Source: William Goodell, *The American Slave Code in Theory and Practice: Its Distinctive Features Shown by Its Statutes, Decisions, and Illustrative Facts* (New York: American and Foreign Anti-Slavery Society, 1853), 321.

Acts Passed at a General Assembly of the Commonwealth of Virginia, April 1831
Chapter XXXIX—An Act to amend the act concerning slaves, free negroes and mulattoes. . . .

4. *Be it further enacted*, That all meetings of free negroes or mulattoes, at any school-house, church, meeting-house or other place for teaching them reading or writing, either in the day or night, under whatsoever pretext, shall be deemed and considered as an unlawful assembly; and any justice of the county or corporation, wherein such assemblage shall be, either from his own knowledge, or on the information of others, of such unlawful assemblage or meeting, shall issue his warrant, directed to any sworn officer or officers, authorizing him or them, to enter the house or houses where such unlawful assemblage or meeting may be, for the purpose of apprehending or dispersing such free negroes or mulattoes, and to inflict corporal punishment on the offender or offenders, at the discretion of any justice of the peace, not exceeding twenty lashes.

5. *Be it further enacted*, That if any white person or persons assemble with free negroes or mulattoes in any school-house, church, meeting-house, or other place for the purpose of instructing such free negroes or mulattoes to read or write, such person or persons shall, on conviction thereof, be fined in a sum not exceeding fifty dollars, and moreover may be imprisoned at the discretion of a jury, not exceeding two months.

6. *Be it further enacted*, That if any white person, for pay or compensation, shall assemble with any slaves for the purpose of teaching, and shall teach any slave to read or write, such person or any white person or persons contracting with such teacher so to act, who shall offend as aforesaid, shall, for each offence, be fined at the discretion of a jury, in a sum not less than ten, nor exceeding one hundred dollars, to be recovered on an information or indictment.

Source: Paul Finkelman, *State Slavery Statutes* (microfiche; Frederick, Md.: University Publications of America, 1989).

Acts of the General Assembly of Virginia, 1849

39. Every assemblage of slaves, free negroes or mulattoes, at any meeting house or other place for the purpose of public religious worship, where such worship shall be conducted by a slave, free negro or mulatto, and every such assemblage for the purpose of instruction in reading or writing, by whomsoever conducted, and every such assemblage in the night time under whatsoever pretext, shall be an unlawful assembly, and it shall be the duty of all magistrates to suppress all such assemblies which occur within their respective jurisdictions; and as often as any slaves, free negroes or mulattoes shall be unlawfully assembled, it shall be the duty of each magistrate within whose jurisdiction the assemblage may be, forthwith to disperse the same, and to that end he may issue his warrant directed to any sheriff, constable,

sergeant, or other person specially designated, commanding him to enter the house or place where such assemblage may be, and seize any slave, free negro or mulatto there found, and it shall be lawful for the magistrate giving such warrant, or any other magistrate before whom the same may be returned, to order any slave, free negro or mulatto so seized to be punished by stripes not exceeding thirty-nine.

40. Any white person who shall assemble with slaves, free negroes or mulattoes for the purpose of instructing them to read or write, or shall associate with slaves, free negroes and mulattoes in an unlawful assembly thereof, shall be punished by confinement in the jail not exceeding six months, and by fine not exceeding one hundred dollars . . . .

Source: Paul Finkelman, *State Slavery Statutes* (microfiche; Frederick, Md.: University Publications of America, 1989).

Other Laws Related to Literacy
Permission to Teach Certain Persons of Color
Acts Passed at the Annual Session of the General Assembly of the State of Alabama, November 1833
An act to authorize the instruction of certain free persons of color therein described.

Whereas, there are now residing in the city and county of Mobile and Baldwin, many free colored Creoles of said city and counties, whose ancestors were residing there in the time of the change of the flag, and to whom, by the treaty entered into between the French republic and the United States of America, in 1803, were secured the enjoyments of all the rights, advantages and immunities of citizens of the United States: and whereas the said colored Creoles have heretofore conducted themselves with uniform propriety and good order, and are anxious to have their offspring educated: therefore,

Be it enacted by the Senate and House of Representatives of the State of Alabama in General Assembly convened, That the mayor and aldermen of the city of Mobile shall have power to authorize and license such person or persons, as they may deem suitable to teach and instruct, for limited periods, the free colored Creole children, residents within the limits of the city and counties of Mobile and Baldwin, who are descended of those persons who were residents of the said city or counties, at the time the treaty made between the French republic and the United States of America, in April, 1803, was ratified: *Provided always*, that none of the colored children shall be so taught and instructed, until they shall first have the permission of the said mayor and aldermen of the city of Mobile, and they shall have recorded the names of such children in a book to be kept by them for that purpose.

Source: Paul Finkelman, ed., *State Slavery Statutes* (microfiche; Frederick, Md.: University Publications of America, 1989).

Acts of the General Assembly of Virginia, 1842
Whereas, it appearing to the general assembly that Henry Juett Gray, of the county of Rockingham, a blind youth of reputable character and exemplary deportment, who has made considerable progress in scientific attainments, is desirous of qualifying

himself to become a teacher of the blind; and that in order to his comfort and extensive usefulness, it is necessary that he should have the services of a servant capable of reading and writing, which object cannot be permanently secured otherwise than by the education of a young slave named Randolph, the property of said Henry Juett: and it further appearing that Robert Gray, the father of said Henry Juett, is willing to indemnify the public against any possible injury which might be apprehended from the misconduct of said slave:

1. *Be it therefore enacted,* That it shall be lawful for the said Henry Juett Gray, or any friend for him, to employ from time to time any competent white person or persons to teach the said slave Randolph reading and writing, and for such white person or persons so to teach said slave without incurring any of the penalties prescribed by law in such cases: *Provided, however,* that this act shall be of no force or effect until the said Robert Gray, or some other responsible person, shall execute before the county court of Rockingham county bond with two or more sufficient sureties, payable to the sitting justices thereof, and their successors, in a penalty to be fixed by said court, but not less than double the value of said slave at mature age, and conditioned for indemnifying the commonwealth and the citizens thereof against any improper use by said slave of the art of reading and writing, and for the sale and removal of said slave by said Henry Juett Gray, or any future proprietor thereof, beyond the limits of this commonwealth, in the event of his conviction of any crime.

Source: Paul Finkelman, ed., *State Slavery Statutes* (microfiche; Frederick, Md.: University Publications of America, 1989).

Slavery and the Common Schools

Acts and Resolutions of the General Assembly of the State of Florida, 1851
Chapter 311.

Be it enacted by the Senate and House of Representatives of the State of Florida in General Assembly convened, That hereafter when any slave or slaves shall be taken up under an order from the Circuit Court, in accordance with the provisions of the act approved November 22, 1829, said slave or slaves shall be considered as belonging to the Common School Fund; and all the money derived from the sale of said slave or slaves, after the payment of the necessary expenses, shall be paid into the Treasury of the State as belonging to the principal of said Fund, and be invested in the same manner as other moneys of said Fund are required to be invested.

[The Act of November 22, 1829, referred to above, provided that any slave manumitted contrary to the provisions of the act, should not be considered free, but instead should be taken up by the marshal or sheriff and sold.]

Source: Paul Finkelman, ed., *State Slavery Statutes* (microfiche; Frederick, Md.: University Publications of America, 1989).

An act amendatory to the Memphis [Tennessee] City Charter passed February 25, 1851; 1860 Edition, Art. IV, Title I, page 157, Memphis City Charter

Section 4. Be it enacted by the General Assembly of the State of Tennessee, that no one shall be admitted as a pupil (in the city schools) but white persons, residing within the city limits, between the ages of six and twenty years.

Source: John Eaton, *Grant, Lincoln, and the Freedmen: Reminiscences of the Civil War with Special Reference to the Work for the Contrabands and Freedmen of the Mississippi Valley* (New York: Longmans, Green, 1907), 192 n. 1.

The Education of Apprentices
Acts of the General Assembly of the State of Arkansas, 1840

An act to restrict the provisions of the second section of an act in the Revised Statutes of the State of Arkansas, under the head of Apprentices.

Be it enacted by the General Assembly of the State of Arkansas, That so much of the second section of a law in the Revised Statutes, of the State of Arkansas as is made applicable to free negro apprentices, be, and the same is hereby, repealed.

Be it further enacted, That in lieu of education, as provided to be given to free negro apprentices in the said second section of the law aforesaid, the master of any free negro apprentice shall be required to give to any male free negro apprentice, on his arriving at the age of twenty-one years, the sum of one hundred and fifty dollars; and to any female apprentice, the following property, or the value thereof in money, viz: one bed, to be worth twenty-five dollars, one cow and calf, to be worth twelve dollars; and one suit of clothes to be worth fifteen dollars; to be paid when said apprentice shall arrive at the age of eighteen years. And in lieu of the provisions of the law to which this is an amendment, as requires the master of any white apprentice to send him, or her, or them to school, one fourth of the time he, she, or they may be bound to service, the master of any such apprentice shall be bound to teach said apprentice, or apprentices, reading, writing and arithmetic, to the rule of three inclusive.

Source: Paul Finkelman, ed., *State Slavery Statutes* (microfiche; Frederick, Md.: University Publications of America, 1989).

Laws of the State of Maryland, 1850
Chapter 221, Section 32.

And be it enacted, That every master of apprentices, and every other person in said county, to whom any white child, between the said ages of six and twenty years shall be bound out to service, shall be required to send each and every such white child so bound to him or them to the district school of the district in which such master shall reside, at least one month in every year, or for such a length of time during the said child's apprenticeship, as shall, in the aggregate amount to the same as one month in every year of such apprenticeship . . . .

Source: Paul Finkelman, ed., *State Slavery Statutes* (microfiche; Frederick, Md.: University Publications of America, 1989).

Revised Statutes of the State of Missouri, 1845

Section 10. When an apprentice is a negro or mulatto, it shall not be the duty of the master to cause such colored apprentice to be taught to read or write, or a knowledge of arithmetic, but he shall be allowed at the expiration of his term of service, a sum of money in lieu of education, to be assessed by the county court.

[This statute was re-enacted in 1856.]

Source: Paul Finkelman, ed., *State Slavery Statutes* (microfiche; Frederick, Md.: University Publications of America, 1989).

NOTES

Abbreviations

The following abbreviations are used throughout the notes.

AMA Mss.	American Missionary Association Manuscripts, 1839–1882, Amistad Research Center, Tilton Hall, Tulane University, New Orleans, La.
FBR	Records of the Bureau of Refugees, Freedmen, and Abandoned Lands, Record Group 105, National Archives and Records Administration, Washington, D.C.
HUA	Hampton University Archives, Hampton, Va.
KKK Reports	U.S. Senate, *Report of the Joint Select Committee to Inquire into the Condition of Affairs in the Late Insurrectionary States: Ku Klux Klan Conspiracy*, 42d Cong., 2d sess., 1872, S. Rep. 41 (Washington, D.C.: Government Printing Office, 1872).
LL	Lilly Library, Earlham College, Richmond, Ind.
NA	National Archives and Records Administration, Washington, D.C.
OR	U.S. War Department, *The War of the Rebellion: A Compilation of the Official Records of the Union and Confederate Armies*, 128 vols. (Washington, D.C.: Government Printing Office, 1880–1901).
RG	Record Group

Introduction

1. Henry Lee Swint, *The Northern Teacher in the South, 1862–1870* (New York: Octagon Books, 1967).

2. Robert C. Morris, *Reading, 'Riting, and Reconstruction: The Education of Freedmen in the South, 1861–1870* (Chicago: University of Chicago Press, 1981), xi.

3. Jacqueline Jones, *Soldiers of Light and Love: Northern Teachers and Georgia Blacks, 1865–1873* (Chapel Hill: University of North Carolina Press, 1980).

4. Ronald E. Butchart, *Northern Schools, Southern Blacks, and Reconstruction: Freedmen's Education, 1862–1875* (Westport, Conn.: Greenwood Press, 1980), xiii, 9.

5. W. E. B. Du Bois, *Black Reconstruction in America* (1935; Millwood, N.Y.: Kraus-Thomson, 1976); James D. Anderson, *The Education of Blacks in the South, 1860–1935* (Chapel Hill: University of North Carolina Press, 1988); Herbert Gutman, "Schools for Freedom: The Post-Emancipation Origins of Afro-American Education," in *Power and Culture: Essays on the American Working Class* (New York: New Press, 1987); Leon F. Litwack, *Been in the Storm So Long: The Aftermath of Slavery* (New York: Alfred A. Knopf, 1979).

6. Michael W. Apple and Linda K. Christian-Smith, *The Politics of the Textbook* (New York: Routledge, 1991), 2.

7. James C. Scott, *Domination and the Arts of Resistance: Hidden Transcripts* (New Haven: Yale University Press, 1990).

Chapter One

1. I have identified statutes that prohibited teaching enslaved and/or free black people in the following states: Alabama, Georgia, Louisiana, Mississippi, Missouri, North Carolina, South Carolina, and Virginia. Statutes in Alabama, Georgia, Missouri, South Carolina, and Virginia prohibited teaching any person of color, whether free or enslaved; the others only prohibited teaching slaves. I have not identified such statutes in Kentucky, Maryland, Arkansas, Texas, Florida, Delaware, or Tennessee; however, Maryland, Arkansas, and Florida did specifically legislate that while masters, though obliged to provide some degree of education to white apprentices, had no such duty toward free black apprentices. See the appendix for the full text of the antiliteracy statutes.

2. Mattie J. Jackson, *The Story of Mattie J. Jackson: Her Parentage—Experience of Eighteen Years in Slavery—Incidents During the War—Her Escape from Slavery. A True Story* (Lawrence, Mass.: Printed at Sentinel Office, 1866), 2; Deborah Gray White, *Ar'n't I a Woman? Female Slaves in the Plantation South* (rev. ed.; New York: W. W. Norton, 1999), 70; Michael P. Johnson, "Runaway Slaves and the Slave Communities in South Carolina, 1799 to 1830," *William and Mary Quarterly* 38 (July 1981): 418–41.

3. Jackson, *Story of Mattie J. Jackson*, 3–6.

4. Ibid., 10.

5. Henry Bibb, *Narrative of the Life Adventures of Henry Bibb, an American Slave*, in vol. 2 of *African American Slave Narratives*, ed. Sterling Lecatur Bland Jr. (Westport, Conn.: Greenwood Press, 2001), 355.

6. John Quincy Adams, *Narrative of the Life of John Quincy Adams, When in Slavery and Now as a Freeman* (Harrisburg, Pa.: Sieg, 1872), 6, 36; Elizabeth Hyde Botume, *First Days amongst the Contrabands* (1893; New York: Arno Press, 1968), 6–7.

7. Booker T. Washington, *Up From Slavery* (1901; New York: Doubleday, 1963), 6.

8. Jackson, *Story of Mattie J. Jackson*, 11. Other former slaves also recalled women in their family who could read well enough to gather information about the war from the newspapers. Minnie Davis reported that her mother would "steal the newspapers and read up about the war, and she kept the other slaves posted as to how the war was progressing." Likewise, Chana Littlejohn's aunt was able to keep other slaves updated on the progress of the war. George P. Rawick, ed., *The American Slave: A Composite Autobiography*, 19 vols. (Westport, Conn.: Greenwood Press, 1972), vol. 12, pt. 1, p. 257, and vol. 15, pt. 2, pp. 57–58.

9. Jackson, *Story of Mattie J. Jackson*, 11.

10. Ibid., 11–12.

11. Regarding the notion of slavery as a negotiated relationship, see Ira Berlin,

Many Thousands Gone: The First Two Generations of Slavery in North America (Cambridge, Mass.: Harvard University Press, 1998), 2.

12. Jackson, *Story of Mattie J. Jackson*, 12. Regarding slave narrators' "undertelling" the horrors of slavery, see P. Gabrielle Foreman, "Manifest in Signs: The Politics of Sex and Representation in Incidents in the Life of a Slave Girl," 76–99, and Deborah M. Garfield, "Earwitness: Female Abolitionism, Sexuality, and Incidents in the Life of a Slave Girl," 100–130, in *Harriet Jacobs and Incidents in the Life of a Slave Girl: New Critical Essays*, ed. Deborah M. Garfield and Rafia Zafar (New York: Cambridge University Press, 1996).

13. Jackson, *Story of Mattie J. Jackson*, 12. No legal precedent existed in the antebellum South for a slave who had escaped from her owners to obtain refuge from a public official. Unlike slave societies such as Cuba, which under Castilian law provided a range of protective legislation placing the state between slave and master, in the slave society of the American South the patriarch of each household reigned all but supreme. Enslaved people sought to transform Union officers into official arbiters in master-slave relationships, ultimately appealing to them for freedom. For a discussion of protections provided by Castilian law, see Herbert Klein, *Slavery in the Americas: A Comparative Study of Virginia and Cuba* (Chicago: University of Chicago Press, 1967), 59–78. See also David Brion Davis, *The Problem of Slavery in Western Culture* (Ithaca, N.Y.: Cornell University Press, 1966), 223–43. Davis argues that these legal protections may have been more theoretical than real, having little if any impact on the brutality of slavery in societies like Brazil and Cuba. For a discussion of master-slave relations and the law, see Peter W. Bardaglio, *Reconstructing the Household: Families, Sex, and the Law in the Nineteenth-Century South* (Chapel Hill: University of North Carolina Press, 1995), 26–31; and Stephanie McCurry, *Masters of Small Worlds: Yeoman Households, Gender Relations, and the Political Culture of the Antebellum South Carolina Low Country* (New York: Oxford University Press, 1995).

14. James C. Scott, *Domination and the Arts of Resistance: Hidden Transcripts* (New Haven: Yale University Press, 1990), 8.

15. Jackson, *Story of Mattie J. Jackson*, 20.

16. See Bruce Fort, "Reading in the Margins: The Politics and Culture of Literacy in Georgia, 1800–1920" (Ph.D. diss., University of Virginia, 1999).

17. 2 Brevard's Digest 243, in George M. Stroud, ed., *Sketch of the Laws Relating to Slavery in the Several States of the United States* (1856; New York: Negro Universities Press, 1968), 60. Georgia enacted a similar law in 1770 that proscribed reading as well as writing.

18. Acts and Resolutions of the General Assembly of the State of South-Carolina, December 1800, in Paul Finkelman, ed., *State Slavery Statutes* (microfiche; Frederick, Md.: University Publications of America, 1989). For a discussion of the Stono Rebellion and its consequences, see Peter Wood, *Black Majority: Negroes in Colonial South Carolina from 1670 through the Stono Rebellion* (New York: Alfred A. Knopf, 1975), 308–26.

19. David Walker, *David Walker's Appeal to the Coloured Citizens of the World*, ed. Peter P. Hinks (University Park: Pennsylvania State University Press, 2000), 34, 2.

20. Peter P. Hinks, *To Awaken My Afflicted Brethren: David Walker and the Problem of Antebellum Slave Resistance* (University Park: Pennsylvania State University Press, 1997), 116–18.

21. Georgia Statutes, 1829, in Finkelman, *State Slavery Statutes.*

22. Acts Passed by the Second Session of the Legislature of the State of Louisiana, January 1830, in Stroud, *Sketch of the Laws,* 61.

23. Regarding gradual versus immediate abolition, see David Brion Davis, "The Emergence of Immediatism in British and American Antislavery Thought," in *Antislavery,* ed. Paul Finkelman (New York: Garland Publishing, 1989), 83–104.

24. Acts Passed by the General Assembly of the State of North Carolina, at the Session of 1830–31, in Finkelman, *State Slavery Statutes.*

25. Ibid. Regarding unequal punishment of free blacks, see Ira Berlin, *Slaves without Masters: The Free Negro in the Antebellum South* (New York: Pantheon Books, 1974), 96. Severely imbalanced punishments could be meted out, as in an 1836 Alabama statute that punished with death black people convicted of robbery or burglary but that punished whites convicted of the same crimes with a fine, or two-year sentence, or whipping, at the judge's discretion. Acts Passed at the Annual Session of the General Assembly of the State of Alabama, 1836, Number 48, Sections 2 and 3, in Finkelman, *State Slave Statutes.* Peter Wood suggests that whipping persisted as a punishment for blacks long after it had been eliminated for whites in part because blacks were less likely than whites to be able to afford a fine. Wood, *Black Majority,* 278.

26. Georgia Penal Code, Section 18, 1833, in Stroud, *Sketch of the Laws,* 61.

27. "Acts Passed at the General Assembly of the Commonwealth of Virginia, April 1831, Chapter XXXIX—An Act to amend the act concerning slaves, free negroes and mulattoes," in Finkelman, *State Slavery Statutes.*

28. Approximately twenty-six of fifty-two black people charged with involvement in Turner's insurrection were convicted. The rest were acquitted or had the charges against them dismissed. Many suspected of being participants never made it to court as whites killed them when caught. Kenneth S. Greenberg, ed., *The Confessions of Nat Turner and Related Documents* (New York: Bedford Books of St. Martin's Press, 1996), 57–58.

29. The statute also severely restricted conditions under which slaves could be brought into the state. Acts Passed at the Thirteenth Annual Session of the General Assembly of the State of Alabama, November 1831. In the aftermath of Turner's rebellion the Virginia legislature considered emancipating all slaves in the state. Greenberg, *Confessions of Nat Turner,* 23.

30. "A Memorial of the General Assembly of the State of Alabama to the General Assemblies of the Several States of the Union, January 1836," in Finkelman, *State Slavery Statutes.*

31. Bernard E. Powers Jr., *Black Charlestonians: A Social History, 1822–1885* (Fayetteville: University of Arkansas Press, 1994), 136; Whittington B. Johnson, *Black Savannah, 1788–1864* (Fayetteville: University of Arkansas Press, 1996), 127–29.

32. Acts and Resolutions of the General Assembly of the State of South Carolina, December 1834, in Finkelman, *State Slavery Statutes.*

33. John W. Cromwell, *The Early Negro Convention Movement* (Washington, D.C.: American Negro Academy, 1904), 7.

34. Edmund Fuller, *Prudence Crandall: An Incident of Racism in Nineteenth-Century Connecticut* (Middlebury, Conn.: Wesleyan University Press, 1971), 58, 76–95; Philip S. Foner and Josephine F. Pacheco, eds., *Three Who Dared: Prudence Crandall, Margaret Douglass, Myrtilla Miner—Champions of Antebellum Black Education* (Westport, Conn.: Greenwood Press, 1984), 20–43. I am grateful to Jennifer Rycenga for her insights on the partnership between Prudence Crandall and black abolitionists. Jennifer Rycenga, "Agitation as Education: Race, Class, and Religion in the Pedagogy of the Abolitionist Educator Prudence Crandall (1803–1890)," paper given at the Center for the Study of Religion at Yale University, New Haven, Conn., Spring 2001. Reminiscent of southern laws, though not as restrictive, the Connecticut statute of May 1833 provided, in part: "Whereas, attempts have been made to establish literary institutions in this state for the instruction of colored persons belonging to other states and countries, which would end to the great increase of the colored population of the state, and thereby to the injury of the people[,] . . . no person shall set up or establish in this state any school, academy, or literary institution for the instruction or education of colored persons who are not inhabitants of this state." It went on to prohibit teaching, harboring, or boarding any black person from another state. General Statues of Connecticut, 1835, Title 53—Inhabitants. For a discussion of similar challenges to black education in Illinois during this period, see Robert L. McCaul, *The Black Struggle for Public Schooling in Nineteenth-Century Illinois* (Carbondale: Southern Illinois University Press, 1987).

35. Nathan Bass, "Essay on the Treatment and Management of Slaves," *Transactions of the Southern Central Agricultural Society of Georgia* (1846/1851), in *Advice among Masters: The Ideal in Slave Management in the Old South*, ed. James O. Breeden (Westport, Conn.: Greenwood Press, 1980), 11–16; A Mississippi Planter, "Management of Negroes upon Southern Estates," *DeBow's Review* 10 (June 1851), in *Advice among Masters*, ed. Breeden, 231.

36. Hurricane, "The Negro and His Management," *Southern Cultivator* (September 1860), in *Advice among Masters*, ed. Breeden, 329–32.

37. Rawick, *American Slave*, vol. 2, pt. 1, pp. 63, 176; George P. Rawick, ed., *The American Slave: A Composite Autobiography: Supplement, Series 1*, 12 vols. (Westport, Conn.: Greenwood Press, 1977), vol. 7, pt. 2, p. 365. See also Leonard Black, *The Life and Sufferings of Leonard Black, a Fugitive from Slavery* (New Bedford, Mass.: Benjamin Lindsey, 1847), 19. On Webster's blue-back speller, see below, chap. 7.

38. Rawick, *American Slave . . . Supplement, Series 1*, vol. 8, pt. 3, p. 1329; Rawick, *American Slave*, vol. 12, pt. 1, pp. 130–31.

39. Rawick, *American Slave*, vol. 2, pt. 1, p. 246; Rawick, *American Slave. . . Supplement, Series 1*, vol. 6, pt. 1, pp. 10–11. Albright was elected to the Mississippi state senate in 1874. Many slaves referred to cutting off a hand or thumb as a potential or actual punishment for a slave who was caught reading or writing. See, for example, the statements by William McWhorter and Tom Hawkins in James Mellon, ed., *Bullwhip Days: The Slaves Remember* (New York: Weidenfeld and Nicolson, 1988), 197–98.

40. Code of Mississippi, Article 3, January 16, 1823, in A. Hutchinson, comp., *Code of Mississippi: Being an Analytical Compilation of the Public and General Statutes of the Territory and State, with Tabular References to the Local and Private Acts, from 1798–1848* (Jackson, Miss., 1848).

41. Lewis C. Lockwood, "Mary S. Peake: The Colored Teacher at Fortress Monroe," in *Two Black Teachers during the Civil War*, ed. William Loren Katz (New York: Arno Press and the New York Times, 1969), 5–16. See also Robert Francis Engs, *Freedom's First Generation: Black Hampton, Virginia, 1861–1890* (Philadelphia: University of Pennsylvania Press, 1979), 13. Engs suggests that white Hamptonians had an exceptionally lax attitude toward slave control, and therefore Mary Peake may have taught both free blacks and slaves without opposition before the Civil War.

42. For example, in 1788 free and enslaved African Americans had established the first black Baptist church in North America. By 1832, blacks in Savannah supported three independent Baptist churches. James M. Simms, *The First Colored Baptist Church in North America* (1888; New York: Negro Universities Press, 1969), 20–21; Johnson, *Black Savannah*, 6–15.

43. Stroud, *Sketch of the Laws*, 63.

44. Susie King Taylor, *A Black Woman's Civil War Memoirs: Reminiscences of My Life in Camp with the 33rd U.S. Colored Troops, Late 1st South Carolina Volunteers*, ed. Patricia W. Romero and Willie Lee Rose (New York: M. Wiener Publishing, 1988), 29–30. Taylor's maiden name was Baker; however, in her book she used the surnames of her two husbands, King and Taylor. For convenience, I refer to her as "Taylor" throughout. Ibid., 25–26.

45. Lucy Skipwith to John Cocke, November 1850, August 1854, May 1855, May 1858, October 1859, March, 1862, March 1863, August 1863, March 1864, and May 1864, in John W. Blassingame, ed., *Slave Testimony: Two Centuries of Letters, Speeches, Interviews, and Autobiographies* (Baton Rouge: Louisiana State University Press, 1977), 65–82. According to Blassingame, Cocke supported African colonization, temperance, and popular education. Although Cocke often denounced slavery, he was one of the largest slaveholders in the country, with plantations in Virginia and Alabama. In the 1830s Cocke, a founder of the American Colonization Society, freed one family of slaves and sent them to Liberia in West Africa. See also Randall M. Miller, *"Dear Master": Letters of a Slave Family* (Ithaca, N.Y.: Cornell University Press, 1978), 35.

46. Acts of the General Assembly of Virginia, 1842, in Finkelman, *State Slavery Statutes*.

47. G. W. Offley, *A Narrative of the Life and Labors of the Rev. G. W. Offley, a Colored Man, Local Preacher, and Missionary* (Hartford, Conn., 1859), 9; James Fisher, "Narrative of James Fisher" (originally printed in *National Anti-Slavery Standard*, April 13, 1843), in Blassingame, *Slave Testimony*, 234; *American Missionary*, April 1866, 75; *American Missionary*, September 1867, 194.

48. Mellon, *Bullwhip Days*, 200; Charles Alexander, *Battles and Victories of Allen Allensworth, A.M., Ph.D., Lt. Col. Retired U.S. Army* (Boston: Sherman, French and Company, 1914), 8–9.

49. Rawick, *American Slave . . . Supplement, Series 1*, vol. 8, pt. 3, p. 1232.

50. Rawick, *American Slave*, vol. 2, pt. 1, p. 50.

51. Peter Randolph, *From Slave Cabin to the Pulpit: The Autobiography of Rev. Peter Randolph—The Southern Question Illustrated and Sketches of Slave Life* (Boston: James H. Earle Printers, 1893), 11.

52. Theresa A. Singleton, "The Archaeology of Slave Life," in *Before Freedom Came: African-American Life in the Antebellum South*, ed. Edward D. C. Campbell Jr. and Kym S. Rice (Charlottesville: University Press of Virginia, 1991), 171. For a monograph on the subject of literacy among slaves, see Janet Duitsman Cornelius, *"When I Can Read My Title Clear": Literacy, Slavery, and Religion in the Antebellum South* (Columbia: University of South Carolina Press, 1991).

53. Wood, *Black Majority*, 278, 314.

54. Interview of Charity Bowery by Lydia Maria Child, 1847–48, in Blassingame, *Slave Testimony*, 267; Offley, *Narrative*, 9.

55. James Curry, "Narrative of James Curry, a Fugitive Slave" (originally printed in *The Liberator*, January 10, 1840), in Blassingame, *Slave Testimony*, 128–44.

56. Fisher, "Narrative of James Fisher," 230–38.

57. Taylor, *Black Woman's Civil War Memoirs*, 31.

58. A. T. Jones interviewed by the Freedmen's Inquiry Commission in Canada, 1863, in Blassingame, *Slave Testimony*, 430.

59. *Wilmington (N.C.) Journal*, February 12, 1863.

60. Curry, "Narrative of James Curry," 128, 130–31. Curry escaped to Canada. When he returned to North Carolina in 1865, twenty-seven years later, he was attacked by enraged whites. The passage Curry cited is found in Acts 17:26.

61. Freedmen's Inquiry Commission interview of C. H. Hall, 1863, in Blassingame, *Slave Testimony*, 416–18.

62. Elijah Marrs, *Life and History of the Rev. Elijah P. Marrs* (Louisville, Ky.: Bradley and Gilbert Company, 1885), 11–12.

63. Ibid.

64. For a discussion of enslaved people's conceptions of freedom, see Thomas L. Webber, *Deep Like the Rivers: Education in the Slave Quarter Community, 1831–1865* (New York: W. W. Norton, 1978), 139–48.

65. Frederick Douglass to Thomas Auld, September 3, 1848, in Frederick Douglass, *Narrative of the Life of Frederick Douglass, an American Slave*, ed. David W. Blight (New York: Bedford Books, 1993), 135.

66. Ibid., 57–60. An "ell" is an old British measurement roughly equivalent to a yard. *Oxford English Dictionary*.

67. Douglass, *Narrative*, 61; Caleb Bingham, *The Columbian Orator: Containing a Variety of Original and Selected Pieces Together with Rules; Calculated to Improve the Youth and Others in the Ornamental and Useful Art of Eloquence* (Boston: J. H. A. Frost, 1831).

68. Bingham, *Columbian Orator*, 245.

69. Ibid., 240–42.

70. Douglass, *Narrative*, 61.

71. Ibid., 62.

72. Margaret Douglass, *Educational Laws of Virginia: The Personal Narrative of Mrs.*

Margaret Douglass, a Southern Woman, Who Was Imprisoned for One Month in the Common Jail of Norfolk, under the Laws of Virginia, for the Crime of Teaching Free Colored Children to Read (Boston: John P. Jewett and Company, 1854), 7–13; Josephine F. Pacheco, "Margaret Douglass," in *Three Who Dared*, ed. Foner and Pacheco, 57–95.

73. Douglass, *Educational Laws of Virginia*, 21–22.

74. Ibid., 33–36.

75. Ibid., 44–50.

76. Ibid., 49.

77. Robert E. Perdue, *The Negro in Savannah, 1865–1900* (New York: Exposition Press, 1973), 40, 43, 70.

78. Jackson, *Story of Mattie J. Jackson*, 2.

79. Ibid., 23.

80. Ibid., 31.

Chapter Two

1. See Ira Berlin et al., eds., *Free at Last: A Documentary History of Slavery, Freedom, and the Civil War* (New York: New Press, 1992).

2. Abraham Lincoln inaugural address, March 4, 1861, in Richard C. Drum and Elon A. Woodward, eds., *The Negro in the Military Service of the United States, 1639–1886: A Compilation of Official Records, State Papers, Historical Extracts, etc., Relating to His Military Status and Service from the Date of His Introduction into the British North American Colonies* (Washington, D.C.: Adjutant General's Office, 1888; microfilm, Washington, D.C.: National Archives and Records Administration, 1963), 398.

3. John Eaton, *Grant, Lincoln, and the Freedmen: Reminiscences of the Civil War* (New York: Longmans, Green, 1907), 173. Edward L. Pierce, an early Union worker among the freedpeople, called it "the mysterious spiritual telegraph which runs through the slave population." Edward L. Pierce, "The Contrabands at Fortress Monroe," *Atlantic Monthly* 8 (November 1861): 628.

4. First report of Edward L. Pierce to Secretary of Treasury Salmon P. Chase, February 3, 1862, in Frank Moore, ed., *The Rebellion Record: A Diary of American Events*, 11 vols. and supplement (New York: G. P. Putnam, 1864), suppl., vol. 1, doc. 51, p. 309.

5. Statement by John T. Washington of Hampstead P.O., King George County, Va., to Confederate Headquarters, Fredericksburg, Va., May 7, 1861, in *OR*, ser. 1, 2:820; Daniel Ruggles, Brigadier-General, Volunteers, Commanding Forces, Headquarters, Fredericksburg, Va., to R. S. Garnett, Adjutant-General, Volunteer Forces, Richmond, Va., May 8, 1861, in *OR*, ser. 1, 2:820.

6. Pierce, "Contrabands at Fortress Monroe," 627; Robert Francis Engs, *Freedom's First Generation: Black Hampton, Virginia, 1861–1890* (Philadelphia: University of Pennsylvania Press, 1979), 18–28; Jack D. Foner, *Blacks and the Military in American History: A New Perspective* (New York: Praeger, 1974), 32–35. It should be noted that "contraband" was not an uncontested term, as it linked people directly to their status as property even after they had achieved a modicum of freedom. The editors of

American Missionary chose to call people escaping slavery "refugees" rather than "contrabands," "freedmen," or "vagrants." "Contraband" they found offensive because it implied property in human beings; "freedmen" was inappropriate because the people who sought refuge with the army were not fully free; and "vagrant" suggested a degradation that the people did not deserve. *American Missionary*, February 1862, 29. However, according to historian Willie Lee Rose, the term "contraband" appealed to northern businessmen for the very reason that it denoted a respect for property rights. Willie Lee Rose, *Rehearsal for Reconstruction: The Port Royal Experiment* (Indianapolis: Bobbs-Merrill, 1964), 15.

7. Benjamin F. Butler to Winfield Scott, May 24, 1861, in *OR*, ser. 1, 2:648–52; "An Act to Confiscate Property Used for Insurrectionary Purposes," August 6, 1861, in Moore, *Rebellion Record*, vol. 2, p. 475; Secretary of War Simon Cameron to Major General B. F. Butler, August 8, 1861, in Moore, *Rebellion Record*, vol. 2, p. 493.

8. Pierce, "Contrabands at Fortress Monroe," 631.

9. Testimony of C. B. Wilder, Superintendent of Contrabands at Fortress Monroe, Va., before the American Freedmen's Inquiry Commission, May 9, 1863, in Ira Berlin et al., eds., *Destruction of Slavery* (New York: Cambridge University Press, 1985), 89.

10. Brigadier General A. McD. McCook to General W. T. Sherman, from Camp Nevin, Ky., November 5, 1861, in *OR*, ser. 1, 4:337.

11. Brigadier General W. T. Sherman to Brigadier General A. McD. McCook, from Louisville, Ky., November 8, 1861, in *OR*, ser. 1, 4:347; McCook to Sherman, from Camp Nevin, Ky., November 5, 1861, in *OR*, ser. 1, 4:337; Major General John A. Dix to Secretary of War Simon Cameron, from Port McHenry, Md., August 8, 1861, in Drum and Woodward, *Negro in the Military Service*, 424. For evidence of fluctuation in policy regarding escaped slaves, see Brigadier General A. E. Burnside, Department of North Carolina, to Secretary of War E. M. Stanton, March 21, 1862, in Drum and Woodward, *Negro in the Military Service*, 487; Brigadier General Alvin P. Hovey to Brigadier General Fred Steele, December 6, 1862, in Drum and Woodward, *Negro in the Military Service*, 690; General Order No. 26, issued by Captain and Assistant Adjutant General W. W. H. Lawrence, Central Army of the Mississippi, June 18, 1862, in Drum and Woodward, *Negro in the Military Service*, 542; D. C. Buell to Brigadier General O. M. Mitchell, Department of the Ohio, March 11, 1862, in Drum and Woodward, *Negro in the Military Service*, 480.

12. J. H. Lane to General S. D. Sturgis, October 3, 1861, in *OR*, ser. 1, 3:516. See also Major General John A. Dix, Department of Pennsylvania, to Secretary of War Simon Cameron, August 8, 1861, in Drum and Woodward, *Negro in the Military Service*; Major General H. W. Halleck to General Asboth, from St. Louis, Mo., December 26, 1861, in *OR*, ser. 1, 8:465; and Order No. 43 of Major General W. T. Sherman, June 18, 1862, in Drum and Woodward, *Negro in the Military Service*, 540.

13. First report of Edward L. Pierce to Secretary of Treasury Salmon P. Chase, February 3, 1862, in Moore, *Rebellion Record*, suppl., vol. 1, doc. 51, p. 303.

14. According to G. P. Reily, an employee of the American Missionary Association, in 1863 would-be contrabands were thrown into jails by local police all over the state of Kentucky. State law, then in effect, provided that slaves should be kept for

eight months before being sold. However, the Kentucky legislature amended the law to permit sale after thirty days in jail, in part because of overcrowding. Union authorities ultimately intervened and released those they found. Many of these freedpeople went to work on fortifications. G. P. Reily to Brother Fee, June 17, 1863, AMA Mss.

15. Vincent Coyler, *Brief Report of the Services Rendered by the Freed People to the United States Army in North Carolina, in the Spring of 1862, after the Battle of New Bern* (New York: Vincent Coyler, 1864); Horace James, *Annual Report of the Superintendent of Negro Affairs in North Carolina, 1864, with an Appendix, Containing the History and Management of the Freedmen in this Department up to June 1st, 1865* (Boston: W. F. Brown, n.d.). Even the camps did not guarantee safety. When Confederate forces attacked New Bern in January 1864, several African Americans lost their lives, and many more fled their homes. Joe A. Mobley, *James City: A Black Community in North Carolina, 1863–1900* (Raleigh, N.C.: Department of Cultural Resources, Division of Archives and History, 1981), 24.

16. Ira Berlin et al., eds., *The Wartime Genesis of Free Labor: The Upper South* (New York: Cambridge University Press, 1993); and Ira Berlin et al., eds., *The Wartime Genesis of Free Labor: The Lower South* (New York: Cambridge University Press, 1990).

17. Berlin et al., *Wartime Genesis of Free Labor: The Upper South*, 97. The 1864 census of blacks within Union lines in North Carolina was as follows: New Bern and Vicinity—8,591; Beaufort—2,426; Washington—2,741; Roanoke Island—2,712; Plymouth—860; Hatteras Banks—89. James, *Annual Report of the Superintendent of Negro Affairs in North Carolina, 1864*, 5–6. Numbers were constantly shifting, however.

18. For studies of emancipation and the freedpeople, see Engs, *Freedom's First Generation*; Louis S. Gerteis, *From Contraband to Freedman: Federal Policy toward Southern Blacks, 1861–1865* (Westport, Conn.: Greenwood Press, 1973); Peter Kolchin, *First Freedom: The Responses of Alabama's Blacks to Emancipation and Reconstruction* (Westport, Conn.: Greenwood Press, 1972); Mobley, *James City*; Rose, *Rehearsal for Reconstruction*; and Joel Williamson, *After Slavery: The Negro in South Carolina during Reconstruction, 1861–1877* (Chapel Hill: University of North Carolina Press, 1965).

19. Northern observers described escaped slaves as famished, ill-clad, wounded, and unhealthy. Some even arrived in camps wearing iron collars around their necks. Newton M Mann, "Condition of the Negroes Who Came into Vicksburg with Sherman's Army," broadside dated March 7, 1864, Massachusetts Historical Society, Boston, Mass.; Testimony of Colonel George H. Hanks, Department of the Gulf, before the American Freedmen's Inquiry Commission, New Orleans, La., February 6, 1864, in Berlin et al., *Wartime Genesis of Free Labor: The Lower South*, 518; Eaton, *Grant, Lincoln and the Freedmen*, 2.

20. Mobley, *James City*, 13.

21. Ibid., 6.

22. Benjamin Quarles, *The Negro in the Civil War* (Boston: Little, Brown, 1969), 79–99; Mobley, *James City*, 6–10.

23. Engs, *Freedom's First Generation*, 38; S. Goodrich Wright to Brother Whipple,

December 28, 1862, AMA Mss. See also W. Perkins to Simeon Jocelyn, June 19, 1863, AMA Mss.

24. In New Bern, North Carolina, for example, Abraham Galloway, who had escaped from slavery and lived in Canada for many years, met with recently freed men to discuss the terms under which they would enlist to serve in the Union army. David S. Cecelski, "Abraham H. Galloway: Wilmington's Lost Prophet and the Rise of Black Radicalism in the American South," in *Democracy Betrayed: The Wilmington Race Riot of 1898 and Its Legacy*, ed. David S. Cecelski and Timothy B. Tyson (Chapel Hill: University of North Carolina Press, 1998), 44–46. In Columbus, Kentucky, some contrabands were so discouraged with their living conditions that they considered returning to the homes of their enslavement. One man urged patience, using the biblical metaphor of Moses leading the children of Israel out of bondage. He told his fellow contrabands that they had now reached the Red Sea. With the Egyptians behind them and the sea before them, they had to have faith that God would send them help through Abraham Lincoln. S. Goodrich Wright to Brother Whipple, December 28, 1862, AMA Mss.

25. Lockwood to Brethren, January 6, 1862, AMA Mss. The Union's failure to pay black laborers was a consistent source of complaint and would later become a major issue once black men were permitted to fight in the army. See for example, C. B. Wilder, Superintendent of Contrabands at Fortress Monroe, to *The Tribune*, May 1862, AMA Mss.; and James E. Yeatman, *A Report on the Condition of the Freedmen of the Mississippi, Presented by the Western Sanitary Commission, December 17, 1863* (St. Louis: Western Sanitary Commission, 1864), 4.

26. Pierce, "Contrabands at Fortress Monroe," 639.

27. First report of Edward L. Pierce to Secretary of Treasury Salmon P. Chase, February 3, 1862, in Moore, *Rebellion Record*, suppl., vol. 1, doc. 51, p. 308.

28. Second report of Edward L. Pierce to Salmon P. Chase, June 2, 1862, in Moore, *Rebellion Record*, suppl., vol. 1, doc. 51, p. 315.

29. Ibid., 322.

30. Chaplain J. P. Rogers to Levi Coffin, December 21, 1862, in Levi Coffin, *Reminiscences of Levi Coffin, the Reported President of the Underground Railroad* (Cincinnati: Robert Clarke Company, 1898), 625. According to John Eaton, poor whites and former slaves were sent to Cairo from Mississippi, Tennessee, and Arkansas by the Union army. Eaton, *Grant, Lincoln, and the Freedmen*, 37.

31. Edward R. Pierce to Simeon Jocelyn, April 9, 1863, AMA Mss.

32. G. L. Rankin to Simeon Jocelyn, March 6, 1863, AMA Mss.

33. Vincent Coyler, *Brief Report of the Services Rendered by the Freed People*, 43. See also G. L. Rankin to Simeon Jocelyn, March 6, 1863, AMA Mss.

34. L. H. Cobb, *Report and Extracts Relating to Colored Schools in the Department of Tennessee and State of Arkansas, November 30, 1864* (Memphis, Tenn.: Freedmen Press Printers, 1864), 6, Massachusetts Historical Society, Boston, Mass.

35. James A. Emmerton, *A Record of the Twenty-Third Regiment, Mass Vol. Infantry in the War of the Rebellion, 1861–1865* (Boston: William Ware and Company, 1886), 96–97.

36. Revered S. C. Wright to AMA Brethren, December 19, 1862, AMA Mss.

37. "Report of the American Freedmen's Inquiry Commission, June 30, 1863," in *OR*, ser. 3, 3:430, 432, 447; Paul A. Cimbala, "Making Good Yankees: The Freedmen's Bureau and Education in Reconstruction Georgia, 1865–1870," in *The Freedmen's Bureau and Black Freedom*, ed. Donald G. Nieman (New York: Garland, 1994), 58; R. M. Manly to T. J. Childrey, November 12, 1866, M803, FBR; R. M. Manly to C. Kennedy, October 1, 1866, M803, FBR.

38. Yeatman, *Report on the Condition of the Freedmen of the Mississippi*, 1.

39. Ibid., 11.

40. Mary S. Peake to Simeon Jocelyn, January 1862, AMA Mss.

41. Lewis C. Lockwood to Brethren, February 4, 1862, AMA Mss.; Lewis C. Lockwood, "Mary S. Peake: The Colored Teacher at Fortress Monroe," in *Two Black Teachers during the Civil War*, ed. William Loren Katz (New York: Arno Press and the New York Times, 1969), 34, 40.

42. Lockwood, "Mary S. Peake," 30.

43. Lockwood to Brethren, March 6, 1862, AMA Mss.

44. Henry Lee Swint, *The Northern Teacher in the South, 1862–1870* (New York: Octagon Books, 1967); Ronald E. Butchart, *Northern Schools, Southern Blacks, and Reconstruction: Freedmen's Education, 1862–1875* (Westport, Conn.: Greenwood Press, 1980); Robert C. Morris, *Reading, 'Riting and Reconstruction: The Education of Freedmen in the South, 1861–1870* (Chicago: University of Chicago Press, 1981); Jacqueline Jones, *Soldiers of Light and Love: Northern Teachers and Georgia Blacks, 1865–1873* (Chapel Hill: University of North Carolina Press, 1980).

45. Rose, *Rehearsal for Reconstruction*, 32–62; Butchart, *Northern Schools, Southern Blacks, and Reconstruction*, 5–6.

46. James D. Anderson makes a similar argument in "Ex-Slaves and the Rise of Universal Education in the New South, 1860–1880," in *Education and the Rise of the New South*, ed. Ronald K. Goodenow and Arthur O. White (Boston: G. K. Hall, 1981), 2. My argument is contra to that made by historian Ronald E. Butchart, who sees education as something imposed upon freedpeople by white northerners in lieu of fighting to get them land and economic justice. Butchart writes, "What did it all mean? The Afro-Americans were on the threshold of freedom. They needed land, protection, and a stake in society. They needed and demanded meaningful power. They were given instead a school. The gift was vastly inadequate to the needs of men and women set free in a vengeful, vindictive society. Indeed, as the school fell under the control of a race and a class with interests opposed to those of the southern blacks, education was not merely inadequate, it was utterly inappropriate." Butchart, *Northern Schools, Southern Blacks, and Reconstruction*, 9.

47. Lockwood to Brethren, March 6, 1862, AMA Mss.

48. Chaplain Chris M. Blake to Simeon Jocelyn, June 30, 1862, AMA Mss.

49. Chaplain J. W. Crumb, Yorktown, Va., to Simeon Jocelyn, August 9, 1862, AMA Mss.

50. Lockwood to Brethren, October 6, 1862, AMA Mss.

51. *American Missionary*, January 1863, 18; ibid., July 1863, 159–60.

52. Ibid., September 1863, 202–5.

53. Lockwood to Brethren, July 17, 1862, AMA Mss.

54. Ibid.

55. *American Missionary*, June 1863, 137.

56. Yeatman, *Report on the Condition of the Freedmen of the Mississippi*, 3.

57. G. W. Offley, *A Narrative of the Life and Labors of the Rev. G. W. Offley, a Colored Man, Local Preacher, and Missionary* (Hartford, Conn., 1859), 9.

58. Peter Randolph, *From Slave Cabin to the Pulpit: The Autobiography of Rev. Peter Randolph—The Southern Question Illustrated and Sketches of Slave Life* (Boston: James A. Earle Printers, 1893), 31.

59. "Report of the American Freedmen's Inquiry Commission, June 30, 1863," in *OR*, ser. 3, 3:447.

60. Booker T. Washington, *Up From Slavery: An Autobiography* (1901; New York: Doubleday, 1963), 5.

61. *New York Times*, January 14, 1862.

62. Second report of Edward L. Pierce to Salmon P. Chase, June 2, 1862, in Moore, *Rebellion Record*, suppl., vol. 1, doc. 51, p. 322. See also Rose, *Rehearsal for Reconstruction*, 87–88. Rose quotes plantation superintendent William Gannett as saying, "The Negroes will do anything for us, if we will only teach them."

63. New England Freedmen's Aid Society, *First Annual Report of the Educational Commission for Freedmen, May 1863* (Boston: Prentiss and Deland, 1863), 12.

64. Appointed by the secretary of war, the American Freedmen's Inquiry Commission consisted of three staunch abolitionists, Robert Dale Owen of Indiana, James McKay of New York, and Samuel G. Howe of Massachusetts, who took testimony throughout the South and produced two reports. The commission recommended the formation of what became the Freedmen's Bureau. See *OR*, ser. 3, 3:73; and Eric Foner, *Reconstruction: America's Unfinished Revolution, 1863–1877* (New York: Harper and Row, 1988), 68.

65. Testimony of Harry McMillan before the American Freedmen's Inquiry Commission, June 1863, in Berlin et al., *Wartime Genesis of Free Labor: The Lower South*, 250–54. McMillan successfully took control of his own life in freedom. In 1863 he borrowed money and bought a plantation on Ladies Island, South Carolina, where he, his wife, two daughters, and twenty-one hired hands planted sixty-five acres of cotton, yielding $1,358 worth of ginned cotton. John W. Blassingame, ed., *Slave Testimony: Two Centuries of Letters, Speeches, Interviews, and Autobiographies* (Baton Rouge: Louisiana State University Press, 1977), 379; Rose, *Rehearsal for Reconstruction*, 314–15.

Chapter Three

1. Elijah Marrs, *Life and History of the Rev. Elijah P. Marrs* (Louisville, Ky.: Bradley and Gilbert, 1885), 18. Marrs was born to a free father and enslaved mother in Shelbyville, Shelby County, Kentucky in 1840. His brother, Henry Marrs, enlisted in the Union army before Elijah did.

2. Compiled Military Service Record of Elijah Mars, RG 94, M1818, roll 233, NA; and review of the Regimental Records of Company L, Twelfth U.S. Colored Troops, RG 94, NA. In his autobiography Marrs spelled his name with two "r"'s, but it is spelled with one "r" in all of his military records. I have adopted Marrs's own spelling.

3. Marrs, *Life and History*, 17.

4. Ibid., 18.

5. Ibid., 20. Marrs mustered in on September 26, 1864, and was assigned to Company L, Twelfth U.S. Colored Artillery. Compiled Military Service Record of Elijah Mars, RG 94, M1818, roll 233, NA. See Peter Bruner, *A Slave's Adventure Toward Freedom: Not Fiction but the True Story of a Struggle* (Oxford, Ohio, 1919), 43, for a similar account of sixteen men meeting on the road to Camp Nelson, Kentucky, and enlisting in the Union army together. Bruner described his motivation for joining the army as follows: "The officers asked me what I wanted there and I told them that I came there to fight the rebels and that I wanted a gun. When I had run off before and wanted to go in the army and fight they said that they did not want any darkies, and that this was a white man's war. After I had been there about a week they made up a regiment and called it the Twelfth U.S. Heavy Artillery." This is the same regiment that Elijah Marrs joined two months later. Robert Anderson, a former slave from Green County, Kentucky, inspired by several friends who had run away and enlisted, followed suit after being punished unjustly. Robert Anderson, *From Slavery to Affluence: Memoirs of Robert Anderson, Ex-Slave*, ed. Daisy Anderson Leonard (1927; Steamboat Springs, Colo.: Steamboat Pilot, 1967), 4.–43.

6. Ira Berlin et al., eds., *The Black Military Experience* (New York: Cambridge University Press, 1982), 13–15.

7. The historiography of education of African American soldiers during the Civil War generally casts the Union army as a schoolhouse in which white chaplains, along with white officers and their wives, taught black men. Historian Dudley Taylor Cornish argues that the Union army had no coherent educational program for black soldiers and concludes that "what schooling the colored soldier received while in federal service was in general the result of the intelligent interest of his officers, who, aware of the Negro's need and desire for education, tried to provide for that need and fulfill that desire." This is only part of the story. African American soldiers had a far more complex relationship to literacy than Cornish and others have suggested. Dudley Taylor Cornish, "The Union Army as a School for Negroes," *Journal of Negro History* 37 (October 1952): 368. John W. Blassingame made a similar argument in "The Union Army as an Educational Institution for Negroes, 1862–1865," *Journal of Negro Education* 34 (Spring 1965): 152–59. More recently, Edward G. Longacre has repeated this limited depiction in his reference to education in black Union regiments. See his "Black Troops in the Army of the James, 1863–1865," in *"Manhood Rights": The Construction of Black Male History and Manhood, 1750–1870*, vol. 1 of *A Question of Manhood: A Reader in U.S. Black Men's History and Masculinity*, ed. Darlene Clark Hine and Earnestine Jenkins (Bloomington: Indiana University Press, 1999), 532–49.

8. Marrs, *Life and History*, 23. According to Adjutant General Lorenzo Thomas,

who was responsible for the administration of the Bureau of Colored Troops, non-commissioned officers were usually appointed from within white regiments, "but as intelligent blacks are found they are made sergeants and corporals." Report of Lorenzo Thomas to Secretary of War E. M. Stanton, November 7, 1864, in *OR*, ser. 1, 4:921–22.

9. Marrs, *Life and History*, 23; Berlin et al., *Black Military Experience*, 13–15.

10. Marrs, *Life and History*, 24–25.

11. Frederick Douglass et al., *Men of Color: To Arms! To Arms!* (Philadelphia, 1863), GLC 2752, Gilder Lehrman Collection, New York, N.Y.; Frederick Douglass, "Why Should a Colored Man Enlist?" (originally published in *Douglass' Monthly*, April 1863), in *Frederick Douglass: Selected Speeches and Writings*, ed. Philip S. Foner, abridged by Yuval Taylor (Chicago: Lawrence Hill Books, 1999), 528–31.

12. Douglass, "Why Should a Colored Man Enlist?" 529–30.

13. Marrs, *Life and History*, 28.

14. Susie King Taylor, *A Black Woman's Civil War Memoirs: Reminiscences of My Life in Camp with the 33rd U.S. Colored Troops, Late 1st South Carolina Volunteers*, ed. Patricia Romero and Willie Lee Rose (New York: M. Wiener Publishing, 1988), 7–11, 33–37; Eve Merriam, *Growing Up Female in America: Ten Lives* (New York: Doubleday, 1971), 161–79. King says that she was not paid for her teaching or nursing duties. It is likely that her work as a laundress was her sole source of income.

15. Taylor, *Black Woman's Civil War Memoirs*, 37–52.

16. F. M. Thomas to George Whipple, July 1, 1864, AMA Mss.; Elizabeth (Lizzie) Edwards Diary, April 19, 1866, Quaker Collection, LL.

17. The First North Carolina Colored Volunteers was later known as the Thirty-fifth United States Colored Troops. Frances Beecher Perkins, "Two Years with a Colored Regiment: A Woman's Experience," *New England Magazine* 23 (January 1898): 537.

18. Ibid., 533, 535–36.

19. See, for example, *Record of the Services of the Seventh Regiment, U.S. Colored Troops from September, 1863 to November, 1866, by an Officer of the Regiment* (Providence, R.I.: E. L. Freeman, 1878), 86–87.

20. Quoted from a April 10, 1865, report by Warren in John Eaton, *Grant, Lincoln, and the Freedmen: Reminiscences of the Civil War* (New York: Longmans, Green, 1907), 208–9.

21. *Freedmen's Journal* 1 (January 1865): 11.

22. John Fee to Simeon Jocelyn, July 18, 1864, August 8, 1864, AMA Mss.; *Freedmen's Record* 1 (December 1865): 12.

23. Handwritten statement of Jason Spratley, Warwick County, Va., n.d., HUA.

24. John McCline, *Slavery in the Clover Bottoms: John McCline's Narrative of His Life during Slavery and the Civil War*, ed. Jan Furman (Knoxville: University of Tennessee Press, 1998), 81–83. After the war, McCline attended a school for freedpeople and became a teacher. For more on Webster's blue-back speller, see below, chap. 7.

25. Sweney enlisted in September 1863 and was promoted to first sergeant in Company F of the Thirteenth Regiment on November 20, 1863. Regimental Rec-

ords, Thirteenth U.S. Colored Infantry, RG 94, NA. Sweney's military service record was missing from the National Archives in Spring 2000. A copy of his service record at the Freedmen and Southern Society Project indicates that he was born free in Greensborough, Kentucky.

26. John Sweney to Brigadier General Fisk, October 8, 1865, in Berlin et al., *Black Military Experience*, 615.

27. Ibid.

28. James Scott, *Domination and the Arts of Resistance: Hidden Transcripts* (New Haven: Yale University Press, 1990), 1–25.

29. When the Civil War began, Turner was pastor of Israel African Methodist Episcopal Church in Washington, D.C., a congregation with several hundred members. He used his prominence in Washington to recruit black men into the Union army, and to reward his efforts, President Lincoln himself appointed Turner the first African American chaplain in the United States Army in September 1863. Edwin S. Redkey, "Black Chaplains in the Union Army," *Civil War History* 33 (December 1987): 331–50; Edwin S. Redkey, ed., *Respect Black: The Writings and Speeches of Henry McNeal Turner* (New York: Arno Press and the New York Times, 1971), viii; Compiled Military Service Record of Henry McNeal Turner, RG 94, M1819, NA.

30. Henry McNeal Turner to Adjutant General, U.S. Army, June 24, 1865, Adjutant General Letters Received, RG 94, M619, 736T, 1865, NA.

31. Ibid.

32. Henry McNeal Turner to Adjutant General, U.S. Army, August 14, 1865, Adjutant General Letters Received, RG 94, M619, 591T, 1865, NA.

33. Henry McNeal Turner to Adjutant General, U.S. Army, August 31, 1865, Adjutant General Letters Received, RG 94, M619, 695T, 1865, NA.

34. William Waring to Adjutant General, U.S. Army, June 21, 1864, Adjutant General Letters Received, RG 94, M619, 876W, 1864, NA; William Waring to L. Thomas, Adjutant General, United States Colored Troops, November 10, 1864, Adjutant General Letters Received, RG 94, M619, 2042W, 1864, NA.

35. Benjamin Randolph to E. D. Townsend, November 1, 1864, in Military Service Record of Benjamin Randolph, RG 94, M619, 972, 1864, NA.

36. Regarding Randolph's attendance at Oberlin College, see Dorothy Sterling, ed., *The Trouble They Seen: Black People Tell the Story of Reconstruction* (Garden City, N.Y.: Doubleday, 1976), 79. Benjamin F. Randolph to E. D. Townsend, November 1, 1864, in Military Service Record of Benjamin Randolph, RG94, M619, 972, 1864, NA; Randolph to Thomas, May 31, 1865, RG 94, M619, 462, 1865, NA. In this second letter Randolph complained that the greatest surviving evil in the regiment was the use of profanity. As some of the white commissioned officers engaged in the practice, it was difficult for the chaplain to preach against it to the men.

37. Francis A. Boyd to Major General B. Butler, January 5, 1865, and affidavit of L. W. Gratigny, January 6, 1865, in Military Service Record of Francis A. Boyd, RG 94, M619, 1861–1865, NA.

38. Francis A. Boyd to Adjutant General Lorenzo Thomas, December 31, 1864, RG 94, M619, 1861–1865, NA.

39. Francis A. Boyd to Colonel O. A. Bartholomew, January 3, 1865, RG 94, M619, 1861–1865, NA.

40. *American Missionary*, December 1864, 295.

41. Ibid., September 1866, 205–6; ibid., April 1866, 88–89.

42. Monthly school report for October 1865, Greensboro, Georgia, M799, roll 20, FBR.

43. Richard Baxter Foster, *Historical Sketch of Lincoln Institute, Jefferson City, Missouri: Full History of its Conception, Struggles, and Triumph* (Jefferson City, Mo.: n.p., 1871), 5–14. When first permitted to enlist, black soldiers earned seven dollars each week in contrast to white soldiers' thirteen dollars. After many soldiers refused to accept unequal pay and some threatened mutiny, Congress equalized the pay of black and white soldiers. Berlin et al., *Black Military Experience*, 16–21.

44. Sexton mustered out of the army on January 8, 1867. Military Service Record and Pension Records of Samuel Sexton, NA.

45. Foster, *Historical Sketch of Lincoln Institute*, 7.

46. W. Sherman Savage, *The History of Lincoln University* (Jefferson City, Mo.: New Day Press, 1939), 1.

47. Foster, *Historical Sketch of Lincoln Institute*, 9–10.

48. Savage, *History of Lincoln University*, 11.

49. For the history of Southland College, see Thomas C. Kennedy, "Southland College: The Society of Friends and Black Education in Arkansas," *Southern Friend* 7 (Spring 1985): 39–69; Thomas C. Kennedy, "The Last Days at Southland," *Southern Friend* 8 (Spring 1986): 3–19; Thomas C. Kennedy, "The Rise and Decline of a Black Monthly Meeting: Southland, Arkansas, 1864–1925," *Southern Friend* 19 (Autumn 1997): 3–29; and Linda B. Selleck, *Gentle Invaders: Quaker Women Educators and Racial Issues during the Civil War and Reconstruction* (Richmond, Ind.: Friends United Press, 1995), 191–217.

50. Eli Jay, "History of Southland College," unpublished manuscript in Southland Collection, LL.

51. Jacqueline S. Nelson, *Indiana Quakers Confront the Civil War* (Indianapolis: Indiana Historical Society, 1991), 2–4; Minutes of the General Committee of Indiana Yearly Meeting of Friends on the Concerns of the People of Color, September 1852, 36, Quaker Collection, LL.

52. Minutes of the General Committee of Indiana Yearly Meeting of Friends on the Concerns of the People of Color, October 1863, 49, Quaker Collection, LL.

53. Minutes of Indiana Yearly Meeting Committee on Freedmen's Relief, September 30, 1864, in Minute Book of Board of Control for Freedmen's Relief Committee of the Ohio, Indiana, Iowa, and Western Yearly Meeting of Orthodox Friends, September 1864 to May 1867, Quaker Collection, LL.

54. Minutes of Indiana Yearly Meeting, Report of Indiana Yearly Meeting's Executive Committee on Freedmen, 1864, 18, Quaker Collection, LL.

55. Ibid.; *Freedmen's Record* 1 (January 1866): 4.

56. *Freedmen's Record* 1 (August 1866): 6.

57. Ibid. (January 1866): 4 (emphasis in original). The *Freedmen's Record* did not

note the location of this action by freedpeople, but the freedpeople's action on their own behalf clearly encouraged the Quakers in their mission. For further evidence of self-reliance on the part of the freedpeople and its effect on Quaker thinking see ibid. (March 1866): 9.

58. Report of the Committee on the Concerns of the People of Color of the General Committee of Indiana Yearly Meeting, October 4, 1851, 41, and September 29, 1853, 31, Quaker Collection, LL.

59. Minutes of the General Committee of Indiana Yearly Meeting—Concerns of the People of Color, 1863, 25, Quaker Collection, LL.

60. Minutes of Indiana Yearly Meeting, Report of Indiana Yearly Meeting's Executive Committee on Freedmen, 1864, 22, Quaker Collection, LL. The Quaker motto as expressed in one issue of the *Freedmen's Record* was "Our duty is, first to relieve suffering, then educate to prevent it." *Freedmen's Record* 1 (December 1865): 6.

61. Regarding dissatisfaction with donating clothing, see *Freedmen's Record* 1 (December 1865): 10. Regarding vocational school see Indiana Yearly Meeting, Second Annual Report of the Executive Committee on Freedmen, 1865, 43, Quaker Collection, LL. Quaker missionaries in Vicksburg, Mississippi, also set up a vocational school to teach women sewing. *Freedmen's Record* 1 (December 1865): 3–4.

62. Marie Jenkins Schwartz, *Born in Bondage: Growing Up Enslaved in the Antebellum South* (Cambridge, Mass.: Harvard University Press, 2000), 172.

63. *Freedmen's Record* 1 (June 1866): 6. These examples are from the Quaker-operated Lauderdale Orphan Asylum in Mississippi. The circumstances would have been similar in Helena.

64. Ibid. (December 1865): 4.

65. Ibid., 7.

66. *Freedmen's Record* 1 (March 1866): 9.

67. Ibid. (June 1866): 16.

68. "Report of Joseph Dickinson and Timothy Harrison," ibid. (September 1866): 12.

69. Ibid. (June 1866): 16.

70. Eli Jay, "History of Southland College," unpublished manuscript, Southland Collection, LL.

71. Bentzoni letter, June 1, 1865, Letters Sent, Regimental Records, Fifty-sixth U.S. Colored Troops, RG 94, NA.

72. General Order No. 8, signed by Charles Bentzoni, Helena, Ark., March 22, 1865, in Regimental Records, Fifty-sixth U.S. Colored Troops, NA.

73. According to the regimental treasurer, the donations came from officers and soldiers as follows: field and staff, $55.00; Company A, $75.00; Company B, $102.00; Company C, $301.40; Company D, $239.40; Company E, $106.00; Company F, $470.00; Company G, $117.00; Company H, $360.85; Company I, $196.50; and Company K, $60.60. *Freedmen's Record* 1 (September 1866): 12.

74. Ibid. The concerts raised a total of $73.

75. Ibid. (April 1866): 14.

76. The land was part of a parcel of eighty acres which had to be purchased as a whole. The regiment purchased thirty acres, and Calvin Clark purchased the re-

mainder from his personal funds. He was later reimbursed by Indiana Yearly Meeting. The full eighty acres cost $2,400. Ibid. (September 1866): 12.

77. Letter from Calvin Clark, ibid. (July 1866): 6.

78. Report of Alida Clark, ibid. (August 1866): 11.

79. "Report of Joseph Dickenson and Timothy Harrison," ibid. (September 1866): 11.

80. Ibid., 6. The men were on the steamship *Continental*. Some had been in Helena, Arkansas; some had been quarantined in St Louis. Regimental Records, Fifty-sixth U.S. Colored Troops, RG 94, NA.

81. *Freedmen's Record* 1 (August 1866): 1.

82. Report of W. W. Wales, June 1866, in ibid., 4.

83. Southland College remained open until 1925.

84. Jack D. Foner, *Blacks and the Military in American History: A New Perspective* (New York: Praeger, 1974), 51.

85. Berlin et al., *Black Military Experience*, 15.

86. Thomas Wentworth Higginson, *Army Life in a Black Regiment, and Other Writings* (New York: Penguin Books, 1997), 42.

87. Compiled Military Service Record of Elijah Mars, RG 94, M1818, roll 233, NA. Elijah Marrs mustered out of the army on April 24, 1866. Compiled Military Service Records of Henry Mars, RG 94, M1817, roll 69, NA. As of the fall of 1865, the U.S. government had paid total compensation of $213,883 to loyal slave owners in Delaware and Maryland. Nearly four thousand owners filed claims in those two states, but not all had been resolved as of the date of the report. Report of Assistant Adjutant General C. W. Foster, in *OR*, ser. 3, 5:139–40.

Chapter Four

1. Elijah Marrs mustered out of the Union army on April 24, 1866. Henry Marrs mustered out on March 16, 1866. Military Service Record of Elijah Mars, RG 94, M1818, roll 233, NA; Military Service Record of Henry Marrs, RG 94, M1817, roll 69, NA.

2. Henry Marrs to Chaplain T. K. Noble, Superintendent of Freedmen's Schools, Louisville, Ky., June 5, 1867, doc. A4394, Freedmen and Southern Society Project, University of Maryland, College Park.

3. Application of the Colored People of Shelbyville to Secretary E. M. Stanton, Washington, D.C., May 14, 1866, doc. A60320, Freedmen and Southern Society Project.

4. Elijah Marrs, La Grange, Ky., to Secretary E. M. Stanton, February 1, 1868, Freedmen and Southern Society Project.

5. My thinking about freedpeople's emergence into the public sphere is influenced by Jurgen Habermas, *The Structural Transformation of the Public Sphere: An Inquiry into a Category of Bourgeois Society* (Cambridge, Mass.: MIT Press, 2000). Also helpful in this regard was Craig Calhoun, ed., *Habermas and the Public Sphere* (Cambridge, Mass.: MIT Press, 1992).

6. Deposition of Colonel George H. Hanks before the American Freedmen's

Inquiry Commission, February 6, 1864, in Ira Berlin et al., eds., *The Wartime Genesis of Free Labor: The Lower South* (New York: Cambridge University Press, 1990), 517–21.

7. Freedmen of Roanoke Island to Mr. President, March 9, 1865, and Freedmen of Roanoke Island to Secretary of War, March 9, 1865, in Ira Berlin et al., eds., *The Wartime Genesis of Free Labor: The Upper South* (New York: Cambridge University Press, 1993), 231–36.

8. Carter Holmes to William M. Beebe, April 27, 1867, in ibid., 346–47.

9. John Richard Dennett, *The South as It Is: 1865–1866*, ed. Henry M. Christman (New York: Viking Press, 1965), 283.

10. Regarding the antebellum convention movement, see John W. Cromwell, *The Early Negro Convention Movement* (Washington, D.C.: American Negro Academy, 1904); and Philip S. Foner and George E. Walker, eds., *Proceedings of the Black State Conventions, 1840–1865*, 2 vols. (Philadelphia: Temple University Press, 1979, 1980), vol. 2. Regarding colonization, see the constitution of the American Colonization Society, quoted in Early Lee Fox, *The American Colonization Society, 1817–1840* (Baltimore: Johns Hopkins Press, 1919), 47, 51–52; and Amos J. Beyan, *The American Colonization Society and the Creation of the Liberian State: A Historical Perspective, 1822–1900* (Lanham, Md.: University Press of America, 1991), 1–15.

11. Sidney Andrews, *The South Since the War* (1866; Boston: Houghton Mifflin, 1971), 120; David S. Cecelski, "Abraham H. Galloway: Wilmington's Lost Prophet and the Rise of Black Radicalism in the American South," in *Democracy Betrayed: The Wilmington Race Riot of 1898 and Its Legacy*, ed. David S. Cecelski and Timothy B. Tyson (Chapel Hill: University of North Carolina Press, 1998), 56–57.

12. Andrews, *South Since the War*, 121, 124; Dennett, *South as It Is*, 149; Roberta Sue Alexander, *North Carolina Faces the Freedmen: Race Relations during Presidential Reconstruction, 1865–67* (Durham, N.C.: Duke University Press, 1985), 24–25.

13. The minutes of the southern black conventions do not list women as delegates or officers. However, it is certainly possible that women were among the spectators who viewed the proceedings of the conventions. Elsa Barkley Brown has written about such black women in attendance at Republican conventions held in Richmond, Virginia, in the 1860s. Elsa Barkley Brown, "Negotiating and Transforming the Public Sphere: African American Political Life in the Transition from Slavery to Freedom," *Public Culture* 7 (Fall 1994): 107–46.

14. Andrews, *South Since the War*, 121, 124; Dennett, *South as It Is*; 149; Alexander, *North Carolina Faces the Freedmen*, 24–25.

15. Dennett, *South as It Is*, 149–50; Andrews, *South Since the War*, 120–21, 131.

16. Andrews, *South Since the War*, 127; Dennett, *South as It Is*, 153.

17. Andrews, *South Since the War*, 129, 125; "State Convention of the Colored People of North Carolina, Raleigh, September 29, 1865," in Philip S. Foner and George E. Walker, eds., *Proceedings of the Black National and State Conventions, 1865–1900* (Philadelphia: Temple University Press, 1986), 179–81.

18. Andrews, *South Since the War*, 159–61.

19. Foner and Walker, *Proceedings of the Black State Conventions*, 298–99, 290.

20. "Proceedings of the Colored Convention of the State of Kansas, Held at Leavenworth, Oct. 13, 14, 15, 16, 1863," Beinecke Rare Book and Manuscript Library, Yale University, New Haven, Conn. Although Kansas was a free state, the men who attended the 1863 convention considered the Emancipation Proclamation an important turning point for them, as they had been tainted by the existence of slavery in the South and particularly in neighboring Missouri. Black men in Kansas did not have the right to vote, for example. Mary Beth Norton et al., *A People and a Nation: A History of the United States* (Boston: Houghton Mifflin, 1998), 399. Black Californians, too, took the opportunity of emancipation to advocate for increased educational opportunities for African Americans. At the 1865 State Convention of the Colored Citizens, delegates urged the state legislature to give every child the privilege of education. The state would not permit black children to attend school with whites and would only establish schools for blacks where there were ten or more children. The delegates found that this practice deprived many of the benefits of schooling. Delegates also pledged support for an African American institute, equivalent to a high school, that had been established in San Jose but was experiencing financial challenges. "Proceedings of the California State Convention of the Colored Citizens, Held in Sacramento on the 25th, 26th, 27th and 28th of October, 1865," in Foner and Walker, *Proceedings of the Black State Conventions*, 2:173–76.

21. "Memorial to the Senate and House of Representatives of the United States in Congress Assembled: Proceedings of the Colored People's Convention of South Carolina, Charleston, November 24, 1865," in James S. Allen, *Reconstruction: The Battle for Democracy, 1865–1876* (New York: International Publishers, 1937), 228–29. See also "Address of the Colored Convention to the People of Alabama, Mobile, May 21, 1867," in ibid., 236–42.

22. "Memorial to the Senate and House of Representatives . . . Proceedings of the Colored People's Convention of South Carolina," in ibid., 228–29.

23. State Convention of the Colored People of Georgia, Augusta, January 10, 1866, in Foner and Walker, *Proceedings of the State and National Conventions*, 233.

24. "An Address of the Colored People of Missouri to the Friends of Equal Rights, October 12, 1865," in Foner and Walker, *Proceedings of the Black State Conventions*, 2:281.

25. Ibid., 2:278–82.

26. State Convention of the Colored People of Georgia, Augusta, January 10, 1866, in Foner and Walker, *Proceedings of the State and National Conventions*, 234; *American Freedman*, April 1866, 11–14; Alan Conway, *The Reconstruction of Georgia* (Minneapolis: University of Minnesota Press, 1966), 40–60.

27. "Proceedings of the Convention of Colored Citizens of the State of Arkansas, held in Little Rock, Thursday, Friday and Saturday, Nov. 30, Dec. 1 and 2, 1865," in Foner and Walker, *Proceedings of the Black National and State Conventions*, 191. Grey had been a slave of Governor Henry A. Wise of Virginia. He was also a minister. Richard L. Hume, "Negro Delegates to the State Constitutional Conventions of 1867–69," in *Southern Black Leaders of the Reconstruction Era*, ed. Howard N. Rabinowitz (Urbana: University of Illinois Press, 1982), 131.

28. "Proceedings of the Colored People's Convention of the State of South Carolina," in Foner and Walker, *Proceedings of the Black State Conventions*, 2:289–90.

Chapter Five

1. John W. Alvord, *First Semi-Annual Report on Schools and Finances of Freedmen, January 1, 1866* (Washington, D.C.: Government Printing Office, 1868), 9, reprinted in John W. Alvord, *Semi-Annual Reports on Schools for Freedmen: Numbers 1–10, January 1866–July 1870* (New York: AMS Press, 1980). Alvord visited, among other places, Baltimore, Maryland; Hampton, Norfolk, Petersburg, and Richmond, Virginia; New Bern, Goldsboro, and Wilmington, North Carolina; Florence, Charleston, and Beaufort, South Carolina; Savannah and Augusta, Georgia; Mobile and Montgomery, Alabama; Jackson, Vicksburg, and Natchez, Mississippi; and New Orleans, Louisiana. He went through most cities twice, on the initial journey as well as on the return. AMA employee D. J. Allen also commented on this observed tendency toward self-reliance. Parents of students were "industrious and scorn the thought of being dependent upon the Government for support." D. J. Allen to George Whipple, March 1864, AMA Mss.

2. School report of Simon Ryall, April 10, 1866, M799, roll 20, FBR.

3. James Smith to George Whipple, October 18, 1865, AMA Mss.

4. J. W. Alvord to George Whipple, October 31, 1865, AMA Mss., emphasis in original.

5. Emanuel Smith to E. P. Smith, April 10, 1867, AMA Mss.

6. Ibid.

7. Emanuel Smith to E. P. Smith, May 1, 1867, AMA Mss. According to Smith, books cost on average between twenty and twenty-five cents each.

8. Emanuel Smith to E. P. Smith, June 29, 1867, AMA Mss.

9. Emanuel Smith to E. P. Smith, October 30, 1867, AMA Mss.

10. The struggle to find trained teachers for freedpeople in Florida continued for some time. In 1869, after the state had established a common school system, the Assistant Superintendent of Education wrote to the AMA requesting teachers for black students. Florida, he said, had been neglected more than most other states in matters of education. In September of the same year, the chairman of the Board of Public Instruction wrote to the AMA to request teachers specifically for the school in Tallahassee. A. J. Wakefield to George Whipple, January 23, 1869, AMA Mss.; C. H. Edwards to E. P. Smith, September 13, 1869, AMA Mss.

11. Robert C. Morris, *Reading, 'Riting, and Reconstruction: The Education of Freedmen in the South, 1861–1870* (Chicago: University of Chicago Press, 1981), 22–26. See also Charles Strong to George Whipple, May 9, 1864, AMA Mss.; and C. L. Tambling to Simeon Jocelyn and George Whipple, May 11, 1864, AMA Mss.

12. Margaret Adams to American Missionary Association, May 9, 1864, June 2, 1864, AMA Mss.

13. Margaret Adams to American Missionary Association, May 9, 1864, AMA Mss.

14. I consulted the 1860 and 1870 U.S. census for New Orleans, New Orleans city directories for 1860 and the years immediately following the war (the directories were not printed during the war), marriage license records, and obituaries in the New Orleans Public Library, Government Documents Section, in July 2000. *Gardner's New Orleans Directory for 1861* in the Tulane University Government Documents Library listed a Margaret Adams who rented furnished rooms at 139 Burgundy. This is probably not the same Margaret Adams, as the address differs from the one Adams gave in both of her letters to the AMA. Her name does not appear in John W. Blassingame's *Black New Orleans, 1860–1973* (Chicago: University of Chicago Press, 1973) or in his research notes in the John Blassingame Papers, housed in Manuscripts and Archives at Yale University, New Haven, Conn. Margaret Adams also does not appear in the records of Oberlin College as having attended or graduated from the school. Student Folders, Oberlin College Archives, Oberlin, Ohio.

15. Morris, *Reading, 'Riting, and Reconstruction*, 27; Margaret Adams to AMA, June 2, 1864, AMA Mss.

16. AMA report signed I.P.W., January 2, 1865, Savannah, AMA Mss., emphasis in original.

17. John W. Alvord, *Fifth Semi-Annual Report on Schools for Freedmen, January 1, 1868* (Washington, D.C.: Government Printing Office, 1868), 5, reprinted in Alvord, *Semi-Annual Reports*; John W. Blassingame, "Before the Ghetto: The Making of the Black Community in Savannah, Georgia, 1865–1880," *Journal of Social History* 6 (Summer 1973): 463–88; Robert E. Perdue, *The Negro in Savannah, 1865–1900* (New York: Exposition Press, 1973), 72; Jacqueline Jones, *Soldiers of Light and Love: Northern Teachers and Georgia Blacks, 1865–1873* (Chapel Hill: University of North Carolina Press, 1980); AMA report signed I.P.W., January 2, 1865, Savannah, AMA Mss.; Richard R. Wright, *A Brief Historical Sketch of Negro Education in Georgia* (Savannah: Robinson Printing House, 1894), 17–18, 20–21. William J. Campbell pastored the First African Baptist Church of Savannah. A former slave, he had been freed by the will of his mistress in 1849. The church had a membership of 1,800 members and owned property valued at $18,000. The trustees of the church were all white. "Account of a meeting of Black Religious Leaders in Savannah, Georgia, with the Secretary of War and the Commander of the Military Division of the Mississippi," in Ira Berlin et al., eds., *The Wartime Genesis of Free Labor: The Lower South* (New York: Cambridge University Press, 1990), 331–37.

18. Susie King Taylor, *A Black Woman's Civil War Memoirs: Reminiscences of My Life in Camp with the 33rd U.S. Colored Troops, Late 1st South Carolina Volunteers*, ed. Patricia W. Romero and Willie Lee Rose (New York: M. Wiener Publishing, 1988), 29–30.

19. AMA report signed I.P.W., January 2, 1865, Savannah, AMA Mss.; William J. Richardson to George Whipple, January 10, 1865, AMA Mss., emphasis in original.

20. Wright, *Brief Historical Sketch of Negro Education in Georgia*, 21.

21. S. W. Magill to AMA, February 6, 1865, AMA Mss.

22. S. W. Magill to AMA, February 26, 1865, AMA Mss.

23. Ibid.

24. Jones, *Soldiers of Light and Love*, 74; Joe Martin Richardson, *Christian Reconstruc-*

tion: The American Missionary Association and Southern Blacks, 1861–1890 (Athens: University of Georgia Press, 1986), 247.

25. Quoted in Leon F. Litwack, *Been in the Storm So Long: The Aftermath of Slavery* (New York: Alfred A. Knopf, 1979), 477.

26. *National Freedman's Relief Association of New York Annual Report of 1865/66* (New York: Holman, 1866), 22.

27. Ibid.

28. Ibid.

29. S. W. Magill to AMA, February 7, 1865, AMA Mss; Jones, *Soldiers of Light and Love*, 76.

30. A. K. Spence to George Whipple, June 21, 1864, AMA Mss.

31. George Candee to George Whipple, June 22, 1864, AMA Mss.

32. M. M. Clark to M. E. Strieby, August 10, 1864, AMA Mss.

33. For an extensive discussion of conflicts between black communities and the AMA, see Richardson, *Christian Reconstruction*, 235–55.

34. Report of J. H. Douglass, Quaker Representative, and R. S. Donaldson, Acting Assistant Commissioner, Freedmen's Bureau, in *Freedmen's Record* 1 (January 1866): 7, 11; letter from Lizzie Bond in ibid. (November 1865): 9.

35. Ibid. (January 1866): 7.

36. Ibid., 7, 11.

37. Ibid. (April 1866): 7.

38. Ibid., 7. African Americans' prosperous condition in Columbus is intriguing as there was no community of free persons before the war. Indeed, the census of 1860 counted only four free blacks in Lowndes County, and two of them were under the age of twenty. U.S. Bureau of the Census, *Eighth Census of the United States Taken in the Year 1860* (Washington, D.C.: Government Printing Office, 1864). Migration into the city following the war may have been a factor. It is also possible that some enslaved people had managed to accumulate a degree of wealth. See Dylan C. Penningroth, *The Claims of Kinfolk: African American Property and Community in the Nineteenth-Century South* (Chapel Hill: University of North Carolina Press, 2003).

39. *Freedmen's Record* 1 (June 1866): 4.

40. Ibid. (July 1866): 6, emphasis in original; Register of Signatures of Deposits in the Branches of the Freedman's Savings and Trust Company, 1865–1874, RG 101, M816, roll 14, NA.

41. *Freedmen's Record* 1 (June 1866): 5.

42. Ibid.

43. U.S. House, Select Committee on Memphis Riots, *Memphis Riots and Massacres*, 39th Cong., 1st sess., 1866, H. Rep. 101 (Reprint; Miami, Fla.: Mnemosyne Publishing Company, 1969), 2–3, 35, 20–21.

44. John W. Alvord, *Fourth Semi-Annual Report on Schools for Freedmen, July 1, 1867* (Washington, D.C.: Government Printing Office, 1867), 43, reprinted in Alvord, *Semi-Annual Reports*.

45. In Jackson, Mississippi, Quakers made plans to sell the freedpeople's schoolhouse and the land on which it stood to the black community so that they could run it

for themselves. *Freedmen's Record* 1 (August 1866): 5. Arguably the Quakers tended to be less intrusive and controlling because they had no interest of recruiting or welcoming African Americans into membership as Friends.

46. To be sure, white Quakers were never fully exempt from feelings of white superiority or paternalism. In the 1770s, for example, when Friends made the bold moral move of excluding from membership anyone who owned slaves, many offered aid to African Americans but always with the expectations that Quakers should exercise control. In the nineteenth century, although most maintained abolitionist sentiments, Quaker groups rarely invited African Americans into church membership or encouraged them to set up separate meetings. Alida Clark in Arkansas was an important exception. Jean R. Soderlund, *Quakers and Slavery: A Divided Spirit* (Princeton, N.J.: Princeton University Press, 1985), 177–87; Linda B. Selleck, *Gentle Invaders: Quaker Women Educators and Racial Issues during the Civil War and Reconstruction* (Richmond, Ind.: Friends United Press, 1995), 167–74.

Chapter Six

1. John W. Alvord, *First Semi-Annual Report on Schools and Finances of Freedmen, January 1, 1866* (Washington, D.C.: Government Printing Office, 1868), 9–10, reprinted in John W. Alvord, *Semi-Annual Reports on Schools for Freedmen: Numbers 1–10, January 1866–July 1870* (New York: AMS Press, 1980).

2. Elijah Marrs, *Life and History of the Rev. Elijah P. Marrs* (Louisville, Ky.: Bradley and Gilbert Company, 1885), 78. John Sweney also taught school when he returned to his hometown of Greensborough, Kentucky. John Sweney to Freedmen's Bureau, June 28, 1866, doc. A4310, Freedmen and Southern Society Project, University of Maryland, College Park.

3. Marrs, *Life and History*, 79.

4. Ibid., 85.

5. Ronald E. Butchart, *Northern Schools, Southern Blacks, and Reconstruction: Freedmen's Education, 1862–1875* (Westport, Conn.: Greenwood Press, 1980) 100; Richard Paul Fuke, "Land, Lumber, and Learning: The Freedmen's Bureau, Education, and the Black Community in Post-Emancipation Maryland," in *The Freedmen's Bureau and Reconstruction: Reconsiderations*, ed. Paul A. Cimbala and Randall M. Miller (New York: Fordham University Press, 1999), 288–314. For additional information on the Freedmen's Bureau see George R. Bentley, *A History of the Freedmen's Bureau* (New York: Octagon Books, 1974); and Donald G. Nieman, ed., *The Freedmen's Bureau and Black Freedom* (New York: Garland Publishing, 1994).

6. Because the Freedmen's Bureau combined figures for Maryland/Delaware and Missouri/Kansas, it is not possible to be certain whether black teachers outnumbered white ones in each of those states.

7. Jacqueline Jones, *Soldiers of Light and Love: Northern Teachers and Georgia Blacks, 1865–1873* (Chapel Hill: University of North Carolina Press, 1980), 210.

8. Joe M. Richardson, *Christian Reconstruction: The American Missionary Association and Southern Blacks, 1861–1890* (Athens: University of Georgia Press, 1986), 191.

9. Report of G. L. Eberhart, October 15, 1866, M798, roll 32, FBR; Freedmen's Bureau school report form, "Circular No. 8," M799, roll 20, FBR. Several sources have provided invaluable information about African Americans in Georgia before and during Reconstruction: E. Merton Coulter, *Negro Legislators in Georgia during the Reconstruction Period* (Athens: Georgia Historical Quarterly, 1968)—despite an extremely negative view of black legislators, Coulter provides some very useful information; Edmund L. Drago, *Black Politicians and Reconstruction in Georgia: A Splendid Failure* (Baton Rouge: Louisiana State University Press, 1982); Whittington B. Johnson, *Black Savannah, 1788–1864* (Fayetteville: University of Arkansas Press, 1996); and Robert E. Perdue, *The Negro in Savannah, 1865–1900* (New York: Exposition Press, 1973).

10. Mary Gale filled out her own school report, although she was included in a school report prepared by a white teacher named Baufield in Columbus. The five white teachers in the report prepared by Baufield taught in the Colored Methodist Church, while Gale taught in the Colored Baptist Church. It is not clear what connected her to the other teachers. Because Gale completed her own report and seemed to act independently from the white teachers, her report is counted as a report for a separate school from Baufield's.

11. The reports prepared by black teachers can be found in M799, roll 20, FBR. One of the subsequent forms asked the person filling it out to indicate how many of the teachers in a school were black and how many were white. This question does not provide much help in assessing black teachers' work, however, because unless all the teachers were black, it is impossible to say that a black teacher was in charge of setting the school's agenda. In any event, most teachers left that question unanswered.

12. B. H. Townsley to G. L. Eberhart, October 20, 1865, M799, roll 20, FBR.

13. Ibid.

14. School report of Smith Varser, June 14, 1866; Edward Petty to G. L. Eberhart, March 27, 1866; Ephraim Rucker monthly report, April 30, 1866; all in M799, roll 20, FBR.

15. Abraham Colby to Dear Brethren, October 1865, M799, roll 20, FBR; School report of Charles Martin, with note signed by Edward Powell, January 1, 1866, M799, roll 20, FBR.

16. Abraham Colby testimony, in KKK Reports, Georgia, 1:699–707; Drago, *Black Politicians and Reconstruction in Georgia*, 37. The Ku Klux Klan whipped Colby for being active in the Republican Party.

17. School report of Jacob Wade, January 1, 1866, M799, roll 20, FBR; report of Thurston Chase, Superintendent of Schools in Florida, and report of J. T. Kirkman, First Lieutenant and State Superintendent of Education, Texas, in John W. Alvord, *Fourth Semi-Annual Report on Schools and Freedmen, July 1, 1867* (Washington, D.C.: Government Printing Office, 1868), 37, 53, reprinted in Alvord, *Semi-Annual Reports*.

18. Johnson, *Black Savannah*, 12, 126–29; John W. Alvord, *Fifth Semi-Annual Report on Schools for Freedmen, January 1, 1868* (Washington, D.C.: Government Printing Office, 1868), 29, reprinted in Alvord, *Semi-Annual Reports*.

19. School report of Jane Deveaux, January 1866, M799, roll 20, FBR.

20. Johnson, *Black Savannah*, 21, 127–29; Perdue, *Negro in Savannah*, 48.

21. School report of Louis B. Toomer, January 1, 1866; School report of James Porter, January 1, 1866; Abraham Colby to Dear Brethren, October 1865; all in M799, roll 20, FBR.

22. School report of William Cole, October 1865; School report of Lewis Smith, October 19, 1865; both in M799, roll 20, FBR. John Ogden became principal of the Fisk School in Nashville, which later became Fisk University. Joe M. Richardson, *A History of Fisk University, 1865–1946* (University: University of Alabama Press, 1980), 9.

23. School report of John L. Bentley and Isaac L. Primus, October 1865, M799, roll 20, FBR. The three teachers who reported that they did not receive a salary were father and son Tunis Campbell and Edward Howard. School report of Tunis Campbell, January 1866, M799, roll 20, FBR. Campbell paid teachers himself. Tunis G. Campbell, *Sufferings of T. G. Campbell and His Family, in Georgia* (Washington, D.C.: Enterprise Publishing Company, 1877), 2.

24. School report of Jack Mallard, June 1866; School report of Lewis Smith, October 19, 1865; both in M799, roll 20, FBR.

25. White northern teachers often could only find lodging with black families, thereby intensifying southern white objections to their presence in the South and their challenge to mores of social separation of blacks and whites. Butchart, *Northern Schools, Southern Blacks, and Reconstruction*, 115–17.

26. See, for example, *American Missionary*, May 1867, 103.

27. Regarding freedpeople building schools, see, for example, James A. Scovill to Brother Shipherd, May 21, 1868, AMA Mss. Regarding the old mule shed and hole in the ground, see John W. Alvord, *Second Semi-Annual Report on Schools and Finances of Freedmen, July 1, 1866* (Washington, D.C.: Government Printing Office, 1868), 10, reprinted in Alvord, *Semi-Annual Reports*.

28. Quoted in Frederic Bancroft, *Slave Trading in the Old South* (New York: Frederick Ungar, 1931), 223.

29. Alvord, *Fifth Semi-Annual Report*, 5; AMA report signed I.P.W., January 2, 1865, Savannah, AMA Mss.; Walter Johnson, *Soul by Soul: Life Inside the Antebellum Slave Market* (Cambridge, Mass.: Harvard University Press, 1999), 164. Appropriation of the former scene of exploitation was not unique to Savannah. In Montgomery, Alabama, the high school for freedpeople met in the old slave auction mart of Fitz and Frazier. The superintendent of education reported that some of the students had once been sold in that mart. John W. Alvord, *Sixth Semi-Annual Report on Schools for Freedmen, July 1, 1868* (Washington, D.C.: Government Printing Office, 1868), 30, reprinted in Alvord, *Semi-Annual Reports*.

30. School report of William Cole, October 1865, M799, roll 20, FBR. Of the sixty-six black and white Georgia teachers who identified themselves by race in the 1866 monthly reports, twenty-seven taught in African American churches. Most teachers indicated that the churches were Baptist or Methodist, but one was Presbyterian, and several teachers wrote "Colored People's Church" without specifying the denomination. For just a few examples of the many black churches serving as schools see *American Missionary*, April 1867, 79; James A. Scovill to Brother Shipherd, May 21,

1868, AMA Mss.; Charlotte Forten, *The Journals of Charlotte Forten Grimké*, ed. Brenda Stevenson (New York: Oxford University Press, 1988), 393.

31. That was the case in Richmond, Virginia, for example, where by law, title to all black churches rested in a white male committee. Elsa Barkley Brown, "Negotiating and Transforming the Public Sphere: African American Political Life in the Transition from Slavery to Freedom," *Public Culture* 7 (Fall 1994): 111.

32. Report of Sargent Free, Major and Assistant. Inspector General, Freedmen's Bureau, Mississippi, October 7, 1865, M826, roll 9, FBR.

33. H. B. Evans and other trustees to M. J. Ringler, September 20, 1865 (emphasis in original); M. J. Ringler to H. B. Evans, September 25, 1865; W. L. S. Sharkey, provisional governor, to Mrs. M. J. Ringler, September 25, 1865; complaint of Henry B. Evans and other trustees of the Methodist Episcopal Church, South for the Jackson Station, September 1865; H. B. Evans to Lt. Donaldson, Freedmen's Bureau, September 29, 1865; report of Sargent Free, Major and Assistant Inspector General, Freedmen's Bureau, Mississippi, October 7, 1865; all in M826, roll 9, FBR. See also John Tate, Clinton, Tenn., to John Ogden, October 1, 1865, AMA Mss.

34. Wesley J. Gaines, *African Methodism in the South: Twenty-Five Years of Freedom* (1890; Chicago: Afro-Am Press, 1969), 5; Reginald F. Hildebrand, *The Times Were Strange and Stirring: Methodist Preachers and the Crisis of Emancipation* (Durham, N.C.: Duke University Press, 1995), 89–100.

35. School report of Edward Petty(written by Harrison Berry on Petty's behalf), February 1866, M799, roll 20, FBR.

36. Testimony of Carleton B. Cole, Judge of the Superior Court of Macon Circuit, KKK Reports, Georgia, 2:1188–89. The Macon church burned in 1869 or 1870. It is possible that this church housed one of the three Macon schools that filed monthly reports.

37. Abraham Colby to Dear Brethren, October 1865, M799, roll 20, FBR.

38. School reports of Simon Ryall, January 1866, April 1866; School report of James Porter, January 1866; School report of Lucinda Jackson, January 1866; all in M799, roll 20, FBR. Teachers who said the school needed books included O. Davie Alexander and John Phillip, Calhoun County; Bartley Townsley, Griffin; and Abraham Colby, Greensboro.

39. School report of Abraham Colby, January 1866, M799, roll 20, FBR.

40. School report of Jacob Wade, January 1, 1866; School report of Louis B. Toomer, January 1, 1866; both in M799, roll 20, FBR.

41. Bartley Townsley to G. L. Eberhart, October 20, 1865, October 21, 1865, M799, roll 20, FBR.

42. J. Clarke Swagle to G. L. Eberhart, January 25, 1866, M799, roll 20, FBR.

43. School report of Lewis Smith, October 19, 1865, M799, roll 20, FBR; School report of Simon Ryall, April 10, 1866, M799, roll 20, FBR; R. M. Manly to Reverend Kennedy, May 8, 1867, M803, roll 1, FBR; *American Missionary*, May 1867, 103.

44. *Colored Tennessean*, July 18, 1866; testimony of Harry McMillan before the American Freedmen's Inquiry Commission, June 1863, in Ira Berlin et al., *Wartime*

Genesis of Free Labor: The Lower South (New York: Cambridge University Press, 1990), 250–54.

45. Joel Perlmann and Robert Margo have called for refinement of the notion of the nineteenth-century feminization of teaching to recognize the role that region and urban versus rural settings played in determining whether males or females predominated in the classroom. Perlmann and Margo demonstrate that by the time of the Civil War, northeastern states employed significantly higher proportions of women teachers than did southern states. The disparity held true even in rural areas, which were less likely to have kept abreast of pedagogical thinking that in the 1840s asserted that women were more nurturing and thus better suited for teaching young children. According to Perlmann and Margo, in 1860 in northeastern states 75 to 83 percent of teachers in rural areas were women. In contrast, in the South only 36 percent of teachers in rural areas were women. Joel Perlmann and Robert A. Margo, *Women's Work? American Schoolteachers, 1650–1920* (Chicago: University of Chicago Press, 2001), 1–8.

46. Ronald E. Butchart, " 'We Best Can Instruct Our Own People': New York African Americans in the Freedmen's Schools, 1861–1875," *Afro-Americans in New York Life and History* 12 (January 1988): 27–49.

47. Coulter, *Negro Legislators in Georgia*, 123; *Proceedings of the Convention of the Equal Rights and Educational Association of Georgia, Assembled at Macon, October 19, 1866* (Augusta: Office of the Loyal Georgian, 1866).

48. School report of Jack Mallard, June 1866, and School report of Edward Anthony, June 1866, both in M799, roll 20, FBR; Perdue, *Negro in Savannah*, 56.

49. Perdue, *Negro in Savannah*, 46–50; report of G. L. Eberhart, October 15, 1866, M798, roll 32, FBR; Drago, *Black Politicians and Reconstruction in Georgia*, 22; Johnson, *Black Savannah*, 13, 21.

50. Report of G. L. Eberhart, October, 15, 1866, M798, roll 32, FBR.

51. Coulter, *Negro Legislators in Georgia*, 121–26; Drago, *Black Politicians and Reconstruction in Georgia*, 82–83; Russell Duncan, *Freedom's Shore: Tunis Campbell and the Georgia Freedmen* (Athens: University of Georgia Press, 1986), 20–25; Campbell, *Sufferings of T. G. Campbell and His Family*, 7. Campbell had an extensive and controversial political career. Historian E. Merton Coulter accused him of being a "carpetbagger, a braggart, an exploiter and a showman." Russell Duncan sees him as a black radical whose work helped blacks in McIntosh County, Georgia, to gain rights that other freedpeople only dreamed of. Raised in New Jersey, Campbell attended school on Long Island and became active on the abolitionist speaking circuit in the 1850s. Early in the war he attempted to enlist, but he was rejected due to his race. In 1863 General Rufus Saxton appointed him superintendent of St. Catherine's Island off the Georgia coast, and Campbell established a government with its own constitution fashioned after the U.S. Constitution. At one point, Campbell barred all white people from entering the island, fearing that they would take advantage of black settlers. He established a militia to enforce his policies. In 1876, when he was sixty-four years old, Campbell was convicted of false imprisonment in his role as a justice of the peace. He was sentenced to hard labor and hired out onto a chain gang under Georgia's convict lease system. Duncan, *Freedom's Shore*, 10, 99–109.

52. School report of Ephraim Rucker, January 1, 1866, M799, roll 20, FBR; report of G. L. Eberhart, October, 15, 1866, M798, roll 32, FBR.

53. School report of Jane Deveaux, January 1866; School report of Lucinda Jackson, January 1866; School report of Jane Deveaux, Lucinda Jackson, James Wilkie, King Thomas, and Ernestine Truchelot, May 1866; School report of Jane Deveaux, Lucinda Jackson, and James Wilkie, June 1866; all in M799, roll 20, FBR.

54. Clarence E. Walker, *A Rock in a Weary Land: The African Methodist Episcopal Church during the Civil War and Reconstruction* (Baton Rouge: Louisiana State University Press, 1982), 48–50; James M. McPherson, *The Negro's Civil War: How American Negroes Felt and Acted during the War for the Union* (New York: Pantheon Books, 1965), 134–35.

55. *Christian Recorder*, February 27, 1864.

56. Ibid., May 30, 1863.

57. Linda M. Perkins, "The Black Female American Missionary Association Teacher in the South, 1861–1870," in vol. 3 of *Black Women in American History: From Colonial Times through the Nineteenth Century*, ed. Darlene Clark Hine (Brooklyn, N.Y.: Carlson, 1990), 1057–58. Joe M. Richardson suggests, however, that "by 1865 the AMA had concluded that black teachers and missionaries were essential to its work." This conclusion Richardson attributes to the AMA's understanding that many black people preferred to have black teachers. Richardson, *Christian Reconstruction*, 191.

58. In his call for normal schools to train black teachers, John Alvord argued that black teachers would be able to go to areas that white teachers dared not enter. Alvord, *First Semi-Annual Report*, 12–13; A. M. Bush to J. W. Alvord, March 19, 1868, M810, roll 1, FBR; R. M. Manly to Robert Carson, American Freedmen's Union Commission, December 10, 1866, M803, roll 1, FBR; R. M. Manly to Crammond Kennedy, November 5, 1866, M803, roll 1, FBR.

59. Dorothy Sterling, *We Are Your Sisters: Black Women in the Nineteenth Century* (New York: W. W. Norton, 1984), 265; Clara Merritt DeBoer, *His Truth Is Marching On: African Americans Who Taught the Freedmen for the American Missionary Association, 1861–1877* (New York: Garland Publishing, 1995), 23–24, 56. Sara Stanley was the great-granddaughter of John Wright Stanley, a prominent white slave owner and shipper in New Bern, North Carolina. His son John C. Stanley, born to a black mother, inherited a plantation and numerous slaves from his father. The son, Sara's grandfather, was active in the manumission movement in New Bern and freed his immediate family as well as eighteen other relatives. Historians have postulated that he may have maintained ownership in other slaves as a way of circumventing a state law requiring newly manumitted people to leave the state. John Stuart Stanley, Sara's father, operated a store and ran a school for free black children. Sara left North Carolina to attend Oberlin College in 1852 at age sixteen. To avoid the increasing persecution of free blacks, Sara's family moved from North Carolina to Delaware, then to Ohio, while she was in college. She taught in Ohio for several years before applying to work with freedpeople in the South. Ellen NicKenzie Lawson and Marlene D. Merrill, eds., *The Three Sarahs: Documents of Antebellum Black College Women*

(New York: Edwin Mellen Press, 1984), 47–49. Well-known African Americans Frances Ellen Watkins Harper, abolitionist writer Maria W. Stewart, and author Harriet Jacobs similarly went south to teach freedpeople.

60. Forten, *Journals*, 3–17.

61. Ibid., June 2, 1854, 65–66.

62. British Emancipation Day, celebrated on August 1, commemorated the emancipation of slaves in some British West Indian colonies. Ibid., August 1, 1854, 92; July 4, 1857, 235; July 14, 1855, 140 (emphasis in original).

63. Ibid., September 5, 1854, 98; November 18, 1854, 111; September 12, 1855, 138.

64. Ibid., August 9, 1862, 374; August 16, 1862, 375; September 8, 1862, 380; September 14, 1862, 381; September 15, 1862, 381. For other examples of a black teacher's articulation of a racially inspired sense of obligation to the freedpeople, see Butchart, " 'We Best Can Instruct Our Own People,' " 27–49; and Perkins, "Black Female American Missionary Association Teacher in the South," 1049–63.

65. Butchart, " 'We Best Can Instruct Our Own People,' " 29.

66. Blanche V. Harris to George Whipple in Sterling, *We Are Your Sisters*, 276–77; Perkins, "Black Female Missionary Association in the South," 1054–57; Lawson and Merrill, *Three Sarahs*, 56–58.

67. Rebecca Primus to Dear Parents and Sister, November 8, 1865, Rebecca Primus Papers, Connecticut Historical Society, Hartford, Conn.

68. *American Missionary*, March 1860, 63; ibid., April 1860, 89; ibid., June 1861, 139.

69. John Fee to M. E. Strieby, May 30, 1865, AMA Mss., emphasis in original.

70. W. W. Wheeler to George Whipple, August 3, 1865, AMA Mss.

71. Petition quoted in ibid.

72. Joseph C. Chapin to George Whipple, October 2, 1865, AMA Mss.

73. Caroline Damon to George Whipple, October 3, 1865, AMA Mss.

74. Quoted in ibid.

75. John Fee to M. E. Strieby, September 30, 1865, AMA Mss.

76. Caroline Damon to George Whipple, October 1, 1865, AMA Mss.

77. DeBoer, *His Truth is Marching On*, 349.

78. E. Belle Mitchell to M. E. Strieby, March 14, 1866, AMA Mss.; John Fee to William E. Whiting, September 15, 1865, AMA Mss.

79. E. W. P. Smith to M. E. Strieby, October 4, 1865, AMA Mss.; E. Belle Mitchell to M. E. Strieby, March 14, 1866, AMA Mss.

80. Butchart, *Northern Schools, Southern Blacks, and Reconstruction*, 116.

81. Alvord, *First Semi-Annual Report*, 8; Rebecca Primus to Parents and Sister, April 8, 1866, Primus Papers.

82. Jacqueline Jones found that black teachers in Georgia were victims of severe violence while whites were usually threatened. Jones, *Soldiers of Light and Love*, 82. Examination of testimony in congressional hearings into KKK activity in the southern states (KKK Reports) bears out this finding in other states as well.

83. Marrs, *Life And History*, 78–79.

84. KKK Reports, Mississippi, 1:492–93, 513, 63, 76, 225–26.

85. Regarding whipping African American women for sassing white women, see testimony of Caroline Smith in KKK Reports, Georgia, 1:400–403.

86. Testimony of Aury Jeter and Columbus Jeter in KKK Reports, Georgia, 1:560–67.

87. Ibid. A fascinating exchange on the matter of race in America took place at the conclusion of Aury Jeter's testimony: "Question: You taught only those of your own color? Answer: That is all—not exactly of my color but those a great deal darker than I am; those of my race, though. Question: When you speak of color you mean the negro race? Answer: Yes, sir. Question: Was your mother a colored woman? Answer: She was half white, and my father and my grandfather were white men; I am three-quarters white. Question: You are what is called a quadroon? Answer: Yes, sir; I am not so light-colored as I have been. I worked out last year a great deal, and I am somewhat sunburnt." Color clearly meant two different things to the questioner, a white man, and the respondent, a very light-skinned woman who nonetheless identified herself as belonging to the same race as other freedpeople much darker than she. The committee member was likely having a difficult time reconciling the story recounted in Jeter's testimony with the seemingly white woman sitting before him.

88. Alvord, *Second Semi-Annual Report*, 11.

89. John W. Alvord, *Third Semi-Annual Report on Schools for Freedmen, January 1, 1867* (Washington, D.C.: Government Printing Office, 1868), 22, reprinted in Alvord, *Semi-Annual Reports*.

90. Bartley Townsley to G. L. Eberhart, October 21, 1865, M799, roll 20, FBR.

91. Alvord, *Second Semi-Annual Report*, 5.

92. KKK Reports, Georgia, 2:1100–1111.

93. Report of J. W. Alvord, Inspector of Schools and Finances, to Major General O. O. Howard, Commissioner, Freedmen's Bureau, October 1866, in Rufus and S. Willard Saxton Papers, Manuscripts and Archives, Yale University, New Haven, Conn.; Alvord, *Fourth Semi-Annual Report*, 66. For other examples of arson of school buildings, see Hugo Hillebrandt to Jacob Chun, August 8, 1867, M844, roll 7, FBR; and KKK Reports, Georgia, 1:10, 2:594.

Chapter Seven

1. James E. Yeatman, *A Report on the Condition of the Freedmen of the Mississippi, Presented by the Western Sanitary Commission, December 17, 1863* (St. Louis: Western Sanitary Commission, 1864), 1, 11; Henry McNeal Turner to Adjutant General, U.S. Army, August 14, 1865, Adjutant General Letters Received, RG 94, M619, 591T, 1865, NA; Emanuel Smith to E. P. Smith, April 10, 1867, AMA Mss.

2. School report of Tunis Campbell, January 1, 1866, M799, roll 20, FBR.

3. School report of Lewis Smith, October 19, 1865, M799, roll 20, FBR. Smith taught in a school that had been promised but had not received support from the Western Freedmen's Aid Society.

4. Ibid.

5. Edward Anthony to G. L. Eberhart, June 23, 1866; School report of Tunis Campbell, January 1, 1866; School report of Jack Mallard, June 1866; all in M799, roll 20, FBR.

6. Statement of Joseph Warren quoted in John W. Alvord, *Second Semi-Annual Report on Schools and Finances, July 1, 1866* (Washington, D.C.: Government Printing Office, 1868), 7, reprinted in John W. Alvord, *Semi-Annual Reports on Schools for Freedmen: Numbers 1–10, January 1866–July 1870* (New York: AMS Press, 1980).

7. School report of Davie Alexander and John Philip, n.d.; School report of Lynch Lamar, January 1866; School report of Jacob Wade, January 1866; School report of Simon Ryall, January 1866; School report of Ephraim Rucker, January 1866; all in M799, roll 20, FBR.

8. School report of Simeon Beard, January 1, 1866, M799, roll 20, FBR. Beard was a delegate to the Georgia Constitutional Convention in 1867. Edmund L. Drago, *Black Politicians and Reconstruction in Georgia: A Splendid Failure* (Baton Rouge: Louisiana State University Press, 1982), 22. I have not been able to locate information about Jacob Danforth.

9. School reports of Jane Deveaux, Lucinda Jackson, K. Saul Thomas, Louisa Jacobs, and Jane Ann Vattal, January 1866; School report of John Bentley, October 1865; all in M799, roll 20, FBR.

10. School report of Abraham Colby, October 1865; B. H. Townsley to G. L. Eberhart, April 4, 1866; both in M799, roll 20, FBR. The "Child's Primer" that Colby included on his list likely referred to a freedmen's primer authored by abolitionist Lydia Maria Child.

11. Harry R. Warfel, *Noah Webster: Schoolmaster to America* (New York: Macmillan, 1936), 76; Paul Leicester Ford, "Webster's Spelling-Book: Early American Text-Books Noah Webster's Great Enterprise," reprinted from the *New York Evening Post*, n.d., Beinecke Rare Book and Manuscript Library, Yale University, New Haven, Conn.

12. Frederick Douglass, *The Narrative of the Life of Frederick Douglass, an American Slave*, ed. David W. Blight (New York: Bedford Books, 1993), 63.

13. George P. Rawick, ed., *The American Slave: A Composite Autobiography*, 19 vols. (Westport, Conn.: Greenwood Press, 1972), vol. 5, pt. 4, p. 149.

14. Ibid., vol. 4, pt. 2, p. 131.

15. Michael W. Apple and Linda K. Christian-Smith, *The Politics of the Textbook* (New York: Routledge, 1991), 5.

16. See Rachel Bryan Stillman, "Education in the Confederate States of America, 1861–1865" (Ph.D. diss., University of Illinois at Urbana-Champaign, 1972), 65–69.

17. C. H. Wiley, *Address to the People of North Carolina* (Raleigh, N.C.: Conference of Teachers and Friends of Education, 1861).

18. *Proceedings of the Convention of Teachers of the Confederate States, Assembled at Columbia, South Carolina, April 28th, 1863* (Macon, Ga.: Burke, Boykin, and Company), 18, in *Confederate Imprints*, 143 reels (microfilm; New Haven, Conn.: Research Publications, 1972), reel 113, no. 4009.

19. Marinda Branson Moore, *The First Dixie Reader: Designed to Follow the Dixie Primer* (Raleigh, N.C.: Branson, Farrar, and Company, 1863), 14.

20. Ibid., 39.

21. Marinda Branson Moore, *The Geographical Reader, for the Dixie Children* (Raleigh: Branson, Farrar, and Company, 1863), 9–10.

22. Ibid.

23. Throughout the textbook Moore presented a surprisingly sympathetic story of white exploitation of Indians. For example, one drill went as follows: "How do the Indians live? By hunting and fishing. Where did they once live? In all America. What has become of them? The white people drove them away and took their lands. Are they all gone? A few of them live in some places but do not seem much happy. Was it wrong to drive them away and take their lands? It was, and God will judge the white man for it. May not some of the wars we have had, have been such judgments? Very likely." Ibid., 38.

24. Ibid., 10.

25. American Tract Society, *The Freedman's Spelling Book; The Freedman's Second Reader; The Freedman's Third Reader*, vol. 2 of *Freedmen's Schools and Textbooks*, ed. Robert C. Morris (New York: AMS Press, 1980); *American Freedman*, May 1866, 32, emphasis in original. Perhaps in response to this criticism, the American Tract Society subsequently substituted "Lincoln" for "Freedman's" in each title. The editors of the *American Freedman* distinguished their own use of the word "Freedman" in the title of the magazine, saying that it was so named because many of the articles concerned the status of freedpeople, but carried no intimation that the magazine was exclusively for freedpeople. Robert C. Morris extensively discusses textbooks for freedpeople in *Reading, 'Riting, and Reconstruction: The Education of Freedmen in the South, 1861–1870* (Chicago: University of Chicago Press, 1981). See also Saidiya V. Hartman, *Scenes of Subjection: Terror, Slavery, and Self-Making in Nineteenth-Century America* (New York: Oxford University Press, 1997), 125–63.

26. R. M. Manly to William C. Child, Secretary, American Tract Society, June 25, 1866, M803, roll 1, FBR.

27. American Tract Society, *Freedman's Spelling Book*, 79; Isaac W. Brinckerhoff, *Advice to Freedmen*, vol. 4 of *Freedmen's Schools and Textbooks*, ed. Morris.

28. Brinckerhoff, *Advice to Freedmen*, 16.

29. American Tract Society, *Freedman's Spelling Book*, 13, 79.

30. Brinckerhoff, *Advice to Freedmen*, 23–24.

31. American Tract Society, *Freedman's Spelling Book*, 85; Brinckerhoff, *Advice to Freedmen*, 15–17.

32. American Tract Society, *Freedman's Spelling Book*, 22; Brinckerhoff, *Advice to Freedmen*, 6–7.

33. Saidiya Hartman argues that this "fiction of debt" was at the "center of a moral economy of submission and servitude and was instrumental in the production of peonage," a system that kept black people working for little or no pay even after slavery ended. Hartman, *Scenes of Subjection*, 131. Georgia Freedmen's Bureau Superintendent of Education G. L. Eberhart reported in October 1866 that he had dis-

tributed over five thousand books and papers from the American Tract Society. Report of G. L. Eberhart, October 15, 1866, M798, roll 32, FBR.

34. See Melville J. Herskovitz, *The Myth of the Negro Past* (Boston: Beacon Press, 1958); Michael A. Gomez, *Exchanging Our Country Marks: The Transformation of African Identities in the Colonial and Antebellum South* (Chapel Hill: University of North Carolina Press, 1998), 154–85.

Chapter Eight

1. London R. Ferebee, *A Brief History of the Slave Life of Rev. L. R. Ferebee, and the Battles of Life, and Four Years of His Ministerial Life.* (Raleigh, N.C.: Edwards, Broughton and Company, 1882), 3–4; Patricia C. Click, *Time Full of Trial: The Roanoke Island Freedmen's Colony, 1862–1867* (Chapel Hill: University of North Carolina Press, 2001), 83, 105–24.

2. George P. Rawick, ed., *The American Slave: A Composite Autobiography*, 19 vols. (Westport, Conn.: Greenwood Press, 1972), vol. 13, pt. 4, pp. 4–5.

3. George P. Rawick, ed., *The American Slave: A Composite Autobiography: Supplement, Series 1*, 12 vols. (Westport, Conn.: Greenwood Press, 1977), vol. 9, pt. 4, p. 1583.

4. F. E. Morgan, January 15, 1867, in *American Missionary*, April 1867, 79. See also C. C. Duncan, Norfolk, Va., July 1, 1864, in ibid., October 1864, 233.

5. Charlotte Forten, "Life on the Sea Islands," *Atlantic Monthly* (May, June 1864), in *Two Black Teachers during the Civil War*, ed. William Loren Katz (New York: Arno Press and the New York Times, 1969).

6. E. E. Johnson, Evansville, Ind., July 16, 1863, in *American Missionary*, September 1863, 206, emphasis in original.

7. E. B. Eveleth, June 22, 1864, in ibid., August 1864, 191; Caroline E. Jocelyn, July 20, 1864, in ibid., October 1864, 238.

8. H. S. Beals, Beaufort, N.C., November 30, 1866, in ibid., January 1867, 4.

9. John W. Alvord, *First Semi-Annual Report on Schools and Finances of Freedmen, January 1, 1866* (Washington, D.C.: Government Printing Office, 1868), 10, reprinted in John W. Alvord, *Semi-Annual Reports on Schools for Freedmen: Numbers 1–10, January 1866–July 1870* (New York: AMS Press, 1980).

10. *American Missionary*, May 1867, 102–3.

11. Ibid., June 1867, 126; ibid., May 1867, 102; ibid., May 1866, 112. Regarding rents, see W. D. Harris, Richmond, Va., February 1, 1867, in ibid., March 1867, 50. Regarding crop failures, see ibid., September 1866, 204; and Alvord, *First Semi-Annual Report*, 15. Regarding sharecropping and other emergent land tenancy arrangements, see Julie Saville, *The Work of Reconstruction: From Slave to Wage Laborer in South Carolina, 1860–1870* (New York: Cambridge University Press, 1994), 125–35.

12. David Todd, Pine Bluff, Ark., to George Whipple, August 1, 1866, AMA Mss.; H. J. Herlman, Pine Bluff, Ark., to C. H. Fowler, January 1, 1866, AMA Mss.; *American Missionary*, April 1866, 77.

13. *American Missionary*, May 1867, 103.

14. John W. Alvord, *Fourth Semi-Annual Report on Schools for Freedmen, July 1, 1867* (Washington, D.C.: Government Printing Office, 1868), 27, reprinted in Alvord, *Semi-Annual Reports.*

15. For example, urban slaves wore better clothing than rural slaves, either because they were hired out and therefore had some money of their own, or because urban owners were more conscious of the opinions of closely located neighbors. Helen Bradley Foster, *"New Raiments of Self": African American Clothing in the Antebellum South* (New York: Berg, 1997), 151; Richard C. Wade, *Slavery in the Cities: The South, 1820–1860* (New York: Oxford University Press, 1964), 125–31. Slaves in states like South Carolina, who often earned income from the sale of produce from their garden plots, could afford to supplement plantation clothing rations. Eugene D. Genovese, *Roll, Jordan, Roll: The World the Slaves Made* (New York: Pantheon Books, 1974), 551–52. Shane White and Graham White argue that African Americans found ways to graft their unique aesthetic even onto drab clothing, particularly that worn on Sundays. Shane White and Graham White, *Stylin': African American Expressive Culture from Its Beginnings to the Zoot Suit* (Ithaca, N.Y.: Cornell University Press, 1998), 13.

16. Wilma King, *Stolen Childhood: Slave Youth in Nineteenth-Century America* (Bloomington: Indiana University Press, 1995), 15–16, 38–39; Foster, *"New Raiments of Self"*, 150–59; Elizabeth Fox-Genovese, *Within the Plantation Household: Black and White Women of the Old South* (Chapel Hill: University of North Carolina Press, 1988), 121; Florence M. Montgomery, *Textiles in America: 1650–1870* (New York: W. W. Norton, 1984), 309, 312–13.

17. Mrs. H. S. Breese, Hilton Head Island, S.C., July 9, 1867, in *American Missionary*, October 1867, 221–22, emphasis in original.

18. Report from Misses Graves, Walrad, and Blood, Raleigh, N.C., in *American Freedman*, January 1867, 153.

19. Mr. C. G. G. Paine, Tyler House, Hampton, Va., January 2, 1866, in *American Missionary*, February 1866, 26.

20. G. N. Carruthers, Corinth, Miss., August 24, 1863, in *American Missionary*, October 1863, 236, emphasis in original; Mr. Bay, Tyler House, Hampton, Va., January 2, 1864, in *American Missionary*, February 1864; J. M. Stradling, February 6, 1868, in *American Freedman*, March 1868, 375. See also Samuel G. G. Cross, Townville, N.C., in *American Freedman*, March 1868, 380; and J. W. Burghduff in *American Freedman*, February 1868, 365. Burghduff estimated that another two hundred children would attend the schools in Trent Camp near New Bern, North Carolina, if they had proper clothing.

21. Report of Sara Stanley to the American Missionary Association, May 1865, in Ellen NicKenzie Lawson and Marlene D. Merrill, eds., *The Three Sarahs: Documents of Antebellum Black College Women* (New York: Edwin Mellen Press, 1984), 109–10.

22. Report of John F. Sprague in Alvord, *Fourth Semi-Annual Report*, 35.

23. Ira Berlin and Leslie S. Rowland, eds., *Families and Freedom: A Documentary History of African-American Kinship in The Civil War Era* (New York: The New Press, 1997), 207.

24. Laura M. Towne, *Letters and Diary of Laura M. Towne, Written from the Sea Islands*

of South Carolina, 1862–1884, ed. Rupert Sargent Holland (Cambridge, Mass.: Riverside Press, 1912), 147.

25. Report on Educational Activities in the Southwest in *American Missionary*, November 1867, 251; *American Freedman*, June 1867, 235.

26. Jacqueline Jones, *Soldiers of Light and Love: Northern Teachers and Georgia Blacks, 1865–1873* (Chapel Hill: University of North Carolina Press, 1980), 128.

27. *American Missionary*, July 1867, 159.

28. Regarding absences in the spring, see the monthly reports of the following teachers: J. W. M. Carr, June 1864; H. R. Starkweather, M. J. Pruitt, March 1868, March 1869, and May 1869; E. S. Grover, April 1868; all in M810, roll 6, FBR; May E. R. Richards, April 1867, M799, roll 22, FBR; and H. B. Greely, St. Augustine, Fla., to George Whipple, April 29, 1864, AMA Mss. Regarding absences in the fall, see the monthly reports of the following teachers: John Wiley, October 1866, M810, roll 6, FBR; T. B. Hobkins, October 1868, and Jerry Brown, October 1868, M799, roll 22, FBR.

29. *American Freedman*, December 1867, 334.

30. Rawick, *American Slave . . . Supplement, Series 1*, vol. 3, pt. 1, pp. 283–84.

31. Rawick, *American Slave*, vol. 6, pt. 1, p. 275. For some of the other freedpeople who attended school for three months at a time, ibid., vol. 11, pt. 7, p. 240, and vol. 6, pt. 1, p. 204.

32. Ibid., vol. 2, pt. 7, p. 211 (Frank Wise); vol. 4, pt. 2, p. 220; vol. 2, pt. 7, p. 219; vol. 2, pt. 7, p. 250 (Hannah Wright); vol. 2, pt. 7, p. 216; vol. 4, pt. 2, p. 171; vol. 13, pt. 3, p. 116. See also biographical essay by Carrie S. Lucas, HUA.

33. Report of General Davis Tillson, Assistant Commissioner of the Freedmen's Bureau for the State of Georgia, September 1865–November 1865, M798, roll 32, FBR; Miss E. A. Easter, Nashville, Tenn., February 1866, in *American Missionary*, April 1866, 88–89; May Close, Brandon, Miss., June 1866, in *American Missionary*, September 1866, 200; Emily Hubbard, Petersburg, Va., in *American Freedman*, April 1867, 205–7.

34. Samuel Spottford Clement, *Memoirs of Samuel Spottford Clement, Relating Interesting Experiences in Days of Slavery and Freedom* (Steubenville, Ohio: Herald Printing Company, 1908), 13; Douglass Wilson quoted in Octavia V. Rogers Albert, *The House of Bondage; or, Charlotte Brooks and Other Slaves, Original and Life Like, as They Appeared in Their Old Plantation and City Slave Life; Together with Pen-Pictures of the Peculiar Institution, with Sights and Insights into Their New Relations as Freedmen, Freemen, and Citizens* (New York: Hunt and Eaton, 1890), 139–40.

35. School report of Reuben Finney, September 1867, M799, roll 21, FBR.

36. *American Missionary*, November 1867, 254.

37. Towne, *Letters and Diary*, 104–8.

38. Miss P. A. Alcott, Charleston, S.C., December 28, 1865, in *American Missionary*, February 1866, 30. See also J. W. Read, Freedmen's Bureau Superintendent, 8th District, Kentucky, to Professor Ogden, July 19, 1866, AMA Mss.; and *American Freedman*, April 1867, 206.

39. Helen M. Dodd, August 3, 1864, in *American Missionary*, September 1864, 212.

40. Lizzie Parson, Columbia, S.C., February 1867, in *American Freedman*, March 1867, 187–88.

41. School report of J. J. Deseker, April 1868, M810, roll 7, FBR.

42. Harriet Taylor, Portsmouth, Va., March 30, 1863, in *American Missionary*, May 1863, 107; Miss E. E. King, Columbia, S.C., in *American Freedman*, March 1868, 382; J. B. Lowery, Yorktown, Va., May 19, 1863, in *American Missionary*, July 1863, 160; Miss E. W. Douglass, Chatham County, Ga., in *American Missionary*, March 1867, 53; *Freedman's Record* 1 (July 1866): 4.

43. Miss P. A. Alcott, Charleston, S.C., December 28, 1865, in *American Missionary*, February 1866, 30.

44. Elijah Marrs, *Life and History of the Rev. Elijah P. Marrs* (Louisville, Ky.: Bradley and Gilbert Company, 1885), 92; Towne, *Letters and Diary*, 23.

45. American Tract Society, *The Freedman's Spelling Book*, in vol. 2 of *Freedmen's Schools and Textbooks*, ed. Robert C. Morris (New York: AMS Press, 1980), 89.

46. Towne, *Letters and Diary*, xv.

47. Edmonia G. Highgate in *American Missionary*, March 1867, 56–67.

48. Rawick, *American Slave*, vol. 5, pt. 4, p. 184.

49. Martha L. Kellog, January 3, 1863, in *American Missionary*, March 1863, 64–65.

50. *American Freedman*, March 1867, 185.

51. J. B. Lowery, May 19, 1863, in *American Missionary*, July 1863, 160; School report of Thomas H. Whitby, November 1866, M810, roll 6, FBR. See also Freedmen's Bureau monthly reports for April–November 1867: T. B. Birch, Bullock County; W. O. Stevens, Fox Creek; W. B. Craven, Prattville; John Danner, Russell County; in M810, roll 7, FBR; and *Freedmen's Record* 1 (June 1866): 8.

52. Frank H. Greene, July 1864, in *American Missionary*, September 1864, 215, emphasis in original.

53. Miss J. A. Shearman, November 29, 1865, in ibid., January 1866, 2–3.

54. Miss A. T. Howard, Quaker Neck, Md., in *American Freedman*, February 1868, 361; monthly report of T. M. Kennedy, February 1867, M810, roll 7, FBR.

55. Forten, "Life on the Sea Islands," 71.

56. Sara Stanley to AMA, June 9, 1865, in Lawson and Merrill, *Three Sarahs*, 115; Sara Stanley to Samuel Hunt, March 1866, AMA Mss.

57. Sara Stanley to Samuel Hunt, May 4, 1866, AMA Mss.

58. Sara Stanley to Samuel Hunt, July 18, 1866, AMA Mss.

59. George M. Fredrickson, *The Black Image in the White Mind: The Debate on Afro-American Character and Destiny, 1817–1914* (New York: Harper and Row, 1971) 2, 74; Emancipation League, *Facts Concerning the Freedmen: Their Capacity and Their Destiny* (Boston, 1863), 3, in "From Slavery to Freedom: The African American Pamphlet Collection, 1824–1909," Rare Books and Special Collections Division, Library of Congress, Washington, D.C.; available online in *American Memory: Historical Collections for the National Digital Library* (Washington, D.C.: Library of Congress) <http://memory.loc.gov/>.

60. Cardozo and Sumner quoted in *American Missionary*, September 1867, 207–8, emphasis in original.

61. Palmer Litts, July 27, 1863, in ibid., September 1863, 209.

62. Frank H. Greene, Baton Rouge, La., July 1864, in ibid., September 1864, 215.

63. Lydia Hess to Simeon Jocelyn, May 4, 1863, AMA Mss.

64. Mary F. Root, February 1, 1863, in *American Missionary*, April 1863, 90–91, emphasis in original.

65. Towne, *Letters and Diary*, 7. Regarding scientific doctrines of race, see Fredrickson, *Black Image in the White Mind*, 71–97; and Matthew Frye Jacobson, *Whiteness of a Different Color: European Immigrants and the Alchemy of Race* (Cambridge, Mass.: Harvard University Press, 1998), 79–83.

66. Fannie Graves, Maggie E. Walrad, and Carrie M. Blood, May 1867, in *American Freedman*, June 1867, 235.

67. *Freedmen's Record* 1 (December 1865): 12, emphasis in original.

68. David Todd to George Whipple, June 4, 1864, AMA Mss.

69. Mary S. Battey in *American Missionary*, September 1867, 198. The belief that being a mulatto was a significant factor worthy of consideration was limited neither to teachers nor to white northerners living in southern states. C. P. Chase of Indiana sought admission to Oberlin College for his employee, a "bright and intelligent mulatto girl that wishes an education"; and Susan K. Wade of Allegheny, Pennsylvania, applied to Oberlin on behalf of a "young mulatto boy" who was employed by her family as a house servant and driver. C. P. Chase, Valparaiso, Ind., to the president of the Oberlin Institution, March 1, 1864, and letter from Susan K. Wade, December 18, 1864, both in Treasurer's Office Correspondence, 1822–1907, Oberlin College Archives, Oberlin, Ohio.

70. Carrie L. Guild to General Armstrong, November 20, 1868, HUA. Leafy and Eliza were from Charleston, South Carolina. *Catalogue of the Hampton Normal and Agricultural Institute, Hampton, Va., for the Academical Year 1871–2* (Hampton, Va.: Normal School Press, 1872), HUA.

71. John De Forest in *American Freedman*, February 1867, 167. De Forest was a northern novelist employed by the Freedmen's Bureau. See James D. Schmidt, " 'A Full-Fledged Government of Men': Freedmen's Bureau Labor Policy in South Carolina, 1865–1868," in *The Freedmen's Bureau and Reconstruction: Reconsiderations*, ed. Paul A. Cimbala and Randall M. Miller (New York: Fordham University Press, 1999), 251.

72. Ferebee, *Brief History*, 3–4.

73. Walter Johnson, *Soul by Soul: Life Inside the Antebellum Slave Market* (Cambridge, Mass.: Harvard University Press, 1999), 150–151. See also Joel Williamson, *New People: Miscegenation and Mulattoes in the United States* (New York: Free Press, 1980), 20.

74. Augustus C. Stickler, Davis Lake, Ark., to Brother Shepherd, July 9, 1867, AMA Mss.

75. M. E. Watson, Darlington, Md., July 1, 1867, in *American Missionary*, September 1867, 194. For doubts as to African Americans' capacity for mathematics, see O. Brown, Superintendent of Contrabands on Craney Island, Va., quoted in Emancipation League, *Facts Concerning the Freedmen*, 6; and J. A. Sherman, Augusta, Ga., June 1867, in *American Missionary*, September 1867, 212.

76. Alvord, *First Semi-Annual Report*, 11.

77. Fredrickson, *Black Image in the White Mind*, 79–80.

78. See James D. Anderson, *The Education of Blacks in the South, 1860–1935* (Chapel Hill: University of North Carolina Press, 1988).

79. William P. Russell, September 3, 1866, in *American Missionary*, October 1866, 221; ibid., April 1868, 162; F. E. Morgan, Athens, Ga., January 15, 1867, in ibid., April 1867, 80; Mrs. A. T. Ayer, Atlanta, Ga., in ibid., March 1866, 63; ibid., March 1866, 59.

80. School report of William B. Cole, October 1865, M799, roll 20, FBR.

81. George P. Rawick, ed., *The American Slave: A Composite Autobiography: Supplement, Series 2*, 10 vols. (Westport, Conn.: Greenwood Press, 1979), vol. 10, pt. 9, pp. 3944–45.

82. Towne, *Letters and Diary*, xv.

83. Rev. S. J. Whiton, Tyler House, Fort Monroe, Va., December 1, 1865, in *American Missionary*, January 1866, 6; Forten, "Life on the Sea Islands," 71.

84. Maria B. King, Beaufort, S.C., July 13, 1864, in *American Missionary*, September 1864, 215.

85. Lawson and Merrill, *Three Sarahs*, 108.

86. Miss Taylor, Norfolk, Va., *American Missionary*, June 1864, 138; ibid., October 1864, 235; Miss Dodd, Portsmouth, Va., December 30, 1863, in ibid., April 1864, 97.

87. Ibid., May 1866, 101, emphasis in original.

88. Ibid., May 1863, 115.

89. Miss Clarke, Norfolk, Va., in ibid., June 1864, 138.

90. *American Freedman*, June 1867, 234.

91. In 1867 New Jersey became the first state to abolish corporal punishment in schools. Massachusetts was next, but not until 1972. Donald R. Raichle, "The Abolition of Corporal Punishment in New Jersey Schools," in *Corporal Punishment in American Education: Readings in History, Practice, and Alternatives*, ed. Irwin A. Hyman and James H. Wise (Philadelphia: Temple University Press, 1979), 62–88.

92. Walt Whitman, "The Whip in Schools," in *Turning Points in American Educational History*, ed. David B. Tyack (Lexington, Mass.: Xerox College Publishing, 1967), 165–67.

93. *American Missionary*, January 1865, 16.

94. Jones, *Soldiers of Light and Love*, 125.

95. Leon F. Litwack, *Been in the Storm So Long: The Aftermath of Slavery* (New York: Alfred A. Knopf, 1979), 482.

96. Towne, *Letters and Diary*, 178; S. G. Wright, June 20, 1864, in *American Missionary*, August 1864, 192.

97. Rawick, *American Slave*, vol. 13, pt. 3, pp. 144, 312.

98. Rawick, *American Slave . . . Supplement, Series 2*, vol. 5, pt. 4, p. 1472.

99. Rawick, *American Slave*, vol. 5, pt. 3, p. 110.

100. Rawick, *American Slave . . . Supplement, Series 2*, vol. 9, pt. 8, pp. 3628–29.

101. Ibid., vol. 9, pt. 8, p. 3694.

102. *American Missionary*, June 1867, 137; *Freedmen's Record* 1 (March 1866): 9.

103. Rawick, *American Slave . . . Supplement, Series 1*, vol. 8, pt. 3, p. 954. See also Rawick, *American Slave . . . Supplement, Series 2*, vol. 9, pt. 8, pp. 3628, 3694.

104. Miss E. P. Bennett, Greenville, S.C., *American Freedman*, February 1868, 368. Bennett may have been influenced by Horace Mann whose educational philosophies helped to shape the New England common school in the 1840s. Mann urged the use of reason to lead children to self-government and self-control. Horace Mann, "Ninth Annual Report" (1845), in *The Republic and the School: Horace Mann on the Education of Free Men*, ed. Lawrence A. Cremin (New York: Teachers College, Columbia University, 1957), 57.

105. Rebecca Primus to Parents, February 23, 1867, Rebecca Primus Papers, Connecticut Historical Society, Hartford, Conn.

106. School report of Esther Pinkney, October 1865, M799, roll 20, FBR.

107. Whittington B. Johnson, "A Black Teacher and Her School in Reconstruction Darien: The Correspondence of Hattie Sabattie and J. Murray Hoag, 1868–1869," *Georgia Historical Quarterly* 75 (Spring 1991): 101. Sabattie was a native of Darien who lived in Savannah for some time before returning to teach in Darien.

108. School report of Simon Ryall, May 31, 1866, M799, roll 20, FBR.

109. John W. Alvord, *Second Semi-Annual Report on Freedmen's Schools, July 1866* (Washington, D.C.: Government Printing Office, 1868), 13–14, reprinted in Alvord, *Semi-Annual Reports*.

110. Alvord, *Fourth Semi-Annual Report*, 8.

111. School report of Esther Pinkney, October 1865, M799, roll 20. FBR; Johnson, "Black Teacher and Her School," 101.

112. John R. Sutton, *Stubborn Children: Controlling Delinquency in the United States, 1640–1981* (Berkeley: University of California Press, 1988), 43. Southern states lagged behind northern ones in the creation of juvenile facilities. Sutton argues that the introduction of juvenile reform institutions was further delayed after the Civil War due to the adoption of convict lease systems by southern states.

113. Mary F. Root, February 1, 1863, in *American Missionary*, April 1863, 90–91. Many adults attended Sabbath schools where they also learned to read and write. Alvord, *Third Semi-Annual Report on Schools for Freedmen, January 1, 1867* (Washington, D.C.: Government Printing Office,), 4, reprinted in Alvord, *Semi-Annual Reports*.

114. *American Missionary*, May 1866, 101.

115. Miss E. E. King, Columbia, S.C., in *American Freedman*, March 1868, 382.

116. Mrs. E. S. Williams, St. Helena Island, S.C., January 9, 1863, in *American Missionary*, March 1863, 65.

117. H. B. Greely, St. Augustine, Fla., to George Whipple, August 7, 1865, AMA Mss.; John R. Rachal, "Gideonites and Freedmen: Adult Literacy Education at Port Royal, 1862–1865," *Journal of Negro Education* 55 (Autumn 1986): 453–69.

118. Reverend E. O. Tade, Chattanooga, Tenn., *American Missionary*, April 1867, 80; F. A. Fiske in Alvord, *Third Semi-Annual Report*, 11.

119. *American Missionary*, September 1867, 197.

120. F. L., Dawfuskie Island, S.C., June 1867, in ibid., July 1867, 176.

121. Palmer Litts, Fortress Monroe, Va., July 27, 1863, in ibid., September 1863, 208; W. T. Richardson, Beaufort, S.C., January 5, 1864, in ibid., March 1864, 66.

122. Reverend E. O. Tade, Chattanooga, Tenn., ibid., April 1867, 80.

123. James McCrea, Beaufort, S.C., January 1863, in ibid., April 1863, 87–88, emphasis in original.

124. Reverend E. O. Tade, Chattanooga, Tenn., in ibid., April 1867, 80; Miss Haskell, Norfolk, Va., in ibid., June 1864, 139; Miss Reed, Norfolk, Va., February 29, 1864, in ibid., April 1864, 98.

125. Susan H. Clark, Slabtown, near Fortress Monroe, Va., January 1867, in ibid., March 1867, 64.

126. Regarding reading the Bible as a goal of literacy, see *American Freedman*, June 1867, 232; *American Missionary*, April 1863, 90–91; *American Missionary*, March 1863, 65; *American Missionary*, May 1863, 115; *American Missionary*, September, 1863, 208; *American Missionary*, August 1864, 190; and *American Missionary*, March 1864, 66. Regarding voting, see *American Missionary*, May 1867, 99; regarding cheating, see *American Missionary*, January 10, 1868, 53.

127. J. W. Burghduff to American Freedmen's Union Commission, January 1868, in *American Freedman*, February 1868, 364.

128. *American Missionary*, April 1867, 85–86.

129. H. S. Beals, Portsmouth, Va., April 1, 1863, in ibid., May 1863, 109.

130. Ibid., January 1868, 7; ibid., April 1867, 89–90.

131. Leslie A. Schwalm, *A Hard Fight for We: Women's Transition from Slavery to Freedom in South Carolina* (Urbana: University of Illinois Press, 1997), 204–11; Noralee Frankel, *Freedom's Women: Black Women and Families in Civil War Era Mississippi* (Bloomington: Indiana University Press, 1999), 75–77. See also Peter Kolchin, *First Freedom: The Responses of Alabama's Blacks to Emancipation and Reconstruction* (Westport, Conn.: Greenwood Press, 1972), 62–63; Saville, *Work of Reconstruction*, 103, 131; Litwack, *Been in the Storm So Long*; and F. W. Loring and C. F. Atkinson, *Cotton Culture and the Old South* (Boston: A. Williams, 1869), 23.

132. J. B. Lowery, Camp Nelson, Ky., to Brother Whipple, September 6, 1864, AMA Mss. See also Mr. C. G. G. Paine, Tyler House, Va., January 2, 1866, in *American Missionary*, February 1866, 27; and J. E. Breadalbane, Jacksonville, Fla., to George Whipple, May 19, 1865, AMA Mss.

133. E. B. Eveleth to Reverend Hunt, March 1, 1866, AMA Mss.

134. *American Missionary*, March 1867, 53, emphasis in original.

135. H. S. Beals, Beaufort, N.C., in ibid., November 1868, 241.

136. Forten, "Life on the Sea Islands," 77.

137. Dora Ford, Fayetteville, Ark., to Friends of the Freedmen, November 18, 1869, AMA Mss.

138. G. N. Carruthers, Corinth, Miss., August 24, 1863, in *American Missionary*, October 1863, 236.

139. Miss A. M. Church, Downey Farm, Fort Monroe, Va., November 1, 1864, in ibid., December 1864, 293.

140. Miss. J. S. Shearman, Norfolk, Va., November 29, 1865, in ibid., January 1866, 3; ibid., June 1864, 139; ibid., May 1866, 101. See also ibid., April 1864, 98.

141. *American Freedman*, February 1868, 362.

142. *American Missionary*, June 1867, 124.

143. Robert Harris, Fayetteville, N.C., May 2, 1868, in ibid., July 1868, 152; H. S. Beals to L. Hunt, June 2, 1866, AMA Mss.

144. Ferebee, *Brief History*, 10.

145. J. Silsby, Montgomery, Ala., to George Whipple, November 2, 1865, AMA Mss.

146. Rev. I. Pettibone, Savannah, Ga., in *American Missionary*, March 1867, 53; G. N. Carruthers, Corinth, Miss., August 24, 1863, in ibid., October 1863, 236.

147. Reports of Superintendents of Education for Georgia and Florida, in Alvord, *Fourth Semi-Annual Report*, 34, 35.

148. Rawick, *American Slave . . . Supplement, Series 2*, vol. 10, pt. 9, pp. 3944–45.

149. Alvord, *Fourth Semi-Annual Report*, 38. The superintendent may have been referring to the Freedmen's Bank. AMA and Freedmen's Bureau employees encouraged freedpeople to deposit funds into the bank. It collapsed in 1874, due in part to mismanagement and fraud. George R. Bentley, *A History of the Freedmen's Bureau* (New York: Octagon Books, 1974), 146–47.

150. William Henry Heard, *From Slavery to the Bishopric in the A.M.E. Church: An Autobiography* (Philadelphia: AME Book Concern, 1928), 31–38.

151. Samuel Armstrong, Fort Monroe, Va., July 10, 1867, in *American Missionary*, September 1867, 194.

152. Alvord, *Second Semi-Annual Report*, 22. See also William P. Russell, September 1866, in *American Missionary*, October 1866, 221; and M. E. Watson, Darlington, Md., February 3, 1868, *American Missionary*, May 1868, 101.

Chapter Nine

1. John W. Alvord, *First Semi-Annual Report on Schools and Finances of Freedmen, January 1, 1866* (Washington, D.C.: Government Printing Office, 1868), 6, reprinted in John W. Alvord, *Semi-Annual Reports on Schools for Freedmen: Numbers 1–10, January 1866–July 1870* (New York: AMS Press, 1980), emphasis in original.

2. *American Missionary*, July 1868, 150.

3. When the University of South Carolina admitted black students in 1873, white enrollment dropped from 100 percent to 10 percent. Edwin L. Green, *A History of the University of South Carolina* (Columbia, S.C.: State Company, 1916), 413.

4. For a comprehensive listing of black colleges founded between 1860 and 1870, see Julian B. Roebuck and Komanduri S. Murty, *Historically Black Colleges and Universities: Their Place in American Higher Education* (Westport, Conn.: Praeger, 1993), 53–96. Histories of individual institutions include James D. Anderson, *The Education of Blacks in the South, 1860–1935* (Chapel Hill: University of North Carolina Press, 1988); Joe Martin Richardson, *A History of Fisk University, 1865–1946* (University: University of Alabama Press, 1980); Rayford W. Logan, *Howard University: The First Hundred*

Years, 1867–1967 (New York: New York University Press, 1969); and Edward N. Wilson, *The History of Morgan State College: A Century of Purpose in Action, 1867–1967* (New York: Vantage Press, 1975).

5. M. M. Anthony to John Ogden, April 3, 1866, AMA Mss.

6. A. B. Clinton Douglas to John Ogden, June 23, 1868, AMA Mss.

7. W. F. Carter to John Ogden, February 17, 1868, AMA Mss.

8. C. S. Schaeffer, Assistant Commissioner, Freedmen's Bureau, to Samuel C. Armstrong, October 28, 1868, HUA.

9. A. Jared Montgomery to Samuel C. Armstrong, December 1, 1868, HUA.

10. Letter from Brooks Turner, November 1, 1868, HUA; Charley Goodyear to Dear General, July 13, 1868, HUA. James Ammon Dungey (also spelled Dungee) graduated from Hampton in 1872. He was a member of the Hampton Singers while a student, and he became a teacher afterward. The Hampton catalogue listed Mary Eliza Dungey in the middle class in 1871–72. Robert J. Dungey, presumably another brother, graduated in 1875. He also taught after graduation. See *Twenty-Two Years' Work of the Hampton Normal and Agricultural Institute at Hampton, Va.: Records of Negro and Indian Graduates and Ex-Students* (Hampton, Va.: Normal School Press, 1893); and *Catalogue of the Hampton Normal and Agricultural Institute, Hampton, Va.: For the Academical Year 1871–2* (Hampton, Va.: Normal School Press, 1872), 8–9; both in HUA.

11. R. G. B. Patten to General Samuel C. Armstrong, January 12, [1869] (this letter is misdated 1868), HUA. Caleb Nelson graduated from Hampton Institute with the class of 1871. He became a teacher in Virginia. In 1881 he owned four acres of land and a home. *Twenty-Two Years' Work of the Hampton Normal and Agricultural Institute*, 26.

12. Letter from E. D. Tilghman, July 27, 1868, HUA.

13. Ibid.; *Catalogue of the Hampton Normal and Agricultural Institute, . . . 1871–2.*

14. Letter from E. D. Tilghman, September 14, 1868, HUA.

15. *American Missionary*, October 1868, 218. Talladega did not accept women students in the first year because there was no dormitory to house them. Male students slept on the floor in cabins. Freed communities sponsored the first class of students by providing them with food. The students then walked as far as thirty miles to get to the school. Philip S. Foner and George W. Walker, eds., *Proceedings of the Black National and State Conventions, 1865–1900* (Philadelphia: Temple University Press, 1986), 300; Maxine D. Jones and Joe M. Richardson, *Talladega College: The First Century* (Tuscaloosa: University of Alabama Press, 1990), 3.

16. Fred Hunt to John Ogden, July 2, 1868; Alice Allen to John Ogden, July 6, 1868; John H. Burrows to John Ogden, July 6, 1868; all in AMA Mss.

17. W. E. B. Du Bois taught a summer school while a student at Fisk in the 1880s. He recounted his experiences in his essay, "Of the Meaning of Progress," in *The Souls of Black Folk* (1903; New York: Modern Library, 1996), 62–88. Charles Chesnutt taught summer schools in Jonesville, North Carolina, and Spartanburg, South Carolina, in 1874 and 1875. Richard H. Brodhead, ed. *The Journals of Charles W. Chesnutt* (Durham, N.C.: Duke University Press, 1993), 10, 59–63. Anna Julia Cooper taught

in rural Chatham County, North Carolina, while a student at St. Augustine's College. Glenda Elizabeth Gilmore, *Gender and Jim Crow: Women and the Politics of White Supremacy in North Carolina, 1896–1920* (Chapel Hill: University of North Carolina Press, 1996), 36.

18. Vanessa Siddle Walker's monograph, *Their Highest Potential: An African American School Community in the Segregated South* (Chapel Hill: University of North Carolina Press, 1996), relates the history of one such institution in Caswell County, North Carolina, in the twentieth century. In his 1901 study, *The Negro Common School*, W. E. B. Du Bois found that 53 percent of college-educated African Americans were teachers. W. E. B. Du Bois, ed., *The Negro Common School* (Atlanta: University Press, 1901), 14.

19. Henry Lee Swint, *The Northern Teacher in the South, 1862–1870* (New York: Octagon Books, 1967), 85. Swint provides a sympathetic discussion of southern white reactions to freedpeople's education, 85–142.

20. W. E. B. Du Bois, *Black Reconstruction in America: An Essay toward a History of the Part Which Black Folk Played in the Attempt to Reconstruct Democracy in America, 1860–1880* (1935; Millwood, N.Y.: Kraus-Thomson, 1976), 700–701. See also David Roediger, *The Wages of Whiteness: Race and the Making of the American Working Class* (London: Verso, 1991).

21. Testimony of Lieutenant Governor Ridgely C. Powers, KKK Reports, Mississippi, 1:589–90.

22. Quoted in *American Missionary*, April 1867, 79.

23. *Wilmington Daily Dispatch*, December 6, 1866.

24. KKK Reports, Mississippi, 1:589–90.

25. See, for example, Report of Brevet General A. C. Gillem, Assistant Commissioner, Mississippi, in *American Freedman*, June 1867, 239. Mr. H. C. Percy wrote from Norfolk, Virginia, "The more intelligent class seem[s] to be favorably disposed towards, if not in perfect sympathy with the educational movement and the efforts to elevate the colored people." *American Missionary*, January 1866, 5–6. John Alvord reported, "A change of sentiment is apparent among the better classes of the south in regard to freedmen's schools. Those of higher intelligence concede that education must be universal." John W. Alvord, *Second Semi-Annual Report on Schools and Finances of Freedmen, July 1, 1866* (Washington, D.C.: Government Printing Office, 1868), reprinted in Alvord, *Semi-Annual Reports*. M. E. Watson from Darlington, Maryland, wrote, "A number of white Marylanders deigned their presence, who, in spite of past and present prejudices, expressed their surprise and satisfaction with the system on which our school was conducted, and the promptness of recitations, especially in arithmetic." She was grateful that the students had made some "converts." *American Missionary*, September 1867, 194.

26. *American Missionary*, April 1866, 79–80. For biographical information on Cardozo, see Joe M. Richardson, "Francis L. Cardozo: Black Educator during Reconstruction," *Journal of Negro Education* 48 (Winter 1979): 73–83.

27. KKK Reports, Alabama, 2:937.

28. Alvord, *First Semi-Annual Report*, 13. See also *American Missionary*, January

1866, 19–20; Report of Brevet General A. C. Gillem, Assistant Commissioner, Mississippi, *American Freedman*, June 1867, 239; and Report of Brevet Major General Davis Tillson, Assistant Commissioner, Georgia, M798, roll 32, FBR.

29. *American Missionary*, March 1867, 57; John W. Alvord, *Fourth Semi-Annual Report on Schools for Freedmen, July 1, 1867* (Washington, D.C.: Government Printing Office, 1868), 49, reprinted in Alvord, *Semi-Annual Reports*.

30. John Eaton, *Report of the General Superintendent of Freedmen, Department of the Tennessee and State of Arkansas for 1864* (Memphis, Tenn., 1865).

31. KKK Reports, Georgia, 1:472–77.

32. KKK Reports, Alabama, 3:1329.

33. *Norfolk Virginian*, July 2, 1866, reprinted in *American Missionary*, August 1866, 174–75.

34. *Raleigh Daily Sentinel*, June 14, 1866.

35. Report of Frank R. Chase, Brevet Major, State Superintendent of Education, in Alvord, *Fourth Semi-Annual Report*, 49; Alvord, *Second Semi-Annual Report*, 1–2.

36. Anderson, *Education of Blacks in the South*, 26, 81–82.

37. Responses to Emancipation League survey by Samuel Sawyer, Chaplain, Forty-seventh Regiment, Indiana Volunteers, and George D. Wise, Army of the District of East Arkansas, in Emancipation League, *Facts Concerning the Freedmen: Their Capacity and Their Destiny* (Boston, 1863), 7, 8, in "From Slavery to Freedom: The African American Pamphlet Collection, 1824–1909," Rare Books and Special Collections Division, Library of Congress, Washington, D.C.; available online in *American Memory: Historical Collections for the National Digital Library* (Washington, D.C.: Library of Congress), <http://memory.loc.gov/>.

38. Hollis Reed in the *Jersey Journal*, reprinted in *American Missionary*, October 1866, 233.

39. Rufus Saxton Copybook no. 2, December 29, 1862–June 15, 1864, Rufus and S. Willard Saxton Papers, Manuscripts and Archives, Yale University, New Haven, Conn.

40. *American Missionary*, August 1864, 204.

41. Emma B. Eveleth to Simeon Jocelyn, February 4, 1865, AMA Mss.

42. Horace James, *Annual Report of the Superintendent of Negro Affairs in North Carolina, 1864, with an Appendix, Containing the History and Management of the Freedmen in This Department up to June 1st, 1865*. (Boston: W. F. Brown, n.d.), 9.

43. *OR*, ser. 3, 3:431.

44. Speech of General O. O. Howard in *American Missionary*, June 1866, 125. AMA employee Enoch K. Miller drew a distinction between what he called, "the unlettered yet industrious poor white men who work small farms on the hills" and the "poor white trash who stay (but can scarcely be said to live) anywhere and everywhere and eke out a miserable existence by fishing, hunting and stealing." Enoch K. Miller, Little Rock, Ark., to Jacob Shipherd, AMA Mss.

45. Alvord, *Second Semi-Annual Report*, 13.

46. John W. Alvord, *Third Semi-Annual Report on Schools for Freedmen* (Washington, D.C.: Government Printing Office, 1868), 4, reprinted in Alvord, *Semi-Annual Reports*.

47. *American Freedman*, August 1866, 79.

48. Letter from Miss Duncan in *American Missionary*, June 1864, 139.

49. *American Freedman*, August 1866, 80.

50. *American Missionary*, June 1867, 127.

51. Ibid., March 1867, 51.

52. Ibid.

53. *American Freedman*, July 1867, 245.

54. For a comprehensive history of public schooling prior to the Civil War, see Lawrence A. Cremin, *American Education: The National Experience, 1783–1876* (New York: Harper and Row, 1980).

55. Carl F. Kaestle, *Pillars of the Republic: Common Schools and American Society, 1780–1860* (New York: Hill and Wang, 1983), 192–95; A. D. Mayo, *The Educational Situation in the South* (n.p., n.d.), 4. See also J. C. Gibbs, "Education in the Southern States," in *The Addresses and Journal of Proceedings of the National Educational Association of the United States, 1873* (Peoria, Ill.: N. C. Nason, Printer, 1873), 82; Joe M. Richardson, *The Negro in the Reconstruction of Florida, 1865–1877* (Tallahassee: Florida State University Press, 1965), 184–87; Harold N. Rabinowitz, ed., *Southern Black Leaders of the Reconstruction Era* (Urbana: University of Illinois Press, 1982), 62; Drew Gilpin Faust, *A Sacred Circle: The Dilemma of the Intellectual in the Old South, 1840–1860* (Baltimore: Johns Hopkins University Press, 1977), 8; and Charles W. Dabney, *Universal Education in the South*, 2 vols. (Chapel Hill: University of North Carolina Press, 1936), 1:23–25.

56. Kaestle, *Pillars of the Republic*, 200–204.

57. C. Thurston Chase in *American Missionary*, October 1867, 223–24.

58. School report of Charles Day, June 1867, M810, roll 6, FBR.

59. Fisk P. Brewer in *American Freedman*, June 1866, 42, emphasis in original.

60. The AFUC, for example, committed itself to work on behalf of "persons released from slavery, and of other needy persons in the southern states" and pledged that "no distinctions of race or color shall be recognized, and especially shall no school be maintained from which pupils shall be excluded on the ground of such distinction." Records of the New England Freedmen's Aid Society, Massachusetts Historical Society, Boston, Mass.

61. H. S. Beals to M. E. Strieby, November 1865, AMA Mss.

62. H. S. Beals to Reverend L. Hunt, February 28, 1866, June 2, 1866, AMA Mss.

63. Beals to Hunt, May 15, 1866, September 15, 1866, AMA Mss.

64. Beals to Hunt, November 30, 1866, AMA Mss.; Monthly report of Amy Chapman, January 1867, AMA Mss.; *American Missionary*, January 1867, 4. According to Samuel J. Whiton, an AMA employee, freedpeople contributed $800 to build Washburn Institute, which contained the finest hall for African Americans in North Carolina. The freedmen, he said, were very proud of the building. Samuel J. Whiton to E. P. Smith, January 1, 1867, AMA Mss.

65. Beals appeared to have the implicit support of AMA general field secretary Edward P. Smith, who visited Beaufort while the white school was in session. H. S. Beals to E. P. Smith, February 15, 1867, AMA Mss.

66. Ibid.; Samuel J. Whiton to E. P. Smith, February 16, 1867, AMA Mss.

67. Memorial from Colored Citizens of Beaufort to the American Missionary Association, March 4, 1867, AMA Mss.

68. Hyman Thompson to George Whipple, March 1867, AMA Mss. Interestingly, Thompson and other freedpeople seemed to have a direct pipeline into communications between Beals and AMA officials. They made very specific references to information included in Beals's letters.

69. Amy Chapman to E. P. Smith, March 16, 1867; Samuel J. Whiton to E. P. Smith, March 4, 1867; Beals to E. P. Smith, April 1867; Hyman Thompson et al. to George Whipple, June 10, 1867; all in AMA Mss.

70. *American Missionary*, May 1867, 109.

71. H. S. Beals in ibid., August 1867, 172–73.

72. L. E. Bemis in ibid., September 1867, 195.

73. Francis L. Cardozo in ibid., April 1866, 79–80. For other examples of freedpeople's schools inspiring influential whites to consider common education more seriously, see E. P. Smith, Memphis, Tenn., in ibid., August 1866, 171; and L. E. Bemis, Smithfield, N.C., in ibid., September 1867, 195.

74. Brodhead, *Journals of Charles W. Chesnutt*, 5–10; Earle H. West, "The Harris Brothers: Black Northern Teachers in the Reconstruction South," *Journal of Negro Education* 48 (Spring 1979): 126–38.

75. *American Missionary*, March 1867, 51.

76. Ibid.

77. Du Bois, *Negro Common School*, 35.

78. Edgar W. Knight, *The Influence of Reconstruction on Education in the South* (New York: Teachers College, Columbia University, 1913), 65–73.

79. There was no uniformity to the constitutions and statutes that established public schooling. Each included its own provisions and restrictions. They all had in common, though, some mechanism for paying for schools. Some imposed property taxes to fund schools; others imposed capitation taxes so that even those who did not own property would pay. In some states black schools were supported only by taxes collected from black people. Works that discuss development of public school systems in southern states include Horace Mann Bond, *Negro Education in Alabama: A Study in Cotton and Steel* (Tuscaloosa: University of Alabama Press, 1994); Knight, *Influence of Reconstruction on Education in the South*; William Preston Vaughn, *Schools for All: The Blacks and Public Education in the South, 1865–1877* (Lexington: University Press of Kentucky, 1974); and Vernon Lane Wharton, *The Negro in Mississippi, 1865–1890* (New York: Harper and Row, 1965).

80. Several witnesses described the outfits Klan members wore on their night visits. Sarah Allen of Mississippi testified, "They wore long white robes, a loose mask covered the face, trimmed with scarlet stripes. The lieutenant and captain had long horns on their head, projecting over the forehead; a sort of devise in front—some sort of figure in front, and scarlet stripes." KKK Reports, 2:778. Joseph Galloway, also from Mississippi, remembered, "They had on long gowns or robes—they looked more like gowns of some kind than anything else. Their masks were pieces of cloth, as well as I could tell, sewed to the seam of the coat on the shoulder, and brought over

the head and fastened under the chin. I could see some parts of their faces. The first time they came to my house some of them had horns fastened to the top of the mask." KKK Reports, Mississippi, 2:663. Charlotte Fowler, a black woman whose husband was murdered by the KKK, testified, "It was all around the eyes. It was black; and the other part was white and red; and he had horns on his head." KKK Reports, South Carolina, 1:388. For a history of the Ku Klux Klan in the Reconstruction period see Allen W. Trelease, *White Terror: The Ku Klux Klan Conspiracy and Southern Reconstruction* (New York: Harper and Row, 1971).

81. U.S. Senate. *Report of the Joint Select Committee to Inquire into the Condition of Affairs in the Late Insurrectionary States.* 42d Cong., 2d sess., S. Rep. 41 (Washington, D.C.: Government Printing Office, 1872), 1:73.

82. Testimony of G. Wiley Wells in KKK Reports, Mississippi, 1:1150; KKK Reports, Mississippi, 1:80. See also testimony of Jefferson B. Algood, KKK Reports, Mississippi, 1:501–2.

83. KKK Reports, Mississippi, 1:271–77, 1:75–77.

84. Kaestle, *Pillars of the Republic*, 148–51, 186–92.

85. Eric Foner, *Nothing but Freedom: Emancipation and Its Legacy* (Baton Rouge: Louisiana State University Press, 1983), 68–70; Ludwell H. Johnson, *Division and Reunion: America, 1848–1877* (New York: John Wiley and Sons, 1978), 248; testimony of Richard W. Walker, attorney and former member of the Confederate senate from Alabama. KKK Reports, Alabama, 2:959–61.

86. Du Bois, *Negro Common School*, 92.

87. Testimony of Oscar Judkins, KKK Reports, Alabama, 2:1042–48; testimony of George Pickett, KKK Reports, Mississippi, 1:466–67; testimony of Peter Cooper, KKK Reports, Mississippi, 1:496; testimony of Joseph Galloway, KKK Reports, Mississippi, 2:664–65; testimony of Sarah A. Allen, KKK Reports, Mississippi, 2:777–79.

88. Testimony of Joshua Morris, KKK Reports, Mississippi, 1:306.

89. *American Missionary*, March 1866, 59.

90. Testimony of James Rives, KKK Reports, Mississippi, 1:548–70.

91. Testimony of Caroline Smith, KKK Reports, Georgia, 1:400–403.

92. C. Vann Woodward, *The Strange Career of Jim Crow* (New York: Oxford University Press, 1966), 70; Gilmore, *Gender and Jim Crow*, 2.

93. Henry Allen Bullock, *A History of Negro Education in the South, from 1619 to the Present* (Cambridge, Mass.: Harvard University Press, 1967), 74–85. Bullock argues that white southerners were willing to soften their opposition to black education if blacks could come to understand that they should be trained to occupy their fixed sphere in society, a sphere that did not contemplate equality with whites. Educators such as Samuel C. Armstrong at Hampton Institute and Booker T. Washington at Tuskegee helped to implement this model of "special education for Negroes," of which white southerners, and some northerners, approved.

94. C. Vann Woodward traces the gradual diminution of African Americans' rights and the imposition of institutionalized segregation in *Strange Career of Jim Crow*.

95. Bullock, *History of Negro Education*, 85–88. For a discussion of constitutional provisions for education in individual southern states, see Charles L. Coon, *Facts about*

Southern Educational Progress: A Present Day Study in Public School Maintenance for Those Who Look Forward (Durham, N.C.: Seeman Printery, 1905), 46–60.

96. Du Bois, *Negro Common School.* See also Charles L. Coon, *Public Taxation and Negro Schools. Paper read before the Twelfth Annual Conference for Education in the South, Held in Atlanta, Georgia, April 14, 15, and 16, 1909* (Cheyney, Pa.: Committee of Twelve for the Advancement of the Interests of the Negro Race, 1909). According to Coon, in eleven southern states black teachers received 12 percent of expenditures for their salaries while white teachers received 62 percent. Coon served as school superintendent in Wilson, North Carolina, and as superintendent of the state's normal schools for African Americans. Gilmore, *Gender and Jim Crow*, 159.

97. W. E. B. Du Bois and Augustus Granville Dill, eds., *The Common School and the Negro American* (Atlanta: Atlanta University Press, 1911), 137–38; J. Morgan Kousser, "Progressivism—For Middle-Class Whites Only: North Carolina Education, 1880–1910," *Journal of Southern History* 46 (May 1980): 169–94; Carl V. Harris, "Stability and Change in Discrimination against Black Public Schools: Birmingham, Alabama, 1871–1931," in *African Americans and Education in the South, 1865–1900*, ed. Donald G. Nieman (New York: Garland, 1994), 87–143; Louis R. Harlan, *Separate and Unequal: Public School Campaigns and Racism in the Southern Seaboard States, 1901–1915* (Chapel Hill: University of North Carolina Press, 1958), 11–14, 40; Horace Mann Bond, *The Education of the Negro in the American Social Order* (New York: Octagon Books, 1966), 391–412. See also Robert A. Margo, *Disenfranchisement, School Finance, and the Economics of Segregated Schools in the United States South, 1890–1910* (New York: Garland, 1985).

98. Du Bois and Dill, *Common School and the Negro American*, 8.

99. Anderson, *Education of Blacks in the South*, 148–85. See also Walker, *Their Highest Potential.*

Epilogue

1. Louisville Mortuary Record, 1910, Book 14, p. 100, Filson Historical Society, Louisville, Ky.

BIBLIOGRAPHY

Primary Sources

Manuscripts and Archives

Amherst, Mass.
  Amherst College Library
Boston, Mass.
  Massachusetts Historical Society
Chapel Hill, N.C.
  North Carolina Collection, Wilson Library, University of North Carolina
    Clippings File
  Rare Book Collection, Wilson Library, University of North Carolina
College Park, Md.
  Freedmen and Southern Society Project, University of Maryland
Columbia, Mo.
  State Historical Society of Missouri
Hampton, Va.
  Casemate Museum
  Hampton University Archives
    Early Students Folder
Hartford, Conn.
  Connecticut Historical Society
    Hartford Freedman's Aid Society Records
    Rebecca Primus Papers
Louisville, Ky.
  Filson Historical Society
    Elijah Marrs File
Memphis, Tenn.
  Memphis–Shelby County Public Library and Information Center
    Memphis Archives
New Haven, Conn.
  Beinecke Rare Book and Manuscript Library, Yale University
  Yale University Manuscripts and Archives
    John Blassingame Papers
    Rufus and S. Willard Saxton Papers, 1834–1934
New Orleans, La.
  Amistad Research Center, Tilton Hall, Tulane University
    American Missionary Association Manuscripts, 1839–1882

Howard-Tilton Memorial Library, Tulane University
  Government Documents
New Orleans Public Library
  Government Documents
New York, N.Y.
  New York Public Library
    Herbert G. Gutman Papers
  Schomburg Center for Research in Black Culture
Oberlin, Ohio
  Oberlin College Archives
    Student Folders
    Treasurer's Office Correspondence, 1822–1907
Richmond, Ind.
  Lilly Library, Earlham College
    Quaker Collection
Washington, D.C.
  National Archives and Records Administration
    Records of the Adjutant General's Office, 1780s–1917, Record Group 94
      (microfilm)
    Records of the Bureau of Refugees, Freedmen, and Abandoned Lands, Record
      Group 105 (microfilm)

Newspapers and Periodicals

American Missionary (American Missionary Association), 1863–69
American Freedman (American Freedmen's Union Commission), 1866–68
Black Republican (New Orleans, La.)
Charleston Advocate (Charleston, S.C.)
Christian Recorder (African Methodist Episcopal Church, Philadelphia, Pa.)
Colored Tennessean (Nashville, Tenn.)
Daily Dispatch (Wilmington, N.C.)
Daily Sentinel (Raleigh, N.C.)
Freedman's Press (Austin, Tex.)
Freedmen's Journal (New England Freedmen's Aid Society, Boston, Mass.)
Freedmen's Record (Indiana Yearly Meeting of Friends, Richmond, Ind.)
Free Press (Charleston, S.C.)
South Carolina Leader (Charleston, S.C.)
Wilmington Journal (Wilmington, N.C.)

Published Works

Adams, John Quincy. *Narrative of the Life of John Quincy Adams, When in Slavery and
  Now as a Freeman.* Harrisburg, Pa.: Sieg, 1872. In *Documenting the American South.*
  Chapel Hill: University of North Carolina, 2000.
  <http://docsouth.unc.edu/adams/menu.html>. April 12, 2004.

The Addresses and Journal of Proceedings of the National Educational Association of the United States, 1873. Peoria, Ill.: N. C. Nason, Printer, 1873.

Albert, Octavia V. Rogers. *The House of Bondage; or, Charlotte Brooks and Other Slaves, Original and Life Like, as They Appeared in Their Old Plantation and City Slave Life; Together with Pen-Pictures of the Peculiar Institution, with Sights and Insights into Their New Relations as Freedmen, Freemen, and Citizens.* New York: Hunt and Eaton, 1890. In *Documenting the American South.* Chapel Hill: University of North Carolina Press, 2000. <http://docsouth.unc.edu/neh/albert/menu.html>. April 12, 2004.

Alexander, Charles. *Battles and Victories of Allen Allensworth, A.M., Ph.D., Lt. Col. Retired U.S. Army.* Boston: Sherman, French and Company, 1914.

Alvord, John W. *Semi-Annual Reports on Schools for Freedmen: Numbers 1–10, January 1866–July 1870.* Vol. 1 of *Freedmen's Schools and Textbooks.* Edited by Robert C. Morris. New York: AMS Press, 1980.

American Tract Society. *The Freedman's Spelling Book; The Freedman's Second Reader; The Freedman's Third Reader.* Vol. 2 of *Freedmen's Schools and Textbooks.* Edited by Robert C. Morris. New York: AMS Press, 1980.

Anderson, Robert. *From Slavery to Affluence: Memoirs of Robert Anderson, Ex-Slave.* Edited by Daisy Anderson Leonard. 1927; Steamboat Springs, Colo.: Steamboat Pilot, 1967.

Andrews, Sidney. *The South Since the War.* 1866; Boston: Houghton Mifflin, 1971.

Bell, Howard Holman, ed. *Minutes of the Proceedings of the National Negro Conventions, 1830–1864.* New York: Arno Press and the New York Times, 1969.

Berlin, Ira, and Leslie S. Rowland, eds. *Families and Freedom: A Documentary History of African-American Kinship in the Civil War Era.* New York: New Press, 1997.

Berlin, Ira, et al., eds. *The Black Military Experience.* Ser. 2 of *Freedom: A Documentary History of Emancipation, 1861–1867.* New York: Cambridge University Press, 1982.

——. *The Destruction of Slavery.* Ser. 1, Vol. 1, of *Freedom: A Documentary History of Emancipation, 1861–1867.* New York: Cambridge University Press, 1985.

——. *Free at Last: A Documentary History of Slavery, Freedom, and the Civil War.* New York: New Press, 1992.

——. *The Wartime Genesis of Free Labor: The Lower South.* Ser. 1, Vol. 3, of *Freedom: A Documentary History of Emancipation, 1861–1867.* New York: Cambridge University Press, 1990.

——. *The Wartime Genesis of Free Labor: The Upper South.* Ser. 1, Vol. 2, of *Freedom: A Documentary History of Emancipation, 1861–1867.* New York: Cambridge University Press, 1993.

Bibb, Henry. *Narrative of the Life Adventures of Henry Bibb, an American Slave. Written by Himself.* In Vol. 2 of *African American Slave Narratives.* Edited by Sterling Lecatur Bland Jr. Westport, Conn.: Greenwood Press, 2001.

Bingham, Caleb. *The Columbian Orator: Containing a Variety of Original and Selected Pieces Together with Rules; Calculated to Improve the Youth and Others in the Ornamental and Useful Art of Eloquence.* Boston: J. H. A. Frost, 1831.

Black, Leonard. *The Life and Sufferings of Leonard Black, a Fugitive from Slavery*. New Bedford, Mass.: Benjamin Lindsey, 1847.

Blackett, R. J. M., ed. *Thomas Morris Chester, Black Civil War Correspondent: His Dispatches from the Virginia Front*. Baton Rouge: Louisiana State University Press, 1989.

Blassingame, John W., ed. *Slave Testimony: Two Centuries of Letters, Speeches, Interviews, and Autobiographies*. Baton Rouge: Louisiana State University Press, 1977.

Botume, Elizabeth Hyde. *First Days amongst the Contrabands*. 1893; New York: Arno Press, 1968.

Brinckerhoff, Isaac W. *Advice to Freedmen*. Vol. 4 of *Freedmen's Schools and Textbooks*. Edited by Robert C. Morris. New York: AMS Press, 1980.

Brodhead, Richard H., ed. *The Journals of Charles W. Chesnutt*. Durham, N.C.: Duke University Press, 1993.

Bruner, Peter. *A Slave's Adventure Toward Freedom: Not Fiction but the True Story of a Struggle*. Oxford, Ohio, 1919.

Califf, Joseph Mark. *Record of the Services of the Seventh Regiment, U.S. Colored Troops from September, 1863 to November, 1866 by an Officer of the Regiment*. Providence, R.I.: E. L. Freeman, 1878.

Campbell, Tunis Gulic. *Sufferings of T. G. Campbell and His Family, in Georgia*. Washington, D.C.: Enterprise Publishing Company, 1877.

Clement, Samuel Spottford. *Memoirs of Samuel Spottford Clement, Relating Interesting Experiences in Days of Slavery and Freedom*. Stuebenville, Ohio: Herald Printing Company, 1908. In *Documenting the American South*. Chapel Hill: University of North Carolina, 2000. <http://docsouth.unc.edu/neh/clement/menu.html>. June 7, 2004.

Coffin, Levi. *Reminiscences of Levi Coffin, the Reported President of the Underground Railroad*. Cincinnati: Robert Clarke Company, 1898.

Coon, Charles L. *Facts about Southern Educational Progress: A Present Day Study in Public School Maintenance for Those Who Look Forward*. Durham, N.C.: Seeman Printery, 1905.

———. *Public Taxation and Negro Schools. Paper read before the Twelfth Annual Conference for Education in the South, Held in Atlanta, Georgia, April 14, 15, and 16, 1909*. Cheyney, Pa.: Committee of Twelve for the Advancement of the Interests of the Negro Race, 1909.

Coyler, Vincent. *Brief Report of the Services Rendered by the Freed People to the United States Army in North Carolina, in the Spring of 1862, after the Battle of New Bern*. New York: Vincent Coyler, 1864.

Cremin, Lawrence A., ed. *The Republic and the School: Horace Mann on the Education of Free Men*. New York: Teachers College, Columbia University, 1957.

De Forest, John William. *A Union Officer in the Reconstruction*. Edited by James H. Croushore and David M. Potter. New Haven: Yale University Press, 1948.

Dennett, John Richard. *The South as It Is, 1865–1866*. Edited by Henry M. Christman. New York: Viking Press, 1965.

Douglass, Frederick. "Free the Slaves then Leave Them Alone," excerpted from "The Future of the Negro People of the Slave States" (1862). In *Afro-American History: Primary Sources*, 130–43. Edited by Thomas R. Frazier. New York: Harcourt, Brace and World, 1970.

———. *Life and Times of Frederick Douglass, Written by Himself.* Secaucus, N.J.: Citadel Press, 1983.

———. *My Bondage and My Freedom.* New York: Arno Press and the New York Times, 1968.

———. *The Narrative of the Life of Frederick Douglass, an American Slave.* Edited by David W. Blight. New York: Bedford Books, 1993.

Douglass, Frederick, et al. *Men of Color: To Arms! To Arms!* (Philadelphia, 1863). GLC 2752, Gilder Lehrman Collection, New York, N.Y.

Douglass, Margaret. *Educational Laws of Virginia: The Personal Narrative of Mrs. Margaret Douglass, a Southern Woman, Who Was Imprisoned for One Month in the Common Jail of Norfolk, under the Laws of Virginia for the Crime of Teaching Free Colored Children to Read.* Boston: John P. Jewitt and Company, 1854.

Drum, Richard C., and Elon A. Woodward, eds. *The Negro in the Military Service of the United States, 1639–1886: A Compilation of Official Records, State Papers, Historical Extracts, etc., Relating to His Military Status and Service from the Date of His Introduction into the British North American Colonies.* Washington, D.C.: Adjutant General's Office, 1888. Microfilm, Washington, D.C.: National Archives and Records Administration, 1963. M858, 5 rolls.

Eaton, John. *Grant, Lincoln, and the Freedmen: Reminiscences of the Civil War with Special Reference to the Work for the Contrabands and Freedmen of the Mississippi Valley.* New York: Longmans, Green, 1907.

———. *Report of the General Superintendent of Freedmen, Department of the Tennessee and State of Arkansas, for 1864.* Memphis, Tenn., 1865.

Emancipation League. *Facts Concerning the Freedmen: Their Capacity and Their Destiny.* Boston, 1863. In "From Slavery to Freedom: The African American Pamphlet Collection, 1824–1909," Rare Books and Special Collections Division, Library of Congress, Washington, D.C. Available online in *American Memory: Historical Collections for the National Digital Library.* Washington, D.C.: Library of Congress. <http://memory.loc.gov/>. April 12, 2004.

Emmerton, James A. *A Record of the Twenty-Third Regiment, Mass. Vol. Infantry in the War of the Rebellion, 1861–1865.* Boston: William Ware and Company, 1886.

Ferebee, London R. *A Brief History of the Slave Life of Rev. L. R. Ferebee, and the Battles of Life, and Four Years of His Ministerial Life.* Raleigh, N.C.: Edwards, Broughton and Company, 1882. In *Documenting the American South.* Chapel Hill: University of North Carolina, 2000. <http://docsouth.unc.edu/ferebee/menu.html>. April 12, 2004.

Finkelman, Paul, ed. *State Slavery Statutes.* Microfiche; Frederick, Md.: University Publications of America, 1989.

Foner, Philip S., and George E. Walker, eds. *Proceedings of the Black National and State Conventions, 1865–1900.* Vol. 1. Philadelphia: Temple University Press, 1986.

———. *Proceedings of the Black State Conventions, 1840–1865*. 2 vols. Philadelphia: Temple University Press, 1979, 1980.

Fonvielle, William Frank. *Reminiscence of College Days*. Goldsboro, N.C.: Edwards and Broughton, 1903.

Forten, Charlotte L. *The Journal of Charlotte Forten: A Free Negro in the Slave Era*. Edited by Ray Allen Billington. New York: Collier Books, 1953.

———. *The Journals of Charlotte Forten Grimké*. Edited by Brenda Stevenson. New York: Oxford University Press, 1988.

———. "Letter from St. Helena Island, Beaufort, S.C." *Liberator*, December 19, 1862, 203.

———. "Life on the Sea Islands." *Atlantic Monthly* (May and June 1864). In *Two Black Teachers during the Civil War*. Edited by William Loren Katz. New York: Arno Press and the New York Times, 1969.

Foster, Richard Baxter. *Historical Sketch of Lincoln Institute, Jefferson City, Missouri: Full History of Its Conception, Struggles, and Triumph*. Jefferson City, Mo.: n.p., 1871.

Goodell, William. *The American Slave Code in Theory and Practice: Its Distinctive Features Shown by Its Statutes, Decisions, and Illustrative Facts*. New York: American and Foreign Anti-Slavery Society, 1853.

Gooding, James Henry. *On the Altar of Freedom: A Black Soldier's Civil War Letters from the Front: Corporal*. Edited by Virginia M. Adams. Amherst: University of Massachusetts Press, 1991.

Harlan, Louis R., and John W. Blassingame, eds. *The Autobiographical Writings*. Vol. 1 of *The Booker T. Washington Papers*. Urbana: University of Illinois Press, 1972.

Heard, William Henry. *From Slavery to the Bishopric in the A.M.E. Church: An Autobiography*. Philadelphia: AME Book Concern, 1928. In *Documenting the American South*. Chapel Hill: University of North Carolina, 2000. <http://docsouth.unc.edu/neh/heard/menu.html>. April 12, 2004.

Higginson, Thomas Wentworth. *Army Life in a Black Regiment, and Other Writings*. New York: Penguin Books, 1997.

Hutchinson, A., comp. *Code of Mississippi: Being an Analytical Compilation of the Public and General Statutes of the Territory and State, with Tabular References to the Local and Private Acts, from 1798–1848*. Jackson, Miss., 1848.

Jackson, Mattie J. *The Story of Mattie J. Jackson: Her Parentage—Experience of Eighteen Years in Slavery—Incidents During the War—Her Escape from Slavery. A True Story*. Lawrence, Mass.: Printed at Sentinel Office, 1866. In *Documenting the American South*. Chapel Hill: University of North Carolina, 2000. <http://docsouth.unc.edu/jacksonm/menu.html>. April 12, 2004.

James, Horace. *Annual Report of the Superintendent of Negro Affairs in North Carolina, 1864, with an Appendix, Containing the History and Management of the Freedmen in This Department up to June 1st, 1865*. Boston: W. F. Brown, n.d.

Jones, Thomas Jesse. *Negro Education: A Study of the Private and Higher Schools for Colored People in the United States*. 2 vols. U.S. Department of the Interior, Bureau of Education, Bulletin No. 38 and 39. Washington, D.C.: Government Printing Office, 1917.

Joynes, Edward S. *Education after the War: A Letter Addressed to Members of the Southern Educational Convention, Columbia, S.C., 28th April, 1863*. Richmond: MacFarlane and Ferguson, 1863.

Keckley, Elizabeth. *Behind the Scenes; or, Thirty Years a Slave and Four Years in the White House*. New York: G. W. Carleton, 1868. In *Documenting the American South*. Chapel Hill: University of North Carolina, 2000. <http://docsouth.unc.edu/keckley/menu.html>. April 12, 2004.

Lawson, Ellen NicKenzie, and Marlene D. Merrill, eds. *The Three Sarahs: Documents of Antebellum Black College Women*. New York: Edwin Mellen Press, 1984.

Leigh, Frances Butler. *Ten Years on a Georgia Plantation Since the War*. 1883; New York: Negro Universities Press, 1969.

Lockwood, Lewis C. "Mary S. Peake: The Colored Teacher at Fortress Monroe." In *Two Black Teachers during the Civil War*. Edited by William Loren Katz. New York: Arno Press and the New York Times, 1969.

Marrs, Elijah. *Life and History of the Rev. Elijah P. Marrs*. Louisville, Ky.: Bradley and Gilbert Company, 1885.

Mayo, A. D. *The Educational Situation in the South*. N.p., n.d.

McCline, John. *Slavery in the Clover Bottoms: John McCline's Narrative of His Life during Slavery and the Civil War*. Edited by Jan Furman. Knoxville: University of Tennessee Press, 1998.

McKim, James M. *The Freedmen of South Carolina*. Philadelphia: Willis P. Hazard, 1862.

Mellon, James, ed. *Bullwhip Days: The Slaves Remember*. New York: Weidenfeld and Nicolson, 1988.

Moore, Frank, ed. *The Rebellion Record: A Diary of American Events*. 11 vols. and supplement. New York: G. P. Putnam, 1864.

Moore, Marinda Branson. *The First Dixie Reader: Designed to Follow the Dixie Primer*. Raleigh, N.C.: Branson, Farrar, and Company, 1863. In *Documenting the American South*. Chapel Hill: University of North Carolina Press, 2000. <http://docsouth.unc.edu/moore/menu.html>. April 12, 2004.

———. *The Geographical Reader, for the Dixie Children*. Raleigh, N.C.: Branson, Farrar, and Company, 1863. In *Documenting the American South*. Chapel Hill: University of North Carolina Press, 2000. <http://docsouth.unc.edu/moore1/menu.html>. April 12, 2004.

National Freedman's Relief Association of New York Annual Report, 1865/66. New York: Holman, 1866.

New England Freedmen's Aid Society. *First Annual Report of the Educational Commission for Freedmen, May 1863*. Boston: Prentiss and Deland, 1863.

Newton, A. H. *Out of the Briars: An Autobiography and Sketch of the Twenty-ninth Regiment Connecticut Volunteers*. 1910; Miami: Mnemosyne Publishing Company, 1969.

Nicolay, John G., and John Hay, eds. *Complete Works of Abraham Lincoln*. 12 vols. N.p.: Lincoln Memorial University, 1894.

Nordhoff, Charles. *The Freedmen of South-Carolina: Some Account of Their Appearance, Character, Condition, and Peculiar Customs.* New York: Charles T. Evans, 1863.

Offley, G. W. *A Narrative of the Life and Labors of the Rev. G. W. Offley, a Colored Man, Local Preacher, and Missionary.* Hartford, Conn., 1859. In *Documenting the American South.* Chapel Hill: University of North Carolina, 2000. <http://docsouth.unc.edu/neh/offley/menu.html>. April 12, 2004.

Olmsted, Frederick Law. *The Cotton Kingdom: A Traveller's Observations on Cotton and Slavery in the American Slave States.* Edited by Arthur M. Schlesinger. New York: Alfred A. Knopf, 1953.

Pearson, Elizabeth Ware, ed. *Letters from Port Royal, 1862–1868.* 1906; New York: Arno Press, 1969.

Perkins, Frances Beecher. "Two Years with a Colored Regiment: A Woman's Experience." *New England Magazine* 23 (January 1898): 533–44.

Pierce, Edward L. "The Contrabands at Fortress Monroe." *Atlantic Monthly* 8 (November 1861): 626–40.

———. "The Freedmen of Port Royal." *Atlantic Monthly* 13 (September 1863): 291–315.

Proceedings of the Colored People's Convention of the State of South Carolina, Held in Zion Church, Charleston, November, 1865. Charleston, S.C., 1865.

Proceedings of the Convention of Teachers of the Confederate States, Assembled at Columbia, South Carolina, April 28th, 1863. Macon, Ga.: Burke, Boykin, and Company, 1863. In *Confederate Imprints,* 143 reels. Microfilm; New Haven, Conn.: Research Publications, 1974. Reel 113, No. 4009.

Proceedings of the Convention of the Equal Rights and Educational Association of Georgia, Assembled at Macon, October 19, 1866. Augusta: Office of the Loyal Georgian, 1866.

Proceedings of the National Convention of Colored Men, Held in Syracuse, N.Y., October 4–7, 1864; With the Bill of Wrongs and Rights, and the Address to the American People. Boston, 1864.

Randolph, Peter. *From Slave Cabin to the Pulpit: The Autobiography of Rev. Peter Randolph—The Southern Question Illustrated and Sketches of Slave Life.* Boston: James H. Earle Printers, 1893.

Rawick, George P., ed. *The American Slave: A Composite Autobiography.* 19 vols. Westport, Conn.: Greenwood Press, 1972.

———. *The American Slave: A Composite Autobiography: Supplement, Series 1.* 12 vols. Westport, Conn.: Greenwood Press, 1977.

———. *The American Slave: A Composite Autobiography: Supplement, Series 2.* 10 vols. Westport, Conn.: Greenwood Press, 1979.

Redkey, Edwin S., ed. *A Grand Army of Black Men: Letters from African-American Soldiers in the Union Army, 1861–1865.* New York: Cambridge University Press, 1992.

Reid, Whitelaw. *After the War: A Tour of the Southern States, 1865–1866.* Edited by C. Vann Woodward. New York: Harper and Row, 1965.

Shaw, Robert Gould. *Blue-Eyed Child of Fortune: The Civil War Letters of Colonel Robert Gould Shaw.* Edited by Russell Duncan. Athens: University of Georgia Press, 1992.

Smith, James. *Autobiography of James L. Smith: Including Also, Reminiscences of Slave Life, Recollections of the War, Education of Freedmen, Causes of the Exodus, etc.* Norwich, Conn.: Press of the Bulletin Company, 1882.

Starobin, Robert S., ed. *Blacks in Bondage: Letters from American Slaves.* New York: New Viewpoints, 1974.

Stearns, Charles. *The Black Man of the South, and the Rebels; or the Characteristics of the Former and the Recent Outrages of the Latter, by Charles Stearns, a Northern Teacher.* New York: American News Company, 1872.

Stroud, George M., ed. *A Sketch of the Laws Relating to Slavery in the Several States of the United States of America.* 1856; New York: Negro Universities Press, 1968.

Taylor, Susie King. *A Black Woman's Civil War Memoirs: Reminiscences of My Life in Camp with the 33rd U.S. Colored Troops, Late 1st South Carolina Volunteers.* Edited by Patricia W. Romero and Willie Lee Rose. New York: M. Wiener Publishing, 1988.

Taylor, Yuval, ed. *I Was Born a Slave: An Anthology of Classic Slave Narratives.* 2 vols. Chicago: Lawrence Hill Books, 1999.

Thomson, Mortimer [Doesticks, Q. K. Philander, pseud.]. *What Became of the Slaves on a Georgia Plantation? Great Auction Sale of Slaves, at Savannah, Georgia, March 2nd and 3rd, 1859.* N.p., 1863.

Towne, Laura M. *Letters and Diary of Laura M. Towne, Written from the Sea Islands of South Carolina, 1862–1884.* Edited by Rupert Sargent Holland. Cambridge, Mass.: Riverside Press, 1912.

U.S. Bureau of the Census. *Eighth Census of the United States Taken in the Year 1860.* Washington, D.C.: Government Printing Office, 1864.

U.S. Congress. House. Select Committee on the Memphis Riots. *Memphis Riots and Massacres.* 39th Cong., 1st sess., 1866. H. Rep. 101. Reprint; Miami, Fla.: Mnemosyne Publishing Company, 1969.

U.S. Congress. Senate. *Report of the Joint Select Committee to Inquire into the Condition of Affairs in the Late Insurrectionary States: Ku Klux Klan Conspiracy.* 42d Cong., 2d sess., 1872. S. Rep. 41. Washington, D.C.: Government Printing Office, 1872.

U.S. War Department. *The War of the Rebellion: A Compilation of the Official Records of the Union and Confederate Armies.* 128 vols. Washington, D.C.: Government Printing Office, 1880–1901.

Walker, David. *David Walker's Appeal to the Coloured Citizens of the World.* Edited by Peter P. Hinks. University Park: Pennsylvania State University Press, 2000.

Walker, Susan. "The Journal of Miss Susan Walker." In *Quarterly Publication of the Historical and Philosophical Society of Ohio,* vols. 7–9. Cincinnati, Ohio, 1912–14.

Washington, Booker T. *Up From Slavery: An Autobiography.* 1901; New York: Doubleday, 1963.

Weaver, C. P., ed. *Thank God My Regiment an African One: The Civil War Diary of Colonial Nathan W. Daniels.* Baton Rouge: Louisiana State University Press, 1998.

Wiley, C. H. *Address to the People of North Carolina.* Raleigh, N.C.: Conference of Teachers and Friends of Education, 1861. In *Documenting the American South.*

Chapel Hill: University of North Carolina, 2000.
<http://docsouth.unc.edu/imls/confteach/menu.html>. April 12, 2004.

Winks, Robin, et al., eds. *Four Fugitive Slave Narratives*. Reading, Mass.: Addison-Wesley, 1969.

Yeatman, James E. *A Report on the Condition of the Freedmen of the Mississippi, Presented by the Western Sanitary Commission, December 17, 1863*. St. Louis: Western Sanitary Commission, 1864.

Yoder, Jacob E. *The Fire of Liberty in Their Hearts: The Diary of Jacobs E. Yoder of the Freedmen's Bureau School, Lynchburg, Virginia, 1866–1870*. Edited by Samuel L. Horst. Richmond: Library of Virginia, 1996.

Secondary Sources

Adams, David Wallace. *Education for Extinction: American Indians and the Boarding School Experience, 1875–1928*. Lawrence: University Press of Kansas, 1995.

Alexander, Roberta Sue. *North Carolina Faces the Freedmen: Race Relations during Presidential Reconstruction, 1865–67*. Durham, N.C.: Duke University Press, 1985.

Allen, James S. *Reconstruction: The Battle for Democracy, 1865–1876*. New York: International Publishers, 1937.

Anderson, James D. *The Education of Blacks in the South, 1860–1935*. Chapel Hill: University of North Carolina Press, 1988.

Andrews, William L., ed. *African American Autobiography: A Collection of Critical Essays*. Englewood Cliffs, N.J.: Prentice Hall, 1993.

———. *Six Women's Slave Narratives*. New York: Oxford University Press, 1988.

Angell, Stephen Ward. *Bishop Henry McNeal Turner and African American Religion in the South*. Knoxville: University of Tennessee Press, 1992.

Apple, Michael W., and Linda K. Christian-Smith. *The Politics of the Textbook*. New York: Routledge, 1991.

Aptheker, Herbert. *Abolitionism: A Revolutionary Movement*. Boston: Twayne Publishers, 1989.

———. *The Negro in the Civil War*. New York: International Publishers, 1938.

———. "The Negro in the Union Navy." *Journal of Negro History* 32 (April 1947): 169–200.

Bacote, Clarence Albert. *The Story of Atlanta University: A Century of Service, 1865–1965*. Atlanta: Atlanta University, 1969.

Bancroft, Frederic. *Slave Trading in the Old South*. New York: Frederick Ungar, 1931.

Barbour, Hugh, and J. William Frost. *The Quakers*. Westport, Conn.: Greenwood Press, 1988.

Bardaglio, Peter W. *Reconstructing the Household: Families, Sex, and the Law in the Nineteenth-Century South*. Chapel Hill: University of North Carolina Press, 1995.

Bentley, George R. *A History of the Freedmen's Bureau*. New York: Octagon Books, 1974.

Berkeley, Kathleen C. " 'Colored Ladies Also Contributed': Black Women's Activities from Benevolence to Social Welfare, 1866–1896." In *The Web of*

Southern Social Relations: Work, Family and Education, edited by Walter J. Fraser Jr.,
R. Frank Saunders Jr., and Jon L. Wakelyn, 181–203. Athens: University of
Georgia Press, 1985.

Berlin, Ira. *Many Thousands Gone: The First Two Centuries of Slavery in North America.*
Cambridge, Mass.: Harvard University Press, 1998.

———. *Slaves without Masters: The Free Negro in the Antebellum South.* New York:
Pantheon Books, 1974.

Bernstein, Iver. *The New York City Draft Riots: Their Significance for American Society
and Politics in the Age of the Civil War.* New York: Oxford University Press, 1990.

Beyan, Amos J. *The American Colonization Society and the Creation of the Liberian State:
A Historical Perspective, 1822–1900.* Lanham, Md.: University Press of America,
1991.

Black Biographical Dictionaries, 1790–1950. Alexandria, Va.: Chadwyck-Healey, 1937.

Blassingame, John W. "Before the Ghetto: The Making of the Black Community in
Savannah, Georgia, 1865–1880." *Journal of Social History* 6 (Summer 1973):
463–88.

———. *Black New Orleans, 1860–1973.* Chicago: University of Chicago Press, 1973.

———. "The Recruitment of Negro Troops in Kentucky, Maryland and Missouri,
1863–1865." In *The Day of Jubilee: The Civil War Experience of Black Southerners*,
edited by Donald G. Nieman, 533–45. New York: Garland Publishing, 1994.

———. "The Union Army as an Educational Institution for Negroes, 1862–1865."
Journal of Negro Education 34 (Spring 1965): 152–59.

Blight, David W. *Race and Reunion: The Civil War in American Memory.* Cambridge,
Mass.: Harvard University Press, 2001.

Bond, Horace Mann. *The Education of the Negro in the American Social Order.* New
York: Octagon Books, 1966.

———. *Negro Education in Alabama: A Study in Cotton and Steel.* Tuscaloosa: University
of Alabama Press, 1994.

Bracey, John H., Jr., ed. *Blacks in the Abolitionist Movement.* Belmont, Calif.:
Wadsworth, 1970.

———. *Free Blacks in America, 1800–1860.* Belmont, Calif.: Wadsworth, 1971.

Brawley, James P. *Two Centuries of Methodist Concern: Bondage, Freedom, and Education
of Black People.* New York: Vantage Press, 1974.

Breeden, James O., ed. *Advice among Masters: The Ideal in Slave Management in the Old
South.* Westport, Conn.: Greenwood Press, 1980.

Brown, Elsa Barkley. "Negotiating and Transforming the Public Sphere: African
American Political Life in the Transition from Slavery to Freedom." *Public Culture*
7 (Fall 1994): 107–46.

Bullock, Henry Allen. *A History of Negro Education in the South, from 1619 to the
Present.* Cambridge, Mass.: Harvard University Press, 1967.

Burkett, Randall K., et al., eds. *Black Biography, 1790–1950: A Cumulative Index.*
Alexandria, Va.: Chadwyck-Healey, 1991.

Butchart, Ronald E. *Northern Schools, Southern Blacks, and Reconstruction: Freedmen's
Education, 1862–1875.* Westport, Conn.: Greenwood Press, 1980.

———. " 'We Best Can Instruct Our Own People': New York African Americans in the Freedmen's Schools, 1861–1875." *Afro-Americans in New York Life and History* 12 (January 1988): 27–49.

Calhoun, Craig, ed. *Habermas and the Public Sphere.* Cambridge, Mass.: MIT Press, 1992.

Campbell, Edward D. C., Jr., and Kym S. Rice, eds. *Before Freedom Came: African-American Life in the Antebellum South.* Charlottesville: University Press of Virginia, 1991.

Cecelski, David S., and Timothy B. Tyson, eds. *Democracy Betrayed: The Wilmington Race Riot of 1898 and Its Legacy.* Chapel Hill: University of North Carolina Press, 1998.

Cimbala, Paul A., and Randall M. Miller, eds. *The Freedmen's Bureau and Reconstruction: Reconsiderations.* New York: Fordham University Press, 1999.

Clement, Rufus E. "The Educational Work of the African Methodist Episcopal Zion Church, 1820–1920." M.A. thesis, Northwestern University, 1922.

Click, Patricia C. *Time Full of Trial: The Roanoke Island Freedmen's Colony, 1862–1867.* Chapel Hill: University of North Carolina Press, 2001.

Clinton, Catherine, and Nina Silber, eds. *Divided Houses: Gender and the Civil War.* New York: Oxford University Press, 1992.

Cohen, William. *At Freedom's Edge: Black Mobility and the Southern White Quest for Racial Control, 1861–1875.* Baton Rouge: Louisiana State University Press, 1991.

Conway, Alan. *The Reconstruction of Georgia.* Minneapolis: University of Minnesota Press, 1966.

Cornelius, Janet Duitsman. *Slave Missions and the Black Church in the Antebellum South.* Columbia: University of South Carolina Press, 1999.

———. *"When I Can Read My Title Clear": Literacy, Slavery, and Religion in the Antebellum South.* Columbia: University of South Carolina Press, 1991.

Cornish, Dudley Taylor. *The Sable Arm: Negro Troops in the Union Army, 1861–1865.* New York: Longmans, Green, 1956.

———. "The Union Army as a School for Negroes." *Journal of Negro History* 37 (October 1952): 368–82.

Coulter, E. Merton. *College Life in the Old South.* New York: Macmillan Company, 1928.

———. *Negro Legislators in Georgia during the Reconstruction Period.* Athens: Georgia Historical Quarterly, 1968.

Cremin, Lawrence A. *American Education: The National Experience, 1783–1876.* New York: Harper and Row, 1980.

———. *Traditions of American Education.* New York: Basic Books, 1976.

Cromwell, John W. *The Early Negro Convention Movement.* Washington, D.C.: American Negro Academy, 1904.

Dabney, Charles W. *Universal Education in the South.* 2 vols. Chapel Hill: University of North Carolina Press, 1936.

Dailey, Jane, Glenda Elizabeth Gilmore, and Bryant Simon, eds. *Jumpin' Jim Crow:*

Southern Politics from Civil War to Civil Rights. Princeton, N.J.: Princeton University Press, 2000.

Davis, David Brion. *The Problem of Slavery in Western Culture.* Ithaca, N.Y.: Cornell University Press, 1966.

DeBoer, Clara Merritt. *His Truth Is Marching On: African Americans Who Taught the Freedmen for the American Missionary Association, 1861–1877.* New York: Garland Publishing, 1995.

Donald, Henderson H. *The Negro Freedman: Life Conditions of the American Negro in the Early Years after Emancipation.* New York: Henry Schuman, 1952.

Drago, Edmund L. *Black Politicians and Reconstruction in Georgia: A Splendid Failure.* Baton Rouge: Louisiana State University Press, 1982.

Du Bois, W. E. B. *Black Reconstruction in America: An Essay toward a History of the Part Which Black Folk Played in the Attempt to Reconstruct Democracy in America, 1860–1880.* 1935; Millwood, N.Y.: Kraus-Thomson, 1976.

——. "How Negroes Have Taken Advantage of Educational Opportunities Offered by Friends." *Journal of Negro Education* 7 (April 1938): 124–31.

——. *The Souls of Black Folk.* 1903; New York: Modern Library, 1996.

——, ed. *The Negro Common School.* Atlanta: University Press, 1901.

Du Bois, W. E. B., and Augustus Granville Dill, eds. *The Common School and the Negro American.* Atlanta: Atlanta University Press, 1911.

Duncan, Russell. *Freedom's Shore: Tunis Campbell and the Georgia Freedmen.* Athens: University of Georgia Press, 1986.

Echoes of Glory: Illustrated Atlas of the Civil War. Alexandria, Va.: Time-Life Books, 1991.

Edwards, Laura F. *Gendered Strife and Confusion: The Political Culture of Reconstruction.* Urbana: University of Illinois Press, 1997.

Engs, Robert Francis. *Freedom's First Generation: Black Hampton, Virginia, 1861–1890.* Philadelphia: University of Pennsylvania Press, 1979.

Faust, Drew Gilpin. *A Sacred Circle: The Dilemma of the Intellectual in the Old South, 1840–1860.* Baltimore: Johns Hopkins University Press, 1977.

Finkelman, Paul, ed. *Antislavery.* New York: Garland Publishing, 1989.

Floyd, Silas Xavier. *Life of Charles T. Walker, D.D.* Nashville, Tenn.: National Baptist Publishing Board, 1902.

Foner, Eric. *Nothing but Freedom: Emancipation and Its Legacy.* Baton Rouge: Louisiana State University Press, 1983.

——. *Reconstruction: America's Unfinished Revolution, 1863–1877.* New York: Harper and Row, 1988.

Foner, Jack D. *Blacks and the Military in American History: A New Perspective.* New York: Praeger, 1974.

Foner, Philip S., ed. *Frederick Douglass: Selected Speeches and Writings.* Abridged and adapted by Yuval Taylor. Chicago: Lawrence Hill Books, 1999.

Foner, Philip S., and Josephine F. Pacheco, eds. *Three Who Dared: Prudence Crandall, Margaret Douglass, Myrtilla Miner—Champions of Antebellum Black Education.* Westport, Conn.: Greenwood Press, 1984.

Forbes, Ella. *African American Women during the Civil War*. New York: Garland, 1998.

Fort, Bruce. "Reading in the Margins: The Politics and Culture of Literacy in Georgia, 1800–1920." Ph.D. diss., University of Virginia, 1999.

Foster, Helen Bradley. *"New Raiments of Self": African American Clothing in the Antebellum South*. New York: Berg, 1997.

Fox, Early Lee. *The American Colonization Society, 1817–1840*. Baltimore: Johns Hopkins University Press, 1919.

Fox-Genovese, Elizabeth. *Within the Plantation Household: Black and White Women of the Old South*. Chapel Hill: University of North Carolina Press, 1988.

Frankel, Noralee. *Freedom's Women: Black Women and Families in Civil War Era Mississippi*. Bloomington: Indiana University Press, 1999.

Franklin, Vincent P., and James D. Anderson, eds. *New Perspectives on Black Educational History*. Boston: G. K. Hall, 1978.

Fredrickson, George M. *The Black Image in the White Mind: The Debate on Afro-American Character and Destiny, 1817–1914*. New York: Harper and Row, 1971.

Fuller, Edmund. *Prudence Crandall: An Incident of Racism in Nineteenth-Century Connecticut*. Middletown, Conn.: Wesleyan University Press, 1971.

Gaines, Wesley J. *African Methodism in the South: Twenty-Five Years of Freedom*. 1890; Chicago: Afro-Am Press, 1969.

Garfield, Deborah M., and Rafia Zafar, eds. *Harriet Jacobs and Incidents in the Life of a Slave Girl: New Critical Essays*. New York: Cambridge University Press, 1996.

Genovese, Eugene D. *Roll, Jordan, Roll: The World the Slaves Made*. New York: Pantheon Books, 1974.

Gerteis, Louis S. *From Contraband to Freedman: Federal Policy toward Southern Blacks, 1861–1865*. Westport, Conn.: Greenwood Press, 1973.

Gilmore, Glenda Elizabeth. *Gender and Jim Crow: Women and the Politics of White Supremacy in North Carolina, 1896–1920*. Chapel Hill: University of North Carolina Press, 1996.

Glatthaar, Joseph T. *Forged in Battle: The Civil War Alliance of Black Soldiers and White Officers*. New York: Free Press, 1990.

Godbold, Albea. *The Church College of the Old South*. Durham, N.C.: Duke University Press, 1944.

Gomez, Michael A. *Exchanging Our Country Marks: The Transformation of African Identities in the Colonial and Antebellum South*. Chapel Hill: University of North Carolina Press, 1998.

Goodenow, Ronald K., and Arthur O. White, eds. *Education and the Rise of the New South*. Boston: G. K. Hall, 1981.

Green, Edwin, L. *A History of the University of South Carolina*. Columbia, S.C.: State Company, 1916.

Greenberg, Kenneth S., ed. *The Confessions of Nat Turner and Related Documents*. New York: Bedford Books of St. Martin's Press, 1996.

Griffin, Farah Jasmine, ed. *Beloved Sisters and Loving Friends: Letters from Rebecca Primus of Royal Oak, Maryland, and Addie Brown of Hartford, Connecticut, 1854–1868*. New York: Alfred A. Knopf, 1999.

Gutman, Herbert. *Power and Culture: Essays on the American Working Class*. New York: New Press, 1987.

Habermas, Jurgen. *The Structural Transformation of the Public Sphere: An Inquiry into a Category of Bourgeois Society*. Cambridge: MIT Press, 2000.

Hargrove, Hondon B. *Black Union Soldiers in the Civil War*. Jefferson, N.C.: McFarland, 1988.

Harlan, Louis R. *Booker T. Washington: The Making of a Black Leader, 1856–1901*. New York: Oxford University Press, 1972.

———. *Separate and Unequal: Public School Campaigns and Racism in the Southern Seaboard States, 1901–1915*. Chapel Hill: University of North Carolina Press, 1958.

Harrison, Lowell H. *The Antislavery Movement in Kentucky*. Lexington: University Press of Kentucky, 1978.

Hartman, Saidiya V. *Scenes of Subjection: Terror, Slavery, and Self-Making in Nineteenth-Century America*. New York: Oxford University Press, 1997.

Harvey, McClennon Phillip. *A Brief History of Paul Quinn College, Waco, Texas: 1872–1965*. Waco, Tex.: Smith, 1965.

Henritze, Barbara K. *Bibliographic Checklist of African American Newspapers*. Baltimore: Genealogical Publishing Company, 1995.

Herskovits, Melville J. *The Myth of the Negro Past*. Boston: Beacon Press, 1958.

Hildebrand, Reginald F. *The Times Were Strange and Stirring: Methodist Preachers and the Crisis of Emancipation*. Durham, N.C.: Duke University Press, 1995.

Hine, Darlene Clark, ed. *Black Women in America: An Historical Encyclopedia*. Brooklyn, N.Y.: Carlson, 1993.

Hine, Darlene Clark, and Earnestine Jenkins, eds. *"Manhood Rights": The Construction of Black Male History and Manhood, 1750–1870*. Vol. 1 of *A Question of Manhood: A Reader in U.S. Black Men's History and Masculinity*. Bloomington: Indiana University Press, 1999.

Hinks, Peter. *To Awaken My Afflicted Brethren: David Walker and the Problem of Antebellum Slave Resistance*. University Park: Pennsylvania State University Press, 1997.

Holmes, Dwight Oliver Wendell. *The Evolution of the Negro College*. Contributions to Education, no. 609. New York: Bureau of Publications, Teachers College, Columbia University, 1934.

Holtzclaw, Robert Fulton. *Black Magnolias: A Brief History of the Afro-Mississippian, 1865–1980*. Shaker Heights, Ohio: Keeble Press, 1984.

Jackson, Broadus B. *Civil War and Reconstruction in Mississippi: Mirror of Democracy in America*. Jackson, Miss.: Town Square Books, 1998.

Jacobson, Matthew Frye. *Whiteness of a Different Color: European Immigrants and the Alchemy of Race*. Cambridge, Mass.: Harvard University Press, 1998.

Johnson, Guy B. *Folk Culture on St. Helena Island, South Carolina*. Chapel Hill: University of North Carolina Press, 1930.

Johnson, Ludwell H. *Division and Reunion: America, 1848–1877*. New York: John Wiley and Sons, 1978.

Johnson, Michael P. "Runaway Slaves and the Slave Communities in South Carolina, 1799 to 1830." *William and Mary Quarterly* 38 (July 1981): 418–41.

Johnson, Walter. *Soul by Soul: Life Inside the Antebellum Slave Market*. Cambridge, Mass.: Harvard University Press, 1999.

Johnson, Whittington B. *Black Savannah, 1788–1864*. Fayetteville: University of Arkansas Press, 1996.

——. "A Black Teacher and Her School in Reconstruction Darien: The Correspondence of Hattie Sabattie and J. Murray Hoag, 1868–1869." *Georgia Historical Quarterly* 75 (Spring 1991): 90–105.

Jones, Jacqueline. *Soldiers of Light and Love: Northern Teachers and Georgia Blacks, 1865–1873*. Chapel Hill: University of North Carolina Press, 1980.

Jones, Maxine Deloris, and Joe Martin Richardson. *Talladega College: The First Century*. Tuscaloosa: University of Alabama Press, 1990.

Kaestle, Carl F. *Pillars of the Republic: Common Schools and American Society, 1780–1860*. New York: Hill and Wang, 1983.

Katz, Michael B. "The Origins of Public Education: A Reassessment." In *The Social History of American Education*, edited by B. Edward McClennan and William J. Reese, 91–117. Urbana: University of Illinois Press, 1988.

Katz, William Loren. *Flight from the Devil: Six Slave Narratives*. Trenton, N.J.: Africa World Press, 1996.

Kelley, Robin D. G. *Race Rebels: Culture, Politics, and the Black Working Class*. New York: Free Press, 1994.

Kennedy, Thomas C. "The Last Days at Southland." *Southern Friend* 8 (Spring 1986): 3–19.

——. "The Rise and Decline of a Black Monthly Meeting: Southland, Arkansas, 1864–1925." *Southern Friend* 19 (Autumn 1997): 3–29.

——. "Southland College: The Society of Friends and Black Education in Arkansas." *Southern Friend* 7 (Spring 1985): 39–69.

Kett, Joseph. *Rites of Passage: Adolescence in America, 1790 to the Present*. New York: Basic Books, 1977.

King, Wilma. *Stolen Childhood: Slave Youth in Nineteenth-Century America*. Bloomington: Indiana University Press, 1995.

Klein, Herbert. *Slavery in the Americas: A Comparative Study of Virginia and Cuba*. Chicago: University of Chicago Press, 1967.

Knight, Edgar W. *Education in the South*. Chapel Hill: University of North Carolina Press, 1924.

——. *The Influence of Reconstruction on Education in the South*. New York: Teachers College, Columbia University, 1913.

——. *Public School Education in North Carolina*. Boston: Houghton Mifflin, 1916.

Kolchin, Peter. *First Freedom: The Responses of Alabama's Blacks to Emancipation and Reconstruction*. Westport, Conn.: Greenwood Press, 1972.

Kousser, J. Morgan. "Progressivism—For Middle-Class Whites Only: North Carolina Education, 1880–1910." *Journal of Southern History* 46 (May 1980): 169–94.

Leloudis, James L. *Schooling the New South: Pedagogy, Self, and Society in North Carolina, 1880–1920.* Chapel Hill: University of North Carolina Press, 1996.

Levy, Barry. *Quakers and the American Family: British Settlement in the Delaware Valley.* New York: Oxford University Press, 1988.

Litwack, Leon F. *Been in the Storm So Long: The Aftermath of Slavery.* New York: Alfred A. Knopf, 1979.

Loewenberg, Bert James, and Ruth Bogin, eds. *Black Women in Nineteenth-Century American Life: Their Words, Their Thoughts, Their Feelings.* University Park: Pennsylvania State University Press, 1976.

Loring, F. W., and C. F. Atkinson. *Cotton Culture and the Old South.* Boston: A. Williams, 1869.

Malval, Fritz J. *A Guide to the Archives of Hampton Institute.* Westport, Conn.: Greenwood Press, 1985.

Margo, Robert A. *Disenfranchisement, School Finance, and the Economics of Segregated Schools in the United States South, 1890–1910.* New York: Garland, 1985.

———. *Race and Schooling in the South, 1880–1950: An Economic History.* Chicago: University of Chicago Press, 1990.

McAfee, Ward. *Religion, Race, and Reconstruction: The Public School in the Politics of the 1870s.* Albany: State University of New York Press, 1998.

McCaul, Robert L. *The Black Struggle for Public Schooling in Nineteenth-Century Illinois.* Carbondale: Southern Illinois University Press, 1987.

McCurry, Stephanie. *Masters of Small Worlds: Yeoman Households, Gender Relations, and the Political Culture of the Antebellum South Carolina Low Country.* New York: Oxford University Press, 1995.

McLemore, Richard Aubrey, ed. *A History of Mississippi.* Vol. 1. Hattiesburg: University and College Press of Mississippi, 1973.

McPherson, James M. *The Negro's Civil War: How American Negroes Felt and Acted during the War for the Union.* New York: Pantheon Books, 1965.

Merriam, Eve. *Growing Up Female in America: Ten Lives.* New York: Doubleday, 1971.

Miller, Randall M., ed. *"Dear Master": Letters of a Slave Family.* Ithaca, N.Y.: Cornell University Press, 1978.

Mobley, Joe A. *James City: A Black Community in North Carolina, 1863–1900.* Raleigh, N.C.: Department of Cultural Resources, Division of Archives and History, 1981.

Montgomery, Florence M. *Textiles in America, 1650–1870.* New York: W. W. Norton, 1984.

Montgomery, William E. *Under Their Own Vine and Fig Tree: The African-American Church in the South, 1865–1900.* Baton Rouge: Louisiana State University Press, 1993.

Morris, Robert C. *Reading, 'Riting, and Reconstruction: The Education of Freedmen in the South, 1861–1870.* Chicago: University of Chicago Press, 1981.

Nelson, Jacqueline S. *Indiana Quakers Confront the Civil War.* Indianapolis: Indiana Historical Society, 1991.

Nieman, Donald G., ed. *African Americans and Education in the South, 1865–1900.* New York: Garland, 1994.

———. *The Freedmen's Bureau and Black Freedom.* New York: Garland, 1994.

———. *The Politics of Freedom: African Americans and the Political Process during Reconstruction.* New York: Garland, 1994.

Norton, Mary Beth, et al. *A People and a Nation: A History of the United States.* Boston: Houghton Mifflin, 1998.

Paradis, James M. *Strike the Blow for Freedom: The 6th United States Colored Infantry in the Civil War.* Shippensburg, Pa.: White Maine Books, 1998.

Patterson, Orlando. *Slavery and Social Death: A Comparative Study.* Cambridge, Mass.: Harvard University Press, 1992.

Penn, I. Garland. *The Afro-American Press and Its Editors.* Springfield, Mass.: Wiley, 1981.

Penningroth, Dylan C. *The Claims of Kinfolk: African American Property and Community in the Nineteenth-Century South.* Chapel Hill: University of North Carolina Press, 2003.

Perdue, Robert E. *The Negro in Savannah, 1865–1900.* New York: Exposition Press, 1973.

Perkins, Linda M. "The Black Female American Missionary Association Teacher in the South, 1861–1870." In Vol. 3 of *Black Women in American History: From Colonial Times through the Nineteenth Century,* edited by Darlene Clark Hine, 1049–63. Brooklyn, N.Y.: Carlson, 1990.

Perlmann, Joel, and Robert A. Margo. *Women's Work? American Schoolteachers, 1650–1920.* Chicago: University of Chicago Press, 2001.

Perman, Michael. *Reunion without Compromise: The South and Reconstruction, 1865–1868.* New York: Cambridge University Press, 1973.

Pickens, William. *Bursting Bonds: The Heirs of Slaves.* Boston: Jordan and More Press, 1923.

Posey, Josephine. *Against Great Odds: The History of Alcorn State University.* Jackson: University Press of Mississippi, 1994.

Potter, Vilma Raskin. *A Reference Guide to Afro-American Publications and Editors, 1827–1945.* Ames: Iowa State University Press, 1993.

Powers, Bernard E. *Black Charlestonians: A Social History, 1822–1885.* Fayetteville: University of Arkansas Press, 1994.

Puryear, B. N. *Hampton Institute: A Pictorial Review of Its First Century 1868–1968.* Hampton, Va.: Prestige Press, 1962.

Quarles, Benjamin. *Black Abolitionists.* New York: Oxford University Press, 1969.

———. *The Negro in the Civil War.* Boston: Little, Brown, 1969.

Rabinowitz, Howard N., ed. *Southern Black Leaders of the Reconstruction Era.* Urbana: University of Illinois Press, 1982.

Raboteau, Albert J. *Slave Religion: The Invisible Institution in the Ante-Bellum South.* New York: Oxford University Press, 1978.

Rachal, John R. "Gideonites and Freedmen: Adult Literacy Education at Port Royal, 1862–1865." *Journal of Negro Education* 55 (Autumn 1968): 453–69.

Raichle, Donald R. "The Abolition of Corporal Punishment in New Jersey Schools." In *Corporal Punishment in American Education: Readings in History, Practice, and Alternatives*, edited by Irwin A. Hyman and James H. Wise, 62–88. Philadelphia: Temple University Press, 1979.

Ransom, Roger L., and Richard Sutch. *One Kind of Freedom: The Economic Consequences of Emancipation*. New York: Cambridge University Press, 1977.

Rawley, James A. *Turning Points of the Civil War*. Lincoln: University of Nebraska Press, 1989.

Redkey, Edwin S. "Black Chaplains in the Union Army." *Civil War History* 33 (December 1987): 331–50.

——, ed. *Respect Black: The Writings and Speeches of Henry McNeal Turner*. New York: Arno Press and the New York Times, 1971.

Richardson, Joe Martin. *Christian Reconstruction: The American Missionary Association and Southern Blacks, 1861–1890*. Athens: University of Georgia Press, 1986.

——. "Francis L. Cardozo: Black Educator during Reconstruction." *Journal of Negro Education* 48 (Winter 1979): 73–83.

——. *A History of Fisk University, 1865–1946*. University: University of Alabama Press, 1980.

——. *The Negro in the Reconstruction of Florida, 1865–1877*. Tallahassee: Florida State University Press, 1965.

Roebuck, Julian B., and Komanduri S. Murty. *Historically Black Colleges and Universities: Their Place in American Higher Education*. Westport, Conn.: Praeger, 1993.

Roediger, David. *The Wages of Whiteness: Race and the Making of the American Working Class*. London: Verso, 1991.

Rose, Willie Lee. *Rehearsal for Reconstruction: The Port Royal Experiment*. Indianapolis: Bobbs-Merrill, 1964.

Savage, Beth L., ed. *African American Historic Places: National Register of Historic Places*. Washington, D.C.: Preservation Press, 1994.

Savage, William Sherman. *The History of Lincoln University*. Jefferson City, Mo.: New Day Press, 1939.

Saville, Julie. *The Work of Reconstruction: From Slave to Wage Laborer in South Carolina, 1860–1870*. New York: Cambridge University Press, 1994.

Schor, Joel. *Henry Highland Garnet: A Voice of Black Radicalism in the Nineteenth Century*. Westport, Conn.: Greenwood Press, 1977.

Schwalm, Leslie A. *A Hard Fight for We: Women's Transition from Slavery to Freedom in South Carolina*. Urbana: University of Illinois Press, 1997.

Schwartz, Marie Jenkins. *Born in Bondage: Growing Up Enslaved in the Antebellum South*. Cambridge, Mass.: Harvard University Press, 2000.

Scott, James C. *Domination and the Arts of Resistance: Hidden Transcripts*. New Haven: Yale University Press, 1990.

——. *Weapons of the Weak: Everyday Forms of Peasant Resistance*. New Haven: Yale University Press, 1985.

Selleck, Linda B. *Gentle Invaders: Quaker Women Educators and Racial Issues during the Civil War and Reconstruction*. Richmond, Ind.: Friends United Press, 1995.

Simms, James M. *The First Colored Baptist Church in North America*. 1888; New York: Negro Universities Press, 1969.

Smith, Jessie Carney, ed. *Notable Black American Women*. Detroit: Gale Research, 1992.

Soderlund, Jean R. *Quakers and Slavery: A Divided Spirit*. Princeton, N.J.: Princeton University Press, 1985.

Soltow, Lee, and Edward Stevens. *The Rise of Literacy and the Common School in the United States: A Socioeconomic Analysis to 1870*. Chicago: University of Chicago Press, 1981.

Sorin, Gerald. *Abolitionism: A New Perspective*. New York: Praeger, 1972.

Spencer, James, ed. *Civil War Generals: Categorical Listings and a Biographical Directory*. Westport, Conn.: Greenwood Press, 1986.

Spencer, Leon P. *Original Resources in Black Studies: A Guide to the Talladega College Historical Collections*. Talladega, Ala., 1972.

Stampp, Kenneth M., and Leon F. Litwack, eds. *Reconstruction: An Anthology of Revisionist Writings*. Baton Rouge: Louisiana State University Press, 1969.

Sterling, Dorothy. *We Are Your Sisters: Black Women in the Nineteenth Century*. New York: W. W. Norton, 1984.

———, ed. *The Trouble They Seen: Black People Tell the Story of Reconstruction*. Garden City, N.Y.: Doubleday, 1976.

Stevens, Michael, ed. *As If It Were Glory: Robert Beacham's Civil War, from the Iron Brigade to the Black Regiments*. Madison, Wis.: Madison House, 1998.

Stillman, Rachel Bryan. "Education in the Confederate States of America, 1861–1865." Ph.D. diss., University of Illinois at Urbana-Champaign, 1972.

Suggs, Henry Lewis, ed. *The Black Press in the South, 1865–1979*. Westport, Conn.: Greenwood Press, 1983.

Sutton, John R. *Stubborn Children: Controlling Delinquency in the United States, 1640–1981*. Berkeley: University of California Press, 1988.

Swint, Henry Lee. *The Northern Teacher in the South, 1862–1870*. New York: Octagon Books, 1967.

———, ed. *Dear Ones At Home: Letters from Contraband Camps*. Nashville: Vanderbilt University Press, 1966.

Talbert, Horace. *The Sons of Allen: Together with a Sketch of the Rise and Progress of Wilberforce University*. Xenia, Ohio: Aldine Press, 1906.

Trelease, Allen W. *White Terror: The Ku Klux Klan Conspiracy and Southern Reconstruction*. New York: Harper and Row, 1971.

Tyack, David B., ed. *Turning Points in American Educational History*. Lexington, Mass.: Xerox College of Publishing, 1967.

Vaughn, William Preston. *Schools for All: The Blacks and Public Education in the South, 1865–1877*. Lexington: University Press of Kentucky, 1974.

Wade, Richard C. *Slavery in the Cities: The South, 1820–1860*. New York: Oxford University Press, 1964.

Walker, Clarence E. *A Rock in a Weary Land: The African Methodist Episcopal Church during the Civil War and Reconstruction*. Baton Rouge: Louisiana State University Press, 1982.

Walker, Jacqueline Baldwin. "Blacks in North Carolina during Reconstruction." Ph.D. diss., Duke University, 1979.

Walker, Vanessa Siddle. *Their Highest Potential: An African American School Community in the Segregated South*. Chapel Hill: University of North Carolina Press, 1996.

Warfel, Harry R. *Noah Webster: Schoolmaster to America*. New York: Macmillan, 1936.

Warren, Donald, ed. *American Teachers: Histories of a Profession at Work*. New York: Macmillan, 1989.

Webber, Thomas L. *Deep Like the Rivers: Education in the Slave Quarter Community, 1831–1865*. New York: W. W. Norton, 1978.

West, Earle H. "The Harris Brothers: Black Northern Teachers in the Reconstruction South." *Journal of Negro Education* 48 (Spring 1979): 126–38.

Wharton, Vernon Lane. *The Negro in Mississippi, 1865–1890*. New York: Harper and Row, 1965.

White, Deborah Gray. *Ar'n't I a Woman? Female Slaves in the Plantation South*. Rev. ed. New York: W. W. Norton, 1999.

White, Shane, and Graham White. *Stylin': African American Expressive Culture from Its Beginnings to the Zoot Suit*. Ithaca, N.Y.: Cornell University Press, 1998.

Williams, Gilbert Anthony. *"The Christian Recorder"—Newspaper of the African Methodist Episcopal Church: History of a Forum for Ideas, 1854–1902*. Jefferson, N.C.: McFarland, 1996.

Williamson, Joel. *After Slavery: The Negro in South Carolina during Reconstruction, 1861–1877*. Chapel Hill: University of North Carolina Press, 1965.

———. *New People: Miscegenation and Mulattoes in the United States*. New York: Free Press, 1980.

Wilson, Edward N. *The History of Morgan State College: A Century of Purpose in Action, 1867–1967*. New York: Vantage Press, 1975.

Wilson, Joseph T. *The Black Phalanx: A History of the Negro Soldiers of the United States in the Wars of 1775–1812*. Hartford, Conn.: American Publishing Company, 1888.

Wolf, Kurt J. "Laura M. Towne and the Freed People of South Carolina, 1862–1901." *South Carolina Historical Magazine* 98 (October 1997): 375–405.

Wood, Peter. *Black Majority: Negroes in Colonial South Carolina from 1670 through the Stono Rebellion*. New York: Alfred A. Knopf, 1975.

Woodson, Carter G. *The Education of the Negro Prior to 1861: A History of the Education of the Colored People of the United States from the Beginning of Slavery to the Civil War*. New York: G. P. Putnam Sons, 1915.

Woodward, C. Vann. *The Strange Career of Jim Crow*. New York: Oxford University Press, 1966.

Wright, Richard R. *A Brief Historical Sketch of Negro Education in Georgia*. Savannah, Ga.: Robinson Printing House, 1894.

INDEX

Abolition movement: and immediatism, 15; and Douglass, 25, 27, 48; and African American soldiers, 48; and Forten, 116; and textbooks, 126, 133, 137

Adams, John Quincy, 9, 10

Adams, Margaret, 1, 83–87, 202, 237 (n. 14)

Administration of schools: and African Americans' conflicts with white northerners, 2, 6; and African Americans' conflicts with missionaries, 3, 42; and American Missionary Association, 3, 83–85, 86, 87, 88, 89, 91–92

Adult education movement, 167, 168–69, 171

Advice to Freedmen (Brinckerhoff), 135–36

African American adults as students: teachers' perceptions of, 2, 167–68; attitudes toward learning, 35–36, 40, 49–52, 55, 56, 60, 65, 81, 93, 139, 154, 168, 169; motivation for learning, 147, 169; progress of, 153, 167, 168; subjects covered by, 169; types of students, 169–71; white employers' resistance to, 181; and power issues, 197

African American children: and literacy, 35; as orphans, 61, 71; and labor contracts, 70–71

African American children as students: teachers' perceptions of, 2; attitudes toward learning, 35–36, 139, 151, 154, 184; Lockwood's claim to inspiration of, 39; progress of, 153; as

parents' teachers, 172; and power issues, 197

African American churches: as sites for schools, 58, 107–10, 121, 241 (n. 30); white trustees of, 108–10; and white southern violence, 123–24

African American ministers: and Union army chaplains' educational mission, 49, 53, 55–56, 230 (n. 29); and Savannah Educational Association, 87; and administration of schools, 87, 89; as teachers, 113, 114–15, 128–29; and white southern violence, 122, 123; as students, 169–70; students read Bible to, 172

African American parents: as adult students, 35, 172; and teacher choice, 83–86, 87, 150; and tuition, 105, 106; and teacher salaries, 106; and education as commodity, 140; and gifts for teachers, 151; and students' enthusiasm for school, 151; and teachers' corporal punishment, 164–65; and white children attending schools for African Americans, 192

African Americans: conflicts with white northerners, 2, 6, 83, 88, 91–92, 96; influence on whites' interest in education, 2–3; role in educational mission, 4; legal status of, 46, 156; viewed by white southerners as inferior, 65, 126, 132, 160, 197, 198, 263 (n. 93); viewed by white northerners as inferior, 90; educability of, 97, 133, 141, 153–57, 160–61, 168, 183–84, 202; and textbook ideology, 131–32, 136; role as laborers in southern

society, 179–80, 182, 195. *See also*
Free blacks; Freedpeople; Literate
African Americans; Schools for African
Americans; Slavery; Slaves
African American soldiers: enlistment
of, 45–46; as teachers, 46, 49, 51, 57,
65, 82; as escaped slaves, 46, 228
(n. 5); education of, 46–47, 49–56,
228 (n. 7); and civil rights, 47, 54, 78;
and building of schools, 47, 55, 56–
59, 62–65, 92; duties of, 47–49, 50,
57; recruitment of, 48, 53, 54, 230
(n. 29); assertiveness of, 50–51, 52;
and payment of teachers, 54; and
funding for schools, 63; and compensation of slave owners, 66; and textbook donations, 129; clothing of,
143; earnings of, 231 (n. 43)
African American students: enrollment
in schools, 49, 102, 140, 185; educational background of, 101, 103; and
tuition payments, 104, 128; sex of,
111, 170–71; and Ku Klux Klan violence, 122; progress of, 127–28, 140,
153–57, 158, 160, 167, 173, 185, 196;
and fuel for schools, 128; clothing of,
138–39, 142–43, 146–47, 250
(nn. 15, 20); enthusiasm of, 140, 151,
172, 173; obstacles facing, 141–42;
motivation for learning, 147, 149;
school attendance of, 149–50; and
white southern violence, 149–50; and
teachers' qualifications, 150; and gifts
for teachers, 151; and exposure to
northerners, 152; teachers' prejudice
toward, 153, 157; and racial hierarchy,
157–60; and teachers' classroom control, 161–65; and corporal punishment, 163–65; and reform schools,
165–67; ministers as, 169–70; as
teachers, 171–72, 186–87; determination of, 200. *See also* African American adults as students; African American children as students

African American teachers: and Union
army, 1, 2, 35; needs of, 2; and clandestine schools, 18–19, 38, 88; and
clandestine learning, 20, 101; and
freedpeople's camps, 37; soldiers as,
46, 49, 51, 57, 65, 82; of African
American soldiers, 49; gender of, 49–
50, 111–13, 114, 115, 118; and self-
help, 51, 79, 82–83; and Quaker
schools, 60; and black conventions,
74; qualifications of, 88, 89, 90, 98–
99, 100, 101–5, 114, 127–28, 182–
83; and administration of schools, 89;
demotion of, 89; and Alvord, 89, 96,
97, 98, 100, 104, 121–22, 244 (n. 58);
and American Missionary Association, 91, 99, 115, 118–20, 244 (n. 57);
and racial discrimination, 91, 118–20,
199, 264 (n. 96); and teaching as
political act, 96–97; and white southerners' hostility toward black education, 96–97, 101, 121–23; and white
southerners, 97–98, 182–83; ratio of
white to black teachers, 98, 99–100;
and Freedmen's Bureau, 98–103, 104,
115, 240 (nn. 10, 11); salaries of, 105–
6; working conditions of, 106–10,
114; partnerships of, 113–14; northerners as, 114–18, 152; motivations
of, 116–17, 118; and integration, 119;
and white southern violence, 121–24,
125, 245 (n. 82); and textbook availability, 126–30; and Confederate
textbooks, 133; and corporal punishment, 164; students as, 171; and
higher education, 178; and poor
whites, 186; determination of, 200
African colonization, 72, 137, 220
(n. 45)
African Methodist Episcopal (AME)
Church, 53, 109, 114–15
Age: and African American adults as
students, 169
Agency of African Americans: in educa-

tion, 3; and initiation of educational movement, 5; and building of schools, 59; demands for, 68; and black conventions, 77

Alabama, 16, 33, 203, 210

Albright, George Washington, 18, 219 (n. 39)

Allen, Alice, 178

Allen, Sarah, 262 (n. 80)

Allensworth, Allen, 20

Alvord, John W.: and self-help, 80–81, 82, 90, 236 (n. 1); and Savannah Educational Association, 87; and African American teachers, 89, 96, 97, 98, 100, 104, 121–22, 244 (n. 58); and white southerners' opposition to black education, 121, 124–25, 181, 259 (n. 25); and textbooks, 129; and freedpeople's insistence on education, 141; and African Americans' intelligence, 160–61; and reform schools, 165–66, 167; and poor whites, 174, 185

American Anti-Slavery Society, 81

American Freedman, The, 134, 248 (n. 25)

American Freedmen's Inquiry Commission, 36, 41, 43, 227 (n. 64)

American Freedmen's Union Commission, 126, 134, 158, 185–86, 188, 261 (n. 60)

American Indians, 133, 248 (n. 23)

American Missionary Association (AMA): and black education, 1, 4, 38, 39; and administration of schools, 3, 83–85, 86, 87, 88, 89, 91–92; schools of, 5; and textbooks, 36, 40, 82, 83, 126, 189; and requests for teachers, 81, 82; and black school boards, 87; goals of, 89; and funding for schools, 89, 92, 98; and African American teachers, 91, 99, 115, 118–20, 244 (n. 57); attitudes toward African Americans, 95, 118–19; and competition for students, 150; and African

Americans' intelligence, 155–56; and corporal punishment, 164; and poor whites, 186, 188, 189–91; and racial discrimination, 189, 190–92

American Tract Society, 129, 134–35, 169, 248 (n. 25)

Anderson, James D., 4

Anderson, Robert, 228 (n. 5)

Antebellum black convention movement, 72

Anthony, Edward, 113, 127

Antiliteracy statutes: and slave resistance, 7, 14–15, 38; and free blacks, 13, 14, 15, 16, 216 (n. 1); and punishment, 15, 16, 18, 27–28; in North, 16–17, 219 (n. 34); and clandestine schools, 104; text of, 202–10

Antislavery literature, 14–15, 16, 17, 24, 28

Apple, Michael W., 4–5

Arkansas, 59–64, 72, 75, 77–78, 92, 157–58, 212

Armstrong, Samuel C., 173, 263 (n. 93)

Ashley, S. S., 193, 194

Asia, 133

Auld, Hugh, 25

Avery, John, 195

Bass, Nathan, 17–18

Battey, Mary S., 158

Beals, H. S., 170, 172, 189–91

Beard, Elkanah, 59

Beard, Simeon, 110, 113, 128

Beasley, Mary, 19

Beecher, Frances, 50

Beecher, James, 50

Benevolent societies: and black education, 3; and black conventions, 74; relationships with African Americans, 83; and funding for schools, 105, 106, 127; and white northern teachers, 114

Bennett, Mrs. E. P., 165, 255 (n. 104)

Bentley, John, 129

Canada, 22, 24

Candee, George, 91–92

Cannon, Nathan, 122

Cardozo, Francis, 156, 159, 180, 192, 193

Carlisle, Edmund, 20

Carter, Jasper, 181–82

Caruthers, Belle, 18

Chapin, Joseph C., 119–20

Chapman, Amy, 190, 191

Chappell, Cornelius, 58

Chase, Thurston, 103

Chesnutt, Charles W., 172, 178, 192, 258 (n. 17)

Chestnut, George, 122

Child, Lydia Maria, 116, 247 (n. 10)

"Child's Primers," 129, 247 (n. 10)

Christian Commission, 56

Christianity: and owners' teaching of slaves, 19, 24; and slave education, 28; and black education, 60; and textbook ideology, 133. *See also* American Missionary Association; Bible; Missionary associations; Missionary teachers

Christian-Smith, Linda K., 5

Civil rights: priorities of, 4, 69, 72, 86; and African American soldiers, 47, 54, 78; and Marrs, 67, 68, 69; and power issues, 68; and black conventions, 76, 125; and constitutional amendments, 79

Civil society: African American participation in, 69, 70, 75, 76, 86, 94, 202

Civil War: and slaves' freedom, 8–11, 30–34, 44, 66; and slaves' information network, 9–10

Clark, Alida, 59, 61–62, 64–65, 92, 239 (n. 46)

Clark, Calvin, 59, 61–65, 92, 232–33 (n. 76)

Clement, Samuel Spottford, 149

Cobb, Lyman, 163

Cocke, John, 19, 220 (n. 45)

Colby, Abraham, 102–3, 105, 112, 129

Colby, William, 103

Cole, Samuel, 63

Cole, William, 105, 107, 161

Common school system: support for, 180, 187, 192, 193, 262 (n. 73). *See also* Public education

Communication networks, 9–10, 31, 68

Compton, John, 150

Compulsory education, 193

Confederacy: and Emancipation Proclamation, 45; and textbook ideology, 126, 130, 133

Confederate army, 33

Confederate officials, 31–32

Connecticut, 16–17, 219 (n. 34)

Contraband camps, 34

Contrabands of war, 32, 33, 222 (n. 6)

Convention of Colored Men of the United States, 17

Convict lease systems, 255 (n. 112)

Cook, Peter, 40

Coon, Charles L., 264 (n. 96)

Cooper, Anna Julia, 178, 258–59 (n. 17)

Cooper, Peter, 122

Cornell's Geographics, 128

Cornish, Dudley Taylor, 228 (n. 7)

Coyler, Vincent, 36

Crandall, Prudence, 17

Crime, 167

Curry, James, 21–24, 25

Damon, Caroline, 120

Danforth, Jacob, 128–29

Davies' Arithmetic, 127, 128

Davis, Charlie, 18

Davis, David Brion, 217 (n. 13)

Davis, Jefferson, 132

Davis, Minnie, 216 (n. 8)

Davis, William, 41

Dawson, Betsy, 62

Day, Charles, 188

Day schools, 99

De Forest, John, 158–59
Delaware, 99
Deskins, Landon, 176
Deveaux, Catherine, 104
Deveaux, Jane, 104, 105, 110, 112, 113, 128, 129
Deveaux, John Benjamin, 104, 112
Dilworth, Thomas, 130
Disenfranchisement, 199
District of Columbia, 18
District of Columbia Orphan Asylum, 71
Dixie Primer, The, 131
Donaldson, R. S., 92–93
Douglas, John Henry, 61–62
Douglass, Frederick, 8, 24–27, 48, 53, 130, 202
Douglass, J. H., 92–93
Douglass, Margaret, 27–28
Douglass, Rosa, 27–28
Du Bois, W. E. B., 4, 174, 178, 193, 196, 199, 201, 258 (n. 17), 259 (n. 18)
Dungey, James Ammon, 176, 258 (n. 10)
Dungey, Jefree, 176
Dungey, Mary Eliza, 176, 258 (n. 10)
Dungey, Robert J., 258 (n. 10)

Eaton, John, 36
Eavesdropping, 9–10
Eberhart, Gilbert L., 100, 101, 102, 113, 129
Economic equality: and literate African Americans, 1; and business establishment, 67, 68–69; and black conventions, 76, 125; and whites' oppression of blacks, 86; and freedpeople's wealth accumulation, 93, 238 (n. 38); and African American soldiers, 231 (n. 43)
Educational Association of the Confederate States of America, 131
Education and power, 5; and freedpeople's relationship with white north-erners, 42–43, 92; and African American soldiers, 47, 53; and black conventions, 75–76, 78. *See also* Right to education
Edwards, John, 93
Edwards, Lizzie, 50, 65
Eighth United States Colored Infantry, 57
Elementary Spelling Book (Webster), 129–30
Elite whites: and schools for poor whites, 3, 179, 188; and inaccessibility of literacy for African Americans, 13, 14; and poor whites' educational achievement, 175; and black education, 180, 183; and private education, 187, 188. *See also* Slave owners; White planters
Emancipation: Lincoln's policy on, 31, 45; and black conventions, 235 (n. 20)
Emancipation League, 155–56
Emancipation Proclamation, 44, 45, 46, 48, 78, 131, 235 (n. 20)
Empowerment: education as, 43, 52, 53
Enlightenment, 7, 163
Epidemics, 64, 142
Equal access, 192
Equality: economic equality, 1, 67, 68–69, 76, 86, 93, 125, 231 (n. 43), 238 (n. 38); political equality, 1, 69, 76, 78, 96, 125; and legal proceedings, 4; and meaning of freedom, 49, 66; and black conventions, 79; and racial etiquette, 118, 189; and African American teachers, 120; and integration, 197; and separate but equal, 199, 201
Eugenics, 157
Eveleth, Emma B., 140, 184, 187
Ezel, Lorenzo, 130

Federal government: and right to education, 69–70, 72; and meaning of freedom, 72; and Reconstruction, 194, 195

Fee, John, 118–20

Ferebee, London R., 1, 138, 139, 140, 159, 172, 202

Fifty-sixth United States Colored Infantry, 58–59, 62–65, 92, 175

First North Carolina Colored Volunteers, 50

First South Carolina Volunteers, Thirty-third Regiment, 49

First United States Colored Troops, 53

Fisher, James, 20, 22

Fisk, Clinton B., 52

Fisk Colored School, 57

Fiske, F. A., 168

Fisk University, 175, 178, 199–200, 201

Florida, 81–83, 211

Former slaves. See Freedpeople

Forten, Charlotte, 116–17, 140, 154, 162, 170

Forten, James, 17, 116

Forten, Mary, 116

Forten, Robert Bridges, 116

Foster, Richard Baxter, 57–58

Fowler, Charlotte, 263 (n. 80)

Free black peddlers, 15

Free blacks: and antiliteracy statutes, 13, 14, 15, 16, 216 (n. 1); and clandestine learning, 19; and passes, 22; in South, 33–34; women's occupations, 34; and freedpeople's intelligence, 156

Freedmen's Address, 74

Freedmen's Aid Society, 93, 94

Freedmen's Bureau: and black education, 3, 36, 74, 79, 98; and murders of African Americans, 68; and labor contracts, 71; protection of, 78; and African Americans' self-reliance, 80–81; and African American teachers, 98–103, 104, 115, 240 (nn. 10, 11); and building of schools, 106, 110, 111; and sites of schools, 108–9; and school burnings, 124; and textbooks, 126–27; and student progress, 128;

and higher education for African Americans, 158; and reform schools, 165–66; and poor whites' attendance at schools for African Americans, 185

Freedmen's Inquiry Commission, 70, 111, 185

Freedmen's Primers, 128, 129

Freedmen's Second and Third Readers, The, 134

Freedmen's Spelling Book, 134, 135, 136, 151–52

Freedmen's Writing Lessons, 129

Freedmen villages, 34

Freedom: and literacy, 8, 22, 23–27, 53, 95; and Civil War, 8–11, 30–34, 44, 66; and telegraph grapevine, 31, 222 (n. 3); as place and concept, 33; meaning of, 43, 47–48, 49, 66, 71, 72, 95; and black education, 43–44, 60, 77; and power issues, 80; anniversary celebration of, 93–94; and integration, 197. See also Slave escapes; Slavery to freedom transition

Freedpeople: role in black education, 1–2, 5, 6, 36, 39–40; and literacy, 34–35; camps of, 37; and payment of teachers, 40, 60, 97, 181; and Quakers, 59–65, 92–95, 124, 232 (n. 57), 238–39 (nn. 45, 46); and funding for schools, 62, 81, 87, 88, 92, 93, 98, 102; and right to education, 69–72, 179, 202; and black conventions, 72–73; school boards of, 82–83, 86, 91–92, 102; and organizing schools, 87, 101, 102; access to books, 126; and textbook ideology, 134–36, 248 (n. 25); immigrants compared to, 167; and right to fair pay, 169; class stratification of, 170; and women as students, 170–71; poor whites compared to, 183–85; and separate schools for poor whites, 190–92; and poor whites attending schools

National Freedmen's Relief Association, 90–91

Nelson, Caleb, 176, 258 (n. 11)

New England Freedmen's Aid Society, 42, 105, 129

New Guide to the English Tongue (Dilworth), 130

New Orleans massacre of 1866, 124

Newton, A. E., 166, 167

New York Reader, 101, 128

New York Society of Friends, 105, 112, 129

Normal schools, 177–78, 183, 201

North Carolina, 15, 33–34, 70, 72–74, 79, 96, 206–7

Northern African Americans: as teachers, 114–20, 152

Northern antiliteracy statutes, 16–17, 219 (n. 34)

Northern Methodist Conference, 109

Nott, Josiah, 161

Oberlin College, 115, 116, 244 (n. 59), 253 (n. 69)

Offley, G. W., 20, 21

Ogden, John, 105, 175, 178

Old field schools, 187

102nd United States Colored Troops, 55

107th Colored Regiment, 57

109th United States Colored Troops, 55

175th Battalion of New York Volunteers, 57

Orr, James L., 180, 194

Our Own Primer, 131

Our Own Spelling Book, 131

Parker, Richard, 20

Paternalism: and white northern missionaries, 1, 89–90, 95; and antiliteracy statutes, 16; and textbook ideology, 131, 136; of elite whites toward poor whites, 179; and Quakers, 239 (n. 46)

Paterson, Preston, 56

Patton, Stephen, 62

Peake, Mary (mother), 18

Peake, Mary S. (daughter), 18, 38–39, 41, 96, 220 (n. 41)

Peake, Thomas, 18

Peck, Solomon, 35

Percy, H. C., 259 (n. 25)

Perlmann, Joel, 243 (n. 45)

Petty, Edward, 102, 109

Phrenology, 157

Pierce, Edward L., 33, 35, 42, 188, 222 (n. 3)

Pinkney, Esther, 165, 166

Pinneo's Grammar, 128

Pit schools, 20

Political issues: political equality, 1, 69, 76, 78, 96, 125; and freedpeople's values, 2; and free blacks, 34; and African American soldiers, 47, 65; and public education, 72; and black education, 86, 178; and African American teachers, 96–97, 112–13; and African American churches, 107; and white southern violence, 122; and textbook ideology, 130, 133, 137

Poor whites: motivation for school attendance, 2–3, 175, 183; and clandestine learning, 20; and textbook ideology, 132; and lack of education, 178–79; and threat of black education, 179, 183; white northerners' attitudes toward, 183–85, 188–89, 260 (n. 44); attendance at schools for African Americans, 185–86, 189, 190–91, 192; textbooks for, 189

Porter, James, 104–5, 110, 113

Port Royal Relief Association, 117

Poverty: and orphans, 61; and black education, 101; of teachers, 105; and tuition payments, 106; and condition of schools, 110, 127; and textbook availability, 127; as obstacle to students, 141–42; and reform movement, 167; and higher education,

175, 176; and poor whites' education, 183, 186. *See also* Poor whites
Powell, Edward, 102, 103
Power issues: and black education, 4–5, 39, 42, 180, 197, 198–99; education and power, 5, 42–43, 47, 53, 75–76, 78, 92; and master-slave relationship, 7, 10, 11; and literacy, 7, 11, 12; and African American civil rights, 68; and black conventions, 77; and freedom, 80; and teacher choice, 87; and administration of schools, 87, 88–89; and African American teachers, 96–97; and teaching as political act, 96–97, 125; and public education, 194–95, 198
Powers, Ridgely C., 179, 180
Prejudice: and black education, 60, 101; and laws and legislation, 74; and civil rights, 76; and white southern violence, 94; and African American teachers, 101; of white northern missionaries, 118–21; teachers' prejudice toward students, 153, 157; and African Americans' intelligence, 168; and separate schools for poor whites, 190, 191; and white children attending schools for African Americans, 190, 192; and public education, 193
Price, George W., 72
Primus, Isaac, 105–6, 129
Primus, Rebecca, 118, 121, 165
Private schools, 91, 102, 186–87, 188, 193–94, 200
Property rights: and slave owners, 22–23, 31, 32, 61–62, 196; and slaves as contraband of war, 32, 222–23 (n. 6), 223–24 (n. 14); and compensation for slaves, 66, 233 (n. 87)
Public accommodations: and racial discrimination, 67, 68
Public education: establishment of, 4, 201; and political issues, 72; black education's influence on, 163, 178,

183, 192–93, 262 (n. 73); and Reconstruction, 193; white southerners' opposition to, 193–96; funding for, 193–96, 198, 199–200, 262 (n. 79)
Public transcripts, 5
Punishment: and antiliteracy statutes, 15, 16, 18, 27–28; discrimination in, 15, 218 (n. 25); of slaves learning to read, 18, 219 (n. 39); of African American teachers, 122; corporal punishment of students, 163–65; and slave rebellion, 218 (n. 28)

Quackenbo's United States History, 128
Quakers: and African American soldiers, 58–59, 62–65, 92; and self-help, 60–61, 92, 94, 232 (n. 57); and building of schools, 62–65, 92–94; relationship with African Americans, 94–95, 238–39 (nn. 45, 46); and white southern violence, 124; and racial hierarchy, 157–58

Racial discourse: and African Americans' intelligence, 29, 97, 133, 141, 153–57, 160–61, 168, 183–84, 202; and black education, 90; and separation of races, 118, 119–20, 189; and textbook ideology, 133
Racial discrimination: and Union army, 54, 66; and black conventions, 67; and public accommodations, 67, 68; and business establishment, 67, 68–69; and African American teachers, 91, 118–20, 199, 264 (n. 96); and segregation, 189, 190–92
Racial mixing, 185–86, 189. *See also* Integration
Racism. *See* Prejudice; Racial discourse; Racial discrimination
Randolph, Benjamin, 55, 230 (n. 36)
Randolph, John, Jr., 72
Randolph, Peter, 30
Rankin, G. L., 36

Ray's Arithmetic, 128

Reconstruction, 74–75, 77, 79, 112, 121, 188, 193–96, 198

Reconstruction Acts, 79, 193

Redeemers, 198

Reform movement, 166–67

Reform schools, 165–67, 255 (n. 112)

Republicans: and schools for poor whites, 3; Radical Republicans, 66, 78; and white southern violence, 123

Richardson, Joe M., 244 (n. 57)

Right to education: establishment of, 2; and government protection, 69–70, 72; and freedpeople, 69–72, 179, 202; and labor contracts, 70–71; and black conventions, 76, 78; and white southern violence, 197

Right to testify in court: and racial discrimination, 68, 69

Ringler, Mrs. M. J., 108

Rives, James, 197

Robinson, Jesse, 66

Root, Mary F., 157, 167

Roper, Ella, 138

Rose, Anna, 202

Rose, William Lee, 113, 223 (n. 6)

Rucker, Ephraim, 102, 113, 128

Runaway slaves, 15, 20

Ryall, Simon, 81, 111, 128, 165, 166, 167

Sabattie, Hattie E., 165, 166

Sabbath schools, 99, 125, 143, 178, 255 (n. 113)

Sanders' Readers, 128

Sanders' Spellers, 128

Savannah Educational Association, 87–89, 105, 114, 129

Saxton, Rufus, 113, 184, 243 (n. 51)

Saxton School, 192

Schools for African Americans: administration of, 2, 3, 6, 42, 83–85, 86, 87, 88, 89, 91–92; African American participation in building of, 2, 4, 36, 40, 98, 261 (n. 64); clandestine schools, 13, 16, 18–19, 20, 21, 38, 88, 90, 104, 183; demand for, 30, 36; African American soldiers' building of, 47, 55, 56–59, 62–65, 92; funding for, 57–58, 62, 63, 81, 87, 88, 89, 92, 98, 102, 105, 106, 108, 110, 159; freedpeople's funding for, 62, 81, 87, 88, 92, 93, 98, 102; Quakers' building of, 62–65, 92–94; African Americans' initiation of building of, 81, 110, 111, 114, 138, 140, 174, 181; trained teachers for, 82–83, 236 (n. 10); freedpeople's organizing of, 87, 101, 102; burning of, 94, 121, 123–24, 174, 198; condition of, 101, 110–11, 142, 162, 174, 199; sites for, 106–10, 241 (n. 29); supplies for, 128, 129, 155; poor whites attending, 185–86, 189, 190–91, 192. See also Textbooks

Scott, James C., 5

Sectional reconciliation, 61, 198

Segregation: and northern African American teachers, 118, 119–20; and racial discrimination, 189, 190–92; institutionalization of, 198, 263 (n. 94); and white southerners' hostility toward black education, 241 (n. 25). See also Integration

Self-determination: as value of freedpeople, 2; education as, 43–44; demands for, 68, 69; and black conventions, 80; and hiring of local teachers, 83, 86; and organizing schools, 88; and administration of schools, 88, 91–92; white northern missionaries' resistance to, 90; and white supremacy, 92; and meaning of freedom, 95; and African American teachers, 111; and Ku Klux Klan, 198

Self-help: as value of freedpeople, 2, 60, 232 (n. 57); and African American teachers, 51, 79, 82–83; and Quakers, 60–61, 92, 94, 232 (n. 57); and black conventions, 75–76, 79, 80; Alvord on, 80–81, 82, 90, 236 (n. 1); and administration of schools, 88; and white supremacy, 92

Series of Confederate Readers, A, 131

Sexton, Samuel, 57

Shaw, Isabella, 164

Shawnee schools, 60

Shropshire, Wesley, 124

Silsby, J., 172

Simms, James, 28

Sixty-fifth United States Colored Infantry, 57

Sixty-second United States Colored Infantry, 57

Skipwith, Lucy, 19

Slave escapes: and gender, 8; and eavesdropping, 9; and passes, 22; and property loss, 22–23; and literacy, 22–24; and challenges to slavery, 24; and Civil War, 31; hazards of, 33, 224 (nn. 15, 19); and enlistment in Union army, 46, 228 (n. 5)

Slave narratives, 8, 12, 28–29

Slave owners: master-slave relationship, 7, 9, 10, 11–12, 13, 18, 217 (n. 13); and teaching of slaves, 19, 25; slave management on Sabbath, 21; and property rights, 22–23, 31, 32, 61–62, 196; and slave escapes, 31; and slave orphans, 61; and compensation for lost slaves, 66, 233 (n. 87); and racial hierarchy, 159; and disciplining of black youth, 167; and recommendations for African Americans' higher education, 177; white northerners' attitudes toward, 183; and fear of black literacy, 202

Slave rebellion, 14, 16, 218 (n. 28)

Slave resistance, 7, 10, 11, 13, 14–15, 38

Slavery: and textbook ideology, 2, 126, 130–32, 133, 136; African Americans' challenges to, 10, 11, 12, 14, 23–24, 26, 27; literacy as threat to, 22, 24,

27, 96; as illegitimate, 25; Lincoln's policy on, 31; Quakers' opposition to, 59; and African American political organizations, 72; and ethnological movement, 161

Slavery-to-freedom transition: and demand for schools, 30–31; and Union army, 32–33; and black education, 39; and African American teachers, 97–98

Slaves: educational vision of, 1; importance of literacy to, 2, 5, 7–8; master-slave relationship, 7, 9, 10, 11–12, 13, 18, 217 (n. 13); and antiliteracy statutes, 7, 216 (n. 1); families of, 8, 12, 22, 32, 61; and access to information, 9, 12, 22, 23; and clandestine learning, 12, 18–22, 24, 25, 47, 49, 65; and clandestine schools, 13, 16, 18–19, 20, 21, 38, 88, 90, 104; punishment for learning to read, 18, 219 (n. 39); and writing supplies, 20–21; and forging of passes, 22; as contraband of war, 32, 222–23 (n. 6), 223–24 (n. 14); clothing of, 142, 250 (n. 15). *See also* African Americans

Smith, Caroline, 198

Smith, E. W. P., 120–21

Smith, Emanuel, 80, 82–83, 126

Smith, James, 81–82, 86

Smith, Lewis, 105, 106, 111, 112–13, 126, 127, 128

Smith, Nancy, 164

Smith, Nellie, 164

Smith, William, 164

Smith's Arithmetic, 101

Smith's Grammar, 128

Social class: and schools for African Americans, 104; and African American teachers, 116–17, 152; and racial hierarchy, 158, 179–80, 183; and African American adults as students, 169, 170; and poor whites' lack of education, 179, 183, 184; and educa-

tion in South, 187. *See also* Elite
whites; Poor whites; Poverty
South: and education and power, 5; and
right to education, 69–70; northern
values exported to, 90–91, 183; and
competing ideologies in textbooks,
126; social structure of, 178–80, 182,
183, 196–98, 263 (n. 93); elite whites'
image of, 180; and education, 187;
and reform movement, 255 (n. 112)
South Carolina, 13, 16, 21, 72, 75, 76,
78, 100, 207–8
South Carolina Colored People's Con-
vention, 76
South Carolina Sea Islands, 33, 35, 39,
49, 60
Southern Conference of the Methodist
Church, 109
Southland Institute, 58–59
Spence, A. K., 91–92
Spratley, Jason, 51
Stalker, Margaret, 153
Stanley, John C., 244 (n. 59)
Stanley, John Wright, 244 (n. 59)
Stanley, Sara, 115–16, 117, 118, 146–47,
154–55, 162, 244 (n. 59)
Stanton, Edwin M., 68
State Convention of the Colored People
of Georgia, 76, 77
State governments: and public educa-
tion, 69; and black conventions, 74;
and white conventions for Recon-
struction, 74–75; and funding for edu-
cation, 79, 178, 187, 198–99; and inte-
gration, 193–94; and taxation, 196
Stewart, Maria W., 245 (n. 59)
Stickler, Augustus, 160
Stono Rebellion, 13, 21
Stowe, Harriet Beecher, 50, 169
Subscription schools, 187
Sumner, A., 156
Sweney, John, 1, 45, 52–53, 54, 65, 202,
229–30 (n. 25), 239 (n. 2)
Swint, Henry Lee, 3

Talladega normal school, 177–78, 258
(n. 15)
Tambling, C. L., 83–86, 87
Tappan, Arthur, 17
Taxation, 193–96, 200
Taylor, Susie King, 19, 22, 49–50, 96,
229 (n. 14)
Teachers. *See* African American
teachers; Missionary teachers; White
northern teachers; White southern
teachers; White teachers
Telegraph grapevine, 31, 32, 222 (n. 3)
Telfair, Georgia, 138, 146
Temperance, 135–36
Tennessee, 59–60, 72, 175, 211–12
Texas, 100, 103
Textbooks: and competing ideologies,
2, 126, 130–37, 248 (n. 25); avail-
ability of, 2, 126–30; need for, 36, 37,
40, 53–56, 101, 110; and American
Missionary Association, 36, 40, 82,
83, 126, 189; donations of, 129; and
Webster, 129–30, 137; for poor
whites, 189; Ku Klux Klan's burning
of, 198
Thirteenth Colored Regiment, 57
Thomas, K. Saul, 129
Thomas, King, 113
Thompson, Hyman, 191, 202
Tilghman, E. D., 1, 176–77
Todd, David, 158
Toomer, Louis B., 110, 113
Towne, Laura, 147, 150, 151, 152, 157,
162, 164
Townsley, Bartley, 96, 101, 106, 110–11,
112, 124, 129, 202
Trimble, Aleck, 164
Truchelot, Ernestine, 113
Tuition: freedpeople's payment of, 60,
82, 93, 104, 128; and schools for Afri-
can Americans, 101, 102, 104, 128;
and teacher salaries, 105, 106, 114; and
poverty, 106; and gifts for teachers,
151; and African American adults as

students, 167–68; for higher education, 175, 176; and poor whites, 192
Turner, Brooks, 176
Turner, Ellen, 8, 10–12, 16, 27, 31, 73
Turner, Henry McNeal, 45, 53–55, 66, 126, 230 (n. 29)
Turner, John, 75
Turner, Nat, 13, 28, 218 (n. 28)
Twelfth U.S. Colored Artillery, 228 (n. 5)
Twenty-sixth United States Colored Troops, 55

Uncle Tom's Cabin (Stowe), 169
Underground Railroad, 28, 104
Union army: and African American teachers, 1, 2, 35; and master-slave relationship, 9, 10, 11, 217 (n. 13); and protection of slaves, 12, 31, 32, 34; and slave escapes, 23, 33; policy toward slaves, 30, 32; failure to pay black workers, 34, 225 (n. 25); and schools for African Americans, 36, 175; enlistment in, 44–48, 227 (n. 1), 228 (n. 5); and African American chaplains, 49, 53, 55–56, 230 (n. 29); officers' wives as teachers, 49, 93; and black education, 52–54; discrimination against African American soldiers, 54, 66. *See also* African American soldiers

Varser, Smith, 102
Vattal, Jane Ann, 129
Virginia, 15–16, 18, 27–28, 32, 33, 60, 72, 100, 124–25, 208–11
Voting rights: and suffrage, 4, 69, 72, 76, 79, 197; and enfranchisement as priority, 69; and literacy, 76, 77, 169; and white southern violence, 182; and disenfranchisement, 199, 201

Wade, Jacob, 103, 128
Wager, John H., 181

Walker, David, 14, 16
Walker, Thomas, 34
Walker, Vanessa Siddle, 259 (n. 18)
Walker's Dictionary, 128
Walton, Caroline Walker, 162, 172
Walton, John, 130
War for Independence, 31
Waring, William, 55
War of 1812, 31
Warren, Joseph, 50, 51, 127
Washburn Institute, 190, 261 (n. 64)
Washington, Booker T., 9–10, 41, 263 (n. 93)
Washington, John T., 31
Watson, M. E., 160, 259 (n. 25)
Watson, Thomas, 63
Webster, Noah, 129–30, 137, 139
Webster, W., 171
Webster's Spelling Books, 101, 127, 128, 139
Wells, G. Wiley, 194–95
Western Freedmen's Aid Society, 105, 106
Western Sanitary Commission, 36–37
Wheeler, W. W., 119
Whipple, George, 82
Whitby, Thomas, 153
White, Graham, 250 (n. 15)
White, Shane, 250 (n. 15)
White children: and African Americans' clandestine learning, 20, 24, 25; and violence against black children attending school, 149; as teachers, 173; white northerners' attitudes toward, 184, 189; and attendance at schools for African Americans, 185, 189, 190–92; black students as teachers of, 186–87; and integration, 197
White conventions, 74–75
Whiteness: education as privilege of, 41–42
White northerners: African Americans' conflicts with, 2, 6, 83, 88, 91–92, 96;

and higher education for African
Americans, 17; and control over
freedpeople, 42–43; and African
Americans in Union army, 53, 66; as
allies of African Americans, 69; and
white supremacy, 89–91, 92, 183;
values of, 90–91, 183; and textbooks,
129, 133–37; and African Americans'
enthusiasm for learning, 172, 174;
attitudes toward poor whites, 183–85,
188–89, 260 (n. 44); and sectional
reconciliation, 198
White northern missionaries: and paternalism, 1, 89–90, 95; and black education, 2, 21, 96; role of, 38, 40, 80,
83; and Southland Institute, 58; prejudice of, 118–21; and poor whites'
education, 175, 183, 187–90. See also
Quakers
White northern teachers: and southern
communities, 3; and black communities, 30; freedpeople's payment of,
40; and African Americans' eagerness
to learn, 50, 151; qualifications of,
90–91, 114, 115; missionary associations' payment of, 98; and white
southerners' opposition to black education, 125; and textbook ideology,
133; and conditions of schools, 142;
and educability of African Americans,
153, 160; and students' progress, 155;
and racial hierarchy, 157–60; and corporal punishment, 164; white southerners' opposition to, 182, 241
(n. 25); and poor whites, 188, 190;
lodging of, 241 (n. 25)
White planters: and black education,
175, 180–83; and private tutors, 187.
See also Elite whites; Slave owners
Whites: African Americans' influence
on, 2–3; and right to education, 69;
historical role in oppression of blacks,
71–72, 75, 76, 86; illiteracy of, 76, 77.
See also Elite whites; Poor whites

White southerners: and black resistance,
42; attitudes toward African Americans, 65, 126, 132, 160, 197, 198, 263
(n. 93); dominance over African
Americans, 68, 69; and black conventions, 73; and freedom of African
Americans, 94; and antebellum power
relations, 96–97; and African American teachers, 97–98, 182–83; and
African American churches, 108–10;
and gender of teachers, 111; and textbook ideology, 130–31; and African
Americans' intelligence, 153; and
racial hierarchy, 159–60; and freedwomen's withdrawal from labor market, 170; and African Americans'
enthusiasm for learning, 174; and
African Americans' role as laborers,
179–80; visits to black schools, 180,
196; education of, 187; and public
education funding, 194; and taxation,
195–96
White southerners' hostility toward
black education: Swint on, 3; and
Quakers' educational efforts, 60, 92,
93, 94; and African Americans' participation in civil society, 70; and
black conventions, 74, 75, 78–79; and
military protection, 82; and African
American teachers, 96–97, 101, 121–
23; and rental property for schools,
106; and African American churches
as schools, 108–9, 121; and burning
of schools, 123–25; and teachers'
classroom control, 163, 166; changes
in, 175, 178, 180, 181, 194, 259
(n. 25); and lack of education for poor
whites, 179; and white northern
teachers, 182, 241 (n. 25); and taxation, 196; and South's social structure,
196–98, 263 (n. 93)
White southern teachers, 131, 163, 164,
182
White southern violence: and black

CPSIA information can be obtained
at www.ICGtesting.com
Printed in the USA
LVHW042342140819
627635LV00004B/362/P

9 780807 858219